UNEASE IN ZION

DISEASE IN ZION, OR

UNEASE IN ZION

Edited by

EHUD BEN EZER

With a Foreword by

ROBERT ALTER

Quadrangle/The New York Times Book Co.

JERUSALEM ACADEMIC PRESS

Distribution of this book is being handled by the following publishers:

For the USA and Canada

Quadrangle/The New York Times Book Co.
10 East 53rd Street
New York, NY 10022

For all remaining areas

Jerusalem Academic Press
P.O. Box 2390
Jerusalem, Israel

Library of Congress Card Number: 79–90166

ISBN: 0–8129–0416–8

QUADRANGLE/THE NEW YORK TIMES BOOK CO.
10 East 53rd Street
New York, NY 10022

PRINTED IN ISRAEL BY JERUSALEM ACADEMIC PRESS

Woe to them that are at ease in Zion,
and trust in the mountain of Samaria,
which are named chief of the nations,
to whom the house of Israel came!

Amos VI: 1

CONTENTS

		Page
ROBERT ALTER	Foreword	9
EHUD BEN EZER	The Price of Zionism	25
SHULAMIT ALONI	Getting Over the Crisis Without Fanaticism	31
SHLOMO AVINERI	Subjugation of the Means to the State's Ends?	49
DAVID BEN GURION	Where There is No Vision the People Perish	67
SHMUEL HUGO BERGMAN	Israeli Synthesis of Humanism and Religion	89
MORDECHAI MARTIN BUBER	Zionism—True and False	103
A. ELI	Lay Not Thine Hand Upon the Lad!	121
BOAZ EVRON	Separation and Equality— Instead of Confused Values	143
YESHAYAHU LEIBOWITZ	Jewish Identity and Israeli Silence	177
YONATAN RATOSH	The New Hebrew Nation (The Canaanite Outlook)	201
PINHAS SADEH	God Speaks to Us With Just Two Words—Love and Death	235
GERSHOM G. SCHOLEM	Zionism—Dialectic of Continuity and Rebellion	263
AKIVA ERNST SIMON	The Arab Question as a Jewish Question	297
AVRAHAM B. YEHOSHUA	Let Us Not Betray Zionism	321
Biographical Notes		340

Foreword*

You see, we would like you to be a Jew for the Jews and not to be a Jew for the Gentiles, because Gentiles reject moralism when it comes from a man without an army.

Uriel Simon, reply to George Steiner at the Sixth Annual American-Israel Dialogue.

The loss of the past, whether collective or individual, is the great human tragedy, and we have thrown ours away as a child tears up a rose. It is above all to avoid this loss that peoples desperately resist conquest.

Simone Weil, *L'Enracinement.*

Back in the mid-60's, in that period which through the violent lurch forward of subsequent events now seems almost at an archaeological distance from us, a young Israeli writer named Ehud Ben-Ezer began to conduct a series of interviews with prominent Israeli intellectuals under the general title, "The Price of Zionism." The publishing history of Ben-Ezer's venture is itself an instructive instance of how the Zionist founding fathers managed to create a society which is far more open to scathing selfcriticism than most outsiders would believe and yet preserves perennial tender spots of national defensiveness. Ben Ezer's interviews appeared in *Moznayim*, the monthly magazine of the Hebrew Writers Association and thus the staidest of union house-organs, an official instrument of an aging cultural establishment. For several months, one could marvel at the paradox of finding sandwiched in between effusive appreciations of octogenarian third-rate Hebrew literati the most uncompromising statements by the subjects of Ben Ezer's interviews on the "fascist mentality" of Israeli leadership, the moral wrongs perpetrated upon the Palestinian Arabs, Israel's betrayal of world Jewry,

* Reprinted from *Commentary*, by permission; Copyright © 1970 by the American Jewish Committee.

9

the capitulation of the Israeli intelligentsia to the blandishments of the governing clique. When, however, an interview with a leading spokesman of the so-called Canaanite movement produced an assault on the idea of Israel as a Jewish state, the editors of *Moznayim* balked, and the publication of "The Price of Zionism" was halted. Within a few months the Six-Day War broke out, and the interviews suddenly became historical documents.

It made a great deal of sense to be taking stock of Zionism during those long months of malaise that preceded the Arab encirclement in the spring of 1967. This was the period, one recalls, when Israelis were talking about a "crisis of values" in the Jewish state. The initial elan of the pioneer generation and the fighters of the War of Independence seemed to have spent itself; the Zionist goal of normalization of Jewish existence had been realized with a vengeance, producing, so it appeared, a way of life devoted chiefly to the creature-comforts of a consumer society; and Israelis were becoming aware of a newly-emerged "espresso generation" of self-indulgent, provincial young people to whom considerations of Jewish history, Jewish destiny, bonds with the Diaspora, were so much antediluvian twaddle. Armed confrontation with the Arabs, once thought to be a transitional stage, now seemed clearly a fixed condition of Israeli life for the foreseeable future; and in a confluence of declining morale and economic recession, emigration was beginning to exceed immigration for the first time since the founding of the state.

It is no wonder, then, that more reflective Israelis began to ask themselves whether, in retrospect, it had all been worthwhile, and Ehud Ben Ezer's questions to leading intellectuals sought from them precisely an articulation of the moral, spiritual, and cultural cost of having fulfilled the ideal of a Jewish state. Had the Jews lost the intellectual breadth and sharpness of perspective generated through their Diaspora position of marginality by becoming in Israel the majority culture of a sovereign state? Surrounded by enemies, pervaded by a "siege mentality" (*toda'at matzor*), isolated from the great centers of Western culture, had they dwindled from a universal people into nothing more than the purblind inmates of an armed province? Had the Jewish state even fulfilled the most basic purpose Herzl conceived for it, the assurance of the physical survival of

persecuted Jews, or, on the contrary, were two million Jews gathered in the Middle East only in order to be threatened continually
with physical extinction, as they were nowhere else in the world?

The early Zionist leaders, we might recall, were divided on the
ultimate rationale of the movement. According to Herzl's political
Zionism, the return to Palestine was above all a solution to "the
problem of the Jews," the only logical means, in an era of exclu-
sionist nationalisms, to provide for the physical security and basic
civil rights of the beleaguered Jews of Eastern Europe. The position
of Ahad Ha-am's cultural Zionism, on the other hand, was that the
purpose of settlement in the Land of Israel was essentially to solve
"the problem of Judaism," to create, that is, a viable autonomous
community which, in a modern secular context, would preserve and
develop whatever was precious in the ethical and spiritual heritage
of the Jews, thus serving as a focus of meaningful national identity
for Jews everywhere. Subsequent events would demonstrate in the
most horrific way the greater realism of Herzl's emphasis, while
the utopian and moralistic aspects of Ahad Ha-am's approach
would come to seem increasingly more dubious; but the two large
goals remain the ones against which Zionist achievement must be
measured, and all that can be asserted with confidence now is that
seven decades of Zionist enterprise in this century have provided no
clear answer either to the problem of the Jews or to the problem
of Judaism. What has happened is that the fulfillment of Zionism
has radically shifted the grounds of both problems, and the nature
of this shift has been especially apparent since June 1967 in regard
to the problem of the Jews.

One incontrovertible fact which is clearer now than ever before
is that the existence of Israel has actually introduced a new element
of threat to the physical security of Jewish populations in many
parts of the world. The hundreds of Jews wasting away in Egyptian
prisons; the Jewish victims of Iraqi public murder dangling in the
squares of Baghdad; the thousands of Polish Jews hounded out of
job, home, and country; the masses of Soviet Jewry subjected to
official campaigns of hatred, risking penal servitude or worse for
any attempt to express their identity as Jews—all these would not
have suffered the harsh fate they have suffered, at least not on the
scale they have, if there were no independent Jewish state. This is,

it would seem, a grim but inevitable price to be paid for Zionism: Israel's existence, after all, has not in itself generated completely new hostility toward Jews in the countries where we now see it expressed, but it has provided a most convenient reason for hostile nativist masses to hold Jews in sharp suspicion, and a ready pretext for official persecution, even as it gives some of these same Jews a new source of pride and hope.

The more crucial arena, however, where the prospects of Jewish survival are in question, is on the soil of Israel itself. Most of us, I suppose, after nearly two decades of Jewish statehood, had come to take Israel's existence more or less for granted. The new and terrible idea that forced itself into Jewish consciousness in those last days of May 1967, as enraged mobs waved skull-and-crossbones banners in Cairo and the incendiary rhetoric of Arab leaders promised "final victory," was the notion that it really was possible to destroy Israel, that a holocaust might yet be a future possibility, not just a trauma of the past. When an unthinkable possibility suddenly becomes thinkable, one's whole imagination of a subject is transformed, and this is, it seems to me, what has occurred in our consciousness of Israel since June 1967.

Certainty, however, is not a quality that really obtains in the realm of history, and it is probably true that Israel's predicament differs somewhat in degree, but not at all in kind, from that of most other nations. Yeshayahu Leibowitz, the intransigently critical neo-Orthodox thinker, may be right in claiming that the whole Zionist notion of guaranteeing Jewish security was based on a 19th-century assumption about collective physical security as an integral part of normal national existence, but that in an age of proliferating weapons of ultimate destruction, no one anywhere can really count on such security, certainly not over a long range of time.

As far as "the problem of the Jews" is concerned, then, national independence could not be a final answer but rather a means of asserting as much autonomous control over the uncontrollable as humanly possible. Against the contention that nothing has substantially changed, that Israel's predicament is merely a replica on a worldwide scale of the situation of East European Jewry, a ghetto surrounded by hatred and suspicion, under the heavy shadow of potential attack, it must be stated emphatically that everything has changed because of the fact of sovereignty. Millions of Jews from the First Crusade to the Final Solution were passive victims because their location as a minority, as resident-aliens on sufferance, made it politically, tactically, psychologically impossible for most of them to be anything but passive victims. By establishing a sovereign state, Jews have resuscitated the possibility of initiating action rather than merely responding to the action of others, of controlling in some significant degree the conditions that are literally matters of life and death to them. If the painfully limited options open to Israel in foreign policy draw our attention to the naiveté of the old Zionist slogan about the Jews being able to "make their own history" again, it is nevertheless true that the State of Israel represents a radical reorientation of the relationship of Jews to history. Israel above all does not *feel* like a ghetto because its citizens have a strong sense of being able to exert a large measure of control over their collective destiny — a stronger sense, ironically, than many Americans are likely to have at this point in history. If the sense of mastery is in part illusory, it is not different in kind from the pragmatically necessary assumption of free will most of us live with as individuals, however illusory *that* may be in the dizzyingly complex and murky interplay of forces that determines our actions. Whether illusion or provisional fact, it has worked, keeping fifty million bloody-minded neighbors at bay for two decades and allowing a new society to develop which, whatever its psychological needs or inadequacies, is remarkably free of fear.

Since I have stressed the value of sovereignty, it is worth pointing out that Israel has escaped the self-hypnotizing fanaticism of many nationalist movements at least partly because sovereignty was not a sacrosanct ultimate principle for the Zionist consensus but rather a highly desirable condition that circumstances eventually made, quite simply, a necessary one. Ben Halpern, in his detailed history of the Zionist idea,* reminds us that the unique situation of Zionism among all the nationalist movements of the past century and a half made possible a certain flexibility in the basic conception of national fulfillment: "Zionism could afford to be ideologically

---

* *The Idea of the Jewish State*, Second Edition, Harvard University Press, 439 pp., 1969.

reasonable, because it was not bound to the nationalist myth of an autochthonous populace aroused to rebellion against foreign rulers. It could regard sovereignty, like any other national aim, either as end or means, according to the circumstances." The nature of circumstances in the twenty years between the Balfour Declaration and the UN Partition Decision made it progressively clearer that sovereignty was the only possible means of attaining even a minimal fulfillment of the most fundamental, and the most morally unassailable, of Zionist goals, saving the lives of Jews. The series of murderous assaults by armed Arab mobs on the Jewish populace of Palestine beginning in 1921; the British Mandatory's abrogation of even the humanitarian aspect of the National Home clause of the Balfour Declaration in cutting off Jewish immigration as Hitler was preparing the gas-chambers; the refusal of the Arabs to cooperate politically with Palestinian Jewry or to consider any bi-national alternative, and finally, their unwillingness to agree to the admission of even 100,000 survivors of the death-camps in 1946 — all these made a sovereign state inevitable if the physical safety and minimal human dignity of Palestinian Jews were to be protected and of a dependable place of refuge anywhere in the world were to be provided for persecuted Jews.

The fact that sovereignty does not have an absolute logical priority in Zionist thought may seem at this historical juncture a matter of purely academic interest, but I think it helps explain something about the distinctive tenor of Israeli nationalism. One should not, of course, pretend that Israelis are never myopically nationalistic, or at least often preoccupied with their own pressing national concerns to an exclusion of any vivid imagination of problems elsewhere. Nevertheless, the fact that national independence has in some respects been conceived as an indispensable means to other ends helps make possible a degree of critical distance from it, allowing an indeterminate middle-point between the extremes of patriotic reflex and disaffected recoil so commonly observable in national states elsewhere. At least one global, and moral, perspective is imposed on Israeli nationalism through the unquestioned sense of obligation it preserves to provide a place of refuge for any Jews in the world who need refuge, no matter what the social, economic, and cultural cost to Israeli society.

The rhetoric and ideology of classical Zionism were emphatically messianic, and one can still encounter in Israel an occasional unreconstructed messianist, like David Ben Gurion, but by far the most prevalent conception of sovereignty among Israelis is instrumental, not messianic. This is, I would contend, the single most reassuring fact about the Jewish state as it has been realized. The history of the past fifty years has made hideously clear what mad realms of uninhibited ruthlessness are opened when a political state imagines itself as the dawning fulfillment of some chiliastic process. Nations obviously relate to one another in terms of power, not morality, but power may at least be qualified or held within certain limits by considerations of morality — provided one does not regard all other nations as instruments of one's own eschatology and thus lose all concrete imagination of the humanity of people on the other side of the border.

Classical Zionist messianism, it should be said, was uniquely humane and gentle-minded among the political messianisms of this century, but the people in whom it most prominently survives in Israel today, the Greater Israel group, however far from resemblance to the ideological butchers of Europe and Asia, are precisely those who find it possible to dismiss the human and national claims of Palestinian Arabs in the interest of a manifest destiny of Jewish rule within "biblical" borders. We have heard again and, alas, again, about the messianic cast of the Jewish mind, in everyone from Marx and Freud to the last Jewish SDS leaders (German or American) at the barricades. Against this rather facile cliché one might well set an observation by Ernst Simon in an essay called "Are We Still Jews?" written in the first years after the founding of the state. The most essential posture of historical Judaism, Simon argued, has been its resistance to false messianisms, its refusal to say with Christianity, with Islam, with Sabbatism, with Marxism, that the redemption was already unfolding. The most Jewish quality, then, of Israel would be its resistance to a messianist conception of its own existence, and what Simon was urging as a moral necessity for the new state in 1952 seems, as we enter the 70's, largely the assumed attitude of the majority of Israelis.

But this brings us from the problem of the Jews to that of Judaism and here the sorting out of assets and deficits becomes even more

complicated because so much of vital importance that cannot be
weighed and measured is included under the second problem. Ahad
Ha-am, a profoundly secular mind of a sort that is no longer so
common, did not of course have the survival of institutional religion in mind when he spoke of the problem of Judaism, but rather
the sustenance of Jewish values, identity, cultural tradition, and
above all, the continuing of the millennial pursuit of absolute justice which, with some apologetic strain, he saw as the distinctive
Jewish vocation among the peoples of the earth. In this very regard,
however, there is one basic question that has become more and
more troubling: Does a Jewish state *belong* in an area where, even
as late as 1947, the majority of the population was Arab? How can
Israel be imagined, even in the most diffuse sense, as a continuation
of the moral heritage of Judaism if its existence depends upon a
manifest historical injustice?

It was the strenuous belief of most Zionist leaders that conflict
between Jewish and Arab nationalism was not inevitable. For a
fleeting moment, in King Feisal's famous declaration to the Zionist
delegation before the Paris Peace Conference in 1919, this belief
seemed to have the possibility of becoming fact. "We are working
together," Feisal had stated, "for a reformed and revived Near
East, and our two movements complete one another. The Jewish
movement is national and not imperialist. Our movement is national and not imperialist, and there is room in Syria (i.e., the region
including Palestine) for both. Indeed, I think that neither can be a
real success without the other." This was precisely the Zionist ideal
of relationship between Arab and Jew, but given the imperative
inner logic of Arab nationalism as an autochthonous movement
of national self-determination, it could not so easily afford to compromise any part of its putative sovereignty over Palestine in this
high-minded fashion, and Feisal himself soon hedged in his own
beautifully diplomatic statement with qualifications and equivoca-
tions.

That Zionists could continue to believe for so long in the com-
patibility of the two nationalist movements was probably, as the
Israeli political scientist, Shlomo Avineri, has suggested, a psychological defense-mechanism on the part of the Zionist leaders.
Humane, idealistic men, many of them fervent socialists, they could

not easily have gone on with their own enterprise in the clear knowledge that it would necessarily mean depriving Palestinian Arabs
of their right to self-determination and would probably lead to
armed conflict as well. It is an essential part of this whole historical
tragedy that Jewish and Arab nationalism were virtually coeval,
a fact that lends to their relationship an almost biblical aspect of
two siblings struggling over a single birthright. One of the siblings,
to be sure, was quite willing to compromise and share the birthright in a variety of ways; but it takes two to make a compromise, and it must be said of the Arabs, whatever the destructive
expressions fanaticism took among them, that there was no clear
legal reason for them to compromise, unless one is misguided enough
or hypocritical enough, to invoke the biblical divine promise of
the Land to the Jews.

There is, then, no easy way out of this moral dilemma for Jews,
but everything depends upon how one balances one's sense of contradictions and opposing claims of justice. I would like for a moment to compare on this issue a view "From Without" — actually
the title of an essay — by George Steiner with one from within by
an Israeli. Steiner's statement appears in an eloquent argument
against nationalism presented as a paper at the 1968 American-
Israel Dialogue,* and I will later refer to it again because it is such
a fine articulation of a universalist reaction to Zionism. After an
initial apology to his audience for presuming to address himself to
these sensitive issues as an outsider, Steiner proceeded to describe
Israel's situation in this fashion: "The existence of Israel is not
founded on logic; it has no ordinary legitimacy; there is neither in
its establishment nor present scope any evident justice — though
there may be an utter need and wondrous fulfillment."

The doubleness of attitude here seems to me just, yet there is
something disquieting in the neat polarity with which the ambivalence is expressed, that yawning gap marked by the disjunctive
dash between the barely, qualified statement of moral censure and
the concessive affirmation of imperious necessity joined with quasi-
theological rhetoric ("wondrous fulfillment"). One's doubts increase
as Steiner goes on to evoke the suffering of the Arab refugees almost

* *Congress Bi-Weekly*, February 24, 1969.

as though Israelis were unaware of it, and to claim that it might
well be "our job in the Diaspora" to be the bearers of Jewish conscience, to preserve allegiance, when Jews have a physical homeland,
to the morally prior Jewish "homeland of truth." (Could Steiner
have been aware that he was echoing, of all people, Lamartine, who
in his fervid French nationalism once asserted, "*La vérité, c'est mon
pays*"?) I would contend that Steiner, for all the honest anguish of
conscience reflected in his position, has taken an easy way out. If
one stops to consider the ambiguities that are involved in personal
morality, not to speak of political morality, one must conclude that
his view of the conflict is not really moral but only moralistic. That
is, he allows himself to describe historical events in absolute moral
terms, and because, obviously, they cannot measure up to these
terms, he must conclude that there is not "any evident justice" in
the establishment of Israel. On the other hand, since, intuitively, he
cannot condemn the actual existence of the Jewish state, since, in
fact, with his Holocaust-haunted vision of Jewish fate in the Diaspora, he positively needs Israel in his world-picture, he has to leap
rhetorically from censure to wondrous fulfillment across a vacuum.

Let me set against this position a very different formulation of
the same dilemma by Shlomo Avineri in his interview with Ehud
Ben Ezer.* After stating quite candidly that Zionism could only
have been realized by subjecting Palestinian Arabs to a manifest
injustice, Avineri continued:

> It is nevertheless possible to see the justification of Zionism vis-à-
> vis the Arab question in morally meaningful terms. Not in black
> and white terms, in the sense, "the country is ours and they have
> no right here," but in terms relevant to the nature of a moral
> choice, that is to say, a choice between two alternatives niether of
> which absolutely satisfies all moral requirements but one of which
> will be a lesser violation of morality than the other. At least after
> the Holocaust I think this much can be said: that if the alterna-
> tives are that the Jews should have a place they can call their own
> at the cost of uprooting several hundred thousand Palestinians
> from their lands and resettling them in another part of the *same*
> Palestine, or that the Arabs should continue to occupy their own

* *Moznayim*, July 1966.

lands while the survivors of the Holocaust have no place to go —
then, it seems to me, the establishment of the State has a justification.

From the viewpoint of a Palestinian Arab, this moral calculus
may seem brutal, but its sober balancing of claims is persuasive,
and it is especially admirable in the way it works out in painstaking
moral terms, as Steiner does not, the problematic connection between "utter need" and evident injustice. The history of Zionism
has been a progressive foreclosure of historical alternatives. Conceived as the only logical solution to the problem of the Jews in
Europe, it was unfortunately a national movement in need of a
territory which arose at a time when the regions of the earth had
already been parceled out, when the indigenous peoples of colo-
nized areas were already beginning to conclude that they had a right
to political autonomy and to the absolute disposition of the lands
where they lived Even if there had been a feasible territorial alternative to Palestine, the profoundly felt historical connection with
the Land of Israel made it the only place in the world that could stir
Jews sufficiently to unite in a national movement and take the steps
necessary to save themselves, as the fiascos of colonizing schemes
in Uganda, Canada, the United States, Argentina, and elsewhere
abundantly demonstrated. With the new restrictive immigration
laws in the U.S. and other Western countries after World War I,
only the nationalist alternative was left open for rescuing the masses
of European Jewry, and only in Palestine. Finally, as I observed
earlier, the complete intransigence of the Arabs during the Mandate
period, supported with increasing thoroughness by official British
policy, made an independent Jewish state the only way to insure
Jewish survival.
   It is easy enough to survey from a distance the great dismaying
panorama of mankind and identify with the suffering humanity
of the Czechs, the Vietnamese, the Biafrans, the Arab refugees, but
it is a far more demanding, and morally credible, business to confront from day to day people who are trying to destroy you, and
still retain some operative awareness of their humanity. Perhaps
the most significant respect in which Zionism has shifted the ground
of the problem of Judaism is in again placing full political power

in the hands of Jews, thus imposing on them the full weight of responsibility for their actions. For Jews outside Israel, especially when they are self-conscious universalists who consider it a higher obligation to remain free of serious allegiance to any nation-state, it is possible to excise historical events from their contexts, abstract them, integrate them into an elegantly consistent moral theory. In Israel, on the other hand, Jews are inexorably forced to confront moral problems in their full historical concreteness, to test the strength of their values against the brutally resistant medium of political actions.

Israel came into being as the embodiment of a historical paradox. The Zionist idea would not have been conceived, could have had no motive force, without a deep emotional and imaginative loyalty to the Jewish past, not only the biblical past, but, in a more complicated way, even to the Diaspora past where, after all, much of the life and memories of the people to be saved was embodied. On the other hand, Zionism was of course a manifesto through action that the previous two thousand years of Jewish history were all wrong, that the national values implicit in the experience of exile, helping to prolong it, had to be radically transformed. In Israel that radical transformation has been consummated, and now it seems, surprisingly, far less radical than some of the early Zionist thinkers had imagined. In other words, the doubleness of attitude of Zionist beginnings continues today in the ongoing ambivalence of Israeli society toward the Jewish past, which alternately appears as an oppressive dream, a haven for nostalgic imaginings, a happy hunting-ground for passionate antiquarians, a rippled, time-pocked mirror of identity, and even, on accasion, a wellspring of values. Ahad Ha-am was both right and wrong about Zionism and the problem of Judaism; the Jewish state has "solved" the problem by keeping it urgently alive, by turning it into an inescapable dimension of the daily life of a nation.

Simone Weil, commenting on the inner collapse of the French nation in the face of Nazi attack, observed that peoples resist conquest to preserve their past, while the French had willfully discarded their own past as a child might tear rose to pieces. The apparent incongruity of the image she chose reflects a fine perception of the facts under consideration. Protecting the past, which is, after all, protecting the integrity of one's identity, may necessitate the use of violent means in a world of violently exercised power. The past itself, however, is as delicate, as fragile and subtle, as a flower; its own intrinsic existence is not in the sphere of power, so it may be protected, but never sustained, by the implements of power, while its possessor can easily destroy it, almost with the casualness of an afterthought. At a time when, in the profound malaise that has beset most Western societies, we proceed to obliterate our past in the most cunning reckless, and smugly self-deluding ways, Israel tends to be set apart by its consciousness of the past as an obscure but peremptory necessity of identity — a necessity felt, moreover, by the younger generation as well as by the founding fathers. Inevitably, it is because of a shared past, onerous yet precious, that these men and women have come together from many lands to live a renewed destiny on this soil. However rapidly Israel rushes into the avant-garde of the new technological future, it continues to feel the gravitational pull of the past from which it so self-consciously derives.

This suggests still another paradox embodied in the realization of the Jewish existence since the breakdown of the old belief-system and the old sequestered social world has been its decidedly ideological character. Zionism, Bundism, Enlightenment Hebraism, Yiddishism, Reform, neo-Orthodoxy, and a good many forms of Jewish political liberalism or radicalism, were attempts to articulate a particular set of cultural, political, social, or theological ideas into a programmatic rationale for continued Jewish existence after the collapse of the traditional world order. Israel came into being through the implementation of one of these ideologies, but the program having been achieved, there is no longer a need for ideology as a sustaining medium of cultural life. Instructively, Israel is the one place in the world now where one needs an ideology in order not to be Jewish — hence the Canaanite movement, which looks back to a pre-Judaic past among the Semitic peoples of the ancient Near East in order to find a historical point of departure for its conception of Israel as a Hebrew-speaking nation fitting into the larger geopolitical "Semitic sphere" (*merhav shemi*), unconnected with the Diaspora or the Jewish past.

I do not mean to imply that being a Jew in Israel, as many Israelis still like to say, is a completely "natural" state. No condition so perplexed, so insistently problematic, deserves to be called natural. But in Israel it is more easily possible to be a Jew without the tendentiousness endemic to ideologies; definitions of Jewishness can be modified empirically instead of being dictated by *a priori* principle. Ideologies all relate to history, though in a peculiar and often unsettling fashion. Beginning with ideas conceived in order to interpret history and to affect its future course, ideologies absolutize the ideas they incorporate, cutting them off from their empirical ground and elevating them into quasi-theological principle. Such principle, moreover, is often treacherously unreliable because, it usually turns out to be a principle of self-justification.

Let me cite a very pure instance of an ideological statement, among the declarations of an anti-Zionist manifesto issued in 1897 by the Executive Committee of the Association of Rabbis in Germany on the occasion of the First Zionist Congress: "Judaism obligates its adherents to serve with all devotion the Fatherland to which they belong, and to further its national interests with all their heart and with all their strength." Deuteronomy does enjoin us to love the Lord our God with all our heart and with all our strength, but surely not to love the Fatherland in identical fashion, and even the accommodationist principle of rendering unto Caesar what is Caesar's is Christian, not Jewish. What the good rabbis were doing, of course, in the crude tendentiousness of this fabrication, was to convert their own political and social self-interest into a theological principle, supposedly grounded in history (or, in this case, tradition) — it was not the rabbis' personal preferences but "Judaism" that required every Jew to be a loyal German.

Virtually anything can be asserted of "Judaism," conceived in this ideological fashion, and in fact George Steiner, acting on a much more ennobling impulse than those German clerics of Mosaic persuasion, has affirmed exactly the opposite — that the Jewish vocation in history is to be a citizen of doubtful loyalty, an eternal guest, a figure who, unlike the benighted nativists of the world, considers a passport as a dissolvable bilateral contract, not a sign of membership in a mystical community. One would hardly want to begrudge George Steiner his personal commitments, but it seems a little suspect for him to insist on elevating a historical predicament into an eternal imperative. Thus, in the crescendo of a universalist credo, speaking on behalf of the historical Jew, he writes: "Yes, I *am* a wanderer, a *Luftmensch;* 'unto the elements free.' But I have made of my harrying, and of the ironies, stress, sophistication, such harrying provokes in the Jewish sensibility, a creative impulse so strong that it has recast much of the politics, art, and intellectual constructs of the age." The language here gives intimations of self-justificatory strain. The Jewish contribution to modern civilization *has* been quite remarkable, but the moment one converts this fact into a Mission ideology, one can easily slip into an apologetic overstatement of even so remarkable a case. To cite the much-exaggerated instance of the Jewish contribution to Western literatures, in perfect candor, it is hard to think of many Jewish writers beside Heine, Kafka, and Babel, who are not, after all, second-rate. In any case, there are clearly no Jews among the giants of Western literature — Homer, Dante, Shakespeare, Milton, Tolstoy — all of whom, in fact, were in their various ways passionate if liberated nationalists. Continuing in this fashion, however, the next, and concluding, sentence of Steiner's credo verges on the maudlin because its tendentiously selective view of historical facts makes it seem what he surely did not intend it to be, a gesture of self-congratulation: "I am a fellow-citizen of Trotsky and Freud; a *Landsmann* of Kafka and Roman Jakobson; I need the same visa as Lévi-Strauss."

Steiner's universalist argument on the intrinsic moral deficits of Jewish statehood is flawed at the core because, having conceived universalism itself ideologically, he posits ideological nationalism as the only kind of nationalism. Working from this premise, he can suggest that the darkest treason of all may be "to yield one's intelligence, one's moral uncertainties, one's instincts, into the hands of the nation-state." But surely this characterization does not fit the relation of the individual to the nation-state as such; what it does describe aptly is the individual's relation to the *totalitarian* state, or at the very least, to a blindly chauvinistic national entity. Fanatic nationalism is a grave moral danger indigenous to the nation-state as a form of human organization, but to equate the two is like equating woods and forest fires. In this age of splintering nationalisms and tribal battles dignified by the name and amplified by the weapons of international war, the terrible danger of forest

fires is all too evident, but it does not follow that they are the necessary consequence of letting forests grow. At any rate, the evidence
on the whole is now more persuasive than ever that it is not granted
to most human beings to identify with all mankind in one great
leap of the imagination. Most men seem to need first the sense of
solidarity with friends, family, clan, class, and nation; and though
far too many emphatically stop at that point, it is surely possible
to move through those spheres to an embracing sense of human
solidarity at large—indeed, arriving at the universal through the
route of particularism may well mean arriving with a fuller, more
realistic sense of what mankind is.

There is no life without potential disease, and all states of being
have their moral dangers. If the nationalist Jew may swell into an
intolerant chauvinist, the wandering internationalist may shrink to
a cultural parasite, protecting himself from the perception of his
condition with a doctrine of elitism. But these are inherent dangers,
not inevitabilities; in both cases, it is a spiritual imperative to work
for what one hopes — that life may prevail over disease. In regard
to Israel, a clear sign of hope is the fact that Jewish nationalism
has largely abandoned its sense of Mission, which leaves it free to
strive for the realizable goal of being humanly decent, trying to
perpetuate admirable cultural ideals rather than embodying an
Ideal. "The life in ideology," Lionel Trilling has written, "is a strange
submerged life in which to ideas we attach strong passions but no
very clear awareness of their consequences." With the translation
of the Jewish state from the realm of ideology to history, the strange
submerged life Zionists led has surfaced in Israel, whose citizens are
daily confronted in a variety of ways with the palpable consequence
of the ideas from which their nation has drawn being and sustenance. It is not an easy confrontation; at times it may seem almost
an unbearable one; but at least it makes unillusioned clarity a necessary element of national existence, and as we try to imagine a
future we would want, for Jews, for all men, perhaps the last thing
we can afford to be is self-deceived.

Robert Alter

The Price of Zionism

"An understanding with the Jewish inhabitants of Israel is within the bounds of the attainable, for it is not the *nation* that is our enemy — in fact, no *nation* is ever the enemy of any other. Rather, the obstacle to understanding between the Jews and Arabs has been created by Zionism and Imperialism."

These were the words of Mahmoud Derwish, an Israeli Arab poet and former editor of *El Jadid*, an Arab-language monthly published in Haifa, written before he put the following question to me, as part of a projected study for his monthly: "If you were an Israeli-Arab writer, what would you write about the attitude of the Israeli authorities to the local Arab inhabaitants?"

"He who rejects Zionism rejects my existence in Israel," I replied. "Why am I a Zionist? Because I have no other alternative. When my great-grandfather and grandfather arrived here in 1878, and plowed their first field in the Arab village of Umlabess (today Petach Tikva) they determined my fate and the fate of my entire family for generations to come. If the Arabs agree to recognize my Jewish nationalism, that of Zionism and the State of Israel, and sign a peace treaty with us, then all of us — nations and states — will be living a life of paradise. If not, we will be condemned to go on fighting in ever-growing hatred — to become each other's nightmare. In short, our lives will be hell.

"In my writing, I have tried to give expression to the malaise of the young Jew in Israel, a malaise resulting from protracted war with the Arabs. The Israeli lives in a state of hostility and nightmare, and cannot fulfill himself as he would wish.

"I am afraid, though, that this may be taken by the Arab readers as a state of despair or of moral crisis, which is not the case. Nor should he forget that the Arab nation and Arab states have to

25

accept at least partial blame for this situation since to this day they have refused to recognize or make peace with us.

"The fact is, the more we, as Jews and Zionists, are driven to a position of despair, the more will our attitude be rigid and unbending. Any faith in our ability to influence the Arabs by our actions good or bad was completely destroyed by the Six Day War."

After leaving Israel, Derwish quoted these passages in an article in the Cairo daily *El Ahram*. It was the first time, I believe, that an Israeli writer was able to present his Zionist credo to the Egyptian public.

Also quoted were some passages from my novel, *Nor the Battle to the Strong*, whose protagonist, an Israeli student, runs amok in front of the Arab lines and is killed. He imagines that solution of the political problem will bring peace to his troubled soul.

It was years before my novel found a publisher willing to risk bringing it out. Meanwhile, however, the Arab nightmare was growing increasingly apparent in the work of my contemporaries. In the words of Prof. Akiva Ernst Simon: "The Arab question has become an internal Jewish question, and the Arab problem can be considered essentially a part of the Jewish problem, just as the Jewish problem was basically a problem of Christianity."

So it was that I began a study of the Arab question and the treatment of the Arabs in Hebrew literature, starting with my contemporaries and going back to the first Hebrew writers of Eretz Yisrael at the end of the nineteenth century. From time to time excerpts from it appeared in Israeli literary periodicals. I came to find that the terror, nightmare and death described in many of the books were to a large extent directly connected with the Arabs and the long war against them. Many of the heroes of our young literature are trapped and molded by this constant war and the fact of being surrounded by Arabs on all sides. From a romantic approach at the beginning of the century through the war of 1948 and moral uncertainties regarding the fate of the Arab as an individual, the image of the Arab has now evolved into a genuine nightmare.

More or less at the same time I decided to put to a number of our leading Israeli intellectuals a question that was troubling me: What has the real price of Zionism been? The resulting interviews

began appearing in *Moznayim*, a monthly put out by the Hebrew
Writers Association, under the title *The Price of Zionism*. Though
the response was considerable, the series was suspended following
refusal by the editor to print my interview with Boaz Evron, while
I for my part refused to submit to censorship. Word of the series,
however, reached Quadrangle, The New York Times Book Co.,
who asked me to complete it. Hence, most of the interviews in
this book, including the complete interview with Boaz Evron,
are now being published for the first time.

During the years I was working the interviews into their final
form (in close collaboration with the interviewees themselves) I
often had the feeling that the protagonist in *Nor the Battle to the
Strong* and myself were one and the same, and that his questions
were my own. For the Israeli, the threat of the Arab and the cumu-
lative pressure of the wars seem to have become the most concrete
expression of an *existential* fear — fear of the meaninglessness
of life and casualness of death.

*

Generally speaking, Israeli literature treats the malaise and
distress of its heroes from standpoints that are either national or
social. Though it is from a religious standpoint that author Pinhas
Sadeh speaks of man's condition of loneliness and individuality,
as we see in the interview "God Speaks to us with Just Two
Words: Love and Death," — his God is beyond good and evil,
and one in whom it is hard to find salvation.

To the young poet E. Eli the necessity of the war with the Arabs,
to which practically every young Israeli can expect one day to be
sent, is tantamount to a latter-day Sacrifice of Isaac. He can find
in himself no God who would countenance the murder of one's
own son as a test for man. It is a covenant whose ideal passes by
way of death. Moreover, from Isaac's point of view his death is
completely without meaning. Hence, if being a Chosen People is
leading us to death, Eli is willing to renounce our "choseness"
and belief in such a God.

In the absence of faith the Israeli regards such a sacrifice as a
meaningless slaughter, the result of an imbroglio of political and

national interests. Zionism seemed to offer spiritual salvation and a normal existence, yet now we are learning its real price. In the words of Prof. Shlomo Avineri, the Jews in Israel today "are bearing the Jewish cross more intensively than any other Jewish community."

From the standpoint of the struggle for Jewish survival, Zionism has yet to provide a safe harbor. And does such a safe harbor even exist? On the other hand, as a national and social — and primarily *secular* — movement, it has not succeeded in replacing the Jewish religion and a belief in God. Hence the sacrifice too is secular, and has no salvation for the soul — no meaning beyond the struggle for national survival.

Is any answer to this existential malaise to be found in the Jewish religion? To Shulamit Aloni, religion is being used as a political means for achieving power, and the result, on the part of the non-religous, is a growing aversion to the religious establishment. In my view, this antagonism has caused one group to seek refuge in diehard conservatism, and the other to reject positive values because of their petrified and anachronistic framework. Both groups, religious and secular, seek in God and the Bible support for a Greater Israel while in the name of this same religion the extremist Neturei Karta denounce the State's very existence. Thus even God has become a national tool and political weapon, and before such a God it is difficult for the individual to open his heart or to engage in a genuine dialogue, as proposed by Buber. Moreover, in terms of a Jewish religion that is so utilitarian, it is hard to arrive at the synthesis of humanism and religion expounded by Prof. Shmuel Hugo Bergman.

Reading the interview with David Ben Gurion you feel a danger of the State's becoming a sole and supreme value, and that from an ideal of spiritual reawakening Zionism will descend to the level of State collective selfishness. In this connection Buber warns that: "Zion is something greater than a patch of land in the Near East. Zionism is the limitless destiny of the nation's soul."

The possibility of the state becoming the supreme value in the life of the individual and nation brings us close to the Canaanite outlook. Poet Yonatan Ratosh, its ideologist, holds that in the Land of Israel there has come into being a new, secular Hebrew nation, one yearning for freedom from the continuum of Jewish history past and present. He gives primacy to territory rather than the nation in the Diaspora. Our history is that of this piece of land, the Land of the Euphrates, rather than that of thousands of years of Judaism and exile. If the Arabs will free themselves of their Islam and Pan Arabism and the Israelis of their Judaism and Zionism, in this Land of the Euphrates there will arise a single great pluralistic nation.

By contrast, Prof. Yeshayahu Leibowitz, from an extreme religious standpoint, claims that the state interests him only to the extent that it is the State of the Jewish People, for otherwise, he feels, it is not only superfluous but harmful as well. To regard the territorial and governmental framework in Israel as a supreme value is a clearcut expression of chauvinism, or to use a stronger term an expression of the fascist mentality. "Why create a State if the Jewish people does not exist?" he asks. "It may be that there will arise here a new, synthetic nation that is defined by its State, like the Nicaraguan nation. But such a nation does not interest me."

In between these two extremes stands Prof. Gershom Scholem, whose view is something of a common denominator for most of the contradictions in this book. Judaism to him is a living phenomenon that does not admit to dogmatic definitions. Dogmatism implies congealment, while the development of Judaism has been a dialectic between continuity and rebellion. Each generation shapes its conception of Judaism anew, and from this standpoint Zionism, secular though it may be, is an inherent part of the continuous development of Judaism and the Jewish faith. Judaism also includes elements that are utopian — both in the past (which has yet to be divulged completely in a non-dogmatic way) and in the future, which has in store for us phenomena which we are as yet unable to recognize or predict.

Author Avraham B. Yehoshua seeks in Zionism its promised tranquillity, but it is only in heroic periods — war and threat to our suvival — he feels, that we have made full use of our potential. With external calm comes internal decay — a poisoning of the self, as in the Lavon Affair. This has been his great disappointment with the implementation of Zionism, and it is the key to understand-

ing many of his stories. He warns us against betrayal of the
Zionist ideal.

Has the Jewish intellectual in Israel lost his critical and creative standpoint as an outsider? To Boaz Evron the Zionist intellectual is subjugated, psychologically speaking, to the men
of action; he has tended to see himself as a part of the very
disease that Zionism set out to cure. He is a servant of national
development. Here in these interviews, however, he shows himself
to be — iedologically speaking — far from a conformist, nor does
he admit of unequivocal or schematic definition.

While these dialogues were in preparation Israel experienced
a period of nervous calm prior to the war of June 1967, a brief and
heroic war of six days, a protracted war of attrition and a cease
fire which we then hoped would persist until the coming of peace.
For several years Israel enjoyed a state of prosperity, development
and relative security within new and larger borders. Many of the
reefs and shoals exposed by these dialogues — painful questions
which are the unavoidable price of Zionism — appeared then as if
less prominent. And I dared not ask myself whether only a new
spark of the conflagration of war or a threat to our survival would
bring these questions again to the fore?

While it was true that the 1967 war and especially the subsequent
war of attrition have attuned our senses to probe these questions
of our survival, of life and death more deeply, yet the periods of
relative calm, devoid of any heroic struggle or imminent risk of
death, might also have produced a fatigue and narrowness of mind,
exaggerated activism that went hand in hand with apathy, overwhelming pride alongside a hidden inferiority complex, excessive
self-confidence together with hostility and aversion to all criticism.

The outbreak of the Yom Kippur war is suddenly laying bare the
roots of the unease in Israel.

Ehud Ben Ezer

Tel-Aviv, October 1973.

Getting Over the Crisis Without Fanaticism

Interview with Shulamit Aloni

(The interview was held in May, 1970)

BEN EZER: Do you think that the Jewish religion in Israel today in fulfilling a positive role?

ALONI: The politicalization of religion is becoming a serious state of affairs. Israel does not have a constitution and there is no clear ruling as regards the limitations of the authorities' intervention in the sphere of beliefs and opinions. At the same time, religion is serving as a political means for gaining positions of power and control. One of Ben Gurion's reasons for not adopting a constitution was that he did not want a cultural war and he hoped that the resolution of the fundamental problems between religion and state, like the question of marriage and divorce, would be postponed. He thought that he would be able to diminish the influence of the religious bloc by means of political manipulation. But it didn't happen that way. The religious parties' extortionary capacity has increased because there are no constitutional norms and there is no majority party that is able or willing to resolve the outcome. As a result, there exists religious coercion in Israel through the agency of a secular Knesset. This state of affairs has produced an enormous appetite in the religious public, and has caused increasing revulsion toward established religion on the part of the non-religious public.

A manifestation of this appetite for coercion may be seen in the Government's attempt, under pressure from the religious parties, to prevent the introduction of Israeli Television broadcasts on Friday evenings. The attempt was thwarted following an Israeli citizen's appeal to the High Court of Justice. Similar pressures were applied in order to pass the "Who is a Jew?" law in the Knesset. Observance of *kashrut* dietary laws in Israel serves

31

as a source of livelihood for the religious parties' "own people."
Supervision of *kashrut* is a source of many jobs, and the strange,
feudalistic regulations, under which a butcher shop in one city
is not entitled to sell meat ritually slaughtered in another city,
arise from the insistence of each religious council on its exclusive
right to issue *kashrut* approval within its own zone. It is clear
that it is not the religious *Halaha* consideration that is decisive
here. To this may be added the use of the national budget for political purposes by the appointment of various religious functionaries
in the religious establishment. The fact that over 80 percent of
the voters for the National Religious Party are also party members,
a percentage that greatly exceeds the proportion in other parties
between the number of party members and the number of votes
received in elections, demonstrates the dependence of the religious
voter on his party. A person who buys a flat in a "Hapoel Hamiz-
rachi" housing bloc, built on national land and in large part with
public funds, is obliged to produce a rabbi's certificate that he is
an observant Jew, a certificate from the National Religious Party
that he is a party member, and has to contribute money to his
party as well. These phenomena have made religion repulsive to
the public at large.

The successes of the religious have caused them to become
less flexible and their demands to grow. *And that is how religion
in Israel has become something not connected with the relations
between man and God or between man and man, nor with questions of
morality — but a complex of ritual and establishmental matters,
with strict observance to the shell and not the kernel.*

BEN EZER: Some people say that religion today is turning to
perilous paths like the sanctification of military power and according divine sanction to the existence of Greater Israel.

ALONI: Following the Six Day War, both religious and secular
circles have been trying to exploit the sentimental, mystical and
messianic residues of Judaism, as well as Jewish "history", for
the purpose of giving extreme nationalistic views an ideological
basis. The success of these circles has been manifest chiefly among
the older and more backward population, and less so among the
educated and the young Israeli-born. That is because the members
of the older generation grew up in a Jewish tradition in the Dias-

pora and they lack a sence of self confidence, while someone born here has more a feeling of belonging and less a feeling of fear.

Forty per cent of the elementary education in our schools is National Religious, with definite indoctrination in all that has to do with establishing grounds for our historic rights to the country on the basis of a divine promise, with hostility towards the other people of the country and its foreign inhabitants. You do not have any general humanistic elements in the curriculum of these schools that could serve as a counter-weight to the nationalistic tendencies. You will not even find there Israel's Scroll of Independence, which assures social and political equality of rights to every citizen of the country without regard to religion, race or sex.

In the General National Schools, too, they are teaching the Book of Joshua and the divine promise for possession of the land, with greater emphasis than is devoted to the equal rights of every citizen of the country — and a negative effect is produced. Even the studies dealing with human equality are sometimes divorced from actual reality and the practical moral that is binding upon every person in our environment.

When, in the days of the First Temple, King Josiah found the book of the law, he did away with all the "high places" in the country. But in recent times we have been witnessing a very serious matter, the renewal of the "high places," for political purposes, of course. Take, for example, the Cave of the Machpelah in Hebron, Rachel's Tomb in Bethlehem, the talk about Bethel. This use of the sacrosanct with regard to sites and tombs is in fact a setting up of "high places," with dangerous appeal to a primitive public that came to this country from the Islamic countries exploiting its susceptiblity to supersitition.

The law that was passed by the Knesset in the "Who is a Jew?" affair rules that a father and his children in Israel today, if the mother has not converted to Judaism, belong to two different ethnic-religious-national groups, contrary to their will, their world view and their way of life. What is absurd about the law is that it explicity prescribes compulsory recourse to the religious establishment in a democratic state, for the purpose of converting the mother, in order to resolve the absurdity in the relations between the father and his child. Marriage of a *kohen* to a divorcee is still to this day forbidden in Israel, and there is no possibility of circumventing the ban except by travelling abroad for a civil marriage (which does not exist in Israel). The *haliza* dispensation is till this day still binding by law, and Jewish women in Israel are subject to it.

You can see how Jewish history and religion are used to impose ritual observance in a manner that borders on infringment of the private domain, as in the question of stopping work, even essential work, and suspending transporation, on the Sabbath. On the other hand, all of the moral and philosophical questions of Judaism, which are essentially universal, are being completely ingored, as are the fundamental tenets set forth in the Scroll of Independence of the state, in the spirit of prophetic vision and of western democratic principles.

BEN EZER: What will be the effect of the phenomena you have mentioned on the future image of Israeli society?

ALONI: We are at a crossroad. The first members of the Zionist movement to come to this country, particularly those who belonged to the workers' movement, considered the quality and character of the society we will have founded to take precedence even over the fact of establishing the state. Today a change has taken place, though the previous values still do exist, and among young people there is a craving to return to them. To what extent this tendency will be sufficiently encouraged for us to be able to get through this period of reactionary crisis without becoming fanatics — is a moot question.

When the principal of a respectable high school in Tel Aviv tells his pupils, in reply to questions that come up among them in connection with the refugee problem, that the suffering of the Arabs is far smaller than the historic suffering of the Jews, and when statements in a similar spirit are also made by an elected representative of the students in Israel — these utterances indicate the awakening of a dangerous attitude. It is upsetting to see that it is just we Jews, who have always been persecuted and tormented, who prove to be insufficiently inhibited the moment we become powerful.

In Konrad Lorenz' book *King Solomon's Ring*, there is an eyewitness account of a savage battle between two wolves. When the stronger of the two overcomes the weaker, and is about to finish him off, the weaker one proffers his throat, exposing the jugular vein — and the stronger one faced with this easy chance to do away with his enemy, withdraws and releases his victim. The author, a student of animals, sums up by indicating that it is precisely the strong that possess inhibitions. He goes on to tell of animals that are considered weak and hunted, like deer or doves, that were put together in cages, and how each fought the other member of its own species with a savagery that knows no bounds. Hence the conclusion that it is perhaps precisely the weak who possess no inhibitions, since they are accustomed to being in the position of the hunted.

The psychology of our always having been persecuted prevents us from seeing where we are using strength illegitimately. There are those among us who today support the settlement of Hebron or Shechem by Jews. In justification they say that if that is wrong for us, it is also wrong for us to live in once-Arab cities like Lydda and Jaffa, which were abandoned by the Arabs after the war of '48. But the truth is that if the Arabs had not fled from those cities — we would not have driven them out. Our claim is that our settlement in such cities came in the wake of the war. Their inhabitants left under the influence of their Arab leaders, and became refugees, while we housed in them a great part of the Jewish refugees who had left the Arab countries — and there was, in this instance, an exchange of population. Moreover, these were the concrete results of a war that we did not initiate. In the Six Day War, the residents of Hebron and Shechem did not flee. Those who say that it is our right today to settle in the heart of Hebron because it is part of our ancient heritage, are forgetting the rights of the residents who have been living there for many generations, and forgetting their own claim that bi-national settlement produces tension, clashes and stark hatred — all the more so today, when all the wounds and enmity of the war are fresh.

This is how, with slogans and rhetoric, an ideology is being built up around the necessary results of reality and war, as well as a tendency to idealize nationalistic goals rather than be realistic about them. The criteria we apply to ourselves are becoming entirely different from those we apply to the Arabs. And to justify all this, we are drawing on the divine promise and the terrible suffering undergone by the Jews of Europe.

Why am I not pessimistic? As long as there are among us people who are disturbed by these things, and are appealing to reason, there is hope. The question is how the alignment of forces will work out, and what the outcome will be. Arguing with the nationalistic sector of the public is extremely difficult. They do not answer the point but resort to the "catcall method." For example when a certain professor attempts to speak logically, he is accused of being a defeatist, and is interrupted with heckling and catcalls. And there is also the technique of hitting below the belt, such as appeared in a recent issue of the morning paper *Ha'aretz*. A paid advertisement was printed, saying: "These, too, oppose settlement in Hebron — Haman, Amalek, Balaam, etc," with a list of all the Biblical foes of Israel. It was signed by: "A father who lost his two sons in the war," and his full name. Had he signed only his name, that would have been a battle of opinions. Adding his bereavement shifts the debate to irrational and unanswerable lines. The debate with Dr. Nahum Goldman, who advanced a proposal that he meet with President Nasser of Egypt, was also not conducted in a pertinent manner. Personal affronts to his reliability were launched by Israelis who had worked with him and trusted him for years.

BEN EZER: George Steiner claims that the mission and message is represented by the universal attitude of the western Jew, while Israelis are becoming increasingly immersed in the problems of a national state. Isn't this, too, part of the price of Zionism?

ALONI: If we are to hold true to the idea that every person has the right to live in liberty wherever he is — then the conclusion that we can suggest to the American Jewish boy disturbed by the evils in his country is not to run away from his country and come to us, but to fight for his rights and for reform of the society in which he lives. If he is aware of his Judaism and is bothered by it — I will suggest that he come here. If Steiner thinks that his role is to reform his present society — I cannot protest against that and tell him to immigrate to Israel. But it seems to me that the Jews can contribute more to themselves and to others as an independent collective, when and where they are not in personal straits because of their status as foreigners, but have a self-identity, an anchor and a home port of their own.

I think that the reason for the difference in evaluation of the Jewish role in Israel and in the Diaspora among Gentiles resides in the fact that here religion is "establishmentalized," and anywhere that politicalization of religion exists — its real value declines. From the time religion and state were separated in France, Catholicism there progressed in religious philosophy. Therefore, the loss of Judaism's universal content is not the price required of us for the consummation of Zionism, but simply the price of political partnership with and political surrender to the religious parties.

My argument with Steiner is not with his cosmopolitan ethical thinking — with which I agree. But I think that a more tenable, stronger, more convincing point of departure for the battle he proposes and for the Jewish role he envisages — is one in which I have a sovereign state of my own. It is also a guarantee that these intellectual forces will be able to remain in existence. In another three generations, England may no longer have a phenomenon like a Jewish Steiner; "Outsiderness" may disappear. On the other hand, in the Jewish state, where the language, culture and world of associations are Hebrew, it will be possible to go on developing these values. It is the Hebrew University that should be the stepping stone towards George Steiner's univeral values.

BEN EZER: But it was precisely students at Hebrew University who broke up Dr. Nahum Goldmann's public appearance. The Tel Aviv Chamber Theatre was recently (May 1970) obliged to remove from the stage "The Queen of the Bath," a caustic and painful political satire, forced by pressures, disturbances and the atmosphere of nationalistic hysteria that the afternoon papers generated against it. The Minister of Defence, Moshe Dayan, who went to see the play, said about it in an interview broadcast by the Israeli radio: "During the play I was thinking what would actually happen were this play to be taken, as it is, and shown to soldiers in the strongholds, to Egyptian soldiers on the other side, on the Western side of the Canal. What tremendous pleasure the Egyptian army would get if they were to be shown the Chamber Theatre of the State of Israel, supported by the Govenrment and the Municipality and cherished by the public... I know that what I am saying might sound like demagoguery... I cannot imagine anything more encouraging, more tremendous for the Egyptian army than to be able to say: This is the State of Israel as they show it, as a satire of course (but the premise is that satire has a basis in reality). That is what I was feeling while I sat in the auditorium, that there couldn't be a performance more encouraging to the Arabs in their hostile view of the State of Israel, than this play. . . Happening to attend this show of the Cameri's I was thinking that they live in a world that is out of touch. I hope all of the people do not live this out-of-touch with life."

The perfomance of the play at Hebrew University in Jerusalem was also broken up brutally. One might say that the demonstraters and hecklers, in both cases, were a small group of extremist nationalist-religious character. But the fact that they were capable of *faits accomplis* on the largest university campus in the country, which is supposed to be, according to what you said, a stepping stone towards Steiner's universal ideas — that fact is very disturbing, because it indicates the beginning of a trend of intolerance, a trend characterized by limiting the freedom of speech and of artistic expression, and the fanning of the passions of the street.

ALONI: We are in a transition period. If the religious forces and the extremist of Greater Israel forces succeed in building up their strength, I have no doubt that we will have to deal with more than solving our own problems as Jews, we will than have to deal with the Arab problem, not just as an upsetting ethical problem, but as a daily preocupation and the single business of our lives! There are also people who are speaking of conquering Gilead in the event Hussein should fall, and some people say that we must annex southern Lebanon, following the increased activity of the terrorists there. With this state of affairs, the Arab problem would not only be an ethical question for us, but our daily fare.

If we reconsider and revert to the earlier Zionist conception of "another dunam, amother goat," — if we stop the cult of the "high places" and sanctity and become realistic, remembering that we must live with and alongside the Arabs forever, as Mapai's approach had been throughout the years — then it is still possible to consider the crisis we are undergoing as only a transition period. But I agree that the questions of culture, ethics and relations with the rest of the world — are today being set aside in Israel. And they are being set aside in a disturbing manner, based on the increasing popularity of two outlooks: the view that we are strong and can take care of ourselves without the aid of others, and the view that we have always been hated and should not count on others at all. The second view brings us back to the previous point, the loss of a sense of proportion.

BEN EZER: Your attitude implies that you believe it is in our power to alter the present situation. I sometimes have the fatalistic feeling that we have lost our faith in the correlation between our good and bad deeds and the Arabs' hatred of us or their willingness to make a peace treaty with us.

ALONI: While political blunders must be paid for, it is still possible even today to achieve changes. Why is it that with all the things we have demanded *for* ourselves, or that we are repeatedly demanding of the world on behalf of Russian Jewry — we are not demanding them *of* ourselves, for example: Recognition of the Palestinians' right to self-determination. We must indicate that a solution is accessible. Much the same is true of the refugees subject. And the argument whether or not we are to blame for creating the problem is unimportant. What is important is the fact that the refugee problem exists as a festering sore and is our Achilles' heel.

What are our good deeds? In point of fact we have not been considerate either of the Arab mentality or of the Arabs' needs. Today the Palestinians are an incipient people, and we are not superior to them by virtue of our considering ourselves the descendants of an ancient people. We have stimulated in them, by our very presence and growth as a national society, their revolt against us and their national crystallization. It may be that prior to the war of June 1967 the Arabs thought that they might succeed in driving us out with a single push. After June 1967 it became clear to them that this was impossible. But our actual handling of things and our information services did not adequately utilize the psychology and trauma of their feelings after defeat, especially in the sphere of our attitudes towards the West Bank Arabs and refugees. And it is they who are the reason for the conflict in the region, and not the neighboring Arab countries.

I am not a fatalist. If there is one per cent of a chance that we may achieve peace by acting differently — we must seize it. For we will not be able to face ourselves ethically if we do not know, day by day and hour by hour, that we are conducting ourselves in our attitude to the Arabs, in our combat policy, and in our diplomatic measures — only because there is no other choice. And when I say attitude to the Arabs, I do not mean something abstract, but men and women and houses and trees and the culture and desires and dreams of the individual and of his ethnic group environment.

Prime Minister Golda Meir's appeal at the authors' convention, for the authors to join the Establishment, is a troubling and amazing symptom. In such a time as ours one may ask writers not to be outwardly against the Establishment, or that they should scourge it gently, with a sympathetic lash — but to join up? To be yes-men in a society in which there is no opposition and no fertile political dialogue? Keeping intellectuals and writers from voicing criticism — that is a dangerous wish.

BEN EZER: It seems to me that the Prime Minister's appeal was superfluous. Most of the authors to whom she appealed in her address on the evening the convention was opened belong to the Establishment anyway. For the most part they rally to raise their organized voice only on subjects that are part of government policy, and in the spirit of that policy. Great is their desire to prove that they are useful to the administration. A large proportion of the young or dissident authors did not show up in any case at the convention, perhaps out of despair, and perhaps because of a lack of faith in the possibility for change. The danger is that a similar thing may recur in the younger generation as well.

ALONI: It is the good fortune of our youth that today a population cannot remain isolated. The world has shrunk, owing to the communications media, films, theatre and television. Young people travel and see many things, and they have access not only to new fashions (dress, hair and pop music), but to new ideas. These ideas reach our younger generation, for whom the word democracy is part of their basic education. (It does not matter what Mrs. Golda Meir understands by that concept; what does matter is the legitimatization of the concept of democracy in Israel). Therefore, this open-mindedness enables the youth to absorb new things and to express their views freely. As long as "our being a democratic society" is part of our self-justification, and is reiterated even by the people with the most anti-democratic tendencies among us — then whoever does care may fight without fear — and there are many such.

BEN EZER: Jewish youth in the western countries have stopped seeing Israel as a challenge. There are those who lean towards the New Left with its various factions, or in some other radical direction, or towards assimilation. What have we to offer to these young people as a Zionist challenge that is relevant to their personal destinies and to their intellectual world?

ALONI: I cannot approach Jewish youth, demanding that they come here just because they are biologically Jewish. It is every person's right to belong where he feels that he does belong, and our psychology here, of demanding immigration and sneering at those who do not want to immigrate, revolts me. I can only approach a Jewish person who feel uneasy where he is because he is Jewish. I have a challenge for him, which is to free himself from that uneasiness and to turn it into a lever. Here in Israel he has the opportunity to set up a new society. I have met groups of hippies and members of the Civil Rights Movement in the U.S., and they always speak of "a rotten society."

In my opinion, their opportunity for a new society is still here. A young student who wishes to contribute his abilities and build himself up in his profession can start here from the beginning.

Young Jews who are not religious are often bothered by the fact of their being Jewish. They can not renounce the collective ego which produces within them a feeling of belongingness, but numerous complexes, as well. In Israel they can find an answer.

BEN EZER: One of the claims of Zionism has been that it brings with it security of Jewish existence. Today there are people who ask how is an armed ghetto in the Middle East, with one set of borders or another, hated by all its neighbors, preferable to Jewish existence in the Diaspora, even at the price of sporadic manifestations of anti-Semitism, but with no physical peril in sight?

ALONI: It is true that in the U.S. today, and even in Russia, the Jew has more physical security than in Israel. But one's evaluation derives from one's point of departure. I do not believe that we will be an armed ghetto for long. I think that the world's hatred of us is our complex. Till the war of June 1967, the English and the French distinguished between Israelis and the Jews living in their countries. They treated an Isreali like a member of a normal people and country, like an Irishman or an Italian, and not like "their Jews," in the Diaspora sense.

BEN EZER: Today, three years after the June 1967 war there is a feeling that the distinction between Israeli and Jew has again become blurred in the eyes of the world. The Jews of Israel are paying with their lives the price of the Jewish struggle for survival, while the Jews of the Diaspora are more and more identified with Israel in the eyes of the world, and held responsible for its actions. In times of stress, particularly as on the eve of the Six Day War, the Israelis have realized that the Jews of the world are the only allies who support them unconditionally.

ALONI: Even today it is wrong to say that the whole world is against us. It is, of course, true that even young people in Israel are not capable of hearing crit:cism without getting an anti-Semitism complex. If a Jew criticizes us, he is charged with Jewish self-hatred and if a Gentile does so — why, he's an anti-Semite. Even our friends among the Gentiles say that it is most difficult to convey criticism to us. And it should be possible to be friends, and not agree with every step of the Israeli government.

When, in her speeches, Golda Meir recalls her childhood and the pogrom atmosphere in her town, it is no wonder that she does not display confidence in Gentiles, since she is carrying with her a stratum of fear and disbelief of them and perhaps of the whole world. And that is the way it is with members of her generation, survivors of the ghettos and the Holocaust. But we, the younger generation, do not have such emotional residues. Nor does the world relate to us in that way. I think that the criticism of Israel's policy made in many circles and countries in the world would be made about the policy af any other state in our situation. I can disagree with criticism, but I can rationally understand its motives and not blame world anti-Semitism for it.

Our conflict with the Arabs is not based on anti-Semitism either, but is a tragic clash between two ethnic groups. A fight for survival is not a value but an exigency (on condition that it is truly a fight for survival). Therefore it should not be judged by the criteria of social and ethical values. In the book of Job it is said: "Skin for skin, yea, all that a man hath he will give for his life." I see the army and the state only as tools and framework to aid in developing values. From that standpoint we ourselves have provided a factual answer to the subject of Jewish survival as a value. Here, Jewish survival is not merely a matter of words and ties among people possessing a common origin, but a fact of life, a world view, a language, a culture and all the rest. Here we have a system of Hebrew education and Israeli culture that enables people to live with a feeling of integrity and belongingness. A Jew in Israel is at home. He can walk around in bedroom slippers. Everywhere else he is obliged to be on his best behavior and wear a necktie.

The best indication of the feelings of a Jew in Israel is to follow the reactions of Jewish tourists who come here from other countries. After a few hours they say, "Why these are our people, *unsere menschen*, *ich bin in haym*, I'm home." This is a sign that there is in Israel a feeling of belongingness — a home for every Jew. You do not have to make an effort and martyr yourself here in order to be yourself. You are simply you.

BEN EZER: Retrospectively, from a historical point of view, how does Zionism's approach to the Arab problem appear to you? Are we not paying today the price of the blindness by virtue of which the state did indeed arise, but without any possibility of peaceful co-existence with the Arab nationalist movement. The romantic, pacifistic approach to the Arabs has always proved itself bankrupt, and only a fatalistic and pessimistic activism, preparing for the very worst, for war, has proven itself tight and proper from our standopint.

ALONI: I agree that we have not been sufficiently aware of the Arabs. It is important to add that the English aided a great deal in exacerbating the relations between the two peoples, as they did in India, too. But, again — I do not accept your fatalistic approach. One of the things that bothers the Arabs most, from the verbal standpoint, is the Israeli Law of Return, which automatically accords Israeli citizenship to any Jew immigrating to Israel. This is actually the repatriation of the Jewish people to its country. It is like the approach of the Russians to the Armenians, or of Germany to Germans. From this derives the justification of the Jewish state, and at the same time for according independence to the Palestinians and recognizing their right to self-determination in part of the country. Retaining the boundaries of the whole land of Israel would oblige us to recognize the return of the refugees, or assume the diadem of conquerors and usurpers. It is impossible to liberate territories while people belonging to an ethnic group other than ours live there. When we recognize that, the conflict will begin to be solved. It will take time, but we, with our policy, are not shortening that time. There is another possibility: The great powers may impose on us a settlement whereby the country will be re-partitioned, and thus the Arabic ethnic group living on the West Bank of the Jordan will be removed from Israeli rule. Such an imposed settlement might perhaps lead to normalization.

I have no doubt that political Zionism did not err in principle. Despite the state of war, Israel is consummating Zionism and providing the answers we have sought from the standpoint of individual and collective survival. At the same time, we have made numerous mistakes, as do all those who function within history. Today we must do everything so that, even though we be right — and in the main we are right — the Arabs as human beings will not be injured and their right to self-determination as a group will be accorded them.

As Europe underwent the emergence of nationalism in the nineteenth century, and we went through that stage at the end of that century and the beginning of this, so the Arabs are going through that stage today. In every transition from a feudal, religious society to a national society, there are extremist nationalist manifestations. The entire process has reached the Middle East late. Therefore there are chauvinistic manifestations on both sides, as there were in Europe years ago. Today when every one of the peoples of Europe has its own national state, young people there are beginning to hold universal outlooks and to regard nationalism as a reactionary word.

If the aim of Zionism has been to set up a sovereign Jewish state then it has succeeded, and Israel no longer needs to justify its existence. It simply exists. But giving up several extremist slogans, and reverting to the values of early Zionism could do a great deal towards bringing peace with the Arabs closer.

BEN EZER: There exists an opinion that Jewish genius has had its origin in a felicitous encounter between the Jewish intellect and one of the rich European cultures. The price of Zionism exists also in the danger of decline in the fertility of the Jewish genius in Israel, owing to the danger of self-circumscription in the national war for survival. You can see a troubling confirmation of this in the fact that Jewish intellectuals in the Diaspora are losing their respectful, appreciative and perhaps self-depreciative attitude towards Israel.

ALONI: In the Middle Ages, during the times when Judaism was improving its breed, Christianity was breeding limitations. Education was accessible only to members of the wealthy classes, while others received education only through the church and the institution of monasticism. But for the Jewish population intellectual activity and study were of tremendous importance. The daughter of the rich man was married to the "prodigy," and they were blessed with the commandment, "be fruitful and multiply." In this sense it may be said that Judaism was engaged in improving the breed. But today there is a democratization of education and advancement all over the world and for all classes. That is the position in Israeli society as well, and it is natural that within several generations Jewish ingenuity will be less exceptional.

At the same time, on the planes of intellectual and scientific creativity that are not connected with politics, Israel's prestige has remained at a high level. Where has the difficulty arisen? In the spheres of thought and *belles lettres*, the spheres that in every state are affected by the conflict among various social and political situations. Israel's political predicament appears to be affecting the ability of its authors and intellectuals to be articulate in the world. And of course there does exist the language difficulty of a small country. A Hebrew author may well ask himself — who am I toiling for?

But in the field of science, Israel's prestige is high, as exemplified by the Weizmann Institute of Science in Rehovot and the Technion in Haifa. We are exporting know-how, and our experts have a great deal of prestige in the world. Those intellectuals, a large proportion of them Jewish, who relate to Israel disparagingly, are basing all their charges on the political sphere, which is clearly the outcome of a specific reality in which we are now placed.

Our courts, where moral problems are coped with untrammeled by political pressure groups, are proving themselves and maintain a high standard. And in the sphere of technology we are highly successful in adopting and adapting technical inventions, developing and improving them. That is the activity of the Jewish genius in Israel today. And all of the rest of the imputations against us are in the nature of political criticism and value judgement, which of course have ramifications in the sphere of thought and ethics.

BEN EZER: How do you see the effect of the Six Day War and the three ensuing years on the educated Is aeli youth who are about to begin army service, and on the young Israelis for whom a state of war had become almost the only prospect for their entire life?

ALONI: I think that the administration does not offer Israeli youth any intellectual encounter. Education is too establishmenta-lized. The classic example is the canvassing of high scool seniors to sign petitions to the Prime Minister. About a month ago, a group of seniors from a Jerusalem high school sent a letter to Prime Minister Golda Meir, in which they wrote:

"We, a group of high school pupils about to be recruited into the Israel Defence Forces, protest against the Government's policy in the affair of the Goldmann-Nasser talks. Till now we have believed that we are going to fight and to serve for three years because there is no alternative. After this affair — it has been proved that even when there is an alternative, though it be the smallest, it is ignored. In the light of this, we and many others are thinking about how to fight in a perpetual war with no future while our Government channels its policy in such a way that op-portunities for peace are missed. We call upon the Government to exploit every opportunity and every chance for peace."

The letter evoked powerful negative repercussions in the Estab-ıɪshment, and in a large part of the public, who trebelled chiefly against young people daring to make their ability and willingness to fight conditional upon their faith in the policy of the Govern-ment. In reply, teachers "spontaneously" canvassed hundreds of seniors in numerous high schools in the country, to sign petitions to the Prime Minister, denouncing the letter of the Jerusalem group of pupils and declaring their loyalty and willingness to fight under any conditions. This organized mass canvassing of signatures shocked me. The Prime Minister was pleased and she was even proud to cite these "spontaneous" petitions at a press conference.

Prof. Chaim Adler of the Hebrew University conducted research in education-to-values in Israeli schools, and the Ministry of Education supressed the work because of its grim findings. It showed chauvinistic tendencies in Israeli youth, particularly in the National Religious Educational stream, and the existence of a strong tendency to judge oneself and one's people by different criteria from those applied to another people. In my opinion, our education is overly nationalistic, and should be changed. In my childhood, the emphasis in Bible study was on the sayings of the prophets. Today, it is on the Book of Joshua and the period of taking possession of the land. The historical rights are the main thing. I hope that the Ministry of Education is aware of these problems, and that it is preparing a broader curriculum for education to universal values.

BEN EZER: Do you feel a danger to the character of Israeli democracy in the phenomenon that it is military men and ex-military men who determine the destiny of the state and reach senior political leadership positions?

ALONI: Most of those military men who are today entering political and economic positions are graduates of the working youth movements. The democratic values that remain from their educational background distinguish them from professional military men in the customary sense. Our tragedy is a different one, and its source resides in the fact that the army has proved itself the most efficient factor in Israel, while there is in the field of politics no imagination, action or thinking to compare with the vigorous drive of the military. It is a troubling state of affairs when people of ability do not enter political life because of the closed structure of the parties, bastioned by a machinery of mediocre individuals. Only the army has become a sort of spring-board that bypasses the long, tortuous path, and enables senior officers to move right into high-ranking political posts. People who come from the civilian world shy away from travelling the long, grey political road, from encountering the reality of political pressure groups and of a proportional elections system in which the nominations are made by the central party leaderships, and the voter has no influence on the choice of his candidates. Particularly today, with the national unity Government and no opposition worthy of the name in the Knesset, there exists a perilous situation in which any dialogue, instead of being conducted in the Knesset, is taking place between the Establishment and the man-on-the-street.

BEN EZER: Do you sense any limitations on the development of women in Israel? Does the anxiety implicit in out existential situation affect her in particular?

ALONI: Women of Western European extraction know how to utilize their rights. But there is an enormous population of women who have come from Oriental countries, countries in which women had an inferior status, and tradition and religion promoted preservation of that inferior status, especially in everything relating to the laws of family life. In their sensitivity to the security situation, there is no difference between the sexes. In a large proportion of young families, the wife has also served in the army, like the husband, and the topic is shared by them equally. But from the standpoint of opportunities for advancement, the situation is as follows: At the higher rungs of the ladder of profession scales, all paths are accessible to the woman. But at middle level jobs and for the weaker strata, a woman's advancement is far more difficult. The degree of a women's freedom rises with her degree of intelligence.

Jewish society's expectations of a woman are first of all that she be a mother and raise children. Today, owing to the demographic problem and the security situation, these demands are addressed more strongly to the woman in Israel. Therefore, the woman today who wants to build herself a career is totally subject to a complex of guilt feelings. Furthermore, owing to numerous religious laws, particularly in the family sphere, an ambivalent attitude towards the woman has remained. After all, there are still many people who pray daily: "Blessed be He who did not make me a woman." And in many schools, religious schools, in which the *Shulchan Aruch* is taught, they still recite that "A person should not walk between two women, two dogs or two pigs, and should not sit between them." That certainly makes it difficult to recognize the equality of the woman and her rights.

Subjugation of the Means to the State's Ends?

Interview with Prof. Shlomo Avineri

(This part of the interview was published in *Moznayim*, July 1966)

BEN EZER: Would it be correct to assert that the feature that distinguishes the Jewish intellectual in the Diaspora from his Israeli counterpart is the former's hypersensitivity and his distinctly universal outlook — in contrast to the circumscribed, parochial outlook and ostensibly normal indifference of the latter? One sometimes has the feeling that the Jew outside of Israel needs his environment to be more just than does his Israeli counterpart, in order to ensure his well-being and his rights.

AVINERI: I perfectly agree that in Israel the intellectual loses the sensitivity which characterizes the Diaspora Jew. In a way this may be what Zionism, with its metaphors of Exile life, has always striven to achieve. All the more so since Zionism, particularly the pioneering sector of Zionism, contained a veiled anti-intellectual bias, although its mainstay has been the intelligentsia.

But it seems to me that the problem is more a structural one, and less connected with the subjective purposes of Zionism. If the Jewish intellectual in the Diaspora does possess a special sensitivity, an intellectual open-mindedness and a creative tension — that is to no small degree because he is living *in two societies and two cultures.* On the one hand he is a Jew, and whatever the objective and subjective significance of the concept may be, it invariably poses questions as to the meaning of his self identity. Therefore the Jewish intellectual, even though he may be at a loss and his Judaism rather blurred, is contending with the problem of what his Jewishness means. On the other hand, as a member of a minority group, he is sensitive to the character of society at large, to its attitude towards him and to his opportunities for fitting into it while retaining his particularity. He is sensitive to the question of how liberal the society at large is, and has the desire to leave something of his own mark on it. Therefore the Jewish intellectual in the Disapora is sensitive both to the meaning of his Jewishness and to the character of society at large. In this way, a specific literature, polemics and philosophy are produced — specifically as a result of what contemporary American sociologists call "marginality."

In Israel, it is an entirely different matter. Since ideology (or at least the vulgar shades of ideology) posits that territorial concentration and national independence are an indication of "normalization" — the question of searching for one's own identity does not exist. We are Jews because we live in Israel, speak Hebrew, learn the Bible and give our children Biblical names. According to this view, we are Jews in the same way that the Englishman is English, the Frenchman French, and so forth. All the sensitivity, the quest for identity, the soul-searching, are no longer there. There is a great deal of irony in the fact that with us the question of who is a Jew has to arise in the course of a debate about the administrative details to be registered in the ID cards of the children of mixed marriages. Throughout the world, the question of who is a Jew is a crucial existential question for every individual Jew. For us, it is an incidental administrative problem.

Nor is there sensitivity to the problem of the character of society at large. It is obvious that the degree of the Israel-educated Sabra's comprehension of the character of the twentieth-century world is less than the average comprehension of his Jewish counterpart in the U.S., England or France. If we add to this the fact that the Jewish intellectual in the Diaspora sometimes lives in two, if not three language cultures (the vernacular, a bit of Yiddish and a smattering of ritual Hebrew), while the Sabra finds it difficult to master even *one* foreign language — then we will realize that much of the linguistic and esthetic sensitivity connected with Jewish writers abroad has also disappeared in Israel.

The ideological view of the function of literature in Israel as an instrument for nation building is also damaging to the possibility of creating esthetic content. We forget that Bialik and Tchernichovsky were *rebelling* against the conventions of the Jewish society of their time by the act of writing in Hebrew, and that a literature which lacks the element of rebellion ceases to have artistic value, while literature in Israel serves as a means to political and ideological ends. Here I am obliged to insert a comment that digresses somewhat from the topic, but belongs to it nevertheless. I have always felt that the great essay about the Holocaust would not be written by a Jew. The victim, however cruel it may be to say so, is not sufficiently aware of the universal significance of the injury done to him. That is why there is a great literary truth embodied in the fact it had to be the German Hochhuth who wrote the work that probably stands as the classic indictment of the silence of the world. In parallel to this, I am of the opinion that the great Hebrew work in Israel can never be a work of identification with the Zionist project — not because the content of the Zionist is at fault, but because the structure of literature is non-conformist.

From this standpoint, Israeli Zionist literature is sometimes reminiscent of Bolshevik "Socialist Realism." It must depict positive characters, and is expected to be constructive. The exception to this is S. Yizhar's short story "Khirbet Khiza'h," written in May 1949, which gives evidence of a universal sensitivity and not of victim sensitivity. But the fact that the very same S. Yizhar, as a member of Knesset in the early 'sixties, voted in favor of retention of Military Government in the Arab-populated areas of Israel — constitutes a classic demonstration of what is likely to happen to the intellectual in Israeli society.

BEN EZER: Jewish self-hatred has usually been considered to be a clearcut manifestation of the anomalous Exilic existence, and there are those who seek confirmation of this in the self-hatred evident among Jewish young people and intellectuals in western countries today. How are we to understand the fact that similar symptoms of Jewish self-hatred are emerging among a considerable portion of the young people and spokesmen of the "healthy" generation of Sabras, as well?

AVINERI: It is true that the Jewish intellectual in the West sometimes possesses a not inconsiderable amount of self-hatred. But self-hatred is merely another expression of extreme self-criticism. From that standpoint, I sometimes get the impression that such Jewish self-hatred is no less current among us. After all, doesn't the desire to be "like all the Gentiles" (whatever the meaning of that expression might be) imply an acceptance of the standards of Gentile society as relevant to Jewish existence? The Jews have not only been persecuted for two thousand years, they have usually been persecuted because they have constituted an elite stratum in each society. In every society, the average standard of living of the Jew has been higher than that of the overall society; the Jewish standard of education has been immeasurably higher than the general standard of education, and the Jewish way of life has been more enlightened and more highly developed than the *average* way of life of the populace.

I hope that I am not being guilty of Jewish chauvinism, but it seems to me that what I have said here is valid, and that one must possess a very high degree of Jewish self-hatred in order to represent the entire Exilic history of the Jews as a chronicle of persecution and a record of a miserable, spiritless, crippled life. The Jews have been persecuted because they have been better educated, wealthier, and more cultured than the average of the societies in which they have lived. Anti-Semitism should be seen not only as the employment of force by the strong against the weak, but also as the jealousy of the average towards achievement and success. Rather than being proud of a Jewish tradition that is aristocratic in the true sense of the word, though its meaning in Jewish life has always contained an element of living dangerously, we are often ashamed of our own history. This means that Jews too frequently have accepted the criteria of an alien society. It has been noted that the image of the Jew in the eyes of the anti-Semite is remarkably similar to that of the Diaspora Jew in the eyes of the Sabra, educated in the vulgarized form of Zionist ideology.

BEN EZER: Why, in your opinion, do Jewish students in the U.S. prefer to devote their idealistic energy and enthusiasm to general liberal causes, such as civil rights, rather than respond to Zionist challenges.

AVINERI: It seems to me that a striking change has taken place in the intellectual Jewish youth's attitude towards Zionism since the establishment of the state. So long as Zionism was a universal movement, not linked with the sovereign interests of a territorial state, it was capable of serving as a cause for idealistic Jewish youth in the Diaspora. From the moment it became an instrument of a state, it underwent a devaluation, a reduction from the universal to the particular. And today it is not capable of providing motivation for a youth who relates to these problems from the standpoint of universal criteria.

BEN EZER: What is the effect of the Israel-Arab situation in shaping the character and concepts of the Israeli public in the country? There are those who think that ultimately there will come into being among us a new type of person, all of whose powers and sensibilities will be mobilized to ensuring physical survival.

AVINERI: I am of the opinion that, in the foreseeable future, our present confrontation with the Arab states will remain more or less within the present frame. I do not believe that the State of Israel is threatened by an Arab attack, so long as the arms balance remains at the present relative level. Nor am I of the opinion that time is working markedly in favor of the Arabs. On the other hand, it does not seem to me that there is any reasonable chance for peace with the Arabs or for open borders with them.

If the present situation is the normal one, and that is in fact my opinion, then it is clear that it has far-reaching ramifications as regards the internal structure of the state. This is already manifest in the metaphoric significance of the word "Arab" in the State of Israel today. It is also manifest in the utter lack of sensitivity to the Arab refugee problem. I should like to stress that I do not think that the State of Israel can permit the return of Arab refugees to its territory. But our public's lack of all sensitivity to the human side of the suffering inflicted on hundreds of thousands of people who were not personally responsible for Arab policy and for the Arab attack in 1948 is so striking that it demonstrates how the present situation generates indifference and callousness.

I am not saying that all of us must be saints, but I do have an uncomfortable feeling about abandoned Arab property, for example; I have never lived and do not think I would ever be capable of living in an abandoned Arab house, or in a building built on abandoned Arab property. I know that it is impossible to behave that way about every single thing, but the fact is that the insensitivity is total.

BEN EZER: Could we have avoided succumbing to this total insensitivity? Could Zionist history have been possible at all, had it not been for the unavoidable Jewish-Arab conflict?

AVINERI: If we view the problem from the viewpoint of historical perspective, then it is clear that *Zionism has failed in its approach to the Arab case.* But I doubt whether there was any alternative. That is really the price of Zionism. It was George Antonius who in the thirties saw things most pungently, when he said that a Jewish state could be established in Palestine only at the price of driving the Palestinian Arabs from their land.

I have no suspicion that there was any Zionist leader, even of the most extreme, who *consciously* thought in these terms. I think that Zionism believed in good faith that it would be possible to make an omelet without breaking eggs. My premise is that there has been a certain functional element in ignoring the concreteness of the Arab question, the fact that there exist two national movements which must of necessity clash during the period of their consolidation. That is to say, had the Zionist leaders not believed that it was really possible to reconcile Zionism with the rights of the Arab people in Palestine, they would have come to the conclusion that the price of Zionism is removal of the Arabs, and since most of the Zionist leaders were idealistic humanists, a large proportion of them even socialists, they would not have been prepared for such a solution. Ignoring the concreteness of the Arab problem was an internal defence mechanism of Zionist consciousness. Had they thought things out, they might have been deterred from Zionism, and only because they clung to a "rosy" idealism were they able to maintain their Zionist outlook.

Nevertheless, it is still possible to view Zionism as justified vis-à-vis the Arab question in terms that are morally meaningful — not in black-and-white terms which would mean we have the country and they have no right at all, but in terms that are relevant to the nature of a moral alternative, that is a choice between two alternatives neither of which entirely satisfies all the moral demands, but one of which is likely to be less morally damaging than the other. It seems to me that it may be said, at least since the Holocaust, that if the alternative is between (a) the Jews having their own roof over head at the price of uprooting hundreds of thousands of Palestinian refugees from their land and resettling them in some other part of the *same* Palestine, and (b) the Arabs of Palestine continuing to live on the land while Holocaust refugees remain homeless — then the moral price of setting up the State is justified. Between the lack of a Jewish homeland following the Holocaust, and the uprooting of part of the Arabs of Palestine to another region in the same country — the moral alternative is clear.

BEN EZER: Securing the survival of the Holocaust refugees and of the Jewish people as a whole has been one of the decisive claims of Zionist ideology. But today there are those who ask: In what respect is an armed ghetto in the Middle East and being hated by all our neighbors preferable to Jewish existence in the Diaspora, even though it might be at the price of sporadic anti-Semitic manifestations. How are we supposed to cope with the fact of the existence of a materially and spiritually rich Jewish life in Western countries, completely contrary to Zionist predictions?

AVINERI: From the standpoint of the State of Israel comprising a solution to the problem of the survival of the Jewish people, there exists a deep tragedy which manifests itself on several planes. First of all, if there is any place in which collective Jewish life is being faced with concrete and constant threat of physical extinction, it is precisely in the State of Israel. The physical survival of the Jew in New York or in London is far more secure than in Jerusalem or Tel Aviv. And if there is any meaning to the uniqueness of the State of Israel (and I always stress this in talks with Jewish friends from abroad), it resides in the fact that only in the State of Israel is my life as a Jew threatened, not in New York or anywhere else. From this standpoint, *we are bearing the Jewish cross more intensively than any other Jewish community.*

Secondly, Zionism is the outgrowth of the plight of the East European Jews, who were being ground between the gears of the parallel processes of disintegration of traditional Jewish community life in the Pale of Settlement and the rise of nationalism in East Europe. It was for this Jewry, and *not for the Jewry of the affluent western countries, that Zionism was created.* This is evident even in the essays of a western Jew like Herzl. The plight of the Jews is *ultimately* the plight of the "Ostjuden," which the "Westjuden" are obliged to assist *in solving.* The tragic paradox lies in the fact that had it not been for the Holocaust, or so it seems to me, the State would not have been founded. Only the shock of the Holocaust could have made possible the moment of international goodwill of November 29, 1947. However, from the time the State was founded, the communities for whose salvation and welfare it was intended *no longer existed.*

Third, the problem of the Jews of Islamic countries raises another aspect of the problem. Islam was free of the anti-Jewish element that was imbedded, in the final analysis, in the very fabric of Christianity. Though the situation of the Jews of the Islamic countries was far from being comfortable, in most cases their problems were a function of the general backwardness and the general discrimination within the retarded Moslem society, and not a problem that arose from a specifically anti-Jewish bias of the Moslem society. From this standpoint it was in fact the founding of the State of Israel that served to introduce an element of hatred of the Jews into a society in which it had not previously existed. The establishment of the State of Israel made the continued existence of Jews impossible in the Arab society after the Arab defeat in 1948. *The uprooting of the Oriental Jews is also one of the prices of Zionism.*

We sometimes tend to attribute genuine meaning to ideology, while ignoring reality. I am referring to the *catastrophe theory* of vulgar Zionism. It is certain that Jewish existence in the United States is problematic, but to claim that one may never know whether there will not be extermination camps in the U.S., as well, is an unparalleled piece of foolishness. But that is why, while the circumstances of the Jews there are constantly improving, there is a tendency among us to dismiss them and to say they are living in a fools' paradise. I am definitely prepared to make distinctions and to concede that there are several places in which the situation of the Jews has become most delicate, as in Latin America and South Africa. But the lack of discernment we are sometimes guilty of is truly astonishing and bears a certain resemblance to the Marxists' dogmas concerning the necessary deterioration of the circumstances of the proletariat. Every time it emerges that the workers' standard of living is rising in the West, the Marxist vulgarizers come forth to say: "Wait and see what the next crisis will be like."

The greater the prosperity, the more severe the crisis is going to be. Such a pseudo-deterministic outlook is only a pace away from desiring to see its realization. And it may be worth mentioning in this connection that in the attitudes towards the Holocaust held by several of the Zionist leaders then in Palestine, there was, or so it seems to me, a seed of ambivalence.

BEN EZER: In retrospect it appears, then, that the consummation of Zionism in Palestine shows indications that at every single stage priority was accorded to the needs of Jewish Settlement and to the "state in the making," sometimes with embarrassing avoidance of responsibility towards the concrete fate of the entire Jewish people. What has been going on here?

AVINERI: The mentality of Zionism consummating itself in this country sometimes exhibits similarity to the structural features of Bolshevik mentality. And from this standpoint, as well, Zionism has demonstrated an affinity to its East European sources. Just as Bolshevik ideology contains an element of the actual, concrete proletariat supposedly serving as a means of accomplishing the ends of the future proletariat, and the revolutionary avant-garde being entitled to impose on the entire working class the conclusions deriving from its ideology — so there are similar nuances in Zionism as it has been consummated in this country. The feeling that we know what is good for the Jews of the world, that under certain circumstances we are entitled to manoeuvre them into a situation that will confirm our prognosis, *that the Jewish entity in Palestine is entitled to view itself as an end which the Jewish Diaspora is obliged to serve as a means* — such nuances and others manifest themselves from time to time in our empirical behavior towards world Jewry.

The deep problematics of our attitude towards the Holocaust and towards illegal immigration to Palestine during the British Mandate are also sometimes linked with these nuances. For example: On September 8, 1939, David Ben Gurion said at a meeting of Hagana activists: "As we now stand on the brink of war, we must clarify to ourselves the path we must follow and the goal towards which we must strive. The First World War in 1914–1918 brought us the Balfour Declaration; this time we must bring to pass a Jewish State."

This was undoubtedly a far-sighted penetration of the mists of the future, but at the same time there is present here a terrible lack of sensitivity to the fear that had engulfed all Jews in September 1939, as regards the physical survival of European Jewry. In this frame of reference, Palestine had stopped being a *solution* to the Jewish problem. World Jewry had become an *accessory* to the Jewish Settlement in this country. And it is possible to produce numerous more up-to-date examples. Our United Nations vote in the matter of South Africa, however right it might have been, did not take into account the significance of this matter for South African Jewry; and when it was decided to kidnap Adolf Eichmann in Argentina, was the significance of this action taken into account from the standpoint of its being a possible spur to anti-Semitism in South America? It seems not.

BEN EZER: It is strange that processes and trends of this sort are almost never expressed in any form of literature, either belletristic, publicistic or scientific.

AVINERI: There is a dearth of substantial works in the field of modern Jewish history, and a connection between the lack of such books and the opinions current in the public about modern Jewish history and the history of the new Jewish settlement in Palestine. This connection, too, is related to the clearly ideological prism through which these subjects are viewed. Even here there exists a projection of the Zionist world view (or the vulgarized application thereof). If Zionism means negating the Disapora, then Zionist education has automatically been associated with an approach which not only highlighted the negative and distorted aspects of Jewish existence in the Diaspora, but even saw the patterns of existence of the Jews of nineteenth century Eastern Europe as characterizing all of Jewish history since the destruction of the Second Temple. One can ask any child in the street about his image of Jewish life in the Diaspora and find that it is a projection of the East European Jewish *stetl* at its decline. This view has submerged any positive content. Instead of representing the Diaspora Jews as an elite group which accomplished splendid cultural and economic achievements in every society into which it was thrust, it has represented them as an unfortunate, itinerant, faceless mass.

We may find an extreme example of this view in the letter of resignation of the first Prime Minister, Mr. David Ben Gurion, addressed to the President, in which he wrote: "We have consolidated human dust, scattered and crumbled throughout the exile ... into the seed of a resurgent nation." In a way, this over-consistent Zionism contains the roots of Canaanitism, which views Jewish history in contemporary Palestine as a direct continuation of the Biblical period, as though the intervening eighteen hundred years were non-existent.

BEN EZER: Is it possible to say, then, that the Canaanite ideology, too, has its source in that same assigning of primacy to the country rather than to the people?

AVINERI: Someone has said that Zionism is *the collective assimilation of the Jewish people*, and indeed it sometimes seems that the roots of Canaanitism lie in overly consistent Zionism. The roots of Canaanitism's hostility towards Diaspora Jewry lie in Zionism's negative approach to Jewish history in the Diaspora, an approach which in its own right was functional, though not essential, to the emergence of a national consciousness in this country. The sense of alienation from the immediate past in the course of a search for a vague identity in the problematic Biblical past is common to the various forms of Canaanitism and radical political versions of Zionism. The manner in which Israeli history and Hebrew literature are being taught in schools in this country, the manner in which from the Bar-Kochba Rebellion till the founding of Petach Tikva (1878) "we have no history," as Yudke says in Chaim Hazaz's novel, constitutes a fine introduction to Hebrewite, Canaanite and other such biases.

Here, too *this* version of Zionism relates to history in the same arbitrary, selective, color-blind manner as does Bolshevism. With regard to the new Jewish settlement in Palestine, as well, the mark of the ideological outlook is apparent in the historiography. Till this day, there is not one good text on the subject. Most of the extant texts are either autobiographies, which are of great value as sources but not as substitutes for historical summary, or political ideology texts bearing the mark of the author's political affiliation. Historical method, self-criticism and perspective are utterly lacking in these essays. As regards the image of the history of Jewish settlement in this country, it is the version which suits the ideology of the Labor Movement that is particularly in evidence. I myself belong to this movement, but I still believe that no movement and no personality can be its or his own historian.

BEN EZER: In recent years, there has been a growing feeling that the two branches of the Jewish people, in Israel and in the Diaspora, are doomed to face the peril of increasing alienation and estrangement, as a result of the lack of possibility of reaching a common definition and a common denominator which recognize and admit the various possibilities of contemporary Jewish existence.

AVINERI: The way to maintain meaningful ties with Diaspora Jewry and particularly with the tremendous Jewish center in America (it is worth remembering that there are 300,000 Jewish students in U.S. universities!) is *for us to recognize the legitimacy of Jewish existence in the Diaspora*, particularly within the framework of the American society.

It is worth understanding and knowing that Jewish existence in the U.S. is entirely different from Jewish existence in Europe. Whatever the situation of the European Jew may be, he has always belonged to a minority ethnic group. The U.S. is itself composed of an inter-ethnic mix and the Jews are one of the components of this mix. Nowhere in Europe may one speak of Judaism as one of the religions of the state. But in the U.S., however apologetic the assertion may sound, Judaism is one of the three religions of the country. This is symbolically manifest in the fact that at Kennedy Airport in New York there are three houses of worship: a Protestant Church, a Catholic Church and a Jewish Synagogue, which today replaces what the Statue of Liberty used to symbolize for anyone entering the U.S. A well known joke has it that Goldberg is an American name. It could not have been a Polish or Russian name.

From this standpoint, it may be that a dialogue is possible between American Jewry and ourselves, if we recognize that American Jewry and Israel, each in its own right, are both *new modes of Jewish existence*, and that both are the fruit of a tremendous revolution. In Israel, the Jews constitute the bearers of national sovereignty, while in the U.S. they are one of the components of a varied, pluralistic national identity. In both societies the situation is different from what it was for the ethno-religious minority of Europe. If we can recognize the legitimacy of this co-existence (and if the American Jews and their intelligentsia recognize that the existence of the State of Israel is not intended to injure them in their present way of life), then there is a chance for a dialogue, which must be based on the two parties not preaching to one another, but communicating with one another.

(This portion of the interview took place in April, 1970).

BEN EZER: How do the price of Zionism and the future of Jewish-Arab relations appear to you in view of the reality that came into being following the war of June, 1967?

AVINERI: After the Six Day War, many people in Israel believed that the magnitude of the defeat would bring the Arabs to the realization that it is not in their power to wipe out the State of Israel, and that there would consequently be many people among them who would sooner or later lean towards reconciliation to the existence of Israel.

This hope appears to have been dispelled, and the results of the Six Day War have been diametrically opposite. There has actually been an intensification of unwillingness on the part of the Arab states to accept the legitimacy of Israel, and the degree of their non-reconciliation with the existence of Israel has been exacerbated. The fact that Israel's borders extend from Mt. Hermon to the Suez Canal has made Israel more concrete — and more threatening — in the consciousness of the Arab public. For the average Egyptian or Syrian, for whom Israel prior to 1967 was in the nature of a vague abstraction even if he did agree with the official policy of hostility toward Israel, Israel has now become an everyday reality which concretely threatens his life. Israeli planes in the skies over Cairo and Damascus do indeed demonstrate Israel's existence and power, but they also assist in mobilizing Arab public opinion against us.

In the course of the Six Day War, those areas of Western Palestine which were still in the possession of the Arabs fell into Israel's hands and a million Palestinian Arabs found themselves under Israeli rule. However liberal Israeli rule in these territories might be, the very fact of these million people under a rule they consider foreign, has reawakened the consciousness of the Palestinians, who since 1948 have been overshadowed by the Arab states, who for their part had treated the Palestinians with demonstrative cynicism. The result has been an intensification of the fight of the Palestinian organizations against Israel. Although this fight has been a military failure and is deteriorating more and more into terrorist atrocity, it may neverthless take some credit for the success in sustaining the fight against Israel even after the crushing Arab defeat of June 1967. It is true that the Arabs' unwillingness to accept Israel is bringing them ruin and destruction, but it is, of course, difficult for the State of Israel, as well.

At the same time, in the wake of the Six Day War, unique conditions for Israel-Arab cooperation were produced. I am referring principally to what is happening in Jerusalem, Judea and Samaria. As a Jerusalemite I can testify for myself that since the barriers between the two parts of the city have been removed, Israeli-Arab contacts have been taking place which have given me a great deal and have indescribably enriched my understanding of the attitude of the other side. The Arabs now living under Israeli rule are beginning to get a more reliable picture of Israel. They will not love us more as a result, but the horrific picture painted by Arab propaganda will disappear, being no longer valid for the Arab living under Israeli rule. We Israelis, too, have learned to know and understand the Palestinian Arab better, and it seems to me that since the Six Day War there has existed in Israel a far greater sensitivity than ever existed previously to the objective injustice that has been the lot of the Arabs of Palestine.

Israel has a unique opportunity to enhance these beginnings if it will be prepared to conduct negotiations with the Palestinian Arabs for the establishment of a Palestinian Arab State in the territories of the former West Bank and Gaza Strip. Since the conflict between the Arabs and ourselves is that between two national movements, a solution can only be reached by means of these two national movements mutually recognizing one another. Both of these national movements, the Israeli and the Palestinian-Arab, have an affinity for what was historical Palestine, and that is why there is no way out, at the initial stage, but to establish two states alongside one each other, Israel and a Palestinian-Arab State.

BEN EZER: Has any essential change taken place in the relations between the Jews of Israel and the Jews of the Diaspora since the war of June 1967?

AVINERI: The picture is quite complex. On the one hand, the Six Day War generated an unprecedented degree of Jewish identification with Israel. This identification extended far beyond the confines of traditional Zionist circles. It was an expression of an existential identification of the Jews with fear for the existence of the Jewish community in Israel. There is no doubt that since the Six Day War Israel has been far more at the center of Jewish consciousness than it was in the past.

But, dialectically, this too has had a price. In those countries where foreign policy has adopted an anti-Israel stand, the situation of the local Jews has been exacerbated. The picture as regards the Jews of the U.S.S.R. and Poland is a clear one. The sympathy that numerous Jews of these countries have entertained for Israel and for Israel's victory has made their situation drastically more difficult. But this picture is not confined to the Communist countries (or to the remnants of Jewish communities in the Arab countries). In France, too, a situation has evolved in which the hostile stance of the French government towards Israel has confronted the Jewish community there with difficult alternatives, all the more so since General de Gaulle in his famous speech incorporated in his criticism of Israel several historiosophical comments on the character of the Jewish people. For the first time since 1945, there is coming into being in France an atmosphere providing a basis for legitimatization of an anti-Jewish approach of sorts. It is not traditional anti-Semitism. But criticism of Israel and of the Jews supporting Israel is likely to turn into an anti-Jewish political weapon. This is the point at which the traditional anti-Semitic Right and the criticisms of part of the extreme New Left are likely to meet. The claim advanced against Herzl by the German rabbis, that the establishment of a Jewish State in Palestine would create a problem of dual loyalty, has been justified to a certain extent, especially in a country like France, which has a monolithic approach to the problem of national identity. It is precisely the successes of the

State of Israel and the degree to which Jews have identified therewith, that is creating new problems for Jewish communities which
had seemingly overcome traditional anti-Semitism.

It is also this great identification of the Jewish community with
Israel that is, to a certain extent, producing a withdrawal among
part of the younger generation of Jews who, in rebelling against
their Establishment-oriented parents, are also rebelling against
the identification of the parent generation with Israel. These nuances also combine with the authentic sympathy the struggle of the
Arabs sometimes evokes in the New Left, the Israel-Arab struggle
being viewed in terms of struggle between the Third World and
European colonialism. If we may add to this the social anti-Semitism which sometimes manifests itself among the leadership of
Black Power in the U.S., together with the disintegration of some
of the classic premises of American pluralism, there is no doubt
that since the Six Day War a situation of polarization has come
into being, which I think will become increasingly acute. In place
of general apathy diluted with non-commital sympathy for Israel,
there is now crystallizing a situation in which powerful, deep
and intensive sympathy on the one hand is being confronted with
severe criticism, if not revulsion, among portions of the younger
generation, on the other.

It should be noted that on the Israeli side of the picture a far-
reaching change in the attitude of the Israeli Sabra towards the Jews
in the Diaspora has also taken place. The Six Day War showed the
Israeli that his only ally is the Diaspora Jew. It was a revelation
that was received with anxiety, and certainly without enthusiasm.
The result is that the typical Sabra arrogance has somewhat
disappeared or been softened. The Sabra has discovered that not
only do the Jews of the Diaspora need him (as his Zionist education
always taught him), but that he, perhaps, may need the Diaspora
no less. And even the most callous of Sabras are beginning to realize
that sometimes the Diaspora Jews have to pay the price of Israel's
success.

BEN EZER: How is the present situation likely to affect the future
and the feelings of Israeli youth, who are obliged to view most
of their life from perspectives of warfare and mobilization? What
will be the affect of this situation on the intellectual future of Israel?

AVINERI: I am sorry to have to admit that the present situation of sustained hostility is likely to go on for a long time. And even if, in the course of time, there should arise a Palestinian Arab State in the territory of what was formerly the West Bank, that would only be the beginning of a solution, and the hostility would not be dispelled instantaneously. The state of siege in which Israel exists is not, to be sure, a new thing, but it is becoming more acute, and what has become even more acute is the *awareness* of the siege and of distress. Till 1967, most Israelis believed that the fundamental problem of Zionism had been solved in 1948, with the founding of the state. Today it has become clear that the picture is far more complex, and that the Arabs refusal is far deeper and more rooted. It has also emerged that every Israeli success has its price, and the fundamental problem of Israel — recognition of her legitimacy on the part of the Arabs — will not be easily solved.

The perils that are implied by this situation are numerous, and all I have said in this respect in our first interview in 1966 applies even more powerfully today. But I should like to concentrate on one specific point and that is the grim prospect sometimes advanced both in Israel, and abroad, according to which a prolonged conflict is liable to lead Israel to the fate of Sparta or Prussia. The fear that we may, as a result of the siege, turn into a second Sparta, living by the sword, is repellant perhaps to any Israeli. But it seems to me that the historical comparison itself is faulty, since it contains a covert premise of historical determinism, which leads any country engaged in a prolonged war into a Spartan situation. From the standpoint of history, there is no such deterministic truth. If we chose to select models from ancient times, I could see Athens as a far more reasonable example for the future of Israel than is Sparta. When we think about Sparta we forget that democratic Athens, in which literature, philosophy, the arts and drama flourished, reached the height of its bloom during a period of ceaseless wars, from the Persian wars to the Peloponesian wars. The Athens of Socrates and Phidias, of Sophocles and of Euripides, the Athens of Pericles' funeral oration, was not at all an Athens of peace and tranquillity, but of ceaseless wars and of empire-building expansion. This does not prove that flourishing culture and war must be interwoven but that various cultures respond differently to the challenge of war. The countries of Latin America have not known war for literally hundreds of years, and it is precisely there that we find military dictatorships, and most of these countries are in a state of cultural stagnation and malaise. There is no determinism linking culture with war, and the choice of Sparta as a model indicates historical ignorance and one-sidedness on the part of its advocate. The question is, what is the social and cultural fabric of the society under discussion. The fact of sustained warfare affected a primitive agrarian society such as Sparta differently from the effect it had on the sophisticated, urban Athenian society. Israel and Egypt are investing more or less the same proportion of their budgets in security. In Israel there prevails parliamentary democracy, which despite all its problems is not about to disappear from the world, while on Egypt's horizons there appears no alternative to the continued existence of a military dictatorship.

It was precisely the Six Day War that evoked in Israel, as I have mentioned earlier, a greater awareness of the suffering and attitudes of the Palestinians. There is today greater understanding of the position of the other side than in any period prior to 1967. Events which occurred in 1948 cannot occur today. Military and security matters which were taboo for public discussion during the administration of Ben-Gurion are today being debated openly. There is today far more criticism and open-mindedness in Israel during a time of severe security pressures, than there were during the fifties and the sixties, in a time of far less stress. In comparison with the Israeli press today, the Israeli press of the fifties seems frightfully conformist. And, too, the stampede to higher education, the openness to the world, are far greater today than in the past, and the generation of sons is far more anchored in the values of western culture — with all its shadows and its achievements — than was the generation of fathers, educated in the *stetls* of Eastern Europe. It seems to me that, without overly idealizing, it may be said that Israel is responding to the challenge of the war and the siege as per the Athenic model, not the Spartan. The opinions expressed by the participants in this volume of dialogues bear witness to this.

Where There is no Vision, the People Perish

Interview with David Ben Gurion

(This part of the interview was published in *Moznayim* in November, 1966)

BEN EZER: Several years ago you said:

"By virtue of the vicissitudes and changes that have taken place in the history of the Jewish people during the past half century, the term 'Zionism' has undergone metamorphoses and alterations. Since the coining of the term, from before the birth of Herzl's political Zionism and till after the establishment of the State of Israel, the term "Zionism" has lost its principal, fertile significance, has been emptied of all real, compelling content, and no longer means to our younger generation in this country (and in the Diaspora, as well) what it meant to its originators and protagonists sixty years ago, and up till the establishment of the State. "Where there is no vision, the people perish. Our literature has not yet epitomized the full value and role of *messianic vision in the history of the people of Israel* from antiquity till our time. It is certain that the laws of nature, the physical and biological laws (and the sociological, if there are such) apply to us just as they do to any other people. But just as there is no one who is free of the natural laws that apply to the entire human race, and nevertheless no person is like another and the intellectual and moral powers of Hillel the Elder, the Gaon from Vilna, Leonardo da Vinci, Newton and Einstein are unique — so, too, peoples distinguish themselves during certain periods, or throughout their existence, by traits and qualities that are not present in most other peoples. The Jews of Yemen, Morocco and Iraq immigrated to this country out of an historical consciousness and a messianic vision and not out of "Zionist" ideology. It is clear that the Diaspora distress was operative here, but not Zionist ideology. They did not buy a "Shekel," did not listen to Zionist

67

speeches and did not read Zionist pamphlets. *The remote past is closer than the past two thousand years,* even than the 60 years the term "Zionism" has existed. Abraham the Patriarch, his son and his grandson; Moses and Aaron; King David and his descendants; the prophets of Israel and all that happened to them and what they said — are closer to us than what was said by Rabbi Ashi and Alfasi and Maimonides and Rabbi Isaac Luria and Joseph Caro, and all Zionist "ideologists" of recent years. *There is a leap in history:* We are living in our homeland, and every excavation in Beit Shearim or in Hazor reinforces our affinity to the homeland and to our past in the homeland."

Furthermore, it seems to me that you have said, on another occasion, that Zionism is the fruit of awful distress and messianic hope. In your opinion, has Zionism ceased to exist?

BEN GURION: It is impossible to clarify any question involving the term "Zionism" without clarifying and elucidating from the outset the various meanings this term has acquired in various mouths and times. The term was coined by Birnbaum (who called himself "another Mattathias") about five years prior to the appearance of Dr. Herzl's pamphlet entitled "The Jewish State," and the creation of the Zionist Federation. Herzl gave this term a clear and correct definition: *"the Jewish people in the making."* For in the first years of his political Zionist activity he believed, or hoped, that he would get a sort of charter for the Land of Israel and transport to there most of the Jews of Europe, who then constituted the numerical and structural majority of the Jewish people in the world. For most of the Zionists of that time, the meaning of "Zionism" was membership and organizational activity in the Zionist Federation and "work of the present" — that is, dealing with the needs of the Jews in their countries of residence in Europe, chiefly in Eastern and Southern Europe. There was only a small minority for whom the meaning of Zionism was the *personal need and will* to immigrate to this country and devote their lives to its economic, cultural and political up-building and development.

Prior to the establishment of the State of Israel there was one difference between Zionists of all kinds and non-Zionists or anti-Zionists. Almost all the Zionists wanted a Jewish State to be set up. Most of the non-Zionists were against it. Following the establishment of the State this difference was eliminated. Except for a negligible minority, almost all Jews, Zionist and non-Zionist, are sympathizers of the Jewish State. But a great change took place even before the establishment of the State, and this change took place in the fate of the Jewish people. In the first half of the twentieth century, two tragic alterations took place in the life of the Jewish people in Europe, which had borne in its heart the dream of a Jewish State and had also laid its first foundations. Before the end of World War I, there took place in Russia a second revolution, the Bolshevik Revolution, which within a few years led to the cutting off of Russian Jewry (about three million Jews) from World Jewry and from the Land of Israel, as well as from Jewish education. In the course of World War II, Nazi Germany exterminated six million Jews in Europe. Jewish centers which in the nineteenth century had sustained all of world Jewry were destroyed. It was European Jewry that had created the *Haskala* (Enlightenment) movement, the new Hebrew literature and Yiddish literature, the Zionist movement, the Jewish workers' movement and the pioneering movement — which latter alone laid the foundations of the Jewish State. The Holocaust destroyed all that.

The quantitative and qualitative center of Disapora Jewry moved from Europe to America. In the U.S.A. there was established a great Jewish center the likes of which had never existed in the Diaspora — not in numbers, not in material and intellectual wealth, not in political status, influence and power.

BEN EZER: I understand that you distinguish between Zionist ideology and national redemption.

Ben Gurion: Zionist ideology, as it was formulated by the three first Zionist thinkers in the nineteenth century — Moses Hess in *Rome and Jerusalem*, Dr. Leon Pinsker in *Auto-Emancipation* and Dr. Herzl in *The Jewish State* — was the fruit of the European reality and of the living conditions of the Jews of Europe. I distinguish between Zionist ideology — the offspring of nineteenth century Europe — and *the messianic longings of the Jewish people for national redemption in the land of their fathers*, which are the fruit of the Prophets of Israel and have existed in the Jewish people throughout all the years. In Europe there have been historical states embodying a single nationality and states embodying numerous nationalites, like France, Italy and England on the one hand, and Austro-Hungary and Russia on the other. Whether or not they had equal rights on paper, the Jews were not considered in any of the European countries as members of the ruling peoples, either individually or collectively. All the peoples of Europe had a political and cultural history of over a thousand years, and the Jews were considered as members of these peoples, but as aliens either tolerated or hated. The power of anti-Semitism was great and strong in most of the countries of Europe, and in several countries the Jews were even denied equal rights on paper.

In the 1880's there began a mass migration of European Jews, the large majority of the migration streaming to the U.S. That country now has close to six million Jews. From its inception, the Zionist movement did penetrate to the U.S., but the Zionist ideology that was brought forth in Europe did not fit the American reality. That country — the U.S. — was fundamentally different from all the European countries. It was not a veteran settlement of many hundreds or perhaps thousands of years that has made its mark and shaped the character of the American people, but rather it was new immigrants who had migrated to America in recent centuries, chiefly in the nineteenth and twentieth centuries up till World War II, who had determined the character of America. As all the American people — excepting the Indian aborigines, whose influence is not in the least evident in America, neither in its language, its culture or its political and economic life — the Jews of America were also immigrants, or the children or grandchildren of immigrants. The late President Kennedy was the grandson of an Irish immigrant. As the rest of the immigrants and immigrants' children from Holland, Germany, Italy, Sweden, Poland and other countries, the Jewish immigrants, too, or their children, exchanged the vernacular they had brought with them from their countries of origin for the English language, which has in practice as in theory become the tongue of the American people. Anti-Semitism was not entirely lacking in America (and by America I mean the U.S.), but it has movements hostile to non-Jewish races as well. The fundamental principle, set forth in the American Constitution, of equal rights for all citizens applies to the Jews as well. There has also been social discrimination, but that did not harm the economic and political status of the American Jews. And the Zionist movement, which penetrated to America too, was from the outset only a movement of aid to European Jewry and the Jews of the rest of the countries outside the U.S. And only exceptional individuals like Dr. Y.L. Magnes and Henrietta Szold were Zionists both in practice and theory — and immigrated to this country.

Following the establishment of the State of Israel, there is almost no ideological difference between the Zionist and the non-Zionist in the U.S. These and those alike do not intend to immigrate to this country, and these and those alike are sympathizers of the Jewish State and are aiding in its development and in its status among nations. The title of Zionist now embraces entirely different things among which there is no connection, and to speak of Zionism per se has no real meaning.

BEN EZER: There are those who claim that your attitude ultimately leads the young Israeli (the Sabra) to feel superior to the Diaspora Jew, with all the grave consequences that entails. On the other hand, shouldn't it be seen as a disturbing symptom that the Jewish intellectual in the Diaspora is beginning to lose his respectful, appreciative attitude towards the State of Israel, and is adopting a contrary tone to the point of casting doubt on the moral value and example of the Jewish State — as for example in the reiterated condemnation by the Jewish intellectuals of the Suez campaign in 1956, and their critical evaluations of the State. Jewish intellectuals in the West view us as pejoratively "normal" and reserve for themselves any degree of sensitivity, mission and message — any disquiet — that the Jews of the world have today. What can be our reply to this trend which looks down at us, dismisses us and is severe in its judgement of us? How do you see the relations between the Jews of Israel and of the Diaspora in this generation?

BEN GURION: There is an unseverable link between Israeli Jewry and Diaspora Jewry, and yet there is a fundamental difference between the two. The Jews of the Diaspora in different countries are different from one another. French Jewry, Moroccan Jewry, South American Jewry or South African Jewry are not like American Jewry — not in their existence, their living conditions or their Jewish tinge. But in comparison with Israeli Jewry, there is one fundamental difference that characterizes all of Diaspora Jewry, with no distinction from one country to the next. The Jew in the Diaspora, whether he recognizes the fact or not, has *a split personality*. In part he is a Jew (and within that part there are numerous, deep differences among various Jews in the same country and in different countries), and in part he belongs completely to the non-Jewish environment in which he dwells. There are countries in which this affiliation to the non-Jewish environment is very great, encompassing almost all of the Jew's life and sensibility, and there are countries in which this affiliation is less marked. In the same country, too, there are differences among various Jews. In language, in everyday actions, in economic and political life, and in almost all of his cultural life — the Jew is similar to the rest of the citizens (in countries where there is no legal discrimination). *In Israel on the other hand the Jew is one hundred percent Jewish and one hundred percent human, that is, a member of the human race.* For he is a member of an independent people which is a member of the family of people with equal rights. Among the Jews of Israel there are differences in "religious" conception, in economic status, in education, in world outlook — like the differences that exist in any independent, free people. But these differences do not arise from an alien environment. In the Diaspora Jew there is a schism — and not just a contradiction — between the Jew in him and the citizen in him, so long as he has not entirely assimilated and abandoned his Judaism. In Israel, this is inconceivable. Even according to the Jewish *Halakha*, Israel is Israel even if he has sinned.

BEN EZER: Is assimilation inevitable?

Ben Gurion: Diaspora Jewry, wishing to avoid the danger of partial or total assimilation, will not achieve its goal unless it observes these three precepts: a. Imparting the Hebrew language to their sons and daughters to the extent of being able to read a Hebrew book or newspaper; b. Imparting a knowledge of the

Bible *in the original;* (The Bible is the most faithful and fertile source of Judaism, and a Jew who does not read the Bible does not have a true concept of Judaism, or of its Jewish and human spirit, riches and greatness. Bialik justly said that reading the Bible in translation, is like kissing a sweetheart through a kerchief.) c. Imparting a knowledge of Jewish history and a knowledge of the latest chapter of Jewish history at its source, that is, by visiting Israel and seeing what is being done, what is being created and what is changing in Israel.

BEN EZER: Judaism, which in the Western countries has become a symbol of the attitude of a sensitive minority, whose fate is a warning to the world, has become in Israel the fashionable topic of "Yiddishkeit," a sort of nostalgia, the symbol of clerical forces whose aim is solely to preserve and who have no "message" for the world, or, what is worse, an instrument in the hands of Israeli national rule. Does not the price of Zionism also reside in the fact that the normalization it has brought in its wake has diminished the universal human vision of Judaism?

BEN GURION: There are those who think — and there are not a few such among the Jews of America — that Judaism is nothing but a religion, like Christianity, Islam, and Buddhism. Those who hold this opinion do not know what Judaism is, and in particular they do not comprehend the deep difference between the Jewish "religion" and other religions. Judaism, even that part which is "religion," is bound up with the history of the Jewish people, of the Land of Israel, of the Hebrew language, of the affinity to this country and to the Hebrew language, of the expectation of the Jewish people's redemption in its country. And at the same time Judaism is a universal, human conception, the likes of which do not exist in any other religion. The holy writs of Christianity start with the history of Jesus, but the Hebrew Book of Books begins with the first human couple created "in the image of God" as set forth in the first chapter of Genesis. Adam and Eve were not white or black or brown, not Jewish and not "Gentiles." That is to say that every person, by the Jewish conception, was created "in the image of God." There is no nobler expression of the unity and equality of the entire human race than this attribute by the prophets of Israel.

The entire book of Jonah was written solely to bring out this idea, and only the Jew-haters — intentionally or ignorantly — falsify the significance of the supreme commandment given in the Law of Israel, "love thy neighbor as thyself," to mean Jews alone. They ignore the passage in the same chapter (XIX) of Leviticus that says: "And if a stranger sojourn with thee in your land... the stranger that dwelleth with you shall be unto you as one born among you and thou shalt love him as thyself: for ye were strangers in the land of Egypt." (King James translation). The prophets of Israel were the first to prophecy that at the millennium "nation shall not lift up sword against nation, neither shall they learn war any more." It was the sages of the Talmud who claimed that God gave his Law to Israel only after all the other peoples had refused to receive it. In the book of Joshua it is explicitly stated that *the people chose God*, as it is written: "And Joshua said unto the people, Ye are witnesses against yourselves that ye have chosen you the Lord, to serve him. And they said, We are witnesses... So Joshua made a covenant with the people that day, and sent them a statute and an ordinance in Shechem. And Joshua wrote these words in the book of the law of God..." (Joshua XXIV).

Judaism differs from all the other "religions" in that it is the most national, the most Jewish, and, at the same time the most universal.

BEN EZER: The intellectual in Israel is under the pressures of siege and sustained danger to the existence of the State, and is therefore obliged, willy nilly, to join the establishment, sharing in the majority's sense of responsibility, and is unable to release himself and examine the reality around him with a critical eye, free of that paralyzing responsibility complex, forfear that his criticism might be detrimental to the State.

BEN GURION: You are afraid that the Israeli intellectual, who is under pressure of a sense of siege and sustained danger to the existence of the State, will not be able to observe the reality around him critically and freely, for fear that his criticism might be detrimental to the State. But in my opinion it is doubtful whether one can speak of Israeli intellectuals, or of any other Israeli unit, in a generalized way. Youth in Israel does not have any single trait, but rather there are differing types among the youth: excellent and execrable, good and bad. And that applies to every type of Israeli. There is a basis to the Talmudic saying (Tractate Megilla XIV:2) "This nation is like unto the dust and like unto the stars. When they descend — *they descend to the dust*, and when they rise — *they rise to the stars.*"

But the intellectual in Israel who fears criticizing things that require criticism, lest the criticism harm the State of Israel, does not understand Israel's needs and Israel's welfare. There is nothing that damages and threatens its existence more than internal faults that are ignored, and that constant efforts are not being made to mend them. And mending starts with seeing the fault and exposing it ruthlessly. For only then can we dispose of it and maintain our intellectual superiority. And only by virtue of that superiority has our people survived under conditions that no other people has withstood.

Upon the establishment of the State, two tasks — that are in fact one — were entrusted to me: setting up the Israel Defense Forces and conducting the War of Independence, which broke out on the very day our renewed independence was declared. The United Nations, which had decided on the establishment of a Jewish State, did not lift a finger when the Arab armies invaded to annihilate Israel, and we had no one to rely on but ourselves. But it was clear, and insofar as I could I explained it to the army and the people, that "reliance on ourselves means two things: *on our strength and on our being in the right.* Just one of these two will not sustain us."

When the Psalmist sang "the mercies of the Lord for ever," and said, "Thou hast a mighty arm: strong is thy hand, and high is thy right hand," he added immediately, "Justice and judgment are the habitation of thy throng: mercy and truth shall go before thy face" (Psalms XXXIX:13–14). Only if we know how to combine courage and justice, daring and truth, will we stand and fear no evil. And an intellectual who does not know the secret of the Jewish people under conditions that no other people has withstood is not worthy of the title of intellectual. We have survived and gotten to where we are only by virtue of our moral and intellectual advantage, and we will damage this advantage and imperil our survival if we ignore the blights and faults in our life and in the life of the State.

BEN EZER: What, in your opinion, is the place of Jewish scholarship in our generation? How do you view the relationship between the first generations of Jewish scholarship whose native land and sometimes even language is foreign, and the new generation of Jewish scholars (and scientists in general) arising among those born in Israel? May one speak of a decline? Of continuity? Perhaps of a Rennaissance and new points of view? Does there not exist a danger that the generations born in Israel, whose only language is Hebrew and whose connection with the Western world comes after a prolonged and difficult struggle with a foreign language and culture, will not be able to preserve the character of Jewish, scholarship, and perhaps of intellectual and scientific life in general, in this country?

Jewish scholarship began tendentially, and with a need for apologetics. In our times it has come to the opposite extreme — of professionalism, a demand for objectivity and preoccupation with details, while tendentiality is considered utterly wrong. Doesn't admiration of the Bible imply something of a return to tendentiality and apologetics?

BEN GURION: The question of "the place of Jewish scholarship in our generation" is a Diaspora-type question. Jews in the Diaspora, as we have said, are split. The Jew in them and the citizen in them are not identical. In Israel, the Jew is always a Jew and always a a citizen. And just as physics, chemistry and biology are taught at Bar Ilan University, founded by the religious party of Mizrachi, so at the Hebrew University in Jerusalem (and in Tel Aviv and Haifa) which has no religious stamp and whose teachers are not Orthodox, Jewish law, Jewish history, the Bible and its commentaries, the Talmud and the Zohar are taught together with all the branches of science and scholarship that are taught in all the universities of the world. And the greatest Kabala scholars at the University are Jews who are called "secular," although there is no justification or true meaning in dividing the people into "religious" and "secular." "Jewish scholarship" in the Diaspora is confined to specific Jewish branches. "Jewish scholarship" in Israel — includes all of human wisdom. But it is precisely the greatest work of the Jewish people — the Book of Books — that was neglected in the Diaspora, and not a few "religious" scholars who knew entire tractates of the Talmud by heart knew only those Bible passages mentioned in the Talmud. Never did a Jewish community in the Diaspora manifest such a great and deep interest in Bible study as do the younger generation and the best of Jewish scholars in Israel.

It is true that Jewish scholarship in the Diaspora was to a great extent a scholarship of apologetics. The genuine intellectual in Israel does not have a Jewish inferiority complex, and has no need to make a case for Judaism. Judaism is not in need of apologetics, but of knowledge and familiarity in the most objective manner. A patriotic Israeli Jew does not need to conceal the handicaps and weaknesses of the members of his people, just as the Prophets of Israel did not. Is there anyone who castigated the Jewish people more than did Isaiah, son of Amoz? "How is the faithful city become a harlot! It was full of judgement; righteousness lodged in it; but now murderers." And what did the prophet demand of his people? "Put away the evil of your doings from before mine eyes; cease to do evil; learn to do well; seek judgement, relieve the oppressed, judge the fatherless, plead for the widow." And then he promised them, "Afterward thou shalt be called, the city of righteousness, the faithful city. Zion shall be redeemed with judgement, and her converts with righteousness." Not apologetics, not tendentialism, but the object of science — of truth; the object of morality — justice.

And if you ask whether there isn't "a danger that the Israeli-born generations will not be able to preserve the character of Jewish and perhaps of intellectual and scientific life in this country in general" — the answer to that has been provided by a non-Jewish, non-Israeli scientist. An American, a planning director of molecular biology in Washington, toured scientific institutions in West European countries, for a year and in Israel as well. The conclusions of his visits were published in the American journal, *Science*, Vol. 133, June 1961. He wrote: "It is well known that in all the countries I visited science is most developed in the British Isles, Israel and Sweden. The territory, population and economic status of a nation determine but little the quality of science in that nation. Science in Israel — a relatively new nation, not much larger than New Jersey, with a population of two million and severe economic and social problems still unsolved—is of the highest quality and more developed than in any country of Western Europe except perhaps Great Britain and Sweden. Israel is the only country that may be qualified to attract American scientists as permanent residents. Israel's scientific tradition is only one generation old. Yet Israel has absorbed and adopted the finest scientific tradition of the West: scientific talent, respect for talent, self criticism and rewards for expertise."

BEN EZER: What is your attitude towards the Cannanites? Following what you have said about the leap in Jewish history and your having defined yourself as not being a Zionist, there are people who consider your position a thoroughly Canaanite one. Are you, too, of the opinion that it is conceivable that a Jewish generation might emerge in Israel that would lack any interest in the history of the Jewish people? Is it conceivable that there will not be any connection between the intellectual (or almost any Jew) in Israel and the members of his people in the Diaspora in the future? Will two different peoples emerge? May it be said that a new "Hebrew people" has been produced in the Land of Israel, whose survival and needs dictate a new set of concepts, will no longer be linked with the Jewish people; for example, in the question of relations with Germany, with the Arab sphere, and in the recurring preference for Israel's interests, in any case, over the interests of the Diaspora Jews; not to speak of the cultural facet that demands "Hebrew" autonomy and a "fresh start"? In your opinion, is the development of life in Israel leading in this direction?

BEN GURION: A new Hebrew people has not emerged in Israel. But what has emerged, or more correctly, what is emerging is a *renewed* Hebrew people, which aspires to and is obliged to combine the supreme Jewish and universally human values (for they can not be separated in Israel) of the prophets of Israel with the new and yearly renewing discoveries of science and technology in our days and in the days to come. And there is now no power that will reinforce and deepen the affinity of the Disapora Jews to the heritage of Jewish history and to Israel like a renewed Israel will. Moreover, it is doubtful whether a renewed Israel can survive and fulfil its historic destiny without deepening and reinforcing its ties with the Jewish people. No one has defined more faithfully, more understandingly and with deeper insight the destiny of Israel than did the prophet Isaiah, when he said, "I the Lord have called thee in righteousness, and will hold thine hand, and will keep thee, and give thee for a covenant of the people, for a light of the Gentiles." (Isaiah XLII:6).

These two interdependent purposes, to be a covenent of the people and a light of the Gentiles, are the purposes that determine the future of the renewed State of Israel. We are faced with two dangers, and only the blind do not see them. Diaspora Jewry faces the increasingly grave danger of partial and total assimilation within the peoples among whom they reside. While this small country is surrounded on all sides by enemies who plot its extinction, (and we, as in ancient times are "the least of all peoples") unless we become "a covenent of the people," unless we deepen the ties between Israel and Diaspora Jewry by drawing the great cream of Disapora Jewry to Israel, unless we deepen the mutual affinity between Israel and Judaism, and between Judaism and Israel, the danger of assimilation will increase. And if Israel does not increase its moral and intellectual superiority to the peak of its ability, and thereby become a light of the Gentiles, we will not ensure our welfare, our survival and our status in the family of peoples. As we have said, this will not be accomplished by power alone.

Almost all the peoples who inhabited this part of the world — now called the Middle East — have been wiped out and have disappeared from the face of the earth. And if the Jewish people, whose independence has been usurped and eradicated for two thousand years, its country falling to foreigners, itself wandering from one country to another, hated and persecuted in every single country, has preserved its faith, its heritage and its expectations despite everything, and after two thousand years it succeeded in returning to its abandoned and ruined country, to re-establish its independence and sovereignty, despite the efforts of its neighbors to annihilate this small, young state — it is only because it has managed to maintain, as in ancient times and throughout the centuries of its exile, its spiritual superiority. But we have not yet arrived at repose and security, and we should know and remember that we are very far from both of them. In the eighteen years that the State of Israel has existed, there have emerged dozens of new states, many of them ten or a hundred times larger than us, and not one of them has succeeded in accomplishing what we have accomplished during this short time. We have stood courageously, a few against many. We have turned human dust, gathered from all over the world, into an independent, sovereign nation, occupying a respectable place in the family of nations. We have given hundreds of thousands of people from all countries, who have returned to their historic homeland, their own national language. We have ensured free elementary education for every boy and girl in Israel from the ages of six to fourteen. We have set up an army that is not just a powerful mainstay of the welfare and sovereignty of the people but a forge for the nation's pioneers and an instrument for the integration of the exiles. In a brief period we have built hundreds of villages and dozens of cities and development towns. We have turned a country abandoned and backward for centuries into a high-ranking center for scholarship, science and research. This small, poor nation has become a very great and welcome aid to new states in Asia, Africa and South America. We have accomplished all of this solely and exclusively by virtue of the intellectual superiority that is latent within us. Only if we combine courage with righteousness, strength with truth, and if we ceaselessly increase and heighten our moral and intellectual superiority, will we become a Chosen People, a faithful bulwark for the Diaspora, an educational example for peoples and a desirable partner for our neighbors on a basis of cooperation for the development of the entire Middle East and for increasing peace in the region and in the world.

BEN EZER: You immigrated to Palestine in 1906. Did your coming to this country alter your approach to Zionism?

BEN GURION: My immigration to this country altered my entire conception of Zionism, Socialism and international problems. Here I understood that everything I had thought of Zionism was vain rhetoric. And everything I had thought of Socialism was miserable phraseology. And the easy solutions then prevalent in Zionism as regards our relations with the Arabs arose from a lack of understanding and unfamiliarity with reality, and out of fuss and bother and drivel. And here, only here, did I understand the meaning of Zionism — if this term, Zionism, is to be used at all, for in the days of Ezra and Nehemia they immigrated to this country without the word "Zionism." And only here did I understand the Bible, and I saw that all I stood for and believed in had its deepest expression in the Bible.

BEN EZER: You said, "relations with the Arabs." When did you begin to realize the nature of these relations and their danger?

BEN GURION: I understood the Arab problem from experience, not from books. When I worked as a hired laborer in Sejera in 1907–1909, I saw for the first time the acuteness and dangers of the "Arab question." It was in 1909, on Passover. Two visitors came for the Seder. On the way, Arabs attacked them. One of the Jews had a Browning. He defended himself. We went out to the spot and saw patches of blood. We knew that it was a grave matter. The Arabs said that an Arab had accidentally shot himself and they took him to the hospital in Nazereth. When he died, they said that the Jews had murdered him. We knew that one of us would fall. We took precautions. We did not go far from Sejera. We walked together. On the seventh day of Passover — it wasn't one that fell, but two. The watchman Israel Korngold found four Arabs in Sejera's graveyard. With Israel was a man born in Safed. He came running to Sejera and said, "They've murdered Israel!" We knew the Arabs had taken revenge. We did not know that they would not be satisfied with their revenge. In the evening the bell in Upper Sejera began to ring, and from Lower Sejera, from the farmers' houses, we began to run up. One young farmer, Shimon Melamed, was running without his rifle. His wife ran after him: "Take your rifle, Shimon!" She never saw him alive again.

When we got up there, we saw Arabs chasing Jews. Shimon Melamed, Shapiro and myself ran towards them. They shouted at us "Get back. The whole village of Sejera (the Arab village) is out!" We began to go back. On the first paces, Shimon shrieked "Ohhhhhh!" He got a bullet right in the heart. And I understood what the Arabs' hatred of us was.

I encountered expression of Arab political opposition in the spring of 1915, after Turkey entered the war as an ally of Germany. Izhak Ben-Zvi and I had been law students at the Turkish university in Istanbul, where I had comrades and friends among the Turkish and Arab students. But we never spoke about Jewish affairs. I had an excellent Arab friend, Yehia Effendi of Jerusalem. We had been friends — without politics.

We came back to Jerusalem at the beginning of August 1914, for the summer vacation, and while we were on the way to this country, the First World War broke out. Jemal Pasha, who was in charge of the Southern Command of the Ottoman Empire, came to Syria and Palestine. He began by repressing the Arab nationalist movement, and in Beirut he hanged several Arab leaders. In Palestine he moved against the Zionist movement, and when our names — Ben-Zvi's and my own — were found among the delegates to the Zionist Congress, we were interrogated by one of the Turkish officers, and Jemal Pasha issued an order to deport us from the Ottoman Empire. We were imprisoned in Jerusalem till our deportation, but as we had been students at the Turkish university they dealt with us pleasantly, and during the daytime we were allowed to walk on the grounds of the Saraya (the govenment buildings, which also included the prison). During the days we would walk free in the yard of the Saraya, and at night they would lock us up. One day I was walking in the Saraya, and there I saw my friend Yehia Effendi. "What are you doing here?" I asked him. "I've got affairs with the government," he answered. "And what are you doing here?" he asked. "The government's got affairs with me," I answered, telling him that we are prisoners and why and that there was an order of Jemal Pasha to deport both of us (Ben-Zvi and myself) from the Turkish Empire — "so that we should never ever come back." And then he replied to me: "*As your friend — I'm sorry. As an Arab — I'm glad.*" And I know that both things were sincere. We spoke Turkish, and that was the first time I had heard a sincere answer from an Arab intellectual. It is engraved in my heart, very, very powerfully.

When I came back here from the U.S., where I spent the war as an exile from Palestine, I looked for Yehia Effendi. I looked for him in every village, in every neighborhood in Jerusalem. I scanned every street. I asked numerous Arabs. I did not find him.

When I was elected to the Zionist Executive in 1933, I said that we must try to talk to the Arabs. I divided the Arabs into two: those who could be bought with money, and those who could not. I decided not to talk to those who could be bought, because after all it was impossible to buy them all. I sought a decent Arab nationalist who could not be bought with money or a job, and who was not a Jew-hater either. I was apprised that there was such a man. His name was Mussa Alami, he was close to the Mufti and was at that time the legal adviser of the British administration. The premise that was then accepted in the Zionist movement was that we were bringing prosperity to the Arabs in the country, and therefore they had no grounds for opposing us. I held the first talk with Mussa Alami in the house of Moshe Sharett (he was still called Shertok then) in Jerusalem. I began with the old tune I had prepared myself: "Look, the Jews will bring prosperity to the Arabs, will make things flourish, prosper, a sound economy, factories," and all that story. The Arab interrupted me: "Listen, listen, *Hawaja* Ben Gurion. I would rather that there be a barren waste here for another hundred years, another thousand years, till *we* can make it flourish and redeem it." And I knew that both Yehia Effendi and Mussa Alami were telling the truth. And the facile Zionism, the verbose fuss, appeared to me more ridiculous than ever.

(To supplement David Ben Gurion's narrative of this meetings with Arab leaders, as he told it to me during that interview, I have drawn upon passages from his book, *Talks with Arab Leaders* [Am Oved Publishers, Tel Aviv, 1967] with the kind permission of the publishers).

(This portion of the interview took place in April, 1970)

BEN EZER: What, in your opinion are the chances for peace between Israel and the Arabs?

BEN GURION: Peace between the Arabs and us will not come quickly. In my opinion, there are two factors that would lead to peace. The first factor is an increment of six to seven million Jews in Israel; the second is a realization by the Egyptian intelligentsia of the needs of the Egyptian people. Most of the Egyptian people are *fellahin*, and their circumstances are deteriorating year by year. Poverty is growing, education is not improving. And the health of most of the people is not all right. It is inconceivable that at least part of the Egyptian intelligentsia should not, in the course of the next eight to twelve years, come to terms with the critical needs of their people, and should not devote themselves to improving the circumstances of the majority of the people. And without peace, they will be unable to do that.

BEN EZER: Does it seem to you the Jewish religion is fulfilling a positive function in Israel these days?

BEN GURION: The danger lies not so much with the religious people, but with the degeneration of the political parties. Most of the people are not orthodox and do not wish religious rule. The danger is the corruption of rule, and the apparatus of rule, which is becoming worse year by year.

BEN EZER: But when the Knesset decided that the Judaism of a person in Israel should be determined according to the Jewish *Halacha*, that was not just a political resolution, but also acceptance of the yoke of the Jewish *Halacha* by a secular state.

BEN GURION: It has been declared in the Knesset more than once that the State of Israel is a State of law and not a State of *Halacha*. Every Jew who is faithful to the *Halacha* should undoubtedly be respected, but the *Halacha* is not binding on every Jew. And only someone who has not carefully studied *Halacha* literature does not know that *Halacha* used to change according to the spirit of the times. In the Bible it is said "An eye for an eye," and it is very clear, without any doubt, what an eye for an eye means. But in a later period the sages came to the conclusion, and it was a correct conclusion, that there was cruelty in an eye for an eye, and they said "an eye for an eye is money" (Talmud, Tractate Baba Kama, p. 83). Anyone perusing that chapter can see how the sages floundered for five or six pages in adapting this interpretation to the Bible source. For in the Bible it is said explicitly, "And if a man cause a blemish in his neighobor; as he hath done so shall it be done to him again" (Leviticus XXIV). And elsewhere it is said, "And thine eye shall not pity; but life shall go for life, eye for eye, tooth for tooth, hand for hand, foot for foot." (Deuteronomy XIX). And there is no doubt as to the meaning these things bear in the Bible text. But the Rabbis realized the cruelty of this punishment, and said, an eye for an eye means money — as though whoever wrote the Bible, had he meant monetary punishment, wouldn't have known how to say so in Hebrew.

BEN EZER: There are people who propose erasing the nationality item from the Israeli ID card and from the census questionnaire, in order to avoid the need to define who is a Jew.

BEN GURION: The proposal to erase nationality from the census might be suitable to the Canaanite conception, if there be such. But not to the viewpoint of the Jewish citizen of the State of Israel. The Jewish people in Israel are a part, and for the time being (for a very long time, if not forever) will remain part of the Jewish people. And erasing nationality from the ID card of a Jew in Israel is the beginning of erasing our being a part of the Jewish people.

BEN EZER: Do you think there is justification for the Knesset decision in the question of "Who is a Jew?" the result of which is that most of the Israeli public agrees to religious coercion?

BEN GURION: There is no doubt that the majority of the Jewish community in this country is not in favor of religious coercion or in favor of the rule of the Chief Rabbinate with the aid of the religious political parties. And this majority undoubtedly is against making mixed marriage difficult — the marriage of people who wish to settle in the land of Israel and consider their children and grandchildren as Jews, and not just as Israelis, that is, citizens of the Jewish State and not part of the Jewish people.

There are also isolated cases (that are known to me) of American Jews who married Gentile wives — and the wives are no less Zionist than their husbands. But these are exceptions. Mixed marriages in Diaspora countries usually lead to utter assimilation, turn the sons and daughters into non-Jews, and in the main into members of a non-Jewish religion, as well. In this country the situation is contrary. A woman who has married a Jew and both of them have come to this country to settle, wishes her sons and daughters to be part of the Jewish people in this country, and the children are circumcised, their language becomes Hebrew, and the second generation — excepting perhaps a solitary exception, if such a case is conceivable — will be Jews without any difference from the rest of the Jewish children.

BEN EZER: What should we, as a Jewish State, do about this question?

BEN GURION: If one or the other party to a mixed-marriage family that has immigrated to this country is utterly without religion, but both wish their children to be Jewish — why should the children not be recognized as Jews, and for what purpose should we bar the way to their mixing and blending in with the Jewish people in its own country, which is why the parents came to the Land of Israel. Have Rabbi Nissim or Rabbi Unterman found that after Ruth the Moabite lay all night with Boaz — even before marriage, as it is told in the Book of Ruth — she afterwards went to the ritual bath and undressed in the presence of three witnesses in order to gain the title of convert, which did not exist at all in the time of Ruth and Boaz? And is there really a Jewish, Israeli or human interest in making it difficult for members of mixed marriages to settle in this country and assimilate into the Jewish people with the greatest speed possible? Can Rabbi Nissim or Rabbi Unterman swear that the Negress whom Moses took to wife, after the handing down of the Law, converted by undressing before three (or two) witnesses at the ritual bath, when even the concept of conversion was not then to be found in the Bible?

Why should religious coercion be imposed on a mother, who

for reasons of human conscience, is not willing to undergo the *Halacha* ceremony of conversion, and her children prevented from assimilating among all the rest of the Jewish children in this country, and kept from bearing the title of Jew, which in this country is a title of honor and great meaning, and no less justified than the appellation of Jew in all the Diaspora countries?

BEN EZER: Perhaps it was feared that without the *Halacha* criterion, non-Jewish elements would assimilate into the Jewish people in Israel. And the name "Jew" would lose its Jewish connotation, just as an "Israeli" is not necessarily Jewish today in the State of Israel.

BEN GURION: The Declaration of the State, in May 1948, was signed by all the Jewish political parties in Israel, and it was unanimously decided that *"We hereby declare the establishment of a Jewish State* in Palestine, the State of Israel." In that declaration we also said that the State "will maintain complete equality of social and political rights for all its citizens, with no difference of *religion, race or sex,"* and every citizen in this state is an *Israeli* citizen, but not every "Israeli" is necessarily a Jew. An Israeli citizen can be an Arab (Moslem or Christian) or a member of another people who has settled as a citizen in this country. And for this reaon several members of the Provisional Council of State had doubts as to whether it was not necessary to give the state a different name in other languages, and not Israel, since Israelite can be interpreted as synonymous with "Jew." But the Council decided to leave the appellation "Israeli" for every citizen, whether Jewish or not. And it decided that the State should be called Israel in all languages. Hence it is clear that an Israeli is not obliged to be a Jew, and Israeli does not mean Jewish, for the decision was passed unanimously. And I do not suppose that anyone in Israel wishes to change or abrogate the highly meaningful passage in the declaration, that the State "will maintain complete equality of social and political rights for all its citizens, with no difference of religion, race or sex," and that it "will ensure freedom of religion, conscience, language, education and culture" for all its citizens, and therefore an Israeli citizen is not obliged to be identified and cannot be identified in Israel specifically

with the Jewish people, since a Christian, a Moslem or a Buddhist
who is a citizen of the Jewish state is also an Israeli. And according
to the declaration "Israeli" is not identical to "Jew."

But the declaration certainly did not intend thereby to detract
from the State's being "a Jewish State," just as Great Britain is a
British state not only for the English but also for the Scotch,
the Welsh, the Irish, the Jews and for other citizens, without
thereby ceasing to be a British state. All of the political parties
in the Knesset signed and are responsible for this declaration. In
it, it is definitely stated that "Even in the midst of the bloody attack
that has been conducted against us for months (today we would
say "for years") we were calling upon the members of the Arab
people who are resident in the State of Israel to keep the peace
and to take their part in the up-building of the state *on a basis
of full and equal citizenship* and on a basis of appropriate represen-
tation in all its institutions, both provisory and permanent."

Israeli Synthesis of Humanism and Religion

Interview with Prof. Shmuel Hugo Bergman

(This part of the interview was published in *Moznayim,* May, 1966)

BEN EZER: Are we not paying too high a price for the realization of Zionism — the price of losing our sensitivity, our sense of humor and satire, our Jewish intellectual "outsiderness," of that "fecund uprootedness" that characterizes the status of the Jewish intellectual in the Diaspora?

BERGMAN: If you are asking about my opinion of our situation in the Diaspora, and about the "price" we have paid, I am obliged to say that I do not at all see our role as intellectuals in the Diaspora in the same way that your question implies. Our role was a parasitic one. I have in mind all of those Jews who were working in Germany before World War I, and especially after it, in the 'twenties. Perhaps they had, certainly they had, a stimulating function vis-à-vis the German people at that time. But as an expression of a people, of the Jewish people and as a contribution to human culture, it seems to me that the sum total is extremely negative. Our role in Germany then, and apparently in America and England today (though I am not a specialist in this) does not make a positive impression on me at all.

It is difficult to explain this to someone who did not live in that period, which was given striking expression, inter alia, in Schwarz-schild's journal, *Tagebuch*, and in Seigfried Jakobsohn's *Weltbühne*, from whose pages, week after week the Jews injected negation and anger into the bloodstream of the German people. They, the Jews, saw a great deal, and owing to their irresponsible position they could afford to expose all the negative aspects of the life of the German people. And they could laugh at the German officer, at the German bourgeoisie and at the German home — and expose all their negative aspects. It started as far back as Heine.

It may be that for the German people this was an invigorating, salutary potion, with its mixture of pain and raillery. But it seems to me that we Zionists were repelled by this role. Of course there were people, among the Gentiles as well, who saw in this role a mission of the people of *Israel*. But if our talent is only sufficient for that — I prefer the smallest positive contribution that we are making, or hope to make, here, to all that world-shaking stuff.

Avinarius, who was editor of *Kunstwort* (a journal that also played an important role in Kafka's development and is now frequently mentioned in his biography), once wrote: "The Jews are the administrators of German literature." And it was true. A great portion of German literature was dependent on Jews. In Prague, my birth-place, there was a German theater whose manager was a Jew (an inspired man named Angelo Neumann). The greater part of the actors were Jewish and the audience was almost entirely Jewish, for there were in fact not many Germans who went to the theater. There was a standing joke in the city: The manager is a Jew, the actors are Jews and the public is Jewish — but it is called a "German national theater."

And it was a very bitter joke. To the Czechs it was painful that a German theater, and especially one on a high level, should exist in the capital of Czechoslovakia. The Jews in this way were performing a national service for the Germans, and, of course, were disavowing outwardly and inwardly, the fact that they were Jews. The theater in this case was a positive contribution, but the overall contribution made by the Jews was one of criticism (as it seems to be in American literature today) and in actual fact there was something parasitic about it.

BEN EZER: Does that mean you feel there is an analogy between the cultural position held by German and Czech Jewry and the role of Jewry in the United States today?

BERGMAN: As far as I have read and know, it seems to me that the analogy is considerable. And if you ask whether we haven't paid too high a price in renouncing this function — the role of *critics of the Gentiles* — upon arriving in the Land of Israel, I feel that the price has not been so great, though of course the world is far more aware of our previous role than it is of our work here in Israel. Moreover, this so-called "function" fostered in the Jews of that time (and I am not certain if this is true in America today) a kind of conceit and feeling of superiority to the Gentiles, even though in fact we were benefitting from their physical and spiritual work. The fact is that in Germany at that time there was a Gentile German literature that the Jews did not read at all — even though we depended on the language. There were writers who depicted the life of the German peasants — something which did not interest the Jews at all. Actually there were two literatures: one in which the Jews were interested and another which they ignored. And what was unhealthy and dangerous in this relationship between the Germans and Jews was that the Jews owned the big newspapers and publishing houses and thus were in control of German literature.

BEN EZER: The "price" of Zionism means inter alia, that the recent generations of native-born Israelis whose only language is Hebrew and who gain contact with the Western world only after a prolonged struggle with a foreign language and culture — may find it difficult to preserve the image of Israel's intellectual life. Your generation was not faced with the problem of this price at all, because your roots were in Western language and culture; perhaps you have not been aware of the severity of this process.

BERGMAN: This is certainly true, but what can be done? Our task and yours, the first generation living here in Israel, in a Jewish atmosphere with the Hebrew language, is to translate as much as possible. Here you have certainly touched on a painful point, but, it seems to me that this is a task that faces every small nation.

In the Czech University in Prague at the beginning of the century there was a Professor of German, an assimilated Czech Jew named Arnost (Oskar) Kraus. (His successor in the post was also a Jew, the poet Ottacker Fischer. And it is interesting that to this day the Jews are for the Czechs the carriers of German culture, like Professor Goldstücker who now holds the post, and is one of the heralds of Kafka. At one time he was the Czech consul in Israel). About the year 1900 Kraus founded a kind of alliance he named "Babel" — an alliance of small nations for the sake of mutual, non-political aid. Each year he traveled to Denmark with a group of Czech farmers in order to establish ties between the two nations and especially to teach the Czechs about the Danish people's university founded by Grundtvig. Grundtvig was a Danish nationalist thinker

— a philosopher and theologian who started a movement that to this day retains its importance in all the Scandinavian countries — an adult education movement. At the ages of 20 or 22 the famers leave their work in the field and go for a period of half a year to study at an adult school of this kind.

Kraus — probably also as a result of a profound Jewish awareness — founded this movement of communication between the two small nations, Denmark and Czechoslovakia. He realized that every small nation must find a way to other small nations, a way leading not to assimilation but to mutual acquaintance, and that in this way a window would be opened on other nations and there would be a greater chance to combat the danger of provincialism.

The importance of Masaryk from the cultural standpoint (and it is greater than from the political standpoint) lies in the fact that he always preached what he called the "opening of windows," especially the opening of windows on cultures quite remote from that of the Czechs, like the English and the Russian. He himself wrote numerous books on this subject and also urged his pupils to follow in his footsteps and make the cultures of other nations accessible to the Czechs.

It seems to me that we in Israel ought to learn from this, especially since today this sort of thing is much easier, as communications media have expanded in to the field of culture.

BEN EZER: Do you think there is any likelihood of a religious revival in Israel? Today for the non-religious person in Israel to adopt a religious way of life is tantamount to passing over to a different camp — so rigid is the division between the two camps in Israel. Could it be that precisely on this point there is room to be influenced by the experience of American Jewry which seeks to answer the needs of present-day reality with its reformist trends? Or can it be that there are signs of such a process here in Israel, in the challenge that the science of Judaism, which is in the main "secular," poses to Judaism, and even Torah Judaism, such as, for example, the historisophic demand that Judaism be considered something dynamic and many-sided. Is it possible that these outlooks, in addition to the exigencies of reality, will lead to a period of fecund renewal in Jewish thought and *Halacha*?

Bernard Levin once published an essay in the *New Statesman* entitled "Am I A Jew?" in which he propounded the opinion that today there are only two possibilities for Jewish living — religious Jewish life (in the Diaspora) and Jewish life (even of the secular variety) in Israel. Anyone else is, like himself, assimilated, or as he puts it, someone who finds no connection with Judaism, who can no longer feel himself a Jew. In this way he paradoxically finds himself sharing the opinion of those "Canaanites" who aspire to disavow their Jewishness (identifying Jewishness with religion) and to assimilate into their "Israeliness" or "Hebrewness." Does this surprising concensus between Jews here and there presage the end of the mission and message of Judaism as such in our nation and in the world as a whole?

BERGMAN: The great advantage of Judaism lies in the fact that it is a tangible national entity rather than an abstract faith and thus an organic part of humanity's overall history. Its deficiency and danger lie in the tension between universalism and national particularism. The great advantage of international religions such as Christianity and Islam lies in the fact that within the church distinctions between the various nations have been abolished. Yet the Church is not a comprehensive social entity like a nation: it does not embrace all areas of living and is to a large extent severed from the concreteness and responsibility of historical life. And there the tension between universalism and particularism has been transplanted from national to religious soil in that there is now a difference, a chasm, between "believers" and "non-believers." This was pointed out years ago by Yitzhak Heinemann. However it is not our concern here to itemize the differences or ask what duties are incumbent on the various "units" of humanity at this moment as regards the danger that is threatening man and humanism.

Only with regard to our Jewishness there is something we must say: from time immemorial there have been competing within our religion, within our nation, the two aspirations that I mentioned, universalism and particularism. This tension is healthy and fecund so long as there is a dynamic equilibrium between the two aspirations, and one does not choke off the other. Our painful history has from time to time resulted in the particularistic trend prevailing to a dangerous degree. Pejorative concepts like "goy," "Edom" and "Amalek" came to dominate the Jewish soul, and our ancestors felt from the Gentile world "a revulsion of fear and a revulsion of pain" (as Binyamin Tammuz said in his article entitled "Nightmare," 1956).

The moment we became a State, a member of the family of nations, the universal aspiration was to a certain extent reinforced, but on the other hand the trends toward isolationism and solitude were also enhanced. This involves a terrible danger for us and for our position among nations. We have been commanded to eradicate the memory of Amalek, but let us not raise with our own hands ghetto walls in this country. Let us be what A. D. Gordon called a *nation of man*, and we will have a recognized place in man's struggle for a new humanism. And who knows if our geographic, historical and psychological situation here in Israel, between East and West, does not equip us to play an important role in this struggle.

BEN EZER: Is such a synthesis possible?

BERGMAN: The question is, what the development of the Jewish religion will be. If those who wish to erect a wall between us and the world are right, and if this is to be the visage of the Jewish religion — then all our aspirations to incorporate the Jewish people in the family of nations will be to no avail. Last Hannukah I read S. Schnitzer's article in Ma'ariv in which, inter alia, he argues, that the Maccabees were not readers of Sophocles and Euripides and if we are continuing to light Hannukah candles in honor of such a movement we should draw conclusions that are consistent.

And indeed, this is the question — does the Jewish nation wish to be a "people dwelling alone"? And what is this "solitude" among the nations, what are we isolating ourselves *for*? And is this self-segregation a means or an end? I of course oppose assimilation, but unfortunately we are witnessing a different phenomenon — many people are making the means an end. The end of the Jewish religion is to be a humanistic religion and to redeem man — and though we have isolated ourselves in order to be able to be more faithful to its message we must not forget that our message is a general one for all humanity. The means of the Jewish religion are not an end in themselves but a means for an end that is exalted and has a very profound religious and human meaning.

The existence of a religious particularism in Israel today is essentially impossible, and since it exists all the same, it is leading, albeit unwillingly, to a Canaanite reaction. Except that Canaanism is also a particularism, though of a different kind — indeed, a worse and emptier kind. I do not think that in our day, when nations are being brought closer together and distances are no longer what they were — that we can live, spiritually speaking, by ourselves alone and consider all of human culture merely "blossoms which do not bear fruit" as Yehuda HaLevi put it. Unfortunately, I am not familiar with the details, but I do not imagine that the education provided in the *Yeshivot* (talmudic academies where five or seven hours a day are devoted to Talmud) can create a healthy man. There is a disproportion between the general human culture and our own culture. And here the problem is extremely difficult — to find a synthesis. Otherwise we really will become two nations from the cultural standpoint: those who see their experience as essentially a human one, and those who scorn the general human culture. Nor are the State and the Hebrew language that we have in common sufficiently strong to bridge the gap.

Here I see the place of Buber in our culture, if we may take the man as a symbol — a man who was on the one hand so deeply rooted in Jewish culture and on the other hand completely rooted in humanity — to the point where he had a message for humanity. I am using his name because I see in him the symbol of the desire for a synthesis. The question is though, is such a synthesis possible. And in my opinion it is on this that everything depends. Various manifestations are not encouraging. It seems that our State Secular School has not succeeded in finding the way. The whole thing is perhaps dependent on the school and whether they can import this knowledge to the pupils. The teaching of Jewish consciousness has apparently not succeeded. And perhaps it has not succeeded for a very fundamental reason — not only because we do not have teachers who know how to teach it, but because it is impossible to teach Judaism as an *object*, without the pupil himself *living* his Judaism. It is not Greek culture that the Jewish child can be taught as syllabus material but rather there has to be something that makes it into a *subject*. For without the observance of religious duties it seems that there is no way of teaching the content of the religious duties.

On the other hand, the State Religious School system does not seem to be succeeding in imparting the *human* values; and both kinds of schools we have in Israel are proclaiming by their very existence that we are not succeeding, and perhaps do not even want to succeed, in creating this synthesis. It is none other than this synthesis that is the aim of both our generation and yours, the young people's.

Before the creation of the State we deluded ourselves that the idea of the State and Zionism would bridge this gap. Hence the degree of disappointment with the establishment of the State that is expressed in the questions and queries of our contemporaries.

BEN EZER: There are those who say that Canaanism is prevailing in Israel not only as an ideological movement but within the broad periphery of superficiality and emptiness. People are disregarding the historic past not for reasons of ideology but because it is easier that way. What do you think of the prospect that this outlook consciously or unconsciously, in politics and intellectual life, will gain a hegemony over the direction of Israel's future development?

BERGMAN: I find it hard to imagine. If Canaanism is triumphant here — and I am trying to imagine your question though I do not wish to talk about such a possibility — it seems to me that if we ever face another serious military test such an outlook will not be able to serve as a real adhesive for the nation. It is difficult to imagine or hope that anyone would make great sacrifices for the sake of such an absence of cultural affiliation.

BEN EZER: But the argument of the Canaanite outlook is just the opposite. Its version is that a new "Hebrew nation" has developed in the Land and State of Israel, one whose existence and needs necessitate a new system of concepts that is no longer tied to the Jewish people and its historic past. This approach would favor the Israeli interest in any area whatsoever over the Jewish interest, such as for example in the question of relations with Germany, or with the Arab Region, to say nothing of the field of culture in which there is a "Hebrew" demand for autonomy and a "new start." Hence Canaanite patriotism may demand for itself a position of preference over Jewish nationalism, which in its eyes is rootless and cosmopolitan.

BERGMAN: What is this Canaanite nationalism — thirty years old or half a century? In the Second World War the French peasants surrendered to the Germans because their national awareness was so meager that they said to themselves, better to live under the Germans than die as Frenchmen. Then Simone Weil wrote a book entitled *L'enracinement* and the theme of it was that one must go to the roots in order to discover the reason for defeat. And on this she constructed a plan for a complete reform of French life. It would be worth taking this book sometime and comparing it with our own situation.

It seems to me that it is clear as daylight that we will be able to live here only if the Jewish faith can free itself from the chains of the ghettos and be a humanistic religion that can absorb all the ideals of humanity, just as it was able to do in the time of the Mishna. On the other hand there is the requirement that those who are called "secular" should repent, to put it simply. From this standpoint we are faced with a giant challenge. It is a great task for us and for all humanity.

BEN EZER: But is this really a challenge for the young Jew in Israel? And is there anything in it to attract the young Jew in the Diaspora? An idealistic Jewish youth in the United States sees a challenge in going to help the Negroes in Mississippi, while Zionism, or religion, seems to say to them nothing, neither here, nor there. The challenges of Zionism and the image of Judaism in Israel seem to have lost their vitality and power of attraction. And if there is indeed, as there seems to be, a Jewish or general human reawakening among American Jewry and its young people — how do we know that its channel will be directed our way?

BERGMAN: This task of finding a synthesis and a new start for religious life in the Jewish people — such a task is no less attractive than going out to demonstrate on behalf of the Negroes (and are there no possibilities here too of "going to the people," of identifying with the downtrodden and oppressed just like in North America?)

I do not know to what extent American Jewry on the basis of its own precedents can help us in the area of religious revival, as you mentioned in your previous question. I have considerable sympathy with the Reform and Conservative movements among the Jews of the United States, but the tasks facing us here in Israel are a lot more concrete, and the problems are such as to put our actual existence much more in jeopardy. There, when you come down to it, no real danger to life exists.

Therefore if we succeed in finding the synthesis, our success would be much more important, fecund and meaningful, but also more difficult to attain, than amongst Jews anywhere else.

BEN EZER: The State of Israel, the Arab question and the chances for peace are bound up together in a knot that seems insoluble. How do you regard this problem in its entirety today?

BERGMAN: Taking into account the rapid pace of history, it seems that we should already be considering the possibility that the East, even the Far East, will be very near in short time. Russia is already in our region, and tomorrow or the day after, perhaps China will be as well. Today there is an apprehension, or prospect, that it is the Arabs who will benefit from this process. But will this really be the case? The security issue, with all the harmful effects that it is liable to and does have on our internal affairs — remains the chief issue, and I do not see any way that this might change.

As regards the past — the creation of the State was beyond the hopes of even the most radical dreamers, which shows how blind we are with regard to history. What has been done here is something no Zionist ever dreamed about. There were among us differences of opinion with regard to the assessment of Arab nationalism when the Brit Shalom was active. At that time the Zionist leaders still regarded the Arabs as an element that could be bought. But no one dreamed the Arabs would leave the country. Only to a very small degree do people have any influence on the shaping of the future, which is why it is so difficult to speak about the future. We must do everything as if the future depended on us but at the same time we must realize that in the final account the future depends on supreme forces — if you wish on the Holy One Blessed Be He.

Luther once said something about the relationship between work and prayer: you must work as if there were no God in the world and everything depended on your work, and you must pray as if your work did not exist at all. So we too must make an effort to think about the future, but at the same time we must try to realize that our thinking is not the final determinant.

Obviously, building "bridges" to our neighbors is the order of the day, and perhaps with time and the continued existence of the State a new generation of Israelis and Arabs will be further away from that victory of ours and that defeat of theirs — and then it will be easier to find the bridge. But to a large extent we are dependent on historical forces that are not in our power or under our control. I think we cannot do much, but what can be done, must be done. And first of all, the simplest thing is to bring the Arabs in the Land of Israel closer to the State of Israel, to adopt such a policy that the Arabs will be prepared to see in the State's existence their own interest as well. The hope is not great, but everything that can be done must be done. It is clear to me that the security issue cannot in the long run be the guarantee of our existence. One cannot base the survival of a small nation on bayonets.

BEN EZER: Yet one of the claims of Zionism was that it brought with it assurance of Jewish survival.

BERGMAN: Zionism was completely mistaken. It did of course rescue us — insofar as we came to settle in Israel. But in a broader perspective, our survival has not at all become more certain. Franz Rosenzweig said that the Jewish people could ensure its survival only step by step, and from that standpoint he considered Zionism an assurance of survival for a brief time only. Its value lay in the fact that it ensured our survival for one more generation. He thought that the Jewish people would be able to ensure its survival only in this way — generation by generation, by means of a specific solution for each period. But this of course was a very un-Zionistic outlook.

(This part of the interview took place in April, 1970)

BEN EZER: How do you view the price of Zionism and the future relationship between Jews and Arabs in light of the reality following the war of June, 1967?

BERGMAN: I have not stopped believing that relations between Jews and Arabs will one day be normal ones, relations of mutual aid and loyal and true cooperation, relations like those foretold by the Prophets of Israel not only in the distant past but in our own times. We have not come to the land of our forefathers in order to be conquerors and ruling masters, but in order to upbuild ourselves while keeping faith with a humanistic Judaism. When the State of Israel was created, the Christian religious philosopher Van Passen wrote that the Land of Israel must and would be a laboratory in which the Jews would solve the problems of cooperative life which plague all humanity. A. D. Gordon wrote that we are enjoined by our history to realize in the Land of Israel the ideal of a Nation of Men, meaning nations living among themselves a life of cooperation just as individual people do.

The war of 1967 has not weakened this faith of mine. I need only mention the repercussions the war had in the hearts of our youngsters who returned from the battlefield without the slightest hint of hatered (see *The Seventh Day: Soliders' Talks about the Six Day War* which gives the testimony of kibbutz youngsters who came back from the war).

And as for the Arab's hatred of the Jews: anyone who saw the Arabs from the Old City of Jerusalem after the war of June, 1967, when the gates were opened and they poured in by the thousands to the Western part of the city to see their Jewish neighbors, embrace them and kiss them, cannot believe that the roots of hatred ran deep.

We must keep faith with the ideal of the Prophets of Isra٬ l. I do not want to quote any verses that seem cheap or bombastic. I will quote only one: "And in that day Israel will be the third with Egypt and Assyria, a blessing in the midst of the earth, whom the Lord of Hosts has blessed, saying, "Blessed be Egypt my people, and Assyria the work of my hands, and Israel my heritage." (Isaiah, 19, 24–25).

BEN EZER: Does it appear to you that the Jewish religion is filling a positive function in Israel these days, or is it entering on dangerous paths like the sanctification of military force, the "Integrity of the Homeland" and the imposition by secular means of religious customs on the non-religious majority of the nation — for example the Knesset decision on the "who is a Jew" question.

BERGMAN: I regret to say that you are right in asking this question. But in order to give an answer that is correct and true it is not enough to trust in political development and combinations of coalition votes. Political combinations come and go. The real danger attending the religious situation in Israel is a religious nihilism that believes in nothing and borrows chauvinistic slogans from the world as a substitute for religion; a religion that has lost it strength and vitality, that has renounced the messianic ideal of the unity of all men, which is the fundamental theme of the beginning of the Book of Genesis.

"If there is no God, then anything goes," said Dostoyevsky, and this is the cynical atmosphere in which we are raising the young generation in Israel. The danger of this cynicism is a genuine one for the entire world and especially in Israel. And in comparison with this danger our struggle against Orthodoxy is something of no importance, or at any rate its importance is trifling. Because here, as I said, it is a matter of random and ephemeral combinations of political parties whereas the nihilism is not ephemeral, because a person does not see the danger and swallows with each and every breath the poison that can kill him.

Incidentally, I see in any link between religion and race an anachronism that runs counter to the spiritual development of man today. I do not deny that such a connection was justified in ancient times, but today it belies the spiritual level which man has attained in his ascent. This was manifested, in a way obvious to everyone, in the German race laws. Anyone who believes, in one way or another, in a connection between blood and religion, must necessarily arrive at materialistic conclusions that set the religious life at naught.

I consider the link between religion and politics a very great disaster, a great disaster for the State of Israel and a great disaster for the Jewish religion. The fact that political considerations, such as coalitions and the like, aspire (or agree) to give religious circles a political and administrative function in the State, must of necessity divide the nation. This development, which is becoming more pronounced in recent months, is fraught with disaster for both Judaism and our State. Yet I stress that all this is said here *en passant*. I do not believe in any "danger" to us from the religious parties. The danger lies in the nihilistic atmosphere in which we are now living — along with the entire world.

Zionism True and False

Interview with Prof. Mordechai Martin Buber

(This part of the interview is based on transcripts of talks between Prof. Buber in his last years and young people from Israeli kibbutzim. The first talk took place in 1961 and was printed in *Shdemot* (the organ of the Youth Department of Ihud HaKibbutzim V'HaKvutzot) No. 7–8, November 1962. The second talk took place in 1963 and was not published. The third took place in 1965, a few months before Buber's death, and appeared in Shdemot, No. 20, Winter 1966. The material is reprinted here with the kind permission of Abraham Shapira, editor of *Shdemot* and a member of Kibbutz Yizre'el, who arranged the meetings and edited the transcripts).

Q. I met a young member of the Habad movement who introduced me to the Hasidic world. I was at the Habad Yeshiva in Lod. It was hard to stay over there for the Sabbath, but apparently something got into me. In the evening I met the "Persuader" — it was all very impressive. They influenced me and we have kept in touch ever since. When I saw their way of life I thought of its implications for life on the kibbutz. Here on certain occasions we lack the feeling of sanctity. A person cannot live in holiness all the time but still, you sometimes feel the need for it. I am looking for the way. I told the Habad people, "I lack your faith." They said, "It makes no difference. Fast on Yom Kippur." So I fasted once or twice and gradually I'm starting to feel that the day means something to me. I live in a secular environment that does not look favorably on kibbutz members attending synagogue — even if it is only on Yom Kippur, once a year. I also miss the sense of the Sabbath — a break in the flow of everyday affairs. You should have a different feeling on that day, but instead you get basketball, football, and you feel that that's just not it. The atmosphere of comradeship that the Hasidim have eliminates the feeling of alienation between men and this too to a certain extent is lacking on the kibbutz.

BUBER: I disagree with what that Habad said — that you can fast without belief.

Q. He didn't put it exactly that way. I said I was searching and he said I should start off by doing something — like refraining from work on the Sabbath, etc. One thing would lead to another. I've found that he was right, but still, when you come down to it, it's not for me. A person may be at peace with himself, but the atmosphere in which he does his searching is also important.

BUBER: I do not think that it is good to carry out religious observances without faith, that is, without intention. I do not think it is good to do anything without intention.

Q. In other words, first you have to be a hundred percent certain?

BUBER: A hundred percent? I do not use that expression. Generally in human life there is no such thing. I do things with intention insofar as I am able. In my opinion the kibbutz and Hasidism share some common ground. Whatever a person does in either context should be done with intention.

Q. But how can this be put into practice? For instance, in the society in which I live I have no way of experiencing the Sabbath.

BUBER: I am referring to something more general — not necessarily religious observances. A man's life is worthy of the name only if everything that he does is done with the utmost intention, done for its own sake. This does not necessarily have to do with religion. In my opinion it is possible to live a life of intention on the kibbutz even without religious content.

Q. On the kibbutz the spiritual side of things is neglected.

BUBER: You are young. You are young and will have influence for many years to come, not by the propounding of theory but by the living example of your life. I don't believe in theories but in human example. Despite all the difficulties — and I realize they exist — a person must live a life of truth — that truth in which he believes. Not the truth as an ideal nor the truth as image, but the truth as action is what Judaism is all about. Judaism's goal is not philosophic theory or artistic creation but Torah as truth.

Q. On the kibbutz we have our principles and our conventions. A person cannot be completely faithful to his truth for it may run counter to the principles of the group.

BUBER: But is it so terrible to live in opposition to the principles of one's group? Live your life in spite of it and gradually the others will be influenced. True influence is always slow in acting.

I know two kinds of influence — two contradictory forces. One is false influence — political influence, propaganda — and it is a tremendous force indeed. The cadence of propaganda is the hurried one; it is the cadence of the newspapers, the radio, speechifying etc. Then there is true influence — education — which is slow-acting. It is a difficult way, but it is the one that prevails in the end. Real history is that of the slow cadence. It is the story of real power. A person lives and implements in his own life that which he would like to teach. Sometimes it takes a whole lifetime. But such a life is worth living. As you would wish others to live, so you must live yourself.

Q. If I, as a teacher, want to teach things about which I have doubts myself, may I share these doubts with my pupils? Take for example education according to Jewish values, does a non-believer have any moral right to impart values to which he has some attachment but does not identify with completely?

BUBER: Let me tell you what I did when my own son and daughter were about twelve years old. Each day I read the Bible with them — in Hebrew of course. Nor did I say to them, "This is the complete and utter truth, you must believe every word that is written here." Rather I said, "It is important that you know what it was that the people who wrote these things believed." And let me tell you something else. Several years later, when my son was serving in the Austrian Army, I took a walk with him one day through the woods. He said to me, "The fact that you taught us the Bible in that way has influenced me very greatly. Especially now, in the Army, it is not as if I could believe what those people believed. But the very fact that they believed with such a strong and total faith still influences me very strongly, each and every day. That those ancestors of mine could believe with such a strength..."

Q. How do you relate to the post-Biblical expressions of Judaism, especially the Talmud?

BUBER: While I spoke of the Bible, it is not the only thing. Nor do I even accept the laws and statutes that are in the Bible. Do you think that by the Bible I mean what it says in Exodus after the Ten Commandments?

Q. It's all one Bible.

BUBER: But I do not believe in any such "oneness." I gave the Bible to my children so that they might in the course of their lives absorb what is good and important for them. I did not put something in their hearts; I assisted them.

Q. Listen to this. We had a symposium and at one of the sessions there was a Rabbi — a man who believes in God. From what he said I gathered that he believed that every single act and event in his life comes from above — that there is someone directing it all. Everything is decreed and it is not for man to decide. So I asked him, "You say everything in your life, no matter how trivial, is decided from above and you have no say whatsoever?" And he replied, "Yes." I can't understand how anyone can think like that. I just don't understand it.

BUBER: *You* don't understand it, yet you want me to?

Q. I want to hear what you think.

BUBER: What that man said even contradicts the Bible. The prophets do not decree but present you with a choice: either-or. The finest example is the Book of Jonah. But all the prophets have it — they are sent not as soothsayers predicting a future that is inevitable but to bring people face to face with choice and decision. Man has a will and can determine what will be in the hour to come. The question is, shall I dare the proven impossible, or resign myself to the inevitable? Shall I dare be other than I am, trusting that deep down inside I really am that other, and only thus shall I prove it — or shall I accept my present inability as permanent? Is our future constantly renewed, or a preordained cul-de-sac?

A living person, who from his own experience is familiar with freedom of choice and its part in changing the objective reality, cannot believe that anything is preordained. Nor can you know the scope and extent of what can be achieved in any desired direction until you have gone in that direction. The powers of the spirit are measurable only in their application. In the criticial moments of our lives neither planning alone nor surprise alone prevails, but even as we are faithfully implementing that which we have planned we are surprised by discoveries and reactions that are rich in mystery. One must always leave room for surprises. He who plans as if they are avoidable really makes them so. Apparently that Rabbi never read the Bible.

Q. Fine, that's one point. Now let's go deeper.

BUBER: Okay, let's.

Q. Religious people believe in something that is supreme — something that is the source of all things. There are those who believe in God the way that Rabbi believes and those who believe differently. Now, the question is in what way do you believe in God?

BUBER: There is no need to go into that here, because practically everything I have ever written has been precisely about that. We are not here to talk about me.

Q. We also spoke to that Rabbi about the Holocaust. We asked him how religious people are able to interpret it.

BUBER: Back at the time I was asked the same thing. I say that we must differentiate between human affairs and the things which nobody understands. In reply to a letter from a young man on this question I wrote that he who believes in God accepts Him as He is. Just as a person in love accepts his beloved as is. God cannot be spoken *about*, but only *to*. Therefore it is not necessary to know about him even all that it is possible to know. Years ago Ben Gurion invited me over one day. While I was still in the doorway he asked me, "Why do you believe in God?" I said to him, "If believing in God means knowing *what to say about him* then I do not believe in God. But if it means talking *to* Him then I do." I do not know if he really understood. He is capable , but does not want to. I tend to the view that not only the Holocaust but all the wars as well are to be understood in terms of human nature. The Holocaust and what caused it should concern the Germans. It is their problem.

Q. But it also concerns us, the victims.

BUBER: So what is your conclusion?

Q. That we must be stronger. But if we take a look at this State of ours against the background of the Holocaust, is there really any value in the Jews defending themselves?

BUBER: There is a sentimental value or a spiritual value. But no factual value. Can any such defense alter the course of history? From the standpoint of history and the nation's destiny it makes no difference.

Q. Can't the fact of our being a state here change a lot as far as our history is concerned?

BUBER: A State is the territorial concentration of a nation, and not for the sake of abnormal times like these but for the sake of true development — in body and soul. Certainly I have a great appreciation for the value of this State. I think that only in three or four generations will we really see just what this value is. It is something that will increase when we see the end of the politization that is now sapping a great part of the nation's strength. In three or four generations the advantage of having the state will be a whole lot greater, and it will be more internal.

Q. The question is, will we be able to survive the *abnormal* times?

BUBER: I am in favor of war when it is necessary. I do not favor passivity. Yet neither do I favor war for the sake of success. As I said in one of my books: "I am not a radical pacifist. I do not believe that one must always answer violence with non-violence."

Q. Still on the subject of the state, should we strive to be a "normal" state, or are we rather a "unique people"? And if we are indeed unique, what is our mission?

BUBER: I do believe there is something unique in us, but it does not lend itself to definition. As I said, it is my hope that in another three or four generations the present situation of over-politization will be altered, and so will our relations with the Arabs. I hope — ah, it won't be easy for those forces to manifest themselves.

Q. Where will they come from?

BUBER: The material exists.

Q. But not the faith.

BUBER: At the moment faith is not necessary. It will manifest itself when we stop wasting all our strength on politics. There will be a renewal, even a religious one. Not a continuation but a renewal. Yet I do not know the forms it will take.

Q. I have absorbed something of the traditional atmosphere in my father's home. How much of this will I be able to hand to my children? And what will they in turn hand on?

BUBER: Internal spiritual revolutions always occur, and when you least expect them. You must be familiar with this — it has been the case throughout history. Not everything that happens is a matter of education. Education can be of assistance when something else already exists which is not based on education. Hope is one such thing — it is not based on education or tradition, etc. Hope is based on the fact that today the young generation is concerned with these problems, and longs for a renewal. Today I see a longing. Yet I must not use the word religion. I must not say this is a longing for a religious renewal, for that word they do not want to hear.

Q. Is there any hope as far as education is concerned? Is there such a thing as the possibility of educating? Educating can be done in two ways — preaching and personal example. . .

BUBER: Not only personal example but also real contact. If you are the solitary type, without contact, you will not succeed.

Q. Our generation is unworthy.

BUBER: A worthy generation — has there ever been something like that?

Q. How can an unworthy generation set a personal example?

BUBER: What is a generation? It is merely an abstact concept. I know only individuals. I am not a perfectionist, in fact I don't believe in perfection. I want to improve and amend whatever is possible. You — and this is typical of every young generation — say either-or. Perfection or bust. I say improve whatever you can, each in his own place and according to his means. He whose eye is open to surprises — not only the bad ones each day brings but the good as well — realizes that it all turns on the quality of people, not the institutions.

The finest institution will solve nothing if its administrators are unworthy. An institution is merely a prior condition.

Q. But how are things to be improved?

BUBER: You want the fast cadence, I know only the slow one, that called education. And first the educators themselves must be educated, which is a difficult task. You think life can be divested of the element of tragedy, but this is impossible.

Once, in the United States, I was asked how the Constitution ought to be amended. I replied that that was not the problem. Things could be done with this Constitution as with any other. Each man is a new creation and must correct his own measure in the world. That which is peculiar to each person alone and to practically no one else is what he should develop and put into practice.

Q. How can one develop himself?

BUBER: On the one hand a person must have a *relationship* with his fellows, while on the other hand *distance* is also important. There can be such a thing as a "crowdedness" that does not permit a person to *see* his fellow, to say nothing of *relating* to him. This is one of the main problems of life on a kibbutz. There are practical aspects too, but we won't go into them here. The basis, however, remains the *mutual relationship*, the person's being open to his fellow.

As I said in one of my books: "Life means to be called, and all we need do is listen. . . Each and every one of us is encased in an armor which from habit we no longer even feel. Only the most fleeting of moments manage to get through, spurring the soul to accept the call."

Such a *dialogue* is also based on a person's being open to surprises. Tomorrow I may have a genuine conversation with a person I haven't had any contact with till now.

Q. How can one educate to dialogue and give educators faith in an encounter?

BUBER: It is difficult not to believe in living reality. If a dialogic reality comes into being, it will be believed. I am not an idealist, in fact I do not know what ideals are. I know things that are tangible and come into being.

As I said in one of my books: "I know no abundance other than that of every passing hour with its demands and its responsibilities. I do not pretend that I can always cope with it. But I know full well that I am subject to the demand and summoned to the responsibility." (*Dialogue*, 1932).

Q. In teaching there is a tension of opposites between the large amount of information the pupil is given and the values (trust, reciprocity, love, cooperation etc.) that he is supposed to develop. There is also a contradiction between the educator and his work and the orientation given in the home.

BUBER: There is a failure to differentiate between the *social* and the *interpersonal*. *Proximity* is not *relating*. We should strive for improvement, not perfection. Every situation is new, every child is a new world and the educator has to learn anew each day. There are no formulas for solving the problems, nor are things to be attained cheaply. I believe not in methods but in personalities. The teacher-pupil relationship is a special one in that there is not complete mutuality, nor is such a thing possible. In our world the educational relationship takes place not between a single teacher and pupil but between a teacher and a number of pupils. Yet all the same there must from time to time be a personal approach to the pupil, nor can anything be substituted in its place. Hence I feel that the profession of the educator is the most difficult and exalted one of all. Yet our society (the entire world) does not yet know this. So much importance is attached to the realm of politics, while that of pedagogy is pushed to one side.

Q. Is it possible to give the pupils a faith in dialogue and encounter?

BUBER: I don't mean faith in an "encounter" but faith in this particular man, the teacher. It is not necessary that, as a child of ten, I know anything about "encounters" or "mutual relationships." But it is necessary that when I am near the teacher I feel that I can tell all to this man. The important thing is that you, the teacher, be the man I can trust.

Teaching that aims at the *what* is not educational. If it aims at the *how*, it is. Education is not a matter of *what* but of *how* — *how* you teach, *how* you introduce things. And this is a very difficult task indeed. Even in technical education, where there may appear to be no place for soul, for experiential contact, there is a *how*. When the pupil is introduced to the world of techonlogy it is important *how* he feels at each and every step of the way. The important thing is to make the technology human, that within technology there should exist genuine relations among people.

Q. Good and evil — I feel I have in me both these worlds. And the better world is masked. I feel I have to give expression to it.

BUBER: Could you illustrate?

Q. In my group I am considered a negative sort of character, with little to recommend him. But inside I feel there is good. I'm thought to be light-headed, a person who doesn't read. But I read a lot, and write too, but whenever somebody comes in I close the book.

BUBER: There is nothing negative about this. I do not have principles. There is what must be done now, and here. I do not have principles. All I have is an orientation and my senses — action according to the given situation.

Q. But our life on the kibbutz is based on principles.

BUBER: In educating young people I explain that there are things worth living for. The true educator has influence even without words. And another thing is *vision*. From time to time to look around and see the conditions, the circumstances. *How* to live now. Even the Ten Commandments need to be translated into the language of circumstances. If I am commanded to honor my father and my mother, from time to time, under varying circumstances, this honoring has to be reinterpreted. And it will not be the same. Yet there is no other way.

Q. You say you are opposed to principles. Yet that in itself is a principle. What do you consider a principle to be?

BUBER: A principle is that one must always do such and such.

Q. Help thy friend — is that a principle?

BUBER: If you make a principle out of it you are mistaken. There are cases where I cannot help, and others in which my friend does not want me to, and I must not give myself the feeling that he does. Each case has to be considered on its own merits.

Q. But there are things which we cannot do without.

BUBER: Open eyes — that is what I propose, and not principles.

Q. But what shall I go by?

BUBER: By your view of the situation. I cannot give it to you any cheaper than that. For the past thirty years I have been trying to follow the development of youth and I have discerned three different stages. When I first arrived in 1938 the most prominent thing was politics. A genuine strong party loyalty, unlike now. A generation which lived a life of exaggerated politization. I understood it, even though I did not approve. Then came a second generation, which was interested in what they called "living" (in America they called it careerism). For even if they belonged to political parties the members of that generation were more interested in themselves, in their work. There was a healthy element in it too — family life.

In recent years I have been witnessing the gradual rise of a third generation, and something about it surprises me — these youngsters know not what is in their hearts. (Though if I should come and say it is such and such they would readily deny it). What I see is a sense of dissatisfaction: Is this the human world? If so, it is very limited, and around it is a large world that has lost its humanity. Talking with these young people I gain the impression of a certain dissatisfaction with political life, as well as with individual life and with the family. There is a striving for something that has no name.

Hence the searching, the sense of helplessness. This is the third stage, that of the young generation of today. Nor is it yet possible to characterize it, the way the first could be described as political and the second as individualistic. The dissatisfaction of these youngsters is readily understandable. They feel that something is rotten. Even though they won't say what, it weighs upon them. The dissatisfaction grows. And there is a yearning, a nameless yearning. I don't mean to apply the stamp of religion to it. It is in the nature of yearning to be the antithesis of any stamp. If I tell them, "Do such and such," they will reply, "Oh, you mean religion." Yet there are those who dream. Certainly they won't come to you and say "Tell us what it is." They are not so foolish. There are those who unburden themselves by asking questions of a more personal nature. It is still all in a formless state, but something seems to have started to grow. Not yet a movement, merely a longing. The real change will come only in two or three generations time. In my heart I have formed a pact with my grandchildren, perhaps my great-grandchildren.

(This part of the interview is based on articles on Zionism and Jewish-Arab relations written by Buber over the course of fifty years. They were collected in *Am V'Olam*, the second volume of *Te'udah V' Ye'ud*, published by *HaSifriya HaTsiyonit*, Jeruaslem, 1964. They are reproduced here with the kind permission of the publishers.)

Q. What is the change that Zionism may bring about in the hearts of the youth?

BUBER: We must strive for nothing less than a concrete transformation of our life as a whole. The process of transforming our inner life must be expressed in the transformation of our outer life, that of the individual as well as that of the community. And the effect must be reciprocal: the change in the external arrangements of our life must be reflected, and renew our inner life time and again. Up to now, Zionist theory has not adequately realized the importance of this mutual influence. The power of the external transformation has frequently been overestimated. Such overestimation cannot, of course, be counteracted simply by confronting it with faith in the power of the spirit. Only he who commends himself to both spirit and earth at the same time is in league with eternity.

Q. It is difficult for people like ourselves to become believers. To change things, change ourselves.

BUBER: The typical man in our day can no longer believe in God, but then neither can he believe in his own self — a self devoid of any foundation or basis. Hence he clutches at a belief in his expanded self — the nation — as the highest reality of all. Lacking any genuine, vital relationship to that truth which is above and beyond his nation, and all nations, the truth that demands its implementation of the nations, he turns his nation into an idol and posits its personality as God; he makes a God of what should be merely a minister, one of the ministering angels. And if there is no degree higher than the nations themselves, no court of appeals beyond the statutes of these nations, the upshot is that the nations and their ministers do battle with every means at their disposal, stopping at nothing, not even annihilation. The secret forces, the ministers, are now nothing more than national ideologies, political myths used by the leaders or their usurpers to warm their selfishness with fancies of pretended idealism. It is the hour when the ministers forget who they are and why they are there and wax arrogant, each imagining hismelf master. But the hand of their Master is upon them.

Q. Is it a negative aspect of Zionism that it has become a nationalistic substitute for religion?

BUBER: In modern Zionism there have been two basically contradictory trends, ever since the beginning. For a long time it was felt only in the sphere of ideology, but with the growing urgency of the political situation and the need for decision, the contradiction has become appallingly real.

In their original form these two trends could be regarded as two different interpretations of the concept of "revival." One strove for the rebuilding and reestablishment of an Israel in which life and the spirit would no longer dwell side by side as two different realms each subject to its own laws, as during the long desert journey of the Exile. Rather, the spirit would build life as a home, even as flesh, for itself. Revival in this sense did not refer merely to a safeguarded existence in lieu of the unsafeguarded one at present, but a life of realization instead of one in which abstract ideals float disembodied in an idealless reality.

The other trend interpreted the term "revival" to mean "normalization." A "normal" nation needs a country, a language, political independence, and once these are acquired the rest will come by itself. How the people in that country will live with one another, what they will say in that language, and what relationship their independence will bear to the rest of humanity — all this has nothing to do with the isssue of revival. Be normal and behold, you are revived.

Never have spirit and life been so remote as now during this so-called revival. Or is what you call spirit merely the collective selfishness that knows no criterion above itself and no law from on high? Where are justice and truth determining our actions, outward or inward? (I say *inward* because external breaches necessarily entail internal ones as well). Such a "Zionism" desecrates the name of Zionism. It is nothing more than one of the vulgar forms of nationalism in our day, one which recognizes no authority other than an imaginary national interest. Put another way, it is a kind of *national assimilation*, one more dangerous than any individual assimilation for the latter affects only the individuals and families concerned, while the former eats at the kernel of Israel's selfhood.

Zion is something greater than a patch of land in the Near East or a Jewish State on this patch of land. Zion implies a memory, a demand, a mission. Zion is the foundation stone, the bedrock and basis of the Messianic edifice of humanity. Zionism is the limitless destiny of the nation's soul.

Q. According to Ben Gurion, the young generation in Israel feels closer to the distant past of the Hebrew nation than to the history of the Jews in the past 2,000 years.

BUBER: Ben Gurion is right in saying that youth in Israel is very much interested in certain parts of the Bible, especially in the stories about the conquest of the land, the stories of the hero-kings and also in some of the words of the Prophets. But on no account are the Prophets to be regarded apart from their historic mission, which sent them to those men who had seized the reins of power in order to summon them to stand in judgment before their God, who made them king provisionally.

What exactly was it that the Prophets censured when they faced the rulers? It was the means which they used to arrive at their ultimate goal (concerning which the Prophets did not differ) —the glory of Israel. These means contradicted the ends, and one of the unexpressed principles of prophecy is that ends do not justify the means. And if the nature of the means is in contradiction to the nature of the end, they desecrate it, poison it and make of it a thing of horror.

Ben Gurion rightly sees in the Messianic vision the second cornerstone of living Judasim. But this also is in need of more concreteness. It is not enough to set "the redemption of Israel" side by side with "the redemption of the human race." The Messianic message is unique in the demand God makes upon the nations of men to realize His kingdom and in this way to take part in the redemption of the world. The message is applied especially to Israel and demands of it that it make an exemplary beginning in the actual work of realization, that it be a nation which establishes justice and truth in its institutions and activities. Therefore, Isaiah not only calls upon the Gentiles to stream to Mount Zion and there to receive the second Torah, the universal one; he supplements this by his summons to the House of Jacob to walk before them in the light of the Lord.

Q. Ben Gurion feels that the term Zionism has lost its germane significance and no longer says to the young generation of Jews in Israel and the Diaspora what it did to the Zionist founders up to the creation of the State. In place of "Zionism" Ben Gurion proposed "the Messianic vision in Jewish history."

BUBER: Behind everything that Ben Gurion has said on that point there lies, it seems to me, the will to make the political factor supreme. He is one of the proponents of that kind of secularization

which cultivated its "thoughts" and "visions" so dilligently that
it keeps men from hearing the voice of the living God. This secularization takes the form of an exaggerated politization. This politization of life here strikes at the very spirit itself. The spirit with all
its thoughts and visions descends and becomes a function of politics. This phenomenon, which is supreme in the whole world at
present, has very old roots. Even some kings in Israel are said to
have gone so far as to employ false prophets whose prophesying
was merely a function of State policy.

Closely connected with all that I have been saying is the problem
of Zionism in our day. Ben Gurion has stated that this no longer has
any real or positive content and that in the eyes of the Israeli
generation in whose name he speaks it has become an ideological
anachronism. Zionism, so his argument runs, means a longing
for Zion, and since this longing has already attained its goal, there
is no rhyme or reason for Zionism anymore. But those who inscribed
the name Zion on their banner, first calling themselves Lovers
of Zion and thereafter Zionists, did not have in mind something
which existed and needed only to be repossessed. I still recall
what this circle of young Zionists to which I belonged some sixty
years ago meant by the name. Had we been asked: "Are you
striving for a country of Jews in Israel?" we would have answered:
"We are striving for Zion and in order to establish Zion we desire
independence for our people in our country." Even today there are
many Zionists who share this feeling, and not only among the older
ones; I myself know a number who came to the country and who
continue to dream this dream which has as yet found no fulfillment,
the dream of Zion. They hope with all their hearts that this country,
as it is, is the first step in the direction of Zion. This quasi-Zionism
which strives to have a country only, has attained its purpose.
But the true Zionism, the love of Zion, the desire to establish something like "the city of a great king" (Psalms 48/3), of "*the* king"
(Isaiah 6/5) is a living and enduring thing. Come, let us awaken
this Zionism in hearts that have never felt it, in the Diaspora as
well as here. For here in this country also we need a movement
which strives for Zion, aspiring towards the emergence of a rebuilt
Zion from the materials at our disposal.

And now Ben Gurion tells us that Zionist thought is dead

but that the Messianic idea is alive and will live until the coming of the Messiah. And I answer him with the question: "In how many hearts of this generation in our country does the Messianic idea live in a form other than the narrow nationalist one which is restricted to the Ingathering of the Exiles?" A messianic idea with the yearning for the redemption of mankind yet without the desire to take part in its realization is no longer identical with the Messianic visions of the prophets of Israel.

Q.   But how can the Messianic ideal of the Prophets be realized in our present situation in Israel?

BUBER: The men of politics think that all they need strive for is the good of the State at that hour, as they see it. Nor do they consider this to be at cross purposes with morality. On the contrary, if someone should come and say their conduct is immoral they will unceremoniously shut him up. They will say it is the very essence of morality, because their means and ends serve the life of the nation. As if group selfishness is any more moral than individual selfishness. In contrast to them you find the men of morality, who quote general principles of right and wrong based on the given situation — without asking each day what can be done under the conditions of that day — and without harm to the nation's life. For such a scrutiny requires the interaction of things — a conscience that is not readily deceived and a trustworthy view of reality.

The politicians lack the supra-political view that alone could show them the nation's true life interest, above and beyond the petty reckonings of the hour. The men of principle on the other hand, lack an eye for what can and should be done and in what degree, at this very hour. They regard politicians as power-mad despots who know no law beyond their own will, while the politicians in turn regard them, these ideologists, as slaves of high-flown utterance better suited to the clouds than a contradiction-ridden earth. Between one and the other, any chance of attaining the degree of right and good permitted by reality is lost.

Q. Ever since your arrival in Israel you have been known as a leader of the pacifists who seek peace with all their might. How do you view our relations with Arabs?

BUBER: During the period of settlement on the land, which in effect amounted to conquest by peaceful means, the finest of us held no hopes of remaining guiltless and unsullied in the war for national survival. Inasmuch as we were ensuring a place for our future generations, we were reducing the space for the future generations of Arabs. Yet our intention was to sin no more than absolutely necessary to gain this objective. And when we were forced by history to replace the selection and training of immigrants with a mass influx and then to strive for international security, our political leadership still held options as to what form that security should take. It was incumbent on us to seek the maximum amount of justice compatible with the exigencies of life. (This was the idea behind the bi-national State and the Near East Federation). And when that hour passed and nothing was done, it paved the way for the refugee problem and an enormous increase in our objective guilt.

It is said that Nordau once came rushing in to see Herzl. "I hear there are Arabs living in Palestine," he cried, "Which means we are not in the right!" If this story is true it reveals a remarkable naivete. By its very essence, life involves injustice. Anaximander even felt that the very fact of our personal existence is an injustice to the Whole, to all the other creatures, and we owe them atonement. At any rate there is no life without the destruction of other life. If you look closely you will see that at each and every moment each and every one of us is stealing the living space of somebody else. In fact if you look really closely you will not be able to go on living. What it means to be a man is that beyond a certain point one begins to take stock of his actions and, as a result, deprives other creatures no more than he must. The degree of necessity in each case may not be easy to recognize because of the intervention of powerful impulses — acquisitiveness and power, yet all the same it can be known. We cannot refrain from doing wrong altogether, but we are given the grace of not having to do more than is absolutely necessary. And this is none other than the grace we are given of being human.

Q. What is the political and practical outlook of this camp to which you belong?

BUBER: As against the outlook of the leadership of the State, which is purely political, and as such defective even politically speaking, we posit an outlook that is both political and moral. Yet beyond this point there is considerable dissension. There are among us those who proclaim a moral principle and demand its implementation, even though if carried through to its logical conclusion it would involve not only a stoppage of immigration but the deportation of Jews who are already here. There are others among us whose attitude is far from being holier-than-thou. They do not raise any banner of unsullied principle or expect it to be obeyed. All they demand is that rectification that is possible under the given circumstances (and not less than that). These circumstances must be examined with care and a plan drawn up specifying how many refugees can be resettled, where and how. This plan may be considered one chapter, the one which we contribute, to an overall solution. Such a solution will not succeed without the cooperation of all parties concerned, yet the initiative for such cooperation, and for the preparatory consultations first of all, must be taken by us. Nor will we be able to do so unless we decide to make our contribution and draw up our plan.

He who would truly serve the spirit must seek to make good all that has been missed; he must seek to free the blocked path to an understanding with the Arab peoples. Today it appears absurd to many — especially in the present intra-Arab situation — to think now about Israel's participation in a Near East Federation. Tomorrow, with a change in certain world political situations which are not dependent on us, this possibility may arise in a very positive sense. Inasmuch as it depends on us, we must prepare the ground for it. There can be no peace between Jews and Arabs that is merely a cessation of war; there can only be a peace of genuine cooperation. Today, under circumstances so manifoldly aggravated the command of the spirit is to pave the way for the cooperation of peoples.

Lay Not Thine Hand Upon The Lad!

Interview with A. Eli

(This interview was held in August 1970)

(For the purposes of this interview I have used passages from *Bein Tz'irim* (Among the Youth) — talks in the kibbutz movement — published by Am Oved, Tel Aviv, 1969. Reproduced with the kind permission of the publishers. I have also used excepts from articles by Eli in *Shdemot*, No. 35, Autumn 1969, and No. 37, Spring, 1970. With the kind permission of the editor, Avraham Shapiro, and the editorial board of Ihud HaKvutzot V'HaKibbutzim. Two passages were also taken from *The Seventh Day: Soldiers' Talk about the Six Day War*, Andre Deutsch, London 1970).

BEN EZER: Eli, in your poem, "This is the Story of Jacob" you wrote:

"A striped blouse is the loveliest present
That Joseph got. Since it was put on him
He's had no rest. He runs around
Like a tiger in a cage, looking
Through the bars..."

This appeared in your first book of poems, published in 1966, a year before the Six Day War. Since then, has your feeling that the "striped blouse" is really a cage grown any stronger?

ELI: A few months ago I attended a giant rally of thousands of Armored Corps personnel. We heard an address by a renowned general who spoke of the lessons learned from the war: "We were not prepared for a war as prolonged as the one that has been going on now for quite some time. We have to get accustomed to the losses as an *item in planning*, to plan on a regular basis the replacement of cadres and replenishment of ranks, to know what percentage will be injured and killed and to make up the losses..."

He spoke in a dry, professional tone, as if the subject were industrial planning, or the improvement of a breed of chickens rather than human lives, as if he did not comprehend at all the terrible significance of what he was saying and doing, as if people's deaths were something natural and self-evident.

Of course he was right — and it is good that we have people who think about such things, who make it their profession — it is thanks to them that we are alive, thanks to the fact that they are dauntless, embedded like roots in the soil and do not retreat or break in any wind — on the other hand, perhaps this is precisely why humanity looks the way it does, because of this excessive confidence, because of a justice that leads to no compromise...

BEN EZER: And you?

ELI: I'll tell you about a conversation I had with a kibbutznik (one whose profound humanity is well known to me and has stood the test of many years) — about what happened to the Czechs in 1968.

"As a nation, they have no right to exist," he said, "now that they have proved they are cowards devoid of all honor. What would the world come to if people were to accept every kind of piggishness and fear for their lives? What would their lives be worth?" "But they didn't stand a chance against the Russians," I replied. "Hundreds of thousands of people would simply have been killed to no purpose..."

"So what? It was essential for the future. It would have shown the way for humanity." Thus, in one breath, he killed a million people — with complete self-confidence...

BEN EZER: And you?

ELI: You must have read in the papers about the reunion of the Harel Brigade that fought in the War of Independence. There were some very "vivid" descriptions there of death and the war in 1948, how every third man was killed, how during that period a certain commander who had a reputation as the brigade's political officer ("politruk") used to stand beside the open graves and exhort those youngsters to go and meet their death. How the man managed to get a single word out of his mouth — despite the justice, despite the belief, that is something I cannot understand.

What does justice do, what does death do to people so that they are prepared to do the most horrible things to others and to themselves, in the sense of "Take now they son, thine only son, whom thou lovest..."

So that the most terrible things of all become beautiful, educational, an example for generations to come...

And they got up and went, in the knowledge that they would die, all of them, that it was only a question of who came first... What came over these young people for whom life had not yet begun... why did they consent? What were they told, what great beliefs, what were they promised, what hopes for the future, what beauty, what exalted things for whose sake it was worth laying down their lives?

To send children to their death? Who can do such a thing? Who can take it upon himself? Who can point to anything worth dying for, apart from the one great and terrible no-alternative? Who can take it upon himself to decide there is no alternative, and won't his voice tremble?

We have to grow accustomed to this, to agree, to plan the replenishment of the ranks with young soliders, who tomorrow will be our own sons, and when war breaks out we will play them "songs of the homeland" over the radio in Hebrew on this side, in Arabic on the other — to remind them there is something "worth fighting for," so they will hurl themselves to their doom with maximum enthusiasm...

BEN EZER: And what is your answer?

ELI: I am not in favor of exaggeration and extremism. In every exaggeration there is evil and distortion, but it seems to me that we ought to consider and examine very carefully all the sanctified values and symbols for which we go to our death. I do not pretend to be at all objective. My standpoint is the result of a sobering-up period after beliefs that were absolute, as it were, and were revealed in all their nakedness and falsehood.

BEN EZER: For example?

ELI: I will tell you a personal story by way of illustration. When I was in the Army and nineteen years old, we were scheduled to go out on a retaliatory raid. The nature of the operation was such that it was clear to me I wouldn't return. For three terrible days (like the days it took Issac to go to Mount Moriah with Abraham) the operation was postponed, and in the end it was cancelled. Actually, I should have died back then. I well remember that terrible naivety. What did that boy know about life, about being a father, for example? Perhaps because of that incident, which takes its significance from the fact that I see it today with hindsight, I cannot break free of the symbol of the Sacrifice.

BEN EZER: A secular sacrifice? Without faith in God? How do you explain it?

ELI: "Take now thy son, thine only son, whom thou lovest..."

When Abraham accepted the commandment he knew a miracle would take place, otherwise he would not have been able to accept it. He knew there was somebody supreme who wanted the good, who cared, who could not make a mistake; and that the outcome — through all the pain and anguish, through the distress and the sacrifice — had to be good. All the same — the legend tells us — "He opened wide his mouth and cried, and moaned loud and long..."

"At that hour," the legend goes on "the ministering angels stood row upon row in the firmament and wept and said to the Master of the Universe: "And thine oath: So shall thy descendants be" — what shall become of it? Said the Holy One Blessed Be He to Michael: "Why are you standing there — do not permit him." (from the Book of Aggadah by Bialik and Ravnitzky).

In other words, somebody is concerned, somebody cares. But today what faith is there? What hope for the good? Can one do such things with such faith today?

I must read you another legend: "And it came to pass after these things that God did tempt Abraham." After what things ? After the words of Satan. Said Satan to the Holy One Blessed Be He: Master of the Universe, this old man (that is, Abraham) whom thou hast granted fruit of the womb at the age of one hundred years, of all the feasts he has made has not offered thee even one dove or fledgling! — Said the Holy One Blessed Be He: Has he not done it all for the sake of his son? If I say to him: sacrifice thy son to me, forthwith shall he sacrifice him. Said Satan: Try him. And immediately — "God did tempt Abraham..." (from the Book of Aggadah by Bialik and Ravintzky).

BEN EZER: And what is your conclusion?

ELI: Reading this legend, I have the feeling that generations of men are dying for some sporting wager between God and Satan. In other words, not for any *objective necessity* but for a death wish buried somewhere deep in man — and for the sake of this game children have to die, there have to be pogroms, a Holocaust... To see if man who was created in God's image can pull the thing off.

BEN EZER: And so?

ELI: So life must not be a game of ideals or a sport of justice and honor. "Lay not thine hand upon the lad!" His life is holier than all the ideals!

I could accept this legend in the sense of a *shared fate*, of a continuity. Sons are not born in a vacuum; there is a responsibility shared between fathers and sons, and this cannot be denied. The son pays for the father's pain, for his ideals and for his shortcomings, but all amidst the terrible forces closing in on them both, amidst a powerful urge to live. Perhaps this is how the world is and this is how life is, perhaps no value, love or beauty can arise unless one is prepared to die for it. This truth too is still very much in doubt — but it is only because of a lack of choice. Are our values more beautiful, our flags redder — merely because more blood has been shed on them?

BEN EZER: Eli, why does the business of the Sacrifice torment you so? Is this the one and only meaning you find in Judaism and our history?

ELI: The symbol of the Sacrifice is not a marginal or incidental tale in Judaism. It is the symbol on which the Jew has been raised for thousands of years. The symbol of the Sacrifice and what it implies are an expression of the meaning of life according to the Jewish conception, and of man's position in the universe — hence I wish to take issue with it.

Actually, even Judaism cannot accept the Sacrifice story in its original form. Piles upon piles of interpretations and legends have been written in order to soften and blunt the bone the reader has to swallow, which is the story's crux:

Abraham received a command from God to offer up his son as a burnt sacrifice and he is prepared to carry out this command without question or argument — and as a reward he becomes the

Father of his Nation, the "Champion of Faith," a paragon and example for the Chosen People, a nation whose uniqueness lies in its faith.

In the story of the Sacrifice, the figure of Abraham is quite different from what it is in the other stories that surround him, where he is seen as a man who tends not to take authority at face value and is not afraid to argue with God when he thinks He is not right. One of the crucial points in this story is that the command is explicitly a divine caprice that is not based on any objective necessity of the kind we are accustomed to seeing in life, where fathers send their Isaacs to be sacrificed because they have no choice, because of the terrible forces closing in on them, and, because sons pay for their fathers deeds and misdeeds — but all because of a desire to survive and live. Whereas here, God will be fulfilled and gain His value if Isaac's blood is spilled, as if without the color of blood He, God, will have no color or substance.

Abraham hears in his soul the voice of the Divine Absolute demanding his son's life. Isaac's life is of no importance in its own right, it is not an aim in its own right and has no value, it is merely in the nature of a test. And this is what various commentaries try to amend — but it sticks in my throat like a bone that I cannot swallow. *What kind of an absolute is this that commands Isaac's death? I cannot find within myself any such God who would think of putting a man to the test of murdering his own son.* In so doing he is making a covenant the ideal of which passes through death. Insofar as I can assume any absolute whatsoever, it is completely and utterly opposed to death, and aimed at life. From this standpoint, as Abraham and his God are reflected in the story, I would not want Abraham as the father of my nation or such a God as my God. God in this story is a Moloch, and Abraham, simply, is an idolator.

But let's get back to the main problem, which is whether there is any absolute in whose name we are permitted to kill, and if there is, can it be recognized and distinguished from all its look-alikes? It seems to me that if there is any lesson to be learned from history, it is that the world is in constant motion and change — and this includes the various "absolute values." Gods rise and Gods fall, concepts of divinity change — not only from period to period and nation to nation but during an individual's own lifetime. I see nothing that is absolute, and if it were, in the light of history we should have to conduct ourselves as if it weren't.

Is there any need, in this day and age, to show what atrocities have been committed in the "name of the absolute" — in the name of the God of Israel and other Gods? How many lives have been taken because people thought they were hearing the voice of the absolute? "My absolute is always righter than the other fellow's." Faith has always been a justification for slaughter. Hitler was a believer; so was Stalin. Isn't it time people stopped sacrificing life in the name of the absolute?

So much for Abraham. And what about Isaac? What is Abraham's absolute for Isaac? Abraham arrived at an awareness of the divine after long years of personal experience and observation of life, just as every man develops a philosophy of life in the course of years, and a system of values on which he builds his life. But the young Isaac does not yet have values, he is still outside his father's values, perhaps at the beginning of the process of their assimilation. He may adopt them in the course of time; he may reject them. To die for them now means to die for empty words which have no reference inside of him; it means to die for a truth that is not his. From Isaac's point of view, Abraham is taking advantage of his childish naivete and the trust he has for him as a son, in order to sacrifice him. For Abraham, the sacrifice has meaning; through it his life confirms its course — but from Isaac's standpoint his death has no meaning at all.

It seems to me that if we are to be honest with ourselves, we must examine our lives and the lives of our fellow men from the standpoint of the dead Isaac, from the standpoint of the dead. It requires a bit of imagination and effort, but if we do it we will be surprised to find that many slogans and values which seemed to us necessary to give life meaning and for which we were willing to die, will suddenly appear to be nonsense. (As Ecclesiastes says, "For a living dog is better than a dead lion...") It seems to us we have large demands as human beings. But when facing the great darkness — how little seems truly essential, how much more than a little sunlight? Perhaps if we understood this, we would be less ready to give our lives or take those of others, in the name of false and inflated values.

This is what I have been trying to explain with the symbol of Isaac and Abraham. A man confronted with the awareness of his own death, or who steps down from the sacrificial altar, has to begin seeking and asking for the meaning of life. The answer "all is vanity" is also possible, but now one cannot but ask.

I heard a psychologist call this stage the "Abraham question" — the stage of maturity at which you begin to see yourself as part of society, of humanity, of the nation. But as I said, the legitimate point of departure is the life of the individual, and when it comes into contradiction with the life of the nation... There is no other nation whose history is strewn with the death of so many individuals. "The Nation of Israel lives!" True, but what answer is that to my friend who fell?

... And when you come down to it, what kind of a Jewish awareness is this that we have been given? We have been taught writings disconnected from reality, we have been raised in the light of a negation of the Exile. So how can one ask people like me to value national survival on truly equal terms with our own human, irreplaceable, lives?

On what has the Jewish child been brought up, been raised these past three thousand years? On the Sacrifice of Isaac, on the sacrifice of man to an ideal, on a life "for the sake of" — it matters not for the sake of what—God, Socialism, Homeland — the "sake of" is more important than life itself. And if I have any complaint against Judaism it is this — its free and willing choice of the Sacrifice, of Moloch. The Jewish people would not survive had it not chosen to be unique. But what is this uniqueness? To what has it brought the nation? Judaism may perhaps be the pinnacle of the human race, but its history has been one of boundless grief, pain and horror. Judaism has led its sons to death rather than to life. And any faith that demands that its people die is an idolatry one.

BEN EZER: And so, in your opinion, is Zionism?

ELI: If Zionism comes to save human lives, then I agree with it. But if it comes to create one more idol, one more faith — I consider it to be an immoral movement.

What are the Bible and the Prophets all about: "Thou shalt not worship strange gods." And what is idolatry, but the attribution to a *thing* the function of godliness... when the sun is not the sun but a God. The sun may be something beautiful and necessary, the State may be something necessary, the Communist Manifesto may be wonderful — but we must not make a cult of them. And we ourselves — in our brief history — have we not worshipped idols? Is the danger completely past?

I admit, life is too precious to me — my own life and that of my son — to sell it for the price of idolatry.

Perhaps one cannot do without a: "Be killed rather than transgress." The world is rather cruel. But we must seek and find our own "Be killed rather than transgress," one that *we* have established — one that is no superstition, and especially not a belief of others.

And now I want to get to the last point: the sacrifice of Isaac as a symbol of the Jewish people's history. There is no need to exaggerate and say that there is no place for faith at all in life. Faith is in the nature of a general orientation in the world, a direction, an attitude toward the future. On the other hand, it seems to me there has never been a believer like the Jewish People, entirely oriented to the apprehension of the Absolute and to a relationship therewith. The Jewish people is "the most daring of dreamers" as in Nellie Sachs's poem — "climbing coils of moonbeams and falling into chasms of light" (going up in smoke...) and from its blood flows the "blood of God." The Jewish people put all its cards on God and in so doing sinned with an extremism that was literally Holocaust-fraught. Its absolute ideals led it to Holocaust that was never-ending. Judaism may perhaps be the pinnacle of the human race — but it has led myriads of its sons to death rather than life.

And if there is any meaning to the Zionist ideal it is this: we no longer want to be "blood of God" and blood for God. We do not want God to be fulfilled by our blood. If the history of the Jewish people proves that in this world recognition of and adherence to the Absolute means extermination, and choosing it means death, then *let there be no choice and no God.*

BEN EZER: I recall that in the poem "Grass" in your second

book, *The Mount of Quietudes* which appeared in 1969 (two years after the war) you said:

"Embraced enemies lie under the green grass,
Hand on earth shoulder, head on dust head,
Above them the poppies are red and don't distinguish
Who was right in the summer. Words rust in the ground.

Roots attach avidly to the soft bodies,
Rising in conquered, conquering stalks,
Are armies of lust, battalions of longing —
Rising to the light, to the warmth, to the last of the leaves..."

ELI: My frame of mind in *Mount of Quietudes* came into being when a few days after the war I read in the newspaper a poem by one of our "national poets," which described our dead sitting in Paradise, and the angles giving them candies... I was posted in Ramallah, and that afternoon I went up to the Mount of Quietudes, and anyone who was there after the war knows what it was like. Why these men, the best and dearest of them all, the cream of the crop (in religious terms I would say these *saints*) — had been swallowed up by the most terrible abyss of all?

Actually, after my first book, *This Is the Story of Jacob*, I wanted to write something altogether different, about the relationship between fathers and sons on the kibbutz. But the war came and diverted me from my purpose. The world interfered...

BEN EZER: How?

ELI: Since the war, a whole lot of questions have been echoing inside me, all the time, propositions for which I am seeking answers. These are feelings for which it is hard to find answers that convince me. I stand appalled in the face of death, in the face of our fallen, trying to digest, trying to understand, to find a justification — and I can't. Perhaps it is because these are the first casualties of our generation in Kibbutz Ein Shemer (till then we had been lucky...) Death at one stroke cut off a slice of life, it cut off Amnon, who was involved in everything, the very essence of life. When you think of Amnon — and you can't help thinking of him, and practically every day — you are assailed with shame at being alive. This is the way you are living, and no justification you can find for yourself will help.

Since the war I've been trying to answer the question, why young boys have to die. And sometimes you come up against a question like this — you're actually infected with it: would I not be willing to trade the entire existence of the Jewish people for those who have fallen? Or: Had the Jewish people been able to assimilate, to disappear at one of the stations along its road... or had there been any other solution that would provide life, and not death...

You might say, "But every nation fights for its homeland, its national existence. Had those same Jews assimilated in the course of the generations they would have been killed as Englishmen, or Frenchmen, or Americans. There are wars elsewhere too, not only here." But the Jewish people, throughout its entire history, has always been surrounded by destruction, by threats to its very physical existence. Is there any other nation that has had to fight for its very life like that? And it's not as if tomorrow we'll get up and move elsewhere. That isn't the problem. The problem has to do with the justification for war. How does a man persuade himself to go out and fight? How? What for? What is it that we die for? Is it possible to give your life without even knowing what for?

Had I been born in the Diaspora — all this might be clearer to me. My psychological make-up would be different. I would have answers. The fact of my living here as the last recourse, the only solution for the nation's survival—would be part of my blood. *But I was born here, without the Jewish complex, without any roots in Jewish culture (in other words — without the Jewish justification). In a reality in which everyone hates me, in which I am surrounded by hatred and can't understand why, what have I done, why am I surrounded by death and wars?*

Of course in a dry intellectual way, ideologically, I understand the tragedy of the Jewish people, the historical laws of anti-semitism, the Holocaust; I have studied the works of Borochov.

I know that the only place for Jews is the Land of Israel. I can declaim it in unison with everybody else — but deep down inside of me it doesn't sit well; it doesn't answer my questions; it doesn't convince me.

I found the same feeling in *The Seventh Day; Soldiers' Talk about the Six Day War*, where one fellow writes: "What did we talk about in years past, the years of childhood and youth? About love of the homeland, about the future of the Jewish People in its own land, the land of the Patriarchs. We talked in every way: history, Bible, geography, excursions and outings to sites of the previous ages, yet I didn't feel it. I was a man divided, I now know, and I have no answer to the question. And all my teachers and educators pass before me and they all admonish me: "What is this question? And the Bible, is it nothing for you?" I lower my eyes and admit: I know, but where are the feelings, the sense of belonging? Because to know is not difficult. But what is the thread that binds me to them—to Moses and the generation of the desert, and Joshua, and after him the wonderful nation with its wars without and within, its days of greatness and exile, the nation of the vision of the Prophets? I am too small to be a part of this nation..."

And against this background we can understand what a girl there says in another interview. She speaks about the people who have already fought in a number of wars and will probably have to be in several more: "How can you bring up people like that? It's really an enormous contradiction. Sometimes I wonder if it wouldn't really be better to give this country up or to give up one war in the world, to renounce a place for war..."

I too am wondering about the same things, and want to find the answer for myself. I am looking for this answer. Because everything that is protection of life, of people, of one's home — that is something I can feel. But I am not infected with this business here — of protecting the Jewish people and the meaning of its unique existence. Because if it were possible to assimilate and find a solution for life, it would be excellent. But apparently it is not possible. But I can feel this only in an intellectual way, ideologically, with a lot less force than I feel the loss of young lives around me.

BEN EZER: But you know that assimilation is not a realistic solution, at least not for a whole nation.

ELI: My mind knows it is not a solution but my heart is divided. I cannot accept such a sacrifice of lives, at any rate not without doubts. We are a generation of doubters and skeptics. We have nothing left but contradictions and shattered beliefs. What is there left to believe in? Once we believed, and once we were taken in — now we no longer consent. They won't be able to deceive us. I want to know and understand where I am going, what I am fighting for. *I do not agree to be an eternal Isaac ascending the altar without asking why, without understanding.* Because the entire lesson of human history is doubt, misgiving, lack of certainty. Too many people have thought they were right and have gone out to die and to kill others. Rightness is a terrible weapon, and must be used carefully...

Are the Egyptians, the El Fatah, always lied to so they will go out to war, and are we always told the truth? Is the enemy always wrong and have we a monopoly on what is right? We have heard how nations have been led out to war. Dosen't this at least require us to check? Not to be so confident? So right? History sometimes turns around and refutes the most sacred truths of all; justifications that seemed unquestionable. Its sense of humor is a very bitter one. And there is only one thing, one evil that can never be rectified: we cannot restore the lives of people who died young in the wars...

BEN EZER: And the Arabs?

ELI: As far as the Arabs are concerned I want to say only one thing: to have to live with the feeling that perhaps our entire historic resurrection, the most beautiful life we establish here, and the most just, will be based on injustice to another nation; that on this we will teach ideals and justice, that it will be the basis of our existence, the soil on which we dwell... to know that we, and perhaps our sons too, will be going out to fight, and perhaps to die — for something that is based on an act of injustice — this doubt, just this doubt alone, is a difficult basis for living. And I ask myself: you have your doubts, but why utter them?

Why weaken the hands of others? For this too I have no answer. But perhaps there are others among us as well, and perhaps they too are secretly troubled by this, and perhaps together we may be able to find the answer...

BEN EZER: But you will accept no ideal, no demand in the name of an idea, in the name of any ideology — as an answer.

ELI: Today, when we believe in nothing, neither the future of humanity, nor man's ability to make a better world, when we know that even a Communist world will not solve the problem of the wars — what have we left as a conclusion, if not human existence? What attains supreme value if not a man's life, his little bit of life on earth, his ties with his family, his parents, his friends...

So if it's to defend these things — life, home, families — that I can understand. But to defend ideals that are one thing today and another tomorrow? To defend a *meaning*? A uniqueness that is more a curse than a blessing? What have we got from three thousand years of seeking the meaning of the Jewish people? A number of geniuses and ... wars and more wars. Slaughter and more slaughter...

If I could identify with the Jewish people, believe in God, in a mission — perhaps this question would not be standing before me. But with the way I think today, the only question that interests me is whether Zionism — in the situation in which it is embroiled today — is saving life or losing it.

BEN EZER: And have you an answer to your question?

ELI: I am looking for one. I want to get to know just what our "self" is, who we are, not only in the negative sense, not only because we are hated, but for ourselves, in a time of trial. What do we carry within ourselves as human beings, as sons of a people?

It may be that Judaism provides an answer to this that is satisfactory and positive — but we are cut off from Judaism and from its answers. Our education trusted that its values would be transmitted on their own – but they haven't. On the contrary: years of education to disparage the Exile have succeeded in severing us from it and from its culture, in which we might perhaps have found an answer to our existential questions — and so it is that we stand as a weakened, fractured link at the end of a chain of Jewish generations, a chain we are unable to continue or hand on to our children.

"Zionism is correct — but for us, who have not drunk directly of the Jewish tradition, it is merely an ideology, and like every ideology it is too meager to provide a release for our emotions or to give meaning and content to our lives. Moreover, it is the Zionist enterprise that has created the reality that gives rise to all our questions." This was said by Dr. Eliezer Schweid.

I face the coming trials with no faith, with no great hopes and with no answers. We are living in a nightmare from which we do not yet see any way out. In this harsh world, we must make our own truths. We must search diligently, rather than hide under lofty words. We must not speculate in hopes and ideas that have no reference inside of us.

Just as we know how to go out and wage war, so must we learn to confront the crucial questions of where we have come to in the name of values and in the name of religion, what really remains after the events of the twentieth century and what have we *not* learned about man.

It may be that freedom is an essential part of man's life, and honor is better than death — but what was the meaning of freedom and honor for those tender children who are martyred? Where are honor and faith in death? Is life in the shadow of never-ending war really freedom? And does our freedom include the Western Wall and the Cave of the Patriarchs as a sine qua non?

We have no way of escaping the question: What are we fighting for?

And I have a number of other questions that many people in Israel think should not be asked, but they haunt me: What drove us into this situation? How have we come to this? Have we not gotten ourselves involved in something unnecessary? Won't our fate be ultimately like of the Crusaders? Will we all be forced to be masters and conquerors, and in the final account a nation of warriors, as in the heartwarming vision of Uri Zvi Greenberg and Yonatan Ratosh? If anybody has it so clear, let him tell me the answer.

BEN EZER: You mention Uri Zvi Greenberg, who is without doubt one of our most prominent poets today. Did you know that he was the only person I turned to who refused to be interviewed? "I cannot fulfill your request," he said in his letter, "Because it is not my custom to participate in symposia, oral or written, neither in one-man interviews nor en masse. I only wish we had fewer pens writing and fewer tongues wagging in mouths at least now at this time, so our enemies won't know everything that is going on in the minds of our "cool-headed intellectuals" in the rear of our sons on the firing line. Because if, God forbid, this militaristic line is breached by only a *few score meters* they, the intellectuals, will suddenly feel what I have been feeling all this time — how shaky is the ground on which we stand, and then all the perverse belletristics and philosophizing will stop. Jews, Israel — now as ever, destined to greatness and catastrophe."

I am very much afraid that to him these questions and doubts of yours are just such unnecessary philosophizing and perverse belletristics. Does this surprise you?

ELI: No.

BEN EZER: Why not?

ELI: Just as animals have tools with which to live — the lion, jaws, the bird, wings — man's chief tool to advance himself and save himself from extinction is his mind. True, our mind is rather weak — but it is all we have. I have no objection to emotions as one of the tools by which man is guided. What I do object to is an *improper balance* when emotions dominate man or nation. One of the wisest of men was no doubt Galileo — or more correctly Brecht — the Communist, humanist and fighter — who wrote a play about him. What does Galileo choose when his foolish disciples expect him to die rather than renounce his theories? He renounces the theories openly and publicly, forgoes being a sterile hero, and utters that wonderful sentence, full of humanity and thought: "Wretched is a country that needs heroes," which is analogous to our own: "The dead praise not the Lord." Secretly, he continues with his research.

BEN EZER: This is in effect the "Czechoslovakian solution" you mentioned at the beginning.

ELI: I'd like to bring you another example from a letter that was written in 1948 by a Palmach man who fell in the War of Independence:

"...What infuriates me in all this is to hear all kinds of people say that 'we become accustomed to so many casualties and I don't get excited about it.' The way I feel, I don't think I'll ever get used to it. Every time it makes me sad and depressed all over again. You'll be surprised to hear this from me, but I feel that if there was some other solution for living that didn't demand so much blood and sacrifice, I would be willing to renounce Zionism. The only trouble is I don't see any such solution that in the final account will cost less, and so *for lack of any choice* I remain a loyal Zionist..."

What conclusion is to be drawn from all this — is it nihilism? Is it despair? No. On the contrary — my conclusion is that man is responsible for his destiny and his actions, and for a constant and careful examination of where he is heading. My conclusion is not a denial of the general human aim, of the flow of life and its meaning, a meaning that does not begin with our birth, nor end with our death. Rather, I am arguing against an improper balance between these two elements of human life. I am arguing against an unnecessary contradiction which does not flow from life itself, a contradiction the absolutist philosophies have brought into it. Sometimes you get the impression man was created for the flag and not the flag for man.

We cannot renounce ideals per se. Ideals are the attempts of various periods to come up with solutions to the problem of man, whereas the difficulty lies in the fact that when you try to realize them they all lead to a contradiction of what is human, and man becomes merely a means and a tool for this realization.

And this perhaps is the tragedy of human life: that the most beautiful and just ideal has no value unless it is accompanied by deeds, and all deeds lead in the end to iniquity and ugliness.

BEN EZER: You seem to be longing for a different and better world. What is that world? A dream of yours? A childhood memory? An attempt at repentance, at a return to Judaism?

ELI: My attempt at repentance is perhaps that inside me I feel a sort of childhood Garden of Eden. And perhaps we kibbutz members really are children of the Garden of Eden, those who encounter no evil from the outside, and live in a world that is good and pampers them, until war comes upon them all of a sudden, and the crisis is also sudden, like the expulsion from the Garden.

I really think that the world in which we lived before the war was the right one. And war, with all its absurdity, negates all the good order of that world. That is why I cannot find consolation for the death of people in war, nor understand it. I did take part in, and experience, the Sinai Campaign of 1956, but then I was apparently too young for it to leave a spiritual impression on me. I had not yet arrived at my conclusions, and it all passed over me like a game.

I think that every man and every poet undergoes the experience of death. It is man's confrontation with his anticipated end, and of all the animals it is what he alone knows. The answer every man gives himself about knowledge determines to a large extent his attitude toward life. Since the war I have not been able to free myself of this experience. It is not as if I were shot at while serving in the Reserves... sometimes the imaginary fear is even more difficult. I think that when a man confronts this experience, his entire world changes. Isaac who has come down from the altar will never again be the same innocent, tranquil, springlike, smiling Isaac who believes without asking. He may smile, his wound may congeal, sprout grass and flowers, but never again will it be the same smile. Inside the terrible death will remain imprisoned like a very heavy stone. Perhaps this moment of descent from the altar is the beginning of a long process whereby Isaac the boy turns into Abraham the man. He begins to ask and to seek answers, and an answer is almost a belief, and a belief is already a new sacrifice. In this way he comes into genuine contact with Abraham's system of values. Every war amounts to a sacrifice of young people who go out to die for beliefs that have yet to become theirs, words which they have yet to learn in the school of their life and assimilate within themselves, words which are still the words of a parrot. What do "Zionism" and "Judaism" mean for young people who are cut off from the Jewish people? Why should one die for the existence of a nation and culture one is not bound to, and whose historical singularity one does not understand? Words and beliefs take on meaning only after considerable life experience. This encounter with death may be the beginning of Isaac's passage down the road to becoming Abraham.

BEN EZER: From what you are saying I gather that war makes the present-day Isaac, the young Israeli, enter the state of Abraham, that is, the state of historical responsibility, national and Jewish. It is as if you are trying to say that this transition from being a son to being a father is a law of destiny. But isn't this the same as claiming a divine justification for war?

ELI: Am I seeking recourse to a divine justification? Divine justification is only possible if you believe in something metaphysical, in another world, a new world. In the past, there were people here who were willing to die for Socialism. But today you know not why or wherefore... and what is Zionism? Is it in the power of this word to answer our questions? To justify the decree of fate? Till now it has been practically a term without a reference. A person has to experience many things personally: exile, anti-Semitism, a Jewish upbringing, *Aliya*, in order for it not to be merely one more "sacrifice of Isaac" which he does not understand. For the concept to have living meaning for him — and not through life experience but by way of intellect and spirit — requires one to have a considerable degree of maturity, both spiritual and human.

We say that culture is an organization of human beings. The solitary man wants to protect himself, and does so by creating a framework: family, society, nation. The supreme objective, the creation of a universal human framework, still seems like a castle in the air. And meanwhile, within the frameworks of nationalism, we encounter a paradox: the individual is insignificant and must sacrifice himself for the group, whereas the basic objective of culture is the individual man. When things reach this point nationalism becomes something I cannot accept nor even understand.

It is true that you cannot identify with the entire world. A man requires a framework to which he belongs. But if nationalism becomes something I must die for, how can I accept it? There is an example in the Bible that I cannot forget: during the great siege of Jerusalem, Jeremiah said, "Give yourselves up to the Babylonians." You might say he was a demoralist, but to him pessimism was a love of life. He wanted to save lives, save the country from destruction and a hopeless war. And I myself, when I write about death and paint a very black picture, within it all one value stands out: life. And perhaps this is the artistic conception wherein against a background of darkness and night a star shines forth.

Life is not a game of ideals. A man who is in the right is the most terrible man I know. What is terrible about faith is that it shuts a man off from other truths. It is terrible the way people shut themselves up in their own vicious rightness. They do not recognize the rightness of the other fellow, and are willing to tear him to pieces. In the final account, what is this just and absolute rightness of ours, a little piece of truth in whose name we judge and tear the other pieces of truth apart. This is the world in which we live, a world of teeth, your only choice is to sharpen yours. The way I see it, every ideal is incomplete and hence contains something of a

lie. The true approach to the world is not that of rational explanation. It is precisely the poet, of whom it is said "he knows not where
he is living," who has a relationship of direct contact with the soil
and substance of the universe. My sensation of the world comes to
me by way of feeling rather than by philosophic method. And
actually, there is no contradiction. Both art and philosophy are
partial conceptions and even "raw" emotions have philosophic
underpinnings.

BEN EZER: Still practically speaking, what is your answer? Have
you chosen a new way of life, one that is motivated by that feeling?

ELI: I have now gone to study Judaism, at Jerusalem, out of a
desire to arrive at a certain crystallization, not that of a rational
position but a deepening of my understanding and feelings. What
is interesting is that Biblical and Jewish themes can appear in a
fellow like me, who placed no stock in Jewish culture. From what
depths do these themes arise? In what strata do they lie hidden? I
have mixed feelings toward them. I am part of this history: I have
no escape from it. One needs a certain foundation of knowledge in
the sense of coordinates for orientation in a cultural field, especially
the culture of one's own nation. The Jewish nation is the People of
the Book. Every Jewish child from the age of three onward is
raised in a way that is symbolized by the Sacrifice of Isaac. At the
dawn of Jewish history somebody chose and set up a certain symbol
which crystallized and passed through every edition and produced
a nation of unusual genius. In the days of Bar Kochba, for example,
a rebellion broke out because the Romans wanted to convert the
Temple into a shrine to Jupiter, and outlawed circumcision. In the
uprising, six hundred thousand Jewish warriors were killed, to say
nothing of plagues and starvation and the total devastation of the
country. Another nation would have been as pliant as a bullrush —
and lived. But the Jew will not betray the tenets of his faith. What is
this faith? It is with tremendous hunger that I am going to learn
about it, to investigate the nature of this faith, for which generations
of Jews have been prepared to die. It may be a faith of genuis and
great truth, or else a terrible and tragic joke, and if so, the most
tragic and stupid joke in human history, one which has devoured
millions of people.

With me, the urge to write is like the urge to pray. Just as the believing Jew finds the time to pray, so the poet wants to find the time to write each day. This dialogue with yourself, with your God, with the specific truth inside of you, is a tremendous effort. For me, writing is a supreme effort, it is a constant birth-giving, a continuous act of discovery. When you write you are in the embrace of a thousand consoling lies, of easy solutions, of a temptation to repeat other people's words, routine formulas. Within all this you search. Then, if you succeed, and there comes a moment of truth — you suddenly discover something. It is a moment of bliss, and it occurs but rarely, amid a lot of failures.

People have different truths. For one, to be a good father is a truth, for another, it is to be a good farmer. Not that one way of life is better than another. Everyone must find his own way. If he doesn't, it is as if he is worshipping strange gods. I think that the God of the artist is a life of relentless searching. There is no such thing as easy writing. The feeling of happiness in life comes when a person utilizes his capacity to the full, and to utilize one's capacity to the full is an effort, a sacrifice, in every field — be it love or farming or scientific research. For Abraham to find his faith he in effect had to sacrifice Isaac. The Jewish people has paid a high price to arrive at the full realization of its faith. I am seeking a direct relationship to the world, to truth, to God. I do not know if I mean this in the religious sense precisely, and I cannot say what God is for me. It is a thing that I cannot define or explain, and a never-ending search is one of its meanings. I feel within me a capacity to live this thing, just as I feel a capacity to live the characters in the Bible, even to converse with them as if I were there. I am not religious in the sense of religion as an escape, an opiate of the masses. My God may also prove to be an opposition to everything that is abstract and above life, and thinking about Him may also lead to a love of earthly experience and of small mortal creatures.

Separation and Equality – Instead of Confused Values

Interview with Boaz Evron

(This part of the interview took place in September 1966.)

BEN EZER: Would it be correct to say that in Israel the Jewish intellectual has lost his outsider status?

EVRON: It is not the Jew who is an outsider, but the intellectual. The Jews' status varies in different countries and periods. In the U. S., with which I am familiar having lived there, the intellectual is an outsider, while the Jew is simultaneously insider and outsider. The Jew diverges a little from Christian culture, and the Jewish intellectual diverges a little more, but only *a little* more, than does the non-Jewish intellectual. The intellectual is, by his nature, somewhat outside of society, because he attempts to evaluate it and to come to formulations as to its intellectual essence. It is difficult to make evaluations from the inside. "Intellectual" and "outsider" are synonymous. Therefore when you ask about the Jewish intellectual in other countries in contrast with the situation in Israel, your possible meaning is that there are no intellectuals in this country. There are only technicians-of-the-intellect, i.e., teachers, pedagogues, propagandists, the entire administrative staff of the society, the engineers of the soul, whose like we saw in preponderance at the recent Hebrew Writers' Congress. All of them are part of the Establishment, which is why they are not intellectuals in the sense we have just denoted — outsiders.

BEN EZER: What is the origin of this phenomenon?

EVRON: Actually, there is nothing essentially new in this atmosphere, which is merely a corruption of the trend that has prevailed in the Hebrew Community since the dawn of the pioneering movement. It was not only the "man of action" of that time who despised intellectuals, but the intellectuals themselves, as well. The proto-

type of the energetic man of action, exhibiting his manhood and
his physicality to the point of exaggeration, with his tousled cowlick
and ferocious moustache, his Russian blouse, his mare and his
rifle, was coupled with the prototype of the bespectacled intellectual,
the butt of ridicule and disparagement, always in doubt as to
whether he was fulfilling any constructive function whatsoever —
certainly no essential function — besides education. And he was
always internally torn, on the one hand seeing himelf as the shadow
and adjunct of the practical man, and on the other hand seething
with natural rebellion against the inferior role assigned to him. To a
certain degree, the reason for this situation resided in the fact that
there was a general consensus on the purpose of the pioneering
activity and on the methods of the activity itself, and it was clear that
that activity was primarily physical and organizational. However,
even under those circumstances, the intellectuals might have fulfilled the function of mentors, passing criticism on what was being
accomplished, in the light of the declared values. They did not do so.
This may be because they lacked faith in the very ability of the mind
and the intellect to serve as a guide to social activity — either under
the influence of the intuitive Romantic approach, which denies the
human intellect and conscious will the capability to influence the
course of historic events or because of the Marxist approach, which
also, in its own way, denies the primacy of the intellect.

Manifestations of the spiritual subjugation of the Zionist intellectual to the men of action, and the rebellion against, it may
already be found in Brenner. You find there the sense of impotence
in the presence of the men who do and act, apparent also in the
literature of the kibbutz movement. It may be assumed that this
reversal was in the nature of a rebellion against the Jewish tradition,
which emphasizes supremacy of the intellect, this tradition now
being viewed as a manifestation of sloth and impotence. We
have observed the repercussions in the Ben-Gurion period. It was
not an anomaly but rather a direct outcome of what was taking
place, that the intellectuals were jumping to attention before the
politicians. Policy-making had become utterly opportunistic, for
it was not being subjected to any true intellectual criticism. As
a result the leadership became utterly arbitrary, without any ideological frame of reference. This trend is continuing, having been exem-

plified in the meeting between Prime Minister Levi Eshkol and Conrad Adenauer, when the latter visited this country. This meeting was an exhibition of the most vulgar practicality, of money grabbing, of an approach that reverts to what we pejoratively term "Diasporism," an eager running after every penny with no reference to the question of how it is acquired. That is how the strictest "pragmatism" is leading us back to the ghetto. It is a significant fact that public objections to that affair arose among academic faculty members, but not from any author's group.

BEN EZER: The special circumstances of Israel, the siege consciousness and the sense of national responsibility which not infrequently paralyze criticism — aren't these the factors which keep the intellectual in this country from adopting an uncompromisingly critical stance?

EVRON: The intellectual's renunciation of his prerogative, of his right to adopt an independent stand in the name of a set of values that is not subordinate to political dictates, is not the result of the conditions of an immigration and settlement country. It is not true that the reason lies in the newness of the country, and the needs of land. Not in every pioneering country have the men of action necessarily dominated. New England of the seventeenth and eighteenth centures for example, was actually a theocracy. The Protestant Pastors enjoyed there untrammeled rule, which greatly affected the character of the people, in both good ways and bad.

The Jewish pioneers in this country made technical and economic activity into an ideal, viewing it *inter alia* as a remedy for Jewish over-intellectualism, thus obliging the intellectual to view himself *as part of the disease that the pioneering movement had set out to cure.* He had a vision of the future society he wished to set up in this country. It contained laborers, farmers, scientists and technicians, but not intellectuals, not himself. Insofar as he did envisage himself, it was as a servant — a servant of the technical, material activity. By virtue of this approach, of course, the Israeli intellectual lost his self-respect from the outset, for it is clear that in those activities which he agreed to consider as genuinely important the men of action outshone him. This sense of self-abnegation before men of action, of paralyzing inner uncertainty, and the suspicion that in their own way men of action comprehend the problems, far better and in a far more immediate manner than intellectuals, who approach things by rational indirection and who suffer from hypersensitivity, are apparent in dozens of books that have been written in this country. This is especially the case with reference to the writing of authors belonging to the Histadrut and Labour Movement. Most of the Israeli intelligentsia renounced in advance its natural social function: the creation of a critical, seminal viewpoint at the opposite pole from practice, the formation of an independent intellectual ethos not bound by businesslike practicality, and the cultivation of a moral pride which is not prepared to surrender to physical pressures. It should be mentioned that this inversion has been quite common in many socialist circles in all countries: the intellectuals have been disparaged while the "healthy instinct" of the worker and of the tiller of the soil has been vaunted. This similarity is a further mark of the Socialist affiliation of broad segments of the Zionist movement.

BEN EZER: It is difficult to dispel the impression that you too are covertly justifying the circumstances that led to the creation of the special situation in which the Israeli intellectual finds himself.

EVRON: The circumstances? Why, they are like the "difficult childhood" rationalization. One can not adduce circumstances as an excuse. They are not an explanation of action but an excuse for failure. The task of an adult person is to overcome circumstances: otherwise those circumstances would cause him to remain for the rest of his life at his parents' board, or at his mother's breast. Insofar as the intellectual in this country is not prepared to relinquish a set of values that is governed by praxis rather than examening it, it is doubtful whether he is worthy of the name. For by this token he gives evidence of not having confidence in the primacy of the intellect. Therefore he is not an intellectual, but rather a servant of the man of action. And the siege situation? It is an excuse too. For the intellectual's criticism of political action might also have guided that action into more positive channels than it has fallen into. It may be that such criticism might have forestalled the state of siege from the outset. The history of the Jewish Settlement in this country is to a large extent the history of lack of criticism. So what does your claim that the circumstances are the cause mean? A lack of wisdom created the circumstances, and afterwards those circumstances have been utilized to gag the wise.

BEN EZER: We are faced with a difficult dilemma. If we still consider ourselves to be part of the Jewish people, then we tend to judge our achievements in terms of how they compare and how they are linked with the culture of the Jewish people in the broadest, most universal sense. On the other hand, there is in evidence a cultural and social phenomenon of constriction of basing our existence on "a fresh start," with comparison only to ourselves. The latter tendency is perhaps a screen against the complex that is likely to result from comparing ourselves with the historic status of Judaism and the intellectual role of the Jew outside Israel today. And this raises the question as to which is preferable: our aspiration to be "a light unto the Gentiles," as Ben-Gurion is fond of saying, or the pessimism of a lack of any intellectual pretensions and the drawing of a tight circle around our precincts? Perhaps there is a certain hypocrisy in defining ourselves as "a light unto the Gentiles," but, on the other hand, retaining this slogan as a value and a purpose implies a challenge to ourselves.

EVRON: A small, closed cultural society in a small country is not in the least capable of being "a light unto the Gentiles," nor even a light unto itself. And that is actually how things have always been. Athens? Florence? Viewing them in isolation is an error of historical vision. Florence was of course a state, but it constituted an integral part of a very broad and open culture, which extended far beyond its narrow political confines. The same is true of Athens. Here in this country, too, there was an open space, not a ghetto. To a large extent, this was a Hebrew speaking region, from here to Mesopotamia. Cultural influences flowed into it from all sides. The atmoshpere in which the ancient Hebrew culture came into being was "cosmopolitan." A small, closed society is likely to lead to a collectivist, tribal situation, a situation in which there is no differentiation, everyone sings the same tune, and there is no encounter of differing opinions and no spur to thinking such as arises from such an encounter. It is a rule that the centers of culture always gravitate to the centers of power, finance and commerce, where there are clashes and encounters of various mutually fertilizing streams. Culture is an urban, not a village product. Only a large society, with universal clashes and contacts, can produce a state of social diversification, proliferation of intellectual and value-judgement criteria, a place in which the outsider can evolve. In a small, tribal society, devoted to uniform mores, the conditions for the evolution of the outsider are negated. And if there is no outsider, there is no intellectual, and in his absence there is no intellectual development.

The aspiration of purists to keep Israel's culture intact and unpolluted is the most certain guarantee of absolute cultural stagnation. Levantinism is produced inside a ghetto, but not when it is opened and a living organism, in contact with the world, is it created. Our authors and scholars who attempt to understand everything about us in terms of Jewish history — as for example that the Canaanites comprise a new Sabbatai Zevi messianism — are utterly artificial in their approach. They are attempting to grasp culture as a closed tradition, a hermetic organism. The younger Hebrew poetry contains influences by T. S. Eliot, Auden, Apollinaire and Mayakovsky that are least as powerful as the influence of earlier Hebrew poets. Nor can Bialik and Tchernichovsky be comprehended exculsively in terms of the Jewish poetic culture, but must also be considered against the background of European Romantic poetry. To comprehend our literature solely from the inside is a vain effort. Such generalizations have not even been attempted as regards our music and plastic arts, for there the international idiom is clear for all to see. Israeli composers sometimes use traditional melodies, but the arrangement is modern, in the spirit of Hindemith and Schoenberg. Only with literature, which is linked with a specific language, can games be played on behalf of a chauvinistic principle.

The great periods of Jewish culture have always been periods of receptivity: the periods of the Second Temple, Spain, Humanism, the West. Our most chauvinistic movements, the most powerful advocates of hermeticism are also clearly echoes of the European nationalistic theories. Of course, there is also a cultural continuity, and external influences come into contact with this continuity. But our existence in this country constitutes a most severe shock to this continuity, perhaps to the point of challenging it, and putting its organic basis in question.

BEN EZER: Jewish intellectuals in the Diaspora claim that if Judaism has a message and a purpose in our time, they are its bearers and not we Israelis.

EVRON: I do not wish to enter into that argument, since I have never claimed that we are the bearers of any message. I might comment, as an observer from the sidelines, that Saul Bellow's *Herzog* is in my opinion a uniquely American product. The fact that it is also popular in non-Jewish circles in the United States indicates that it is a Jewish aspect of the American milieu and not an American aspect of the Jewish cultural milieu.

And actually, who are we? *You are taking as an axiom that our milieu is Jewish, and I believe it is not.*

Of course, nothing begins from nothing. The U.S. is a good example. People came to America bearing with them a certain culture. The American culture is a European, English culture that was transplanted to America. Today it is easy to see that the United States is not England. But the States has been so bound up with English culture that until the end of the last century the only literature taught there was English literature. That is to say, from the ancient racial stem has grown a new, different branch, the result of new conditions. The affinities are not sealed off. Even in England itself there has existed an autochthonous literature only since the thirteenth and fourteenth centuries. Prior to that, it is difficult to distinguish between the literature of England and that of the Continent. A national literature did not yet exist. In most cases, then, the end product differs from the source, turning it into an independent organism.

BEN EZER: What is the analogy that derives from what you have said?

EVRON: Something similar is happening in this country. The English nation of today is a conglomeration of Gauls, Britons, Saxons, Scandinavian Vikings, Normans and French. Till the fourteenth century, the English considered themselves to be French princes. Things crystallize slowly. The Jews who migrated and came to Palestine and founded here a new society, changed their status. Throughout the world, the Jews are an ethno-religious minority defined by a tradition that is distinct from the tradition of the majority. The moment their status as a minority is revoked, they

are in the situation of a ruling majority whose tradition is dominant, and their entire status is altered. This change of status, of
necessity brings about a quintessential change. Zionism has provided an admirable definition: converting the potential people into
an actual people. So why is anyone surprised that that section which
has come here and changed feels alien towards those who have
remained outside? Why, that is what Zionism has wanted — a severance, the creation of a new national entity. Had such an estrangement not been produced, it would have been an indication that
the experiment did not succeed, and that all the work had been
pointless. What is the purpose of creating another Jewish community, if not to create something new?

BEN EZER: Your position seems to imply a severe criticism of
the identification of the State of Israel with the concept of a
Jewish State.

EVRON: At the root of Israeli-Jewish relations lies the problem
that is poisoning both parties, i.e. the national problem. According
to Zionist theory, the Jews are a people and not a religion. The
religion is only one of the attributes of Jewish nationality, though
exilic conditions have highlighted religion as a primary attribute,
by way of being the main thing defining Judaism. The absence of
further national attributes, according to this theory, has made
Jewish exilic existence incomplete. The exilic Jew, according to this
definition, is a damaged human being, if we examine him solely in
terms of his Judaism. Only in Israel can he became a complete and
genuine Jew, by developing his national existence, as a religious or
non-religious individual. The question of how this national quintessence has been conveyed from generation to generation over
hundreds of years without any national framework to support it
has been solved by the explanation that in reality the religion was a
national framework *in statu nascendi*. The national festivals were
still celebrated therein, the cycle of seasons in Palestine was retain-
ed, and the Passover supper was concluded with the words "next
year in Jerusalem." That is why even the atheistic and secular
Zionist factions have been alarmed about the decline of the Jewish
religion in the Diaspora, recognizing that the religion is the most
convenient framework for uniting the Jewish people until it is
reassembled in its homeland. In Israel, so they claimed, a person

may discard his religion since it is merely an external form of nationality.

There is no need to dwell on the intellectual embarrassment that has arisen from this exegesis of the religion, which has never been accepted by orthodox Judaism. This exegesis has made possible the worst, most vulgar type of sacrilege. The Messiah, who is supposed to appear and redeem his people at the Millennium, when the dead will rise from the grave and the Almighty will sit in judgment on the world, has been identified by some with the personalities of leaders of the State. The introduction of contemporary meanings into the framework of absolute, sacred values has desecrated the sacrosanct and has blunted the distinction between the holy and the profane. Religion is tied up with the Absolute. *If you substitute nationalism for religion*, raison d'etat *becomes the sole absolute value*.

BEN EZER: What, then, should Zionism have done?

EVRON: The Zionist conception has been fundamentally at fault in one respect. It has considered Jewish existence in the Diaspora to be a flawed existence, and stressed that a Jew can be a genuine Jew only in Palestine. That is to say that anyone who is here is a more complete Jew than anyone who stays there.

The strangeness Israelis feel toward Diaspora Jews sometimes leads them to interpret it as a sense of superiority. If the Zionist view is correct, and it is only in Israel that a Jew can be a complete person and true to his Judaism, then the Israeli is a more complete Jew, a more complete person, than is the Diaspora Jew. Israelis tend to believe this, since it flatters them and it provides an explanation for their sense of alienation from the Diaspora Jews. If this premise is accepted, then any Israeli loafer or pimp is quintessentially superior, as a Jew and as a human being (the distinction between the two concepts tends to become blurred,) to Maimonides, Einstein, Kafka, Rabbi Nahman from Wroclaw, or the Gaon from Vilna.

Had we understood from the outset that one way of life is as legitimate as the other, that the social framework in which a person exists has not the slightest bearing on his value as a human being, perhaps a different attitude might have evolved. After all, the justification for immigration to Israel is also absurd. Is individual physical safety greater in the homeland? Why, we are speaking morning, noon and night about the danger of being annihilated by the Arabs. The Disapora has survived far longer than has any framework of Jewish political sovereignty, which has been of brief duration in our long history.

BEN EZER: One of the claims of Zionism is that it is making the existence of the Jewish people secure.

EVRON: There is no such thing as security in history. Numerous countries have been destroyed and their population killed or exiled by invaders. Territorial national sovereignty is no guarantee against ruin. Purely from the standpoint of safeguarding Jewish survival it might be safer not to have a Jewish territorial concentration, since such a concentration might be destroyed in the course of historical upheavals, while dispersion forestalls simultaneous destruction in all centers. If we accept the view that from a qualitative Jewish standpoint, or from the standpoint of securing survival, Jewish existence in Palestine is not preferable to Jewish existence any place else, then Judaism is safer in the Diaspora.

BEN EZER: Does that mean that you envisage a chance for healthier relations only through an absolute breach in the Jewish nation between what is termed "the new Hebrew people" or "the new people of Israel" and the Jewish people in the Diaspora?

EVRON: "The Jewish nation" is the most problematic and vague term current in our society. Actually, Jews possess none of the distinguishing marks of a nation. They do not have a common territory, a common language, common secular institutions, a common culture. The things they do have in common are a religious tradition, now in the process of dissolution; intrenchment in the middle strata of the countries in which they reside; and a more or less marked, discriminatory attitude towards them on the part of the non-Jewish population in those countries. But these common marks are not necessarily linked with nationality. I will only be belaboring the obvious if I mention that the Jewish Settlement in this country during recent generations did not come into being solely for Zionist reasons, but as part of a mass migration of Jews out of Eastern and Central Europe, caused by the anti-Semitic

pressures and outbursts there. This is not the first instance of persecuted peoples migrating from developed countries to backward or barren territories. So long as there were countries open to
Jewish migration, only a small percentage of the emigrants came
to Palestine. There is no doubt that had there been in this country
a developed and dense Arab society, the country would not have
been able to absorb a large Jewish influx, and the identification of
the country of migration with the Holy Land of the religious tradition would have disappeared.

If we accept these conclusions, it seems that we will be able to
explain logically the reason for the Israeli public's loss of Jewish
affinity, and even to understand that this is a process of an ineluct-
able historic character, and not the fortuitous outcome of faulty or
tendentious education. If the Jews are not a nation, but an ethno-
religious community, then the Hebrew public in this country,
which possesses many of the properties of a nation (common language, territory and national institutions) has already outgrown that
framework. Judaism can occupy part of the Israeli's existence in so
far as he is a religious Jew or cherishes sentiments towards various
Jewish traditions. But in most of the areas of his life, he functions
not as a Jew but as an Israeli, and Israel has a concrete existence
and concrete interests that are not in the least in the nature of functions of Judaism. In view of the fact that the Jew in Israel does not
suffer from the pressure he is subjected to in other countries because
of his denominational difference, and in many cases here in Israel
he is even uprooted from the middle classes, he loses two of the
characteristic traits of the members of the Jewish community in
the Diaspora. And if he is not even concerned with the Jewish
tradition, then from a functional and existential standpoint he has
ceased to be a Jew. It is clear that here and there he will still retain
loose, weakening traces of the intellectual profile formed by Judaism, but these will be doomed to obliteration. And so we see that
the moment we define Judaism properly, the Hebrew's sense of
strangeness towards Judaism becomes comprehensible as having
been dictated by the circumstances. It may very well be that this
hypothesis is incomplete, that it does not explain all the pertinent
phenomena, but in any case it explains them better than does any
other hypothesis of which I know.

BEN EZER: How would your hypothesis explain the survival of religious Judaism in Israel, all indications being that it is not declining or weakening?

EVRON: There is no contradition. Its status is the same as the status of Jewish survival abroad. A Jewish Israeli is conceivable, just as is a Christian Israeli. One must only oppose the imposition of Jewish religious norms on the state. But if these norms be imposed and our political behaviour dictated by them, they may well undermine the State. The religious principle and the political principle are fundamentally contradictory. The Jewish religion is anti-political in its very essence.

BEN EZER: Aren't you of the opinion that it is just such a Canaanite approach as yours, which accords primacy to the country and its inhabitants over all the rest of the Jewish nation, that is capable of leading to the cynical utilization of the dispersion of the Jewish people to benefit the interests of the State?

EVRON: No. This cynical utilization arises from the Zionist approach, and not from the Hebrew (also termed Canaanite) approach. It is Zionism that has produced this attitude. It has provided Israel with a rationalization for relating to the Jews in the Diaspora as though they were her instruments, as though they were "human dust" devoid of any independent status, with whom it is permissible to do anything that appears necessary for Israel's political interest. The Israeli ideologists attempt to explain away such things as Israel-German relations, the lack of neutrality between the world blocs, the severance of relations with the Verwoerd government contrary to the interests of the Jewish minority in South Africa — with the argument that since Israel is the sole homeland of all the Jews the interests of Israel are ultimately the true interests of the generality of the Jewish people, even if they seem to stand in opposition to the short-range interests of the Jews. But since, according to all realistic forecasts, most of the Jews will go on living in the Diaspora, this claim greatly resembles the old Stalinist claim — that the U.S.S.R. is the homeland of the working class throughout the world, and that anything which advances the interests of the U.S.S.R., in the long run serves the cause of the world proletariat to the same extent, even though it might sometimes appear to the superficial observer that this progress harms and damages part of the proletariat.

We must recognize that the interests of the State of Israel do indeed sometimes conflict with the interests of certain Jewish communities. Only if an *identity* is assumed can there be produced a moral mandate for the exploitation of the Jewish people by the State of Israel.

BEN EZER: The complaints you have advanced against Zionism are usually voiced against what is termed the Canaanite position. What is the difference between the two outlooks?

EVRON: The Zionist approach implies two interlinked claims: The State of Israel is not an end in itself but an instrument and a means to something else, and were it not for this justification the establishment of the State would be an absurdity. The essential difference between the Zionist approach and the approach that might perhaps best be called the *Hebrew approach* is that Zionism considers Judaism as axiomatic, and the State as a function thereof, a function that requires justification. Hence the growth of the Zionist theories about "the return to Zion by right and not by sufferance," and so forth, and the need to *justify* the establishment of the State as an instrument for the ingathering of exiles.

The adherent of the Hebrew outlook considers his Hebrew nationality, his state, as axiomatic, and does not feel any need to *justify* its and his own existence. This link between the speakers of Hebrew and their land and State is a primary category of his social consciousness, to which all other affinities are secondary. He was born or grew up here. He makes his living, loves, fights and dies here. He is *here* and nowhere else, and he *has* no other place. The Israeli, as an Israeli, has no other place, because there is no other place where he can be an Israeli.

We may find a fine parallel to this, again in the chronicles of the United States. The Puritans who migrated to New England did so in order to set up a society according to their own lights, and that was certainly their only justification to themselves for this action. But for an American of subsequent generations, it does not matter in the least *why* his forefathers came to the New World. His being an American is an *axiom* of his existence, and the ideals of the Founding Fathers are to him mere rhetoric.

For someone who has grown up in this country, it does not matter at all, ultimately, whether someone once thought that his country should "play a role in the life of the Jewish people" or not. The association between Zionism and the Israeli sense of homeland is a quintessential one, but there undoubtedly exists an interim phase, during which the attitudes of loyalty are confused, and a person attempts to solve the confusion in an artificial manner by means of definitions such as "Israel and the Jewish people are one," which is sheer nonsense. Or he senses one loyalty which determines his conduct, while he renders lip-service to the other, often without even understanding that there is any contradiction.

BEN EZER: It would seem that the two, the new Hebrew spirit and the Jewish spirit, are hostile to one another.

EVRON: Our line of reasoning leads us to the recognition that the new Hebrew spirit, or Israeli and the Jewish spirit do not have to be hostile to one another. A member of the Hebrew people may be a religious Jew, as he may be a member of another faith. The Hebrew entity only comes into conflict with Judaism when the latter demands national authority for itself and attempts to impose what has turned out to be a false national approach on the authentic Israeli nationalism. Since two national entities can not wear the same crown, an attitude of alienation and hostility towards Judaism has been produced in the Israeli. It is an attitude that is merely an expression of a person's instinctive rebellion against an attempt to falsify his spirit. The very moment this attempt to falsify the spirit ceases, alienation and hostility will disappear too. They may be replaced by indifference. It is also possible that a symapthetic interest will be evoked, and even *lead to religious and cultural, but not national, identification with the Jews of the world.*

The moment the areas are delimited clearly, religion is likely to profit a great deal thereby. The attempt to which religious Judaism has lent its support, to its material benefit, to combine a religion possessing trans-historical and trans-geographic traits with narrow national aims has led to the furor of intellectual perplexity and glib rhetoric so prevalent in our lives. Thus, with the tacit agreement of religious circles, a theory has been produced according to which "it is the religion that has safeguarded the survival of the people." That is to say, the religion too as a *means* for the safeguarding of that ineffable and undefinable essence which in Zionist terminology has usurped the place of God. Thus, organized religion in Israel has itself led to its own moral bankruptcy. It may be that those deeply sincere religious persons who are pained at the way religious Judaism is backsliding into political dealing, dues-collecting and "schnorring" will conclude that the way to purify and change religious values is precisely by helping to distinguish clearly between the domains of God and of Caesar.

A person who considers himself a national Hebrew or a national Israeli, and is not a "bridge-head" of Judaism, is *the only one who can regard the Jews of the Diaspora as equals*, whose way of life possesses its own justification. Only in this way can Diaspora Jews be not "raw material" of "human dust" for the utilization of the Zionist-Israeli leadership, but a way of life in its own right, possessing intrinsic content and value, no less than does the State of Israel.

BEN EZER: There are those who view the situation from a diametrically opposed point of view: It is only by reinforcing the Jewish essence that there exists a chance to safeguard the moral norms of the State, while a tendency like yours, which considers the isolated new Hebrew nationalism as an exlusive, determining value, will ultimately justify the State in all it shortcomings, and lead to chauvinism, precisely because the intellectual base has become immeasurably narrow. On what do you base your nationalism — on territory and language?

EVRON: Until this day the Jewish entity has not reinforced the moral norms of the State. On the contrary, it has caused obscurantism and corruption of norms. "Isolated" nationalism in itself, on the other hand, is neither moral nor immoral. It will be moral if it is required to conduct itself morally. A political framework in itself is morally neutral. It depends on what those who are directing it seek to achieve. But my opinion is that nations are not capable of behaving as isolated units whose sole justification is in themselves. International law and morality are a necessity, and that has no connection with Judaism. It is a world-wide requirement. That is why states should be considered in terms of their behavior and their internal regimes. I am personally of the opinion that I need not accord supreme primacy to the State. If any state sins against the elementary values of justice, freedom and morality, one must fight its regime. It is the duty of every freedom-loving person, if he lives in a State that represses freedom, to fight the regime, and if the circumstances do not permit doing so from within, it may be that he is entitled to act from the outside.

BEN EZER: How is that to be done?

EVRON: The view of the intelligentsia that would limit its role to guiding action and supervising implementation, is merely a more demanding formulation of the view of the intelligentsia's role as purely service, subordinate to the ends of social and economic policy. The intelligentsia has a far more important role: that of determining the social goals and developing a system of humanistic values. Only then will there be created criteria for practical action, according to which it will be possible to mantain a critique of activity. But even then, the men of action are powerful, and in the struggle for the achievement of social goals, they are likely to complicate things with the claim that the ends justify the means: a devastating trap that does away with ends by justifying means. A set of human values is required, then, for supervising the means.

The ability to determine social goals and to develop a set of humanistic values ultimately derives from the fact that the true intellectual is not merely an educated person, but a man of the spirit, a quality that frequently has no connection with education, and derives from deeper sources in the mind than the rational faculty The test of this quality is the ability to do something for its own sake, beyond any considerations of loss or gain, success or failure, because there is a categorical imperative to act so. In certain areas this quality manifests itself as the faculty of the creative artist, who created things for their own sake, according to their own system of rules, to which he submits joyously. In other fields it is manifested as obedience to the inner moral imperative, with a willingness to come out *against* society, not for any social utility, even the most remote, but for the sake of absolute values — even if it is clear that they are damaging to the social interest, whether short-range or long-range.

BEN EZER: Jewish intellectuals in the West are claiming, and such claims are also being voiced among us, that without a close identification with the Diasporas of the Jewish people we are condemned to the perils of parochialism, Levantinism, and a dearth of fertility and creative replenishment in all areas.

EVRON: Our contact with the Jewish people does not strengthen Judaism, nor does it weaken it. It has no relevance to the spiritual significance of Judaism, Our contact with Western Jewry, for example, is not just with Jewry but with the entirety of the Western world. It is not in Judaism that we see a source of fertile intellectual contact — but in Western culture (and it is a pity that our contacts are only with the West). This means that our contacts with the Jews or the West are only a part of our affinities with the Western world, and they have no specific Jewish intellectual significance.

But it seems to me that you are mistaken from the outset in asserting that the Jewish intellectuals of the West are demanding of us identification with the Jewish Diasporas. From reading reports of dialogues with them, I have received a very different impression. On the other hand, this demand is being voiced by our leadership here. And this demand is quite odd in view of the fact that the fundamental attitude of part of our leadership towards the Jewish people is one of scorn and disparagement. I have been told that one of the architects of Israeli policy till recent years expressed this attitude in a statement that if we were to make peace with the Arabs tomorrow, every single Israeli would be running way to do business in Beirut and Damascus, and the entire people of Israel would disintegrate as though the State had never existed. Here again we find the "human dust" approach. *One of the guiding factors in certain streams of the Zionist movement is a disparaging attitude towards the Jewish people.*

BEN EZER: What you are saying seems to imply that it is the Zionist approach that is preventing our integration in the Middle East Region. But it seems that no expression or act of good will on our part would make us more acceptable to Arab nationalism, unless we agreed to self-extermination.

EVRON: It is precisely against Arab nationatlism that we have to wage our war, for it is the quintessential enemy of all groups existing in the region. In so far as this region is to be Arabic — it has no future. Arab nationalism would have to fight against Kurds and Israelis, to preserve inter-Arab equilibrium, and to take the Turks and the Persians into account. Even Egypt's Arabism may well be a passing phase. This is not an Arab region. And the only form in which it can arrive at any consolidation within a more comprehensive framework is by the waiver of any Israeli or Arabic primacy, and the setting up of a federative structure in which all peoples will allow one another to live. This region is by its very nature multi-national, a mosaic of peoples, and so it has always been. Our integration into the region will not necessarily be a cultural integration. Everyone knows that it is necessary to adjust to Western conceptions, for only in their terms is it possible to agglomerate power. It may be that a feudal society is entitled to equal consideration and respect with a bourgeois society from the standpoint of its intellectual achievement and values, but it is certainly impossible to create modern power systems without higher education, without the multi-faceted functions that modern technology produces. Without centralized and delicate administrative management of the social mechanisms, a modern society is not possible, and our regional culture will of necessity accept these patterns. We are more subject to determination by them than we are to the Jewish, Christian or Islamic tradition.

BEN EZER: The desire to establish new patterns in this region is likely to evolve into the view that we must agglomerate power and force in order to compel our neighbors to accept us. Then the process you are proposing would not be in the least different from that which Zionism has been practising and is practising for almost as long as it has existed.

EVRON: If we consider our existence in terms of power, we shall perceive that our fundamental problem is the very narrow organizational principle of the State of Israel. There is no doubt that reliance on three or even five million people as an organizational basis has little future in contemporary terms of power and territory.

What is the solution? The most crude and simplistic solution is conquest, whether within the framework of the bounds of the Anglo-French Mandate, as once held by the Revisionists and by the Herut Party of today, or within a broader framework, contemplated by the fanatics of the type that dream of "the Kingdom of David." But such a "conquest" would only be a miniature repetition of old-style imperialism, which has proven a failure, for the increment of territory containing an oppressed and hostile population can only bring added weakness. Nor would we be able to drive out that population, since the great pow'rs would see to prevent that. For any division and dissension within the region enables them to intervene and impose their will. The weak party in the conflict, who is in danger of his life, will always appeal to assistance from outside factors, who will always be happy to provide it in order to win positions of influence. But unity in the region, which would make it possible to eliminate foreign influences, would clearly rule out in advance any possibility of wars of "conquest" within it. Nationalistic programs of "conquest" contain within them the seeds of their own undoing, since the division and fear they produce within the region lead to reliance on powers outside the region, who will effectively see to prevent any such harmful steps. In the realm of practical diplomacy we have seen what this meant at the time of the Sinai Campaign in 1956. Ben-Gurion preferred to give up the Gaza Strip, which Egypt was actually prepared to relinquish, rather than have to assimilate the population of the Strip within the Israeli system. The narrow organizational principle of the State, which bases itself solely on the Jewish people, did not make such assimilation possible. And the "indigestion" this would have caused, on the basis of this principle could only have meant weakening the State. Hence on this basis of Judaism and Zionism we have no possibility of expansion or of increasing power.

BEN EZER: What are the other solutions?

EVRON: A far subtler solution is that of Yonatan Ratosh and part of the Canaanites. Dispensing with the religious common denominator and dispensing with the insistence on Jewish tradition achieves two ends.

First, it creates an integrative principle based solely on language, culture and a territorial framework, that is, a flexible principle possessing an immeasurably broader integrative capacity than the Jewish-Zionist principle. Second, it affords a more concrete approach, that of a national *territory* as the basis for creating a people, (rather than the concept of a people seeking a territory, as in the traditional Zionist outlook). The theory that all the inhabitants of the Fertile Crescent are originally Hebrews, upon whom an alien Islamic culture has been imposed and who should be brought back to their Hebrew origins. So it will be possible, theoretically, to create a broad human and territorial base, without which there can be no real independence and power within the world power system.

The drawback of this approach, in my opinion, is that this nationalistic principle would stand in direct conflict with the Arab nationalistic principle, which is also theroetically non-religious. And since the two principles are equivalent, they are doomed to a stalemate. A higher organizational principle is necessary, which will be able to incorporate within itself both the Hebrew nationalistic principle and the Arabic nationalistic principle and bring them into a symbiotic coexistence.

The solution offered by people like Prof. Eri Jabotinsky, i.e., forging an alliance with the other minority groups in the region and thereby creating a bloc that could defend itself and withstand the pressure of Arab nationalism, has two drawbacks. First, the entire region is the minimum reasonable unit that could serve as a power base, and splitting it into two blocs would weaken the entire region. Furthermore, the struggle itself would lead to penetration of the influence and hegemony of the major powers into the region, and to the weakening of all the factors struggling within it. Neither would be allowed to overcome its adversary, since such an outcome would mean unity, and elimination of alien influence.

It seems that the establishment of a confederative structure, not on a religious, national or language basis, with mutual respect among all the various constituent elements, is the only course of action that offers hope for the creation of a single organizational principle. However, such a structure would also involve numerous, grave problems.

BEN EZER: Is a confederative stucture the magic formula that might also have redeemed Zionism at its inception?

EVRON: That is a grave question, because the fundamental approach of Zionism has been incorrect. It was an approach that ignored the local population. Had half of the resources used for purchasing and developing land been channeled to setting up a joint agency with the Arabs, and taking care of the previous settlers, perhaps the situation might have been different. By creating such a symbiosis, the security burden might have been avoided. My approach may be optimistic, perhaps, in practice, it would have been impossible to adopt from the outset. But it is one way that has never been tried, till this very day.

BEN EZER: How has the influence of Zionism expressed itself on the character of the Jewish community in this country?

EVRON: Zionism brought with it all the deeply rooted suspicion and fear of what the "Gentiles" attitude towards the Jews might be, without freeing itself of them. On the one hand, it accepted the Jewish stereotypes created by the Gentiles (by defining Jewish existence in exile as "alienated" and "parasitic"), and itself also created stereotyped images of the Gentiles that were divorced from reality. Zionism implied an aspiration to create a new Jewish person, resembling the "simple, healthy" Gentile. The ideal confronting people like Dr. Sheib (Eldad) and the poet Uri Zvi Greenberg is in fact the Polish or Ukrainian peasant they still remember in dread. The Zionist ideologists have forgotten that it is not the "simple," "healthy" *muzhik* who is the mainstay and creator of Russian culture, nor is he the guarantee of achievements, criticism and innovation.

When I read descriptions of the years of our struggle for independence written by Englishmen who were here in this country, and compare them with the image that we have had of the British, it seems to me that they do not relate to the same kind of person. The English were not "simple minded" and ignorant. They understood very well what was happening and what was about to happen here. They were extremely sensitive and complicated in their attitude towards us, although we were their enemy. It was we who were one-sided, simple and simplistic. They saw all the complexity of the situation, and realized that it was not a study in black and white, in which we were the only sufferers, as we portrayed it to ourselves.

The Zionist approach to the non-Jew has not depicted him as a human being with weaknesses and complexes. That is why, here in Israel, Zionism is producing a false picture of the world surrounding us. The Arab people across the border are also seen in certain recurring schematic clichés. The Arabs appear as bloodthirsty, or sub-human monsters, with whom there is no possibility of communication. And so, the holders of this view have created a great ghetto with "self-defense," since, it being impossible to talk to such monsters, we can only cut ourselves off from them and remain on the alert.

BEN EZER: What has this approach led to?

EVRON: One of the outcomes of this approach is the *worship of force* which is implicit in all our conduct here in this country. It is a primitive view that by means of force alone it is possible to solve all the problems of our existence. It is an attitude characteristic of people who are lacking in political instinct and understanding. It is precisely the powerful States that do know that the use of force is an extreme last resort. Only infrequently, and after exhausting preliminary, more complex, delicate and subtle measures do they resort to it. The worship of force also arises from the self-disparagement of the Jew in exile in the face of the force exercised against him, from whence we have fallen into worshipping the man with fists, and assuming that the fist can solve anything. But force alone can not bring victory. From the standpoint of force, the State of Israel faces no concrete danger in the next few years. This is particularly so because a nuclear balance may be coming to the region, which would turn any war or any use of force into a matter of mutual annihilation, in which there would be no victor and no vanquished.

BEN EZER: Without this "Zionist blindness," perhaps we should have despaired from the outset. The fact is simple and unequivocal — we were not wanted here from the start. Had it not been for that blindness, the State might not have arisen.

EVRON: It may be that the Zionist blindness has also, to a great extent, produced the Arab reaction to it. It may be that had it not been for the blindness the reaction might not have been produced. But even if we accept your premises as to the past, I still believe that it is possible to change and to mold a different reality. We are an independent entity that must follow its own path, and not remain shackled by the past.

There is something fundamentally problematic in our very existence, something which is present for every people who settles in a country already occupied by members of another people.

As a matter of fact, practically every people dwells in a country that was once inhabited by others. Almost everywhere, there has been conquest followed by assimilation. The Americans, the Spanish, the French and the English are all examples of this historic phenomenon. We are part of a process, bearers of original sin, but we must not be subjugated by it. The conception and birth of all peoples, as of all individuals, is in "sin." Nevertheless, man must not remain subject to his original sin, but must liberate himself and establish his own law. The time has come for us to establish our own law, to which we may submit.

BEN EZER: What you are saying is likely to lead to a masochistic identification with the fate of the Crusaders in Palestine.

EVRON: No. The unshakable certitude in your right to any place, in your national-territorial survival, is a matter of time. The Franks invaded Gaul — and it is now named after them. The justification for our existence here does not reside in the fact that the Jews were once in this country, for almost every people once lived in a different country. Nor does it reside in the religious faith, since for that purpose one must believe in the Covenant with God and be a totally religious Jew. And most of us are not religious and do not accept the religious conception. Therefore, one of the essential constituents of our right to this country is our admission of the rights to it of the members of the other people, and our ability to achieve a peaceful *modus vivendi* with them.

(This portion of the interview took place in April, 1970.)

BEN EZER: Have the war of June 1967 and the events following it altered any of your opinions concerning the link between Israel and the Jewish people in the Diaspora?

EVRON: I must admit that the events have imposed upon me a certain revision of my previous views. I have come to a slightly different evaluation of the link between Israel and Judaism, of Zionism and of the Israeli national entity. It now seems to me that the things I had said in the previous interview, prior to the Six Day War, were said on the basis of covert premises whose existence I was unaware of at the time. One of these covert premises was that the situation of the Jews of the world from 1945 till the middle

of the '60s, in fact till the war of June '67, was a permanent one.
My assumption was that the anti-Semitic potential had been dis-
charged and used itself up in Nazism and the Holocaust. Of
course, I knew that the philo-Semitism that was so fashionable
after the Second World War was a transitory phenomenon, confined to the intelligentsia and politicaly conscious circles. However,
it seemed to me — and my own naivete in this respect amazes me
till this day — that the problem of Jewish survival in exile had
actually been solved. To be sure, "the Jews are different," but so
are the Catholics, too, different from the Protestants, and in the
United States, for example, where I lived for a number of years,
it was clear to me that the Jews "belonged" far more than the
Negros or the Mexicans, for instance. It may be that it is true,
despite everything, as regards the United States (though troubling
indications have appeared there, as well). But it has emerged
that this confidence had no substantial basis with regard to the
Soviet Union and the other Communist countries; and even in
France there is a re-awakening of anti-Semitism. The unique status
of the Jews in the liberal sector and in the intellectual leadership of the United States as well as their relatively high income
level, have exposed them as an object of hostility of extremist
circles both of the Right and of the Left.

Despite my fundamentally rationalistic world outlook, it
seems to me that sociology and economics will not suffice to explain the unique status of the Jews among the Christian peoples.
The appearance of traditional anti-Semitic response patterns, with
the traditional diabolic images of the Jew, in the "anti-Zionist"
propaganda of Communist countries or in the mediaeval-style
anti-Jewish hysteria that broke out in Amiens, France, prove that
there are here factors in operation which ostensibly non-historical
sociological analyses are not capable of explaining. What is most
amazing is the phenomenon of anti-Semitism without Jews, which
we have witnessed in present-day Poland. This does not mean, as
several Zionist ideologists claim, that anti-Semitism is "inexpli-
cable." But it is clear that the rational explanations advanced to
date are partial and sometimes superficial, and ignore the historic-
psychological dimension. A "more rational rationality," deeper
and more comprehensive, is needed in order to explain the phenom-

enon of anti-Semitism. It emerges, then, as the fathers of Zionism have claimed, that the "Jewish problem" is not the outcome of a particular socio-economic constellation, which can be solved by altering that constellation. It is an historically meaningful phenomenon — an identity that is preserved throughout the vicissitudes of social constellations. This identity, so it appears, even shapes these constellations to a significant extent, so that their alteration is determined *inter alia* by it. It is not fortuitous that many of the prophets of social change during the past two hundred years have been Jews, and their revolutionary role again cut them off from the non-Jewish masses with whom they desired to mingle.

Though it would seem that there is no connection between my conception of the processes creating the new Hebrew people in its homeland, and the problem of anti-Semitism, it has introspectively become clear to me that such a connection does indeed exist. The premise that the problem of the survival of the Jewish people in the Diaspora had actually been solved, had released me from a sense of responsiblity for the fate of the people, and enabled me to accept the doctrine of a Hebrew people that is not linked with Judaism and not responsible for Jewry. However, if there does indeed exist a "Jewish problem" then Zionism has been right in its definition of the situation of the Jews in the world. And then Israel is not exempt from responsibility for their fate. I sense in myself a refusal to detach myself from the strata of the past that reside within me, which have to a decisive degree shaped me. It would be an act of self-emasculation.

I will add that in my opinion Zionism has been only partially right. Its claim that assimilation has failed is only partially true. Very large portions of the Jewish people have inter-married and disappeared. The Nazi outburst followed over a hundred years of successful assimilation, which is continuing with growing impetus till this day. But for those Jews who consider Judaism a positive thing and wish to continue being Jews, or who live willy nilly in Jewish social frameworks which imprint their stamp upon their character, there always exists the threat of discrimination and of becoming involved in the "Jewish problem," and hence the need for Zionism. And besides, why must it be precisely the Jews who should disappear in the "just society of the future?" Are others required to disappear? Is there talk of the Christians disappearing? Is Judaism such a negative thing? Must a minority always inter-marry with the majority in order to be accepted on equal terms? I do not believe that Judaism is a more positive or negative thing than Christianity, Islam or Buddhism, and so I do not see any good purpose served in its ceasing to exist. I do not believe that the "just society of the future" is obliged to be founded on regimented uniformity. In my eyes, such a society would be utterly unjust, since it would do violence to the human uniqueness of its members. I find present day society preferable to that.

BEN EZER: I have noticed that you are using the term "the Jewish people," which you avoided using in our previous interview. Then, you defined Judaism as a mere denomination.

EVRON: I am afraid that in this respect, as well, I was guilty of over-simplification. To a large extent, my position was influenced by formal definitions of nationality, which were accepted in Europe following the French Revolution — based on common territory, government and language. In that connection, religion was considered irrelevant.

This approach is overly formal. It ignores the fact that the religious community and ethnic affiliation are still among the decisive components of national existence. A Christian Frenchman is just a Frenchman. But a Jewish Frenchman is a Jewish Frenchman. By no means can the tradition of the European nations be separated from the background of their growth as Christian states, with immeasurable complex associations with Catholicism and Protestantism, Reformation and Counter-Reformation, relations between Emperor and Pope, between King and Archbishop, the fabric of the culture and the social organization created by the Catholic Church, and the persistence of certain of its patterns in the Protestant states, as well. And, in the same way, the tradition of Islam can not be separated from the Arab states, or the Confucian and racial tradition of China from its existence as a modern Communist, national state. In the present Soviet insistence on ideological hegemony may be heard clear overtones of a continuation of the Orthodox Church's aspirations to becoming a Third Rome. There is a profound identification of this church with the Russian people in the writings of Tolstoi and Dostoyevsky — an identification which has recurred, surprisingly, in the current writing of Solzhenitsyn. With the Armenians, too, we may find a clear identification of Church with nation, and no one is accusing them of not being a nation. Catholicism is one of the clear cut characteristics of Irish and Polish nationalism. Patterns of thought and religious responses, which lack any formal content of religious faith, may survive for decades and centuries after the disappearance of a faith. So, for example, do the Jews persist in their diligent scholarship, the fruit of generations of Talmud and Gemara study and of despising illiteracy, even after having become totally assimilated — or converted to another faith. The patterns of Talmudic intricacies of thought and discourse continue to appear in writings that have nothing to do with Judaism. The priest who interprets the parable of the Doorkeeper of the Law in Kafka's *The Trial* is elaborating a typical structure of Talmudic sophistry.

One need only separate, then, the national *organizational principle* — which is indeed territorial and based on the application of a set of law and unified political-economic action of all the inhabitants of a certain territory — from the community principle. The latter is intertwined with extremely complex elements of religious and ethnic traditions, and sometimes racial traditions, as well (as in the countries of Black Africa and the Far East), which together have produced an operative group possessing common traits and identity. When such a group seeks to consolidate as a state in the modern sense of the word, a contradiction arises between the state structure and the parent ethnic structure. But this need not invalidate the ethnic structure. I do not believe that England is a "theocratic-racial" state, as per the definition attached to Israel by her enemies. But up until relatively a short time ago, only Christians were admitted into the House of Lords, England has its own national church, the Anglican Church, and the King is also the head of that church.

Therefore it is a mistake to deny existence of the Jewish people. But the paradox was created the moment this people established its state. At that moment the state principle, based on territory and language, began to operate. Just as religion dictated that all members of the religious denomination be included in worship and in the religious institutions, so does the state dictate inclusion within the framework of law, of rights and duties, for all the inhabitants of the territory under the jurisdiction of that law. The religious, ethnic principle is fundamentally voluntary. The state principle is the law that is binding on the territory. The attempt to join the two principles, of necessity creates grave contradictions, particularly in those countries, and they are the majority, in which there are a number of religious and ethnic groups. These contradictions exist till this day in many countries, and they are sometimes severe to the point of "cultural war." In this, we are not different in principle from other states known to history.

I believe that with us, too, the state principle will ultimately and of necessity triumph over the religious-ethnic principle, since the victory of this principle is essential for the survival of any state. That is to say, the people creates the state, but the state in turn alters the character of the people. I can say, that I have not changed my views fundamentally, but that now I perceive their partial character, and the fact that they relate to a dynamically changing situation. There does exist a Jewish people. There does exist a necessity for Zionism and for the establishment of a state for the Jewish people. The Jewish people has set up its state, and it must be open to any Jew who wishes to settle in it. But from the moment the state has been established, the logic of a state begins to operate within it, and it is entirely different from the national logic that brought it forth. It dictates, for example, conducting a foreign policy that is not in accord with the interests of the Jewish people but in accord with its own interests: as, for example, the severance of diplomatic relations with South Africa in order to maintain good relations with Black Africa, despite the interests of the Jews of South Africa and their close ties with the state (and other instances that I cited in our previous interview).

I am not asserting that the state principle is more "progressive" than the religious. It may even be the reverse. We have seen what can come of the cult of the state in the style of Nazi Germany, for example. But the state principle is essential for the existence of the state. Therefore I believe that the Jewish people's act of auto-emancipation of necessity gives issue to a state bearing a character which its prophets could not have anticipated. For even if the basis of the state's historic consciousness be Jewish, as the basis of the American historic consciousness is English and Christian, the *modus vivendi* will be that of a secular, not a Jewish state. Actually, it is such at present. It may well be that Hebrew-speaking Moslems and Christians, and there are many such in Israel today, will always feel themselves as outsiders, to some extent, even after receiving completely equal rights and duties, just as the Jews feel themselves to be outsiders in the Western nations, which are basically Christian. But ultimately these Hebrew speaking non-Jews will become Israelis in all respects. The law will prevent all discrimination, for or against them (as it already does today), even though the social segregation persists (as it does to a certain extent even among the Jews themselves). They will serve in the army, in the Government, etc. Already today, while Israel and the Arab states are at war, there are Moslem Arabs in Israel who are Deputy Ministers. Druse, Christian and Moslem Beduin soldiers are fighting in the ranks of the Israel Defence Forces. And this is only the beginning of the process. Even in the field of personal-status law, which is becoming progressively more absurd every year, we will ultimately arrive at secular legislation. These things will not occur in a revolutionary manner, but I am confidently certain that they will occur. Everything indicates such a trend.

BEN EZER: Before the war of June '67, your attitude towards the position of Israel vis-à-vis the Arabs was extremely critical.

EVRON: At that time I considered the process of conflict between the Arabs and ourselves to be to a large extent the outcome of a lack of criticism of our courses of action, on the part of the intellectual and critical circles in the state. I thought that this process was to a large extent subject to volitional decision and choice on our part, and that there was at the time another alternative, oriented to peace, which we had missed. Today I am not as certain of this as I once was.

One of the phenomena that became utterly clear to me at the time of the war and afterwards is the sincere aspiration of the majority of the Israeli public to live in peace with the Arabs. The great hardening of stance which came a year or two after the war, and the extreme chauvinistic approach that came with it, were produced to a large extent by the Israelis' desperation, and the sense of there being no one to talk to on the Arab side. For a long time, despite the chauvinistic pressure of extremist circles, there was in Israeli political circles great opposition to the currency of this line. Even today, concessions to the chauvinistic attitude are merely marginal. I have a clear impression that had there been chances for a true settlement, a settlement that would have alleviated the fears for Israel's security, then even today there would be considerable willingness to make concessions on the part of most circles in Israel.

BEN EZER: How does the Six Day War appear to you today?

EVRON: The war proved the complete lack of correlation between Israeli society and Arab societies. The Israeli victory was not the result of technological superiority. The Arabs had superiority in machines, But Israel's superiority is the result of a clash between a dynamic society of a developed western model and semi-feudal societies with entirely different conceptions of life, and a pace of development that is immeasurably slower than the Israeli. There is a lack of essential structural balance in the contact between the two civilizations: Israeli and Arabic. And the very contact between them of necessity constitutes a death potion for the weaker of the two. Any time the Arab countries come into contact with Israel, in peace or in war, a social revolution takes place within them and they are ruined. Israel, on the other hand, changes much less, and is shaping them.

It may be that their enmity and hatred towards Israel is analogous to the desperate opposition of traditional, patriarchal societies against coming into contact with modern civilization. An expression of this phenomenon is to be found in the extremely ramified literature written in the last century, during the transition from an agrarian economy to an industrial economy in Europe and the United States. With us, the social conflict has become identical with the national conflict, making the pangs of transition far more severe.

BEN EZER: How do you see future relations between Israel and the Arabs under her rule?

EVRON: It is an extremely strange thing that to date there has not developed any effective underground resistance to Israeli rule. The opposition to us is chiefly coming from across the border, despite the existence of ideal conditions for the creation of an underground: open bridges, ties across the border, the support of foreign powers. All the underground cells that have been operating till now have achieved meagre results and have been caught. The explanation lies perhaps in the fact that there has taken place a drastic change in the social structure of the Arabs now under our rule. The farmers and laborers in the West Bank (I am not speaking of Gaza, which is a different case) benefit from our rule. Their circumstances have been improved.

A friend of mine, a Jewish intellectual from Iraq, has told me that he has the impression that the same thing is happening to the Palestinian population that happened to the Jewish immigrants from Iraq. The intelligentsia, the ruling classes, to which he himself belongs, on coming to Israel encountered an established governmental power system that did not take them in and was not opened to them. But the laborers, the clerks and the tradesmen gained by having immigrated to Israel. That is, while the intellectual leadership was eliminated, there took place a social revolution that brought about a shift in the lower classes, and afforded a greater opportunity for equality and social progress.

BEN EZER: What have been the effects of the war on Israeli society? Hasn't the process of loss of capacity for self-criticism been heightened? And what about the ability of the intellectual to be an outsider?

EVRON: There is in the Israeli press a great deal of debate and criticism, a great deal more than there was in the Ben-Gurion period. If we take into account the fact that we are subjected to the pressures of a struggle for survival, it seems to me that it is quite positive that we have still mantained such a considerable degree of criticism. Of course, it may be that I myself have been drawn into the conformism of a society at war.

A state at war is far more difficult to criticise. For many years we have been poking fun at Zionism. On the eve of the war, we began to hear the broadcasts of the Arab stations, their assurances that they would annihilate us and our families and the "advice" broadcast by Damascus Radio to the Syrian soliders, that they should slaughter the Jewish children in front of their mothers' eyes. Suddenly, my country, Israel, and the Zionist propaganda slogans ("another cow and another acre") began to assume a different significance. I said to myself: another acre, another cow and another village — this is my homeland, which those murderers want to lay waste.

And so, not all of my criticism of Israel is earmarked for export. I can laugh at "another acre and another cow," but it's a family joke. Because this country, this state, are the basis of my past and of my present reality.

Extreme criticism is always in fashion in countries that do not face any danger. It is part of the permissible abandon that a people may allow itself if it is absolutely assured of its survival. But here in Israel you suddenly realize that even your sharpest criticism of what is going on here is based on assent at the deepest levels.

Israeli criticism must realize that it is linked with the Israeli reality in a dialectical manner. Despite the dissent there is also identification at the deepest stratum. Suddenly you see that your criticism is of secondary and not of quintessential things. For example, now that the Russians are decrying Zionism as the root of all evil, asserting that the Zionists are to blame for the mass murders in Babi Yar — now that the Kremlin gang is saying things like that I am not capable of declaring myself to be an anti-Zionist. If I were to be an anti-Zionist now, I would be their partner, the partner of the Russians. *Therefore, now for the purposes of the war, I am a Zionist.* I am obliged to admit that I am an offspring of Zionism.

BEN EZER: What will be the political and state framework of the two peoples, the Hebrew and the Arab?

EVRON: The federative solution is essential today, too. My view has not changed. So long as a federative solution is not forthcoming there will be no escaping the intervention of foreign powers in this region. The solution is a merger that will permit each of its constituents maximum autonomy and self-determination,

BEN EZER: How is this to be achieved?

EVRON: Here we come back to the question of the lack of structural balance between the two societies. There may come into being a situation in which the federative framework will be, at least at the initial stage, that of Israeli hegemony. But that would be better than Israel's technological superiority destroying the greater part of the region. Actually, in all federative states it is the most industrialized and developed region that is dominant to start with, till development spreads to the other regions. But we must only prevent the evolution of an Israeli neo-colonialism, and promote the awareness that energetic development of all the sectors of the federation will benefit all the other sectors, as well. Of course, conditions of political equality must be maintained, which will serve as a brake to Israeli expansionist tendencies.

BEN EZER: Does what you are saying imply an answer to the criticism being voiced against Israel, particularly since the Six Day War?

EVRON: I do not think that Israel, in order to justify her existence, must be a "light unto the Gentiles." No state needs to or is required to justify its existence. Why must we? We are a state that was founded in order to solve part of the problems of the Jewish people. No one casts doubt on the right of existence of a state like Saudi-Arabia, which is racial, religious and tribal, and where slavery is still in existence. Even the Germans — no one cast doubt on their right to exist as a state, even during the Second World War. Who, then, has the right to demand that we justify our existence with good deeds? Our existence is the justification for our existence. Even an utterly negative State of Israel is justified from the standpoint of its existence. The question of what the image of that state will be, is already a different question. Does anyone from the New Left dare cast doubt on the justice of the existence of Moslem Pakistan, which is racial, religious and grossly unenlightened?

I sometimes hear the complaints of Jewish youth from abroad. They demand of us that we prove that we are a society that is consummating social justice. As a leftist and a socialist, I have a great deal of sympathy with their wishes. At the same time, I consider a great deal of their charges to be infantile. In the matter of orientation to social justice and progressive experiments in the social sphere, Israel is without any doubt one of the most progressive countries in the world. And it is immeasurably ahead of any Arab country that sees fit to call itself "socialist" or "revolutionary." But the consummation of social justice is not at all in the nature of a justification of our existence. Our existence, as I have said, is justified because we exist — period.

Jewish Identity and Israeli Silence

Interview with Prof. Yeshayahu Leibowitz

(This part of the interview appeared in *Moznayim*, February 1966)

BEN EZER: How would you define Zionist ideology?

LEIBOWITZ: Zionism is not an ideology but a complex of activities that were carried out in order to restore independence to the Jewish nation in its own land. There exist only *anti-Zionist ideologies* to the effect that the Jewish nation is not a nation. But anyone who thinks that Zionism is a solution to the problem of the Jewish nation is mistaken; it is nothing more than the complex of those activities that resulted in the Jewish nation reattaining national sovereignty in its own land. The major problems of the Jewish nation are not those of Zionism.

BEN EZER: Does that mean that from the Jewish standpoint you are disappointed with Zionism?

LEIBOWITZ: I am not disappointed with Zionism, because I never imagined that it would provide a solution to the Jewish people's problems. Moreover, man's essential problems are not political ones. Any solution of social and political problems solves nothing but the problems with which it deals, rather than man's problems from the standpoint of his essential being.

BEN EZER: Would it be correct to conclude from this that your main concern is the Jewish people and the essence of the Jew?

LEIBOWITZ: You ask if I am concerned with the Jewish people? I am concerned *only* with the Jewish people. The State of Israel interests me only insofar as it serves as the State of the Jewish people, for otherwise it is not only superfluous but even harmful. Look, the State itself is a burden on and aggravation of international problems; we are an element of unrest, one that causes conflicts in the world. Hence if the State of Israel is merely the State of Israel it is something harmful, whereas if it is the State of the Jewish people I don't care if it causes unrest. For someone who

177

is not Jewish the Jewish people's very existence is in the nature
of a disturbing element. Had Hitler been successful, to their way
of thinking he would have freed humanity of a lot of problems.
The Diaspora and exile were themselves brought about by the Jewish
people's uniqueness, and if it does not have a uniqueness it will cease
to exist. The same goes for the Jewish people in the State of Israel.

As far as disappointments go, let us take the kibbutz as an example. Who has been disappointed with it? He for whom the kibbutz
has not provided what he expected — namely the salvation
of man. If anyone expected it would, he is a fool and there
is no sense in arguing with him. Values can be attained only
directly. If someone aspires to the moral rectification of man, he
must engage in it directly and not imagine that improvement will
be brought about by creating a given social regime. The kibbutz
has fulfilled its objective — it implemented the form of settlement
which made possible the conquest of the country under conditions
of an Arab majority and foreign rule. It makes no difference
whether or not this was the conscious and original intention of the
kibbutz's creators. Obviously it was not their conscious intention;
neither A. D. Gordon nor Shlomo Lavi had this aim in mind.
Retrospectively, this stands out with surprising clarity, but I admit
that at the time even to me it was not as obvious as it is today:
that the only way of gaining control of the country was by quasi-
military settlement, like the colonies that the Romans founded
when the little Roman Republic took over all of Italy. From here
there arises the question of whether the kibbutz still has a raison
d'etre today or has it turned into a parasitic growth in the body of
the State and nation. And the moral is that one must not attribute
to any social or political movement qualities that do not arise from
its activity as such. The question is not what the people with the
highest level of all in the movement were thinking, but what the
activity was in actual fact; in our case it was the creation of a
regime that enabled a man to be a farmer and solider at the same
time. There was considerable naivete, bordering on folly, in the
belief that altering social relationships would alter the nature of
man. This notion is unconscionably absurd. Likewise we can say
that the essential problem of the Jewish people is that of Judaism,
while Zionism is not a solution of the Jewish problem but rather

what we defined it as at the beginning — the restoration of the Jewish people's national sovereignty.

BEN EZER: What is your view of the relationship between the State of Israel and the Jewish people?

LEIBOWITZ: The Jewish people as a whole, as it is, will not concentrate in the State of Israel. It can do so only as a result of the factor of Judaism. Of course the factor of Judaism has not become dependent on the existence of the State, but only genuine Jewish content is what can bring the Jews to return to the Land of Israel. Zionism is merely part of a broader complex — Judaism.

The Jewish people's situation today is such that with the great majority the Jewish essence has been lost; nor must one disregard the fact that the Jewish people today is in effect a nation consisting entirely of remnants, because though the majority exists, the chief part has been destroyed. The central question is to what extent the State of Israel is a means for bringing about the renewal of Jewish essence among Jews — and thus to bring them to concentrate in their own land, which amounts to pulling oneself up by one's own bootstraps.

And in order to bring about this revival the State has done nothing; it has contributed nothing to Judaism. I am far from any naive idea that the State will provide the answer to the problem of Judaism; yet on the other hand it is obvious to me that the State should be the *arena* in which the struggle for Judaism takes place. It seems to me that this is the only possibility at present for bringing about a Jewish reawakening among the Jews in the diaspora. And unfortunately, the true struggle for Judaism is not taking place in the State of Israel. The State of Israel is a governmental and administrative apparatus that is devoid of all content.

BEN EZER: Isn't this true of every State?

LEIBOWITZ: It may be the content of every State — and as far as other States are concerned it may even be possible, because an ordinary State identifies with the nation that resides in it, something which is not true of the State of Israel if it is viewed as the State of the Jewish People. To consider the State as an entity in its own right, and its problems of survival and its system of administrative and political relationships as values in their own right, is of the essence of Canaanism. And it makes no difference if people do not use this term explicitly. It is obvious that all the forces and public bodies that rule the State will reject any association with Canaanism with all their might; the majority even do so with total subjective sincerity, but this does not alter the fact that what in effect is before their eyes is not the Jewish people as represented by three thousand years of history but the territorial administrative framework we have erected in the past generation. I myself have no interest in this framework as such, and I consider any presentation of it as a value a clearcut expression of a chauvinism that is part naive, part brutal, or to use a stronger term — an expression of fascist mentality.

BEN EZER: Isn't there a danger that even the objective interests, which are of the Jewish essence of the State, will also lead to extreme manifestations of the kind you mentioned?

LEIBOWITZ: The question is, what do I want as a Jew, not what are the Jewish people's "objective interests." There are no *objective* interests, because an interest is nothing other than what an interested party wants. We waged a war, we shed blood, we drove tens of thousands of refugees out of the country. None of these things is cause for rejoicing. But it was the *war of the Jewish people*. I know, this is no justification — no non-Jew will see any justification in it. But for the Jew it is a justification.

BEN EZER: The existence of this justification, even with a Jewish essence to it, still does not alter the feeling of siege in which we live and the heavy price we are paying, psychologically and morally, for our political situation.

LEIBOWITZ: A feeling of siege? On the contrary, it seems to me there is a general feeling of well-being, of self-satisfaction. And even those who see the danger are being bribed by the comfort in the present situation to the point where the fact that they see it does not induce them to change anything, even if they do understand that basically the situation is a catastrophic one. The situation really is catastrophic, but all the same at this hour it is possible to derive a great deal of enjoyment from it, and so even those who understand how catastrophic it really is lack the motivation to do anything in the way of change.

Take an example from the recent election campaign. Finance Minister Pinhas Sapir proclaimed that in 1969 our balance of

payments gap would reach 800 million dollars. What is the meaning of the gap? To my mind it is an index of the parasitic nature of
the nation in the State of Israel and of its life as a kept woman of
vested interests of the world, such as German bandits, American
politicians and Jews who wish to remain in the Diaspora and
assimilate among the Gentiles. Who took any interest in the fact
that the gap, which now stands at between four and five hundred
million dollars, would double within the next four years? Moreover, recognition of this terrible fact — which means the total
corruption of the nation — does not prevent Mr. Sapir from continuing to be one of the pillars of the regime and administration
responsible for this situation.

And for example from a different area, five years ago Yigal
Allon stated publicly that the launching of the Israeli rocket
Shavit 2 amounted to a sabotage of the State interest for the sake of
a certain party's election propaganda, but this did not prevent him
subsequently from joining a Cabinet consisting of people for whom
the chief concern had not been the Homeland's security; and it is
likewise characteristic that the latter did not refrain from bringing
into their cabinet a man who had accused them of such and even
worse things. And a final example will be the Suez campaign of
1956 — perhaps in the hour that preceded that unfortunate episode
there was a hint of a prospect of negotiations between ourselves and
the Arabs, and we have destroyed this for a long time to come
because of the lust for power that informed every action of our
leadership.

BEN EZER: Let us get back to the basic question — will the
"Jewish content" and Jewish essence of the State insure us against
these dangers?

LEIBOWITZ: Jewish content insures Jewish content and nothing
else. Just as by solving a constitutional problem we will not solve
any spiritual or moral problem, solving a spiritual or moral problem will not solve a strategic problem nor will that solution of the
latter solve any economic problem. Only charlatans think there is
an answer to a given question that will solve all other questions.
This is the great psychological error of Marxism, for example. I
repeat, the notion that the solution of a social problems embodies

the solution to all human conflicts is a serious psychological error.

BEN EZER: A "psychological error" of this sort — that the construction of a just, modern society in the Land of Israel will bring us near to the Arabs, was one of the tenets of the Zionist outlook and an integral part of its mythology.

LEIBOWITZ: Not everyone believed it. Weizmann and Brandeis certainly did not; perhaps A. D. Gordon did believe in it — but it only goes to show that he did not have a high intellectual level. One might say, in general, that the attainment of any values always brings about new and stronger conflicts.

BEN EZER: In other words, Zionism has not solved the problem of insuring the Jewish people's survival?

LEIBOWITZ: There is no assurance of survival in the world. Perhaps there is assurance for the Chinese people, because it is almost impossible to destroy them. But do the Poles have any assurance? A generation ago no one imagined it was possible to destroy a nation. But in a Third World War — who knows? Perhaps in another generation, in the southern part of Africa — South Africa and the new Rhodesia — they will make a "final solution" of the white problem, the physical destruction of men, women and children, the way that Hitler understood it. And on the other hand, perhaps the white Afrikaaners will strike first, while they still have an overwhelming preponderance of strength, and destroy the African population, just as the Spaniards destroyed the Indian population in the Antilles. In human life today there is no assurance, therefore the entire problem is a theoretical one. Zionism's demand for a guarantee of security arises from the nineteenth century outlook which considered security one of the normal characteristics of human life. But in our day we can see — if only from science fiction — that the majority of the human race feels its life is hanging by a thread. Hence trends and aspirations today are not measured by the criterion of whether they add security or not. Perhaps life for a Jew in the State of Israel is more dangerous than in Brooklyn or New York, but I want to be a Jew in Israel and not in Brooklyn, among the American nation, therefore the entire problem of security does not exist for me and is no criterion for me.

BEN EZER: What do you think the attitude of Zionism was toward the Arab question from the outset?

LEIBOWITZ: Here one can say that Zionism harbored an almost mythological illusion. Both Herzl and even Jabotinsky, and there is no need to add, the creators of Socialist Zionism had the impression that the national interests of the Jewish people and the Arab people could coalesce. And if this seems absurd to us today, it is not because we are wiser than the first generation of Zionists but that they, for obvious psychological reasons, did not want to see the truth and did not realize they were deluding themselves and their fellows. The Jewish-Arab conflict was not brought about by incorrect tactics or even an incorrect policy, but is an expression of the essence of the Jewish people's historic tragedy. The fact is that the country which is *our* homeland and *our* country became the homeland of another nation; and neither side can nor will it be able — nor from its standpoint does it even have the right — to rei ounce its claim. It is not the problem of the refugees, that stands between us and them but the fact that the State of Israel's very existence prejudices the historic estate of the Arab nation. There are nations that live in permanent conflict with their neighbors, and it may be that we too will have to live generation upon generation in a permanent conflict. On the other hand, perhaps common interests will develop which will shift the essential historical contradiction to one side. Perhaps in the mid-fifties — from 1954 to 1956 — there was such a moment, and we deliberately let it slip by. Not everything is up to us, and solving the moral problem will not solve the political one, but obviously if there is something like the Kafr Kassem incident, it aggravates matters which are difficult in any case.

And here I must make two distinctions: essentially speaking it may be that even an ideal regime will not solve the conflict or bring about peace. But I have no doubt that everything being done by the present regime runs counter to the aim of attaining peace. It is obvious that the entire policy being followed by the State of Israel, both internally and externally, in keeping with the political interests of its leaders, has resulted only in an exacerbation and worsening of the situation.

It is an illusion to think that making concessions to the Arab minority will endear us to them. There is no reason why they should not be a fifth column in the State. Yet all the same it is obvious that the Military Government is merely a continuing course of aggravation and provocation. It is designed not to serve the security of the State but to insure its rulers the election of four or five Arab Quislings to each and every Knesset to help them remain in power, perhaps even against the wishes of the majority of the Jews. There were cases in which the government was saved by these very votes. Can you imagine anything more disgraceful — the Jewish government of the State of Israel being enabled to carry out its policy by virtue of bought Arab votes and against the majority of the Jewish people as represented in the Israeli Knesset.

To take an example from the concepts of biology: if a person has in his body a defect that cannot be corrected he has to live with it — provided there is no medical possibility of its correction. It makes life difficult, but there is no alternative. The fact that we have an Arab minority in Israel that by nature has been and will be an enemy of the State — this fact is part and parcel of our State. It is like one shortage of water: there is no alternative — we cannot choose another country where water is abundant. And the same goes for the twelve percentage of our citizens to whom we cannot attribute unconditional loyalty to the State.

The danger will increase if after a generation the twelve percent becomes twenty percent, and in two generations a third of the population, if not more. And this development will result not from the nature of the Jewish-Arab relationship, but from the way of life that the Jew in our land has adopted for himself, one that is turning us into one of the biologically decadent islands of humanity. I refer to our low birthrate. Today throughout the world there is a high rate of natural increase but there are also islands of humanity which biologically speaking are decadent, i. e. having a low birth rate; and within three generations the Arab minority may become the majority in Israel.

BEN EZER: What in your view is the ideal image of Israel as a State whose chief content is the question of Jewish identity?

LEIBOWITZ: I do not say the State should give one answer or another, but that its entire justification (not from the moral or political standpoint) would arise from the fact that it became a framework in which the struggle for Jewish identity takes place, and this would arouse something in the hearts of those Jews in the world who have an interest in the fact that they are Jewish. And my protest against this short-coming is aimed at every group in our midst, both what is known as the "Right" and what is known as the "Left," what is known as "Religious" and what is known as "Secular." Instead of a struggle over religion there is an agreement on all sides that there shall be no real struggle over religion — by maintaining a secular State that is publicly known to be religious, and a clericalistic-atheistic coalition — just as there is no struggle over any other matter of substance either. If someone took the trouble to read all the party platforms prior to the last elections, he would have seen that were it not for the heading he would have no way of knowing which party is which, and we see a similar phenomenon after the elections: all forms of coalition are possible. There is no basic reason for any party not to enter a coalition with any other party, so as long as an agreement is reached regarding the distribution of power.

BEN EZER: If so, what struggle is desirable?

LEIBOWITZ: There is a profound contradiction between the concept of Judaism that is based on its historic essence and the Canaanite conception. Let us take for example the case of the abduction of the lad Yossele Schuhmacher. The law and the courts of the State, in accordance with the concepts of justice prevailing in our society, accept the elementary right of the individual to educate his children as he pleases. On the other hand, from that standpoint of everything that is embodied in Judaism, parents have no right whatsoever to educate their children, but must train them to the Torah and the observance of religious duties. And in the historical tradition that embodies the Jewish people's uniqueness the Jewish community of Mainz, Germany is considered holy because of the parents there who slaughtered their children in order to prevent their forced apostasy. According to all the concepts prevailing in the present society of the State of Israel, this was an act that was criminal and insane. Nor can these two viewpoints be bridged. If the debate were about this, and if there were a religious Jewry standing in opposition to the entire regime (and not to a certain chance coalition) — it would give the State content, in the

form of a struggle between the values of the world of Torah and
religious duties and the values of the Declaration of the Rights of
Man and of the Citizen.

Not all of the Jewish nation in exile has yet lost the desire to
be part of Judaism. It is true that a large part has indeed lost this
desire, and are lost to Judaism, especially in the small Jewish communities which will disappear by intermarriage within one generation. But there is still a large sector in which this desire is not yet
lost, and who want to fill it with specific Jewish content that requires
exertion and struggle. A Jewish State per se, as a value in its own
right — does not interest them because today it does not interest the
modern man in the western world. It interests the Zambesians
and Tanganikans, nor is this to their discredit, because they are
now in their phase of nationalisim, but today it does not interest
the educated Frenchman or Dutchman or the like. The latter have
readily surrendered their empires and are no longer moved by the
desire that a large part of the world be printed on the map in the
color of their State. The Jewish people in the West has become a
nation of intellectuals whom nationalism does not excite and by its
very nature nationalism cannot interest the class of intelligentsia
in the West to which the majority of our people belong.

Not so long ago I met for talks with groups of young Jewish
intellectuals from France and discovered how remote they are
from every political and philosophical stripe which seems important here in Israel, and how remote the issues that are
important in their eyes are from our public awareness. The
young Jewish intellectual is not excited by the fact that our
ambassador too is received in a State ceremony by President De
Gaulle, whereas he will not find in the flag of the State of Israel
what he is seeking, his Jewish identity. This is not what interests
him. And if we say to him that here we are creating an equitable
social regime (which is a lie in itself) — this avowed accomplish-
ment does not interest him either, because this is something that
was and is being done by the Fourth and Fifth French Republics,
and the Labor Government in England, and there is nothing specifically Jewish in it. But if he has any dim feeling that he belongs or
wants to belong to the Jewish people, then we must show him that
belonging to the Jewish people is expressed in struggles over matters

that are specifically Jewish and that are not part of the reality of the non-Jewish world. And I do not mean Torah and religious duties as the sole and exclusive way in which to belong but rather a social and political reality in whose center the struggle over specific Jewish matters is a real struggle, rather than coalition agreements, over the affirmation or negation of Torah and religious duties.

What is so remarkable about the economic themes with which we occupy ourselves? Our entire kibbutz movement has done less for social justice than has Johnson, the millionaire from Texas. The kibbutz movement has been a lot more egoistic and one of the factors, in it, consciously or unconsciously, has been an aspiration to evade responsibility for the real situation of Jews in the world. And an even more important question is to what extent Zionism express-es a tendency (decidedly unconscious) to flee from the real Jewish people under a guise of Jewish nationalism. Even the revival of the Hebrew language involved the factor of an escape from Yiddish, which was the language of the real Jews.

One might say that Mr. Uri Avneri, M.K. in his extreme anti-Jewish and anti-religious approach — is giving explicit expression to what is in the souls of the majority of our public leaders. Some of them however try to deceive themselves as regards their com-plete detachment from the history of the Jewish people and the Jewish people itself, whereas others aim to deceive — they know that they have no connection with Judaism or the Jewish people but seek to deceive the Jews in this regard. They are interested in the United Jewish Appeal as a permanent institution, which prevents the Jews in exile from developing a spiritual link with the State of Israel, because it soothes their conscience rather than *arousing the problems of their Jewishness*.

And to go back to the example of the kibbutz as an escape from the Jewish people: it has been conspicuously proved that the kibbutz is unable to absorb masses of Jews, for whom it has remained something entirely alien. Any thinking person could have known beforehand that this way of life would not solve the problems of the Jewish people. Yet those who initiated it created a wall, which exists to this day, and it is they who wanted it. It seems to me that one of the standpoints from which we should judge the kibbutz's *raison d'etre* is the fact that it is not absorbing Jews today. Hence what justification is there for maintaining this form as a national asset after it has stopped taking in Jews? The problem of the kibbutz is also the problem of the idea of socialism as an educational ideology and as a factor that attracts Jews. The highest level of human emancipation that has been achieved to date has been achieved by the laborer in Sweden, Norway, England, America, Holland, Switzerland — countries with "capitalist" regimes, nor do we find any correlation between collectivity and human freedom. On the contrary — we find that under collective regimes man is less free. And I emphasize once again — no social amendment can embody any specific Jewish content. Hence how is it to attract the Jews in the Diaspora?

BEN EZER: How do you view the position of the Jewish intellectual in Israel? Can he maintain the position of a "stranger," an outsider? Does he have the possibility of developing a Jewish essence that will present a challenge to the educated Jew in the Diaspora?

LEIBOWITZ: The Kafr Kassem incident where an Israeli army unit mistakenly massacred a group of Arab villagers, could happen anywhere in the world. "Blood runs cheaps" is a general human phenomenon today. But the shocking thing is that our public acquiesced and those responsible for it have all remained in their posts. In any well-run State the Minister of Defense would have resigned immediately, and the Chief of Staff would have resigned, and even those responsible on the lower echelons, and the entire nation would have accepted their resignation — because it happened under their administration. Yet here the public did not demand this. There are signs of baseness in our intelligentsia here, more so than in other countries. Stalin was able to rule only by executing and imprisoning millions of people; only thus was he able to silence the Russian intellectuals. Whereas with us all that is needed is the threat that a writer, professor or member of a given academy will not receive an invitation to lunch with the President or some other ceremonious sign of honor in order to bring him to silence.

BEN EZER: What do you think is the possibility of the State of Israel becoming a Jewish State in essence and content. From the political and practical point of view.

LEIBOWITZ: I am convinced that the United Jewish Appeal is needed not to maintain the State but to maintain it under a certain regime. I have no doubt that the Appeal and most of the grants (apart from aid for defense requirements from the United States) as well as the majority of the funds from Germany do not come to fill the needs of the State but to fill its needs under a given regime. For its vital requirements every State today obtains support — assistance in development of agriculture and industry, and even military assistance. But we receive support in order to maintain a standard of living by virtue of which the regime can enjoy popular support. Our leading economists hold that the flow of free money inhibits the possibility of developing a healthy economy and as a layman this seems to me reasonable — free money distorts the normal process of development, to say nothing of additional negative phenomena which it entails such as an ever increasing gap between the First and Second Israel (established old timers and new immigrants from underdeveloped countries). Nor is the negative influence limited to internal phenomena: it is also destroying our entire relationship with the Jewish people in the Diaspora. The course we are following is not one that creates a relationship of belonging to one people but one of givers and receivers of handouts, which creates a greater psychological gap. It is the complete opposite of a fate shared in common.

A few weeks after the Suez campaign of 1956 the Chief of Staff at the time, Moshe Dayan, visited South Africa on behalf of the United Jewish Appeal. One may dispute the campaign's necessity but the fact remains that scores of Jewish boys, scores of young officers, were killed in it. And what demand did the Israeli Chief of Staff make of South African Jewry? Did he ask them for so-and-so many Jewish boys in place of those who had fallen? No! He asked them for money. Further contributions to the United Jewish Appeal. That was his demand!

Instead of inciting the Jewish youngster in the Diaspora to rebel against his parents, instead of putting him in a state of conflict with them, with himself and with his Jewish identity, we come to his parents as seekers of handouts — and take their money in order not to do the very things that would set their children against them, cut them off from them and bring them to Israel. Those who give the money know full well why they are giving it — to save souls — the souls of theirchildren in the Diaspora. And so from a movement raising children up in rebellion against their parents, Zionism and the State of Israel with it have become a movement resting on the parents' generation and taking handouts from them in order not to do precisely what is incumbent upon it. The United Jewish Appeal, as an expression of the State of Israel's course among Diaspora Jewry, is a denial of the State's Jewish essence and of the possibility or the demand that this essence may someday be able to attract young Jews from the Diaspora to come and settle here.

And were I asked from a political and general standpoint on how Israel ought to stress the fact that it is the State of the Jewish people, I would say — in order to put the idea into sharper focus — that from the outset we should never have joined the United Nations. Switzerland for example, has not joined because of a historic political tradition of neutrality — something which is embodied in its constitution and which prevents it from participating in decisions or votes which amount to adopting a stand in international disputes or casting its votes on the side of a given state or bloc against another State or bloc. This position has gained the esteem of the entire world, in that it expresses Switzerland's unique historic and political essence, nor does anyone accuse that country of isolationism or of apathy. Now if the State of Israel had a true "Jewish consciousness," if it considered itself as representing the Jewish people and its unique historic destiny, and if it proclaimed — to itself and to the entire world — that in accordance with this historic and national uniqueness it was the State not only of its inhabitants but responsible for the fate of all the Jews in the world, even those who did not recognize it as representing them — it would have announced as soon as it was created that it could not join the U.N. lest it be compelled on some occasions to vote in such a way as might harm Jews in any place whatsoever. Such a position would have strengthened the awareness of Jewish uniqueness among Jews throughout the world, and would also have been received with understanding and respect by the Gentile world, which at the time of the State's creation clearly felt the uniqueness of the event. From the standpoint of the political interests of the State and Jewish people this too would have helped us greatly. As a member of the U.N. we are whether we like it or not a satellite of the West, whereas were we neutral it might soften the attitude of the Soviet Union toward us and even toward its own Jews. Under such conditions it might be easier to achieve a rapprochement with the Arab world. All these opportunities have been lost because of our lust for the State to be like any other and the nation dwelling in it a territorial nation like any other, rather than the center of the historic Jewish people.

This severance from the Jewish people's history and any consideration of the State of Israel's significance in the continuation of this history is seen in our relationship with Germany. If our leaders had in their hearts the slightest hint of Jewish historical feeling or concern for the shaping of Jewish national consciousness in the future, no consideration of present profit would have brought them to accept a harlot's gift from Germany and establish normal diplomatic relations with it in this generation thus exonerating it before humanity and history. The State of Israel has betrayed Jewish history and the Jewish people for the benefit of its rulers who bribe its inhabitants with the means they acquire by this betrayal.

BEN EZER: As a natural scientist and an observant Jew, what is your position between these two worlds? Do you not arrive at substantial contradictions in your own inner world — as a religious man who is at the very heart of modern-day scientific development?

LEIBOWITZ: The religious conception of the Torah does away with the entire problem of a contradiction between it and the knowledge and awareness we have acquired from science — and without any tenuous explanations or sterile debates. The entire matter of a confrontation between science and religion and all the attempts to verify the Torah through the findings of scientific research (be it natural science or philological and historical research) and especially the ludicrous attempt to "rescue," as it were, the veracity of the Torah by casting doubt on the certainty of the results achieved through use of scientific method or by explaining that a "scientific truth" is not a certainty but merely a probability whereas the truth of the Torah is absolute — all this is a total misunderstanding of the nature of science and involves serious errors from the religious standpoint as well.

Anyone who engages in this confrontation is attesting that he treats the *holy Torah* the way he treats a textbook in physics, geology, biology and the like. That is to say, he considers it from the standpoint of its value as a *source of information for man*; and if he is a person who considers himself religious, the only difference he sees between the Torah and textbook of science is that the information provided by the Torah is more reliable.

In actual fact, this approach is a thoroughly profane one — that of a person who is completely unaware of the meaning of the concept *holy scripture*, which is in a purely a religious category. Any matter of providing man with information — like any matter of supplying a human need or realizing a human value — is something profane rather than sacred, and in this connection there is no difference between information about the weather and information about the universe and the essence of nature and man.

The concern of religion — the category of holiness — is above and beyond all these things, and in a certain sense also completely foreign to them, to all human needs, interests and values. The concern of the Torah and all the holy scripture is the recognition of man's position before God ("I have set the Lord always before me") with the requirement being that man worship God — and not the imparting of knowledge about the world, nature, history or even man himself.

Just as the precepts of the Torah are the program for the worship of God, rather than the program for the social moral or intellectual process of man or humanity, so the statements of the Torah are not descriptions of nature or stories of history but one of the many forms of the expression "I have set the Lord always before me;" and the same goes for the *Halacha* (religious law) and Oral Law. The first words of the *Orah Hayim*, (the first section of the *Shulhan Aruch* — code of Jewish law by Rabbi Yosef Karo) are "He shall prevail as a lion to rise each morning to the worship of God" and not "to rise each morning to learn something about the world, nature or man." To know how and when the universe came into being, if it came into being — is important from the standpoint of scientific research; to know the quality and nature of man is important from the standpoint of philosophical anthropology; whereas *both kinds of knowledge are irrelevant from the standpoint of faith and religion.* Man's position before God is not defined as part of natural reality — nor are the duty to worship God — and recognition of this duty — dependent on or conditioned by whether the universe is primeval or renewed, whether, when and how it was created and what has been its history and the history of humanity. The aspiration to know these things is *human concern,* and these are concerns dealt with by *science,* whereas religion and faith, the Torah and its commandments, have "concerns" that are altogether different — "concerns" of the kind formulated in that first chapter of the *Shulhan Aruch.* It is completely ridiculous to suppose that the Torah was given in order to teach man something about natural science or history, that the Divine Presence descended on Mount Sinai in order to perform the function of a teacher of physics, biology, astronomy etc; or that the Lord Blessed Be He is merely a better professor than the one in the university! The notion is not only ridiculous but blasphemous as well. He who approaches the Torah from the standpoint of scientific information it does or does not provide attests that it is not his intention to worship God but rather that God should (as it were) worship him and serve his needs in the way of providing knowledge. To put it another way, he approaches the Torah and its Giver not from the standpoint of faith for its own sake but a faith for the sake of his needs. The person who truly believes (in the sense of the faith of *halachic* Judaism, the Torah and its commandments) does not expect the Torah to teach him anything about the universe, nature, man or history; if he is interested in these problems he takes the trouble to investigate them, insamuch as science enables him to do so and he does not have the impertinence to trouble the Lord Blessed Be He with it. From the Torah the true believer expects one thing only: guidance in the ways of worshipping God. Therefore he understands that everything the Torah says about the world and history is not said in order to impart knowledge to man (something which is profane rather than sacred) — but for religious reasons which have nothing to do with the interest of science.

The Lord Blessed Be He is not a functionary of the world nor the Demiurge of Plato, nor can we draw any inference between what we know about the world from science to what the Torah has seen fit to tell us.

(This part of the interview took place in April 1970)

BEN EZER: How do you view Zionism and the future relationship between Israel and the Arabs since the war of June 1967?

LEIBOWITZ: As far as the foreseeable future is concerned an Arab-Israeli peace does not seem a realistic possibility. We are condemned to live for a period that cannot be foretold in advance without peace and hence without security. The choice customarily presented is connected with the problem of the territories conquered in the war of 1967: peace (in other words, surrender of the territories) or security (in other words occupation of the territories) does not exhaust all the possibilities. A lot more probable is a state of neither peace nor security. We are now in a state of latent war, which any day can take on extremely serious proportions. And we will be required on a permanent basis to pay for our existence in human lives and in sacrifices in the economic sphere, as well as many other areas which can only be developed on the basis of a flourishing economy. There is no doubt that this price will rise from year to year, perhaps even from month to month. And in the final account there is no guarantee how long we will be able to survive under these conditions — except that we are clearly and firmly determined to survive to the limit of our ability.

BEN EZER: Should we not therefore ask ourselves why we are taking this future upon ourselves?

LEIBOWITZ: The only answer that permits us to acquiesce in this future is that we are doing it for the sake of our Jewish State, in the context of which the problems of the historical continuation of Jewish people and Judaism will be resolved. If the State will not serve as a framework for this objective — that is, if it will not be a Jewish State, then there is no sense maintaining it. A State is not a value in itself but an instrument, an instrument that is needed for the realization and implementation of things that do have value. As far as we are concerned the value is the Jewish people and its Jewishness.

A State that includes a forty or fifty percent non-Jewish population, all of whose problems will be how to maintain its rule over this population — will not be a Jewish State but merely an apparatus of administration and control that is in the hands of Jews. The exaltation of the State as an apparatus of administration and control, irrelative of its character, and content, is Fascism. The State of Israel's survival has no meaning unless it continues the history of the Jewish People. And if it does not do so there is no meaning to its existence, nor does it even have any right to exist.

BEN EZER: But there are no indications that the present situation is likely to change in the foreseeable future.

LEIBOWITZ: If the present situation, that is the keeping of a million and a half Arabs under our control, becomes stabilized, the results will be: first — the destruction of the State of Israel; second — the destruction of the entire Jewish people as a result of the severance of the State from the Jewish people and its total concentration on the problems of retaining control; third — the subversion of the entire democratic and social structure of our society, both from the standpoint of the State's being transformed into a police (or more correctly *secret-police*) State and by the creation of a laboring class of Arabs ruled over by Jewish foremen, supervisors, officials, policemen and soldiers.

BEN EZER: What are we to do?

LEIBOWITZ: Since there is no prospect of achieving peace we must at once this very night, get out of the territories inhabited by a million and a half Arabs, barricade ourselves in our Jewish State and invest our entire strength in maintaining it. There is another possibility, a remote one, that a settlement will be imposed on us by the great powers, America and Russia, and perhaps that will result in relative quiet for a short period. What will come afterwards cannot be foreseen.

BEN EZER: Your point of departure is the religious one. But there are religious circles in Israel that consider the Six Day War, the conquest of the Western Wall and Old Jerusalem and the other places holy to Judaism the first act of our redemption. They tend to regard the Jewish religion in a Messianic light, to sanctify military strength and to attach a religious value to the Greater Israel and the integrity of the homeland — in other words to Jewish dominion over all the territories conquered in the last war.

LEIBOWITZ: This is the latter-day Sabbataism, a modern incarnation of false prophets, a prostitution of the Jewish religion in the interest of nationalist cannibalism and lust for power. It is the religion of people for whom the nation has become God, the home-land — the Torah, and national sovereignty — that is, administrative power — something sacrosanct. Military victories in themselves have no religious significance whatsoever. The Six Day War is no different from the wars of King Jeroboam the son of Joash, who "restored the borders of Israel from the entrance of Hamath as far as the Sea of the Arabah," which did not prevent the Prophet of God from uttering his harsh prophecy against that wicked King and his nation: "Jeroboam shall die by the sword, and Israel shall surely be led away captive out of their own land."

The current comparison of the Six Day War to the war of the *Hashmonaim* (Hasmoneans) which was essentially a civil war within the Jewish nation between adherents of the Torah and the Hellenists is a complete distortion, for this time the Temple had been liberated not by the Hashmonaim but by the Hellenists. As for the messianic vision — it is one that cannot be implemented. The cases of implementation of Messianism are Christianity and Sabbataism. When the soap-bubble of Sabbataism eventually burst, Judaism, which had been taken in by the messianic bluff, suffered a blow from which it has not recovered. And when the modern Sabbataian soap bubble bursts it will result in a spiritual and psychological collapse that may liquidate Judaism altogether.

BEN EZER: Has there been any essential change in the relations between Israel and Diaspora Jewry since the Six Day War?

LEIBOWITZ: In my opinion there has been no essential change. The involvement of large parts of the Jewish youth with the New Left is merely a continuation of the process of alienation from Judaism, assimilation into the world of the Gentiles and involve-ment in ways of thinking and values that are current there — a process that began several generations ago, and one which the State of Israel has never succeeded in stopping.

In actual fact, the nation living in the State of Israel today has not been interested in preserving the continuity of the Jewish people's history, which is why the State has not been able to stem the process of the Jewish people's collapse, disintegration and assimilation.

The enthusiasm of the Jews abroad for the State of Israel is a kind of cover-up for a situation in which there is no real desire to fundamentally alter the reality of assimilation. This reality is disguised by demonstrative events which do not change the essence of the situation. The sentimental awakening that followed in the wake of the last war has not been transformed into an existential one, and this is not surprising, because from a sentimental awakening no existential revolution can ever come about.

BEN EZER: Does it appear to you that the Jewish faith is fulfilling a positive function in Israel today?

LEIBOWITZ: Faith does not exist in order to "fulfill a function." The Jewish faith is either an end in itself or it has no validity whatsoever. And this is the distinction that traditional Jewish religious thinking makes between "Torah for its own sake" and "Torah that is not for its own sake." It is written that "Torah that is for its own sake become an elixir or life whereas Torah that is not for its own sake becomes an elixir of death" (Talmud, Tractate *Ta'anit*, p.7).

BEN EZER: What do you think of the Knesset decision on the "*Who is a Jew?*" issue? — a decision that is largely based on Jewish religious law.

LEIBOWITZ: Who is a Jew? The entire issue is absolutely irrelevant. The State of Israel does not represent Judaism and can make no decisions about Judaism. No State past, present or future has, is or will represent Judaism.

Therefore the Knesset decision is relevant only as regards the State, not as regards Judaism. As regards Judaism all that is relevant is the fact that a person who from the standpoint of the fundamental concepts and lawful provisions of Judaism is a violator of the covenant, a wilful aspostate and an infidel — is nonetheless entitled to be an officer in the Israel Defense Forces and to command Jewish soldiers. And this right of his is unassailable from the standpoint of the essence of this State, as agreed to by both the religious and the irreligious. I am not a Jew according to the definition in the law of the State of Israel. Therefore I do not care who is or is not registered as a Jew in the lists of the State. There is no copyright over the word "Jew" and anyone who wants to use it can do so at will. The essential meaning of the word is known to me and to those who share my outlook and opinion, and it remains unaffected by the laws and regulations of the State. If the Knesset tomorrow should decide by a majority of sixty-one to fifty-nine that anyone who smears green paint on his nose is a Jew, it will be a law of the State. But for me it is not relevant. Anyone who accepts democracy acquiesces in the possibility that a piece of folly will be enacted by a majority vote.

BEN EZER: In your opinion what is the ideal, or utopian, image of the State of Israel? Would you be in favor of a *halachic* State?

LEIBOWITZ: I am not able to answer this question. It is not I who establish facts. The majority of the Jewish people think along lines that are completely different. It is a hypothetical question and cannot be answered. There never has been and never will be a *halachic* State. The struggle between religion and the secular nature of the State is eternal.

I do not worship the sacred cow of "national unity." I know nothing of value that was achieved by unity. Everything of value has been achieved only by extremely severe struggles, even to the point of bloody civil war. Even today the Jewish faith is something that divides the nation. Everything that is of value divides people. Values are something for which one must struggle and fight: one can by no means unite. Plundering and looting—those are things on which people can unite.

BEN EZER: In other words Jewish *halacha* and the Jewish State are like two parallel lines which never meet? Must there always be antagonism between them?

LEIBOWITZ: For the religious person the religion is a value, that is, an end in itself. But no State is an end in itself. A State, as I said, has instrumental meaning only. The question of the meaning of the Jewish people never arose before the rise of Zionism, and the fact that it arises today gives room for doubts as to whether the Jewish people has any future. And if there is no future, then the State is not only superfluous, it has no raison d'etre. It is nothing but an apparatus of coercion and violence that exists for its own sake. Why create a new "Hebrew nation," a body with the power to fight, to kill and to be killed? Why create a State if the Jewish people does not exist? It may be that there will arise here a new, synthetic nation that is defined by its State, like the Nicaraguan nation. But such a nation does not interest me; I have no need to belong to an artificial construction.

Today there is a process of disintegration, collapse and assimilation of the Jewish people, a process that is going forward with giant steps. I think that we are heading for a schism in the Jewish people. It is of the essence of religion to be in opposition to the State, in opposition to any State; religion is the eternal criticism of the State, of nationalism, of sovereignty, of government and rulers, and never will it identify with the State and its institutions. Today in Israel, in the present situation, where religious Juadism is incorporated in the secular regime, religious Judaism does not represent any values but is merely a factor that interferes with values that the secular State might develop.

BEN EZER: Young people in Israel today, who go to serve in the Army, speak of a feeling of a secular "Sacrifice of Isaac." They have the feeling that the generation of their parents, and the State, are sacrificing them, but without any compensation or consolation of the religious faith in an afterlife, in the eternal and divine meaning of life.

LEIBOWITZ: A "Sacrifice of Isaac"? I know of only one — the temptation of Abraham. The sacrifice of Isaac was the annulment of human values for piety and love of the Lord, whereas what these young people are referring to is the renunciation of life for another, and purely human, value that is known as patriotism. This renunciation — the preference of one human value over another — is the very contradiction of the Sacrifice of Isaac. It is a very wide-spread phenomenon. Even the Nazis were of the opinion that the Fatherland and Nation had priority over human life, that a person should lay down his life for the sake of the Nation and Fatherland. It is a very widespread human phenomenon, and it is not to be marveled at one bit. *"Dulce et decorum est pro patria mori"* — this is not the Sacrifice of Isaac. Some people value their country more than their lives, and some value their lives more than their country.

A man must know how to fight just as he must know how to work. Defending the homeland and fighting are not values, just as work is not a value. They are only in the nature of supplying needs.

BEN EZER: In your opinion, is there any difference between the feeling of a secular Jewish soldier as compared to that of a religious Jewish soldier when both are on the front lines, placing their lives in jeopardy for the survival of the State?

LEIBOWITZ: There is no difference. The only difference is that one considers that it is his duty to worship God in his lifetime while the other does not recognize this duty. As regards the defense of the homeland, they are both equal.

The New Hebrew Nation
(the "Canaanite" outlook)

Interview with Yonatan Ratosh
(This interview took place in July 1970)

BEN EZER: There is currently an opinion that the Jewish "genius" characteristically has its origin in a felicitous encounter between the Jewish intellect and some of the rich European cultures. Isn't the danger of curtailing the fertility of the Jewish "genius" in Israel, the danger of circumscription, included in the price of Zionism? Can the fact that Jewish intellectuals in the Diaspora are losing their respectful and admiring attitude towards the State of Israel — be considered a troubling confirmation of this fear?

RATOSH: I may assume that Jewry — as a primarily urban denomination, mercantile, unstable, alert, the individual learning and advancement of whose members has enabled them to achieve a most respectable status — has quite naturally played a part in the intellectual life of European and American countries that is out of all proportion to its percentage of their respective populations. But your question, asking about the origin of the "Jewish genius," is utterly irrelevant and alien to the way I see reality, alien to me and alien to the new Hebrew nation to which I — to which we in this country — have the honor to belong. With all due respect to every Jewish intellectual for his intellectualism, the greatest peril I see lies in all the "Jewish consciousness" and "Zionist consciousness" that all sorts of Jewish and Zionist parents, teachers, functionaries and intellectuals have been trying to implant here, among the native-born, for all these years.

I am afraid that when you referred to "the price of Zionism" you meant what *Judaism* has lost because the population of this country, the State of Israel, is preoccupied with settlement, with the national economy, with the military — with the state's sovereign national life. But I can not help thinking about the mental, intellectual and ideological distortion that is being imposed on the Hebrew youth by the Zionist version of Jewish education that is pressed upon it through all the phases of the educational system and all the media of mass communication. The Jewish attitudes of the administration in Israel today are alien to the very essence of nationalism, to the principal group quintessence of the youth, who in the nature of things belong to a new nation, a normal nation, the new Hebrew nation.

BEN EZER: The education of the members of my generation in this country's schools was founded on two implicit premises. One was the rejection of exilic existence, from which in the course of time arose the cruel implication that the Jews of Europe had been "to blame," so to speak, for their terrible fate, since they had not surmounted their "negative" nature in time by emigrating to Palestine. The other premise was that the normalization of Jewish national existence, towards which Zionism strives, would exempt us, the young generation born in this country, from all the distortions and suffering of the Diaspora Jewish heritage.

As I grew up, numerous doubts assailed me. Is the Jewish exilic existence really so fundamentally negative and wrong? Perhaps our Zionist education and literature had misled us and twisted our minds, to make us see the Jewish holocaust in Europe through the pin-hole of the Zionist solution, without comprehending the other religious, philosophical, historic and political implications of the Holocaust.

The other, graver doubt came when I realized that Zionism had not exempted us from the Jewish fate, a fate that had been brought home to us by the sustained war, by the Arabs' hatred of us, and by our being immured in a sort of "armed ghetto" in the Middle East. I feel myself today to be *a Zionist for lack of an alternative*. So long as I live in Israel I can not escape the Jewish and Zionist fate that pursues me, and that is brought home to me most forcefully by the Arabs' hatred.

RATOSH: One of the Sinbad the Sailor stories tells of an old man who asks a young fellow to take him across a river. The young fellow takes the old man piggy-back on his shoulders, and crosses the water to the opposite bank. But when he comes up onto the shore, the old man does not release him, but tightens his grip around his neck, and keeps on riding him. If you have decided to give Judaism and Zionism a ride on your shoulders — what can I do to help you? You yourself are choosing your own fate. Dislodge Zionism and Judaism from your back, and they will stop strangling you.

BEN EZER: What, then, are the tenets of the Canaanite outlook that you propose as an alternative?

RATOSH: I shall attempt to summarize in outline form, as concisely as possible, our Hebrew (or Canaanite, as it is commonly called) approach:

As has occurred in many immigration-based countries in recent centuries (for example, Australia, Mexico and the U. S.), there emerged in this country at the turn of the last century a new nationality namely that of the new Hebrew nation.

This new nationality emerged within the geographic and linguistic framework of the classic Hebrew nation, which antedates Judaism. Quite naturally, a process of national resurgence, such as quite a few ancient nations have undergone, coincided with the process of emergence of the new Hebrew nation. Hence the first new Hebrew generation, at the turn of the century, could be and was already imbued with a sense of Hebrew identity and Hebrew consciousness.

The territory of the State of Israel is a natural and integral part of the Euphrates country. This is merely a contemporary version of the classic Hebrew term '*ever ha-nahar*. '*Ever* in this context means "the land of," while *ha-nahar*, "the river" with the emphasis on the definite article, can only refer to the Euphrates River. This, then, is the classic land of the Hebrews. The Hebrews, *ha'ivrim*, are the people of this land ('*ever*). The fate of the Euphrates country, which extends from the Egyptian frontier to the Tigris River, bounded by Egypt, the Arabian peninsula, Iran and Turkey, and the fate of the Israeli territory are one. In fact, willy nilly, it is for the future of the entire Euphrates country, the cradle and heart of Pan-Arabism, and all its inhabitants that the new Hebrew nation is fighting. It is fighting against the repressive, alien, Pan-Arabism, which condemns the country and its inhabitants to medieval servitude at home and foreign domination from without.

Our victory, and in the long run our very existence, is possible only if we take our place at the head of all those who strive for independence and progress in the entire Euphrates country, being the pioneer and nucleus of its resurgence on a secular, national, non-denominational and non-racial basis, with reliance on the classic ancient Hebrew background shared by all the inhabitants and ethnic groups of this country prior to the emergence of Judaism and the rest of the religions that factionalize the population today. (We are speaking of an essentially historic process the particulars and stages of which, naturally, cannot be determined in advance).

Zionism, in all its aspects, is and has been primarily a Jewish ideology, arising from the emotional problems and needs of the Jews in the various countries of their dispersion. In this country it has initiated nothing, innovated nothing. In this country, it has since its inception sought only to dominate — to dominate immigration, education, the economy, politics, and the entire life of the country. To the best of its ability, it has imposed "Jewish consciousness" to inhibit the natural development of the new Hebrew nation, to sap its vital force and threaten its very existence. Zionism has imposed a rule that is alien to the spirit, character and very being of the new Hebrew generation. This was clearly demonstrated, for example, in the confrontation between the Zionist government and the Hebrew army in May 1967. (In contrast to the Israeli Government, which is composed chiefly of elderly East European Jews, with a small admixture of younger local disciples, the Israeli army *is* the Hebrew nation in arms. It is almost entirely composed of Israeli-born and educated youths, all Hebrew speaking and thinking — a young, non-professional, reserves-based fighting force, whose top commanders are little over the age of forty).

The Zionist regime is in fact a missionary one, designed to divide permanently the inhabitants of the country denominationally, in order to establish here a brand of Holy Land, whose geographic and geopolitical location is irrelevant. The very existence of this Holy Land must by its nature consist of commerce in sacraments. It is a Holy Land for the benefit of the Jewish Diaspora, a sort of center that draws its sustenance from the Jewish Diaspora, is integrated into it, and to a large extent relies upon it and is kept by it.

The Hebrew resurgence in the Euphrates country should be viewed in the context of the national awakening of all Near Asia, ever since the national principle reached here in the course of the nineteenth century, having spread eastward since the French Revolution. Its principles are identical in all the resurgent countries here, the same for us as for Iran and Turkey, for example: national and territorial self-determination, a casting-off of racial, community and religious discrimination and a reliance on a classic national period.

This national self-determination is an essential condition for making it possible to absorb masses of people within this national, secular, resurgent framework and to rehabilitate the country. These are the fundamental problems of the new and renascent nation. Without this clear-cut self-determination, no national society can realize itself, and the extent to which national self-determination is complete, governs the extent to which the renascent society will in fact realize itself.

BEN EZER: What are the practical points of your program, within the context of the State of Israel?

RATOSH: Gradual absorption of all the inhabitants of the country into an open, uni-national Hebrew society, which predicates equality of obligations and rights for all, without difference of extraction, faith or denomination.

Uniform secular Hebrew schooling (with optional religious lessons) for all inhabitants of the country, without difference of extraction, faith or denomination.

Gradual conscription into the Israel Defence Forces of all inhabitants of the country, without difference of extraction, faith or denomination.

Immigration as required by the country, according to personal qualifications alone, without difference of extraction, faith or denomination.

BEN EZER: How will we be able to absorb the Arabs into the framework of the new Hebrew nation?

RATOSH: If we have integrated Yemenite Jews with Kurdish Jews, together with Jews from Germany, for example, (groups of people who had nothing in common) why shouldn't we be able to integrate Arab *fellahin*? The only question is that of the basis on which to integrate. Today, we are integrating on a denominational basis. On this basis, we are even integrating people for whom denominational mentality as a basis for the life of the state is in itself alien, as for example those from Western Europe. If we establish integration on a national, secular — Hebrew and not Jewish — basis, there is no reason why we should not be able to absorb non-Jews as well into the broad national framework, without difference of extraction, faith, or denomination. Perhaps I should stress here that in fact the main question is not that of the adults, who might seem to be the candidates for absorption into the Hebrew national society, but of their children, who are going to grow up as Hebrews.

BEN EZER: Why should the Arabs agree to this?

RATOSH: We will open to them secular, Hebrew-language kindergartens, elementary schools and secondary schools. We will conscript them into the Israel Defence Forces. And when they are demobilized from the army we will ask them. Then you will see what their answer will be. They will have grown up as Hebrews. Even under today's conditions, there are already such among them. And there are not a few among them who are demanding such schooling. For them, for all the inhabitants of this country, this is in fact the only real chance to get out of a medieval milieu and be liberated from a repressive Pan-Arabism. In any case, the situation in Israel today is intolerable, with Agudath Yisrael running religious schools in Yiddish, and non-Hebrews having a separate school system in Arabic. The Druse, the Maronites and the Nuseiri, *inter alia*, are no more "Arabs" than were the Jews of Yemen or Iraq. Zionism's sectarian approach is actually intended to create frameworks for ghetto living here, Jewish and Arabic apart.

BEN EZER: Your program is somewhat of an imposition as regards the natural rights of the Arabs who are Israeli citizens.

RATOSH: What would they say in the U.S. if you were to impose Spanish-language schools on part of the citizens of California, claiming that Spanish is the former language of that part of the population? What would the Jews of the U.S. say were the state to oblige them to be educated in separate schools, not in the English language? Would they not consider it an attempt to make second-class citizens of them? And that is exactly what we are doing to the non-Jewish citizens of this country when we impose Arabic schools upon them. The only result of such an approach may well be that instead of bringing them up as fellow citizens, with equal obligations and rights, we will be bringing up here not a few people who will view themselves as belonging, for example, to Pan-Arabist Egypt.

In the first years of the state, there were in the town of Tarshiha, in the Galilee, two categories of residents, in approximately equal numbers: Rumanian-speaking members of the "Mosaic faith" and Arabic speaking members of the "Mohamedan and Christian faiths." We set up two separate schools there, in Hebrew for the former, and in Arabic for the latter despite the fact that they wanted their children to go to the Hebrew school. We thereby perpetuated their status as second-class citizens. This approach is a legacy of the ghetto mentality of Eastern Europe.

It might seem that this was a wrong course of action — to reject a population that explicitly sought to be integrated. But from the denominational point of view it is quite right. If one considers the state and the society to be a denominational state and society, it follows that any portion of the population that does not belong to the proper denominational community will be considered unfit to perform any function other than the lowest and most marginal. This, by the way, is why the non-Jewish intelligentsia in Israel is so frustrated. Moreover, it follows as a matter of course that all the non-Jewish inhabitants of the country are considered to be part of the Arab world, necessarily committed, at least at heart, to owe their allegiance to the Arab world and its inimical attitude towards Israel. They are thus thrust into the arms of Pan-Arabism.

The Jewish leadership, which is not in the least interested in absorbing non-Jews into the society, fears, and justly so, that if non-Jews be afforded the opportunity of equal education at an early stage and *then* find that most of the opportunities open to

Jews are closed to them, they will be far more embittered and furious, and the Hebrew education they will have will make them far better equipped to harm the security of the state. From this standpoint, according to this approach, it is therefore appropriate to shut them out from the outset.

BEN EZER: Why shouldn't we assimilate among the Arabs?

RATOSH: There is no Arab nation to assimilate into. Till this day, the language spoken in the homes of many of the Jews who have come from countries in the Arab speaking world is Arabic. The large majority of these were as assimilated among the Arabs as it was possible to be. And what does that prove? Had there existed an Arab nation, a Hebrew nation could not have arisen here from the outset, as there has not arisen a new nation among the Jewish emigrants in Egypt, in Whitechapel, in Argentina or in the U.S. From the standpoint of nationality, there was a vacuum here, and only within such a vacuum could there have been room for a new nation to come into being.

BEN EZER: Do you mean to say that the new Hebrew nation could not have come into being had there been a secular, democratic, developed Arab nation of a Western type?

RATOSH: Not necessarily. In Palestine there existed no national entity whatsoever. Had there been, the Jews would have assimilated into that nation here, as they have done all over the world, surviving at the most as a separate denomination.

BEN EZER: But the Arabs, from their point of view, see "Arab unity" as a national idea.

RATOSH: The people who want to see it that way are chiefly European observers and other outsiders, who naturally try to force the so-called Arab world into a framework of concepts and terminology that is alien to it — or so-called "Christian Arabs" seeking grounds for their "Arabism" which Moslems treat with such great reservations. By the way, that is probably the chief reason for the vociferous extremism of not a few Christian leaders in the Arab-speaking world, for example George Habash, the leader of the Popular Front for the Liberation of Palestine, the extremist group that is responsible for the policy of hi-jacking planes and that is an outright advocate of Pan-Arabism.

The so-called Arab world is living in the Middle Ages. Its situation is parallel to that of medieval Christian Europe. Were a united "Arab world" capable of realization — it might be comparable to a hypothetical unification of the Latin-American continent in a unified Catholic political framework, with the exclusive use of classic Latin mandatory in schools, on the radio, in the press, in literature and on billboards, combined with an attempt to unite also with Roman Catholic Europe (excluding the cultural development of that Europe). Such a union would doom the region to protracted medievalism at home, and hence to imperialistic subjugation from outside, as well.

BEN EZER: What is the function of the Arabic language, from a national standpoint?

RATOSH: The classic Arabic language, that is, *literary Arabic* — has about the same function as Latin did in medieval Europe. Nobody speaks it, and the uneducated do not understand it either. Its function is to prevent the evolution of national languages and national cultures. The Pan Arabist movement vigorously opposes the development of spoken languages — which differ in every Arab country, often to the point of mutual unintelligibility — and their promotion to the status of national languages. It is Pan-Arabism that hinders national consolidation in every single locale. Egypt has a splendid past of its own, and could rely upon its classic past for the purpose of national resurgence, but this tendency is strangled by Pan-Arabism. Pan-Arabism (in contrast with our Hebrew, pre-Jewish past) has no territorial, national, pre-Moslem past. Therefore Pan-Arabism is incapable of serving as a basis for national resurgence. Perhaps, in the course of long generations, there might arise *new* nationalities in the so-called Arab world, but Pan-Arabism hinders this.

BEN EZER: Why, according to your outlook, couldn't there be, for example, a democratic, secular, Arab nationalism, whose language is Arabic?

RATOSH: The very quintessence of Arabism is based on Arabist-Moslem sectarianism, and the Pan-Arabist movement is based on a Moslem-sectarian foundation. The other denominational communities, the Christians, for example, are tolerated or exploited solely for propaganda purposes. The Copts in Egypt are one of the most natural protagonists of an Egyptian resurgence. It is precisely for that reason that they are being oppressed, and that Egyptian public opinion considers them first and foremost as Christians. The Pan-Arabist world employs the slogan of "a democratic, secular state" only for externally oriented propaganda. At home they know that it is impossible for them, and they talk about the fact. They possess no secular-national social stratum that is likely to effect a revolution. It is, as we have said, a medieval society. They themselves do not take the slogan of a democratic, secular state seriously, and use it only for foreign consumption. They speak of "a pluralistic democratic state, that will be part of the Arab nation." "Nation" in Moslem terminology (*Umma*) is not at all what we mean by the word "nationality," but rather a religious community, a congregation of believers. Pan-Arabism is not capable by any means of leading to a democratic, secular state of the type of the United States, for example. The real Pan-Arabist solution to the "Israeli question" is the massacre and expulsion of at least the great majority of the population. That is what the official spokesmen of Pan-Arabism declared to the world in 1967. That is how, as we know, the Moslems solved their "Assyrian problem" in Iraq upon the inauguration of Iraqi independence at the beginning of the thirties: massacre.

BEN EZER: Why shoudn't the function of Arabic be like the function of the English language?

RATOSH: The English language does not entail the same kind of denominational structure, does not entail a religious faith. One cannot at all compare the social function of the English language in the English speaking world with that of the Classic Arabic language in the so-called Arab world, just as it is impossible to compare the function of English in its world with that of Latin as the language of the Church in the Catholic countries of the Middle Ages.

BEN EZER: Why do you think that it is precisely the Hebrew language and nationality that offer a solution to the problems of the "Euphrates country?"

RATOSH: Despite the alien Jewish rule, we have a developed secular-national identity. I am convinced that the only form of national identity possible for the Euphrates country is a Hebrew resurgence. If there will be differing degrees of local autonomy, and of other languages alongside Hebrew — it will make no difference. Allow me to stress that Hebrew is also the early language of the Maronites in Lebanon, and the ancestral language of principal portions of the population in the Euphrates country. It is the early language of this country prior to the existence of Judaism. The language of Canaan was spoken in Jerusalem, in Rabat-Amon, in Beirut, in Damascus, in Allepo etc. and all the inhabitants of this country are going to accept, as we in Israel do, the Hebrew resurgence as the resurgence of their own cultural past. "Thank you for having preserved our Hebrew language," is what the Maronite priest at Gush-Halav said on the anniversary of the founding of the state.

BEN EZER: How can your outlook stand to reason when we are a minority in the Arab world and in the "Euphrates country?"

RATOSH: The standard figures are the fruit of prejudices built on misconceptions. In the historical land of Canaan, for example, between the Mediterranean shore and the longitude of Damascus, only one-third of the population are Suni Moslems (urban, rural and refugees). Another third are Israeli citizens registered as Jews. And to the last third belong the other religious-ethnic minorities, whose common ground is the opposition of them all to Pan-Arabism. Chief among these, each numbering several hundred thousand, are: The Maronites, the predominant community in Lebanon; the Druse, scattered through Lebanon, Syria and Israel, with their main body populating the region south of Damascus which bears their name, Jebl Druse; the Nuseiri, populating the mountainous coastal region of Syria, from Turkey to Lebanon; and the various Bedouin tribes, scattered throughout the inland and desert regions, comprising the dominant community in the Hashemite Kingdom of Jordan, and quite numerous in Iraq. (Strictly speaking, the Bedouin are the only true Arabs. In their view, any non-Beduin is a foreigner, whatever his denomination, occupation or language; and this also applies to non-Beduins who are Arabic speaking Moslems.)

But it is not the figures that matter. It is an objective fact that in 1948 the numerical ratio was far more to our disadvantage. We here were a civilian population of little more than half a million, with only a militia. And against us were massed quite a number of regular armies, trained to the limits of their capacities. We won, nevertheless, because what took place here was a war between a modern national society and the Middle Ages.

It is an unalterable fact that this same modern national state arose here in Hebrew. I personally can only thank my lucky stars that I am a member of the Hebrew nation, but objectively it is irrelevant. The grandchildren of all the inhabitants of this country, who are today warring against one another under demoninational colors, are going to be members of this resurgent nation in the Euphrates country. The other population, which is not Hebrew speaking, is not in the least doomed, but is also going to emerge from the medieval palings and be absorbed as well into the modern Hebrew national framework. What is taking place here is actually *a civil war among the citizens of the Euphrates country*, with the Egyptians but seeking to exploit this war for their colonial ends.

BEN EZER: What you are terming liberation is liable to appear to others as an aspiration for expansion and conquest.

RATOSH: From a Jewish point of view (and in fact from any denominational approach) it might look like expansion and conquest. But it is not at all like that. I consider the Euphrates country to be one country, from every real, historical, geographical and political standpoint. This is the country that Israel, whether "smaller" or "greater," can not help being an integral part of. Naturally, I aspire, and must aspire, to redeem my country, my entire country, from the darkness of the Middle Ages and from the yoke of foreign, imperialist subjugation. From this point of view and sensibility it is not in the least a matter of expansion and conquest.

BEN EZER: You claim that the same question of religious-community hegemony also exists in Israel today. Why, then, do you prefer Hebrew nationalism to Pan-Arabism?

RATOSH: In the so-called Arab world, Pan-Arabism is not backed up by any secular, modern developed entity or element. So, too, in the social structure, there is no rift between the leadership and the bulk of society, no internal, essential contradiction between them. The leadership is part and parcel of the society. That denominational hegemony — actually tyranny — faithfully reflects the social milieu. With us, that denominational hegemony is in fact in the nature of a foreign, missionary rule. Although the ideologies in Israel are characteristically denominational, and contain all the shortcomings and backwardness of a denominational approach, the quintessence of Israeli society and the historic role that it is fulfilling are chiefly secular and nationalistic. Its level of scientific, technological and social development naturally impels it more and more towards such development. And willy-nilly it is over the character and future of the entire Euphrates country that we are fighting. Thus, the only hope for a positive change in the entire Euphrates country is here.

BEN EZER: A reading of your poem, "The Walker in Darkness," gives the impression that you see war as a metamorphosis in which the Israeli individual discards the relics of his Diaspora Jewish heritage and become part of the proud and ancient Hebrew people. You say:*

> "I am calling to the Hebrews
> To every son of ancients' thew
> Each who strives for truth and glory
> Every son of true eye
> To open eye and heart
> Root out of heart all alien
> Till there be one single heart
> To all this wretched skulking folk
> Human dust in its defilement
> Shattered sects in suffocation
> The noble scion despised
> The mighty folk despoiled —
> To vomit up that poison
> Sucked in with mother's milk
> And all of senility's foreign wisdom
> Threadbare with mold and barreess."

* The following translation, while it is faithful to the sense of the original, is far from doing justice to Mr. Ratosh's strict rhythmic structure, completely Biblical use of language and inspired Psalmic style—Tr.

About war, you write:

> "And every loyal heart and true
> Will mark his brow with blood
> With blood will mark his right hand
> And with heart's blood say amen —
> And consecrated for day of battle
> And consecrated in blood and soul
> In communion with all his brethren
> Brother to brother will show forth
> Brother to brother will speak out
> A pact of brethren each will vow."

And then:

> "And all this wretched, skulking folk
> Whose soul is licking up the dust
> Whose heart is with the hypocrites
> Whose pledge is given to the stranger —
> Will rise like Baal from his blood
> Like Tammuz come back to life,
> See his country goodly and
> Primeval, navel of the world,
> Extending from sea to sea
> From rivers till the ends of earth..."

And further on:

> "Cursed be the sword that shrinks from
> blood
> And cursed be he who cheats his task..."

Tell me, do you really consider constant war in our region to be a good thing?

RATOSH: It seems to me that the question itself arises from a distortion of the meaning of the poem. Since the inception of the new Hebrew nation, we have been embroiled in a triple war or, if you like, in *three wars*. *The first war* is the war inside Palestine, and latterly inside the State of Israel, over the essence of the state: *Hebrew*, i.e. national-secular, or *Jewish*, i.e. denominational-theocratic. This war has taken the form of a constant religious-secular struggle inside the state. It remains within the bounds of a latent war, first of all because the national-secular side is waging it without being clearly conscious — but in the main it is remaining latent because of the second war.

The second war is being waged over the land of the Euphrates and its future — between the new Hebrew nation and Pan-Arabism. This war, too, is being waged from the Hebrew side unwittingly, without a lucid consciousness. (By the way, the Arab side, too, is split over it, both among the states and within each of the states, among the various communities and organizations which are permanently embroiled in hot and cold wars).

The character of this second war is obscured because it is being waged on a denominational basis between Judaism on the one hand and Pan-Arabism on the other, therefore assuming the form of an eternal, immanent war. "Holy War" ("*Jihad*" in Arabic) is an integral part of the Pan-Arabist ideology, while the Jews have the concept of the "War of Commandment" ("*milhemet mitzva*" in Hebrew). The Jews' declared aim is self-defence against Pan-Arabist aggression, and coexistence therewith, which is in the realm of the impossible. The outcome of a Pan-Arabist victory would be the perpetuation of denominational medievalism at home, and imperialist subjugation from outside. Actually, as we have said, in whatever forms it may appear, this is a war over the emergence of a national, secular, democratic society in the entire Euphrates country, of which Israel is but an integral part.

The third war is the war against imperialism from the outside. Initially, it was the Ottoman Empire, then the British Empire, and today it is Egyptian and Russian imperialism. It should be stressed that, within the Euphrates country, only the Hebrew nation has liberated itself under its own power, following the rebellion against the British Empire. Iraq and the Hashemite Kingdom were set up by the British out of imperialist considerations; it was the British who expelled the French from the Levant, not local rebels.

The first-person voice heard in the "Walker in Darkness" psalms is that of the Hebrew warrior who is committed, from birth, to all three of these wars, and it is naturally a poem about this triple war. But its subject is not at all war for its own sake, let alone war under a Jewish banner. The protagonists of this war are not necessarily the descendants of Jews by virtue of being such.

This is the concrete triple war of liberation we have spoken of —
for liberation of the Hebrew nation and the Euphrates country as
a whole from foreign imperialism, from Pan-Arabism and from
Zionism. I might mention that in the Israel Defence Forces there
are serving Druse, Bediun, all kinds of Christians and Moslems,
and people of other extractions, as well, who from a denominational standpoint do not belong to the Jewish community at all.

War as a question of principle seems to me, for us at least, to
be abstracted from all reality, hence irrelevant. The concrete question is always whether a specific war is in line with or runs counter
to historical development and progress. The Hebrew war of libera
tion is without doubt in line with historical development and
progress. Of course, it is not out of the question that wars may
break out in the future between the conflicting interests of a democratic, secular, national Egypt and a Hebrew state possessing a
similar social structure. But that would be like any other war, for
example, between two European states, and not at all a "holy war"
as it is today. I have no pretensions to solving the problem of
eternal peace, from a pacifist standpoint. The war I am speaking
of is, as has been stated, a war of liberation from the yoke of Pan-
Arabism, as well as from the yoke of Zionism and Judaism.

BEN EZER: Don't you fear that the emergence of a new Hebrew
nation in the entire Euphrates country might cause the Jews to
become a "people of overlords" in the region?

RATOSH: You can only say that, viewing the process from a
Jewish point of view, on a denominational basis. From the point of
view that I have the privilege to represent, this war is not a process
of domination, but a process of liberation, of the redemption of
the human being in the Euphrates country on a modern, national,
secular basis. From this point of view, the actual formation of a
new Hebrew nation in the entire Euphrates country is a process
which will embrace more or less all the inhabitants of the country.
It will put an end to any denominational political grouping
(whether Jewish, Pan-Arabist or other) as a surrogate for a shared
national existence. Any thought of a "Jewish people of overlords"
under these circumstances is utterly misguided.

BEN EZER: What in your opinion are the realistic chances for a
peace settlement with the Arabs?

RATOSH: There is no brief for peace with Pan-Arabism. There is no brief for a settlement between "Arabs" and "Jews," between Zionism and Pan-Arabism. It is impossible to make peace with Egypt, for example, so long as it is ruled by Nasser, who is first and foremost the greatest enemy of his country. He has introduced Pan-Arabist self-determination into the constitution of Egypt. This is a severe setback for Egyptian resurgence, completely opposed to the country's character, line of development and progress. All the progenitors of modern Egypt were nationalist Egyptians, explicitly opposed to identification with Pan-Arabism. There is no brief for any peace with a Pan-Arabist movement, which is not and will not be able to be a genuine national society, just as Judaism, too, can not by its very nature be such a society. The foundations of medieval community grouping, whether Zionist or Pan-Arabist, must be demolished, and the whole population be absorbed in one secular, national framework, without difference of extraction or denomination, so that peace may prevail here.

BEN EZER: From its inception, could Zionism's approach to the Arabs have been different?

RATOSH: Zionism, by its very nature, could not have adopted a different approach. What characterizes the Zionist approach (which, as stated, represents grouping on a denominational basis) is a lack of immanent comprehension of the very essence of the new Hebrew nation and of the realities of the Euphrates country, including the essence of the Pan-Arabist world.

BEN EZER: Are you not afraid that the protracted war in which we are engaged will shape a new Israeli human type, all of whose powers are mustered to ensure his physical and national survival, while no universal moral problem concerns him — a human being with narrow horizons?

RATOSH: As for narrow horizons, in so far as that phenomenon exists, it is a denominational curtailment of horizons, the outcome of sectarianism. As for "universalism"—just as no one is biologically simply human, but either a man or a woman, unless he be androgenous, so no one is simply human from a sociological standpoint. Every persons is a member of a certain society, whether it be family, tribe, denomination, community, class or nation. In every period there are progressive social principles and regressive ones.

In our period, in any case with regard to the world outside Europe and North America, it is the national principle that is the progressive and liberating one, while the cosmopolitan course, which for some reason seems to you to be more "ethical," offering broader horizons, is actually a drifting, sterile and, in practice, reactionary course. In any case, that is its actual significance for us. Here, in our part of the world cosmopolitanism is explicitly a reactionary, unrealistic cause, for it does not contribute to, but rather impedes, a national solution and national consolidation. Those who attempt to understand what is going on in our region in terms of some cosmopolitan approach, and to propose solutions in such a spirit, are absolutely mistaken, and ultimately they are supporting imperialist domination from without and medieval backwardness, socially and culturally, at home. Perhaps that is why these cosmopolitan circles have such sympathy for those concepts of Zionism (or Judaism) on the one hand and of Pan-Arabism (or "Palestinism") on the other, which are so utterly muddled from any valid theoretical standpoint.

BEN EZER: What is your stand on the question of the Arab refugees?

RATOSH: In the world of today, there are several tens of millions of refugees, all of whom have been uprooted from the places they lived following international and civil wars. All of them had been inhabitants of their countries for quite a large number of generations. For example, there are about ten million Germans who were uprooted by the last world war; at least fifteen million Indians following the partition of India after the British evacuated; millions that no one has bothered to count in Africa, following the withdrawal of the imperialist powers; as well as all those in Korea and Vietnam. To these may be added entire ethnic populations in the U.S.S.R.: Germans and Tartars who were uprooted from the regions they inhabited and transported, against their will, to east of the Ural River after the Nazi invasion. Israel itself took in hundreds of thousands of refugees from Eastern Europe, and even more from the so-called Arab countries. It is perhaps worth mentioning that the American War of Independence produced a tremendous number of refugees at the time. I believe that about one quarter of the inhabitants of the thirteen colonies adhered to the British Crown and removed, as refugees, to the Crown Colonies in Canada.

The special status of a handful of "Palestinian" refugees is itself based on a fallacious, unrealistic attitude, shared by Zionism on the one hand and Pan-Arabism on the other. It is as though Zionist "invaders" had come from the outside, driven out the inhabitants of the country and settled in their place. What actually happened was *a civil war* (under denominational banners on both sides, as we have stated) between natives of the country come to grips. The real protagonist of the war was the Hebrew generation of natives of the country (with a denominational Zionist leadership, which the Hebrew generation practically forced to declare the establishment of the State). In this civil war, the new Hebrew generation defeated medieval Pan-Arabism. What has made a handful of "Palestinian" refugees, the refugees of this civil war, unique among all the millions of refugees in the world, is the result of that Pan-Arabist and Zionist attitude and the product of international money, especially American money, which provides for entire camps of refugees and perpetuates their existence as professional refugees whose livelihood depends on persisting in their refugee status. This status, or rather plight, was produced by a political refusal on the part of Israel's neighboring states — those same states that inavded Israel at its inception in order to get whatever territorial gains they could, but were defeated — a refusal to asborb these people and normalize their existence, as all the refugees of the world have usually been dealt with. The most patent example of this was in the Gaza Strip, where Egypt ruled as though it were an alien conquered zone, under a military regime with a permanent night curfew, with strict discrimination between its inhabitants and Egyptians, and a ban on emigration to Egypt — all in order to perpetuate, with American funds, the "Palestinian problem." Israel, for example, even as it is presently constituted, is solving the problems of the refugees in Gaza — absorbing them into work, making them into productive human beings. To solve the problems of the refugees it is not necessary, it is just not possible, to bring them to the State of Israel of 1967. The State must be brought to them.

BEN EZER: Is there any place in your outlook for the "Palestinian entity?"

RATOSH: "Palestine" in the so-called Arab world is merely the de-
signation of the province extending from the Jezreel valley and south-
ward, west of the River Jordan. It was in the sense of "province"
that the Arab word "*balad*" was used to designate "Palestine."
There is not here, and there never has been a nationality, a nation,
a political tradition or an ethnic entity. (By the way, almost all the
Arab inhabitants of the valleys, and the coastal region, and a
large proportion of the urban population are the descendants of
immigrants of recent generations). To date, there is nowhere any
clear distinction between a Palestinian movement and a Pan-
Arabist movement. The case on behalf of the "Palestinians" and
the "Palestinian people" was itself introduced in recent years and,
like the slogan of "a pluralistic, democratic, secular state," for
purely propaganda purposes. It is designed to please the Western
ear, a claim based on ostensibly national-territorial grounds in a
manner acceptable to Western political thinking. This case was
worked out following the advice and under the guidance of the
Algerian F. L. N. and was developed by the professional advertising
agencies of Madison Avenue. The sort of "pluralistic, democratic,
secular state" the F. L. N. set up in Algeria is well known:
actual expulsion of the entire non-Moslem population of over half
a million people (and about a million Arab refugees to boot) with
expropriation of their property; and the establishment of a pure
Moslem Pan-Arabist state, practising repression of the Berber
minorities at home and Pan-Arabist imperialism vis-à-vis all
neighboring North African states.

The "Palestinian" slogan has been a felicitous propaganda
stratagem, especially against a Zionism based on Jewish sectarianism. But it can not make something out of nothing. It is based on
the refugee camps, whose continued existence is utterly artificial —
the result of pressure from the so-called Arab states, and maintained
by American funds. In practice, the "Palestinian question" in the
political arena is actually just a question of what the fate of the
districts of Samaria and Judea will be, what state they will belong
to or among which states they will be divided. And too — what
will be the fate of the Jordanian Hashemite Kingdon and the future

of its regime, or, perhaps, more precisely, among which states will it be divided, and how?

Incidentally, the advocates and quasi-advocates of a "Palestinian entity" in Israel mean in fact only a denominational *apartheid:* a weak, Arab-speaking Bantustan, with an Israeli security border on the Jordan, so that Israel's political life will not have to take in a large non-Jewish population, which would hamper Jewish sectarianism in the state. This in practice, is also the background for the "open bridges" policy of the State of Israel, which orients the thinking of the inhabitants of the West Bank towards Amman.

BEN EZER: How does your outlook take in the fact of the existence of Arab terrorism, which they allege to be part of a national war?

RATOSH: Contrary to a prevalent image, which the Arab terror movements are cultivating in their propaganda, these movements are not in the least underground, but are sponsored organizations. They were founded by Nasser Egypt as an instrument to serve his ends, and were recruited by the Egyptian authorities, with personal threats and promises, from the refugee camps in the Egyptian zone of conquest in Gaza. The principal portion of these organizations' budgets comes from the coffers of the governments of of the so-called Arab world, from their inception till this very day, and they operate openly, relying on the cooperation of these governments. The only place in which they are really obliged to operate underground is under Israeli rule, and their operations here are most feeble. They are far less in evidence than the criminals and rioters in American metropolises, for example, and the danger they pose here is far smaller. Their standard of operations and the solidarity among their members are extremely poor. Almost everyone caught invariably informs on all his comrades. The meagre operational capability that the terrorists do have in Israeli territory is based chiefly on their terrorizing the Moslem street by the usually indiscriminate murder of men, women and children. Even this ability to terrorize is founded, to a critical extent, on the Jewish denominational policy that motivates non-Jews to identify with the common enemy. Since Israel did not immediately annex these areas, their populations have reason to worry about the possibility of their being returned to their previous rulers. The return of the Gaza Strip to Egyptian rule in 1957 serves as a stern warning to them. The Egyptians at that time executed and tortured everyone who had previously cooperated with the Israelis.

The terrorist organizations actually exist in only two countries — in the Jordanian Hashemite Kingdom and in Lebanon. In the rest of the so-called Arab states — Egypt, Syria and Iraq — they are either not allowed to function or they are in the nature of irregular troops, under orders to the governments of each of the states and more or less within the frameworks of their armies. They are able to operate in the Hashemite Kingdom and in Lebanon primarily because these are the weakest and smallest of the so-called Arab countries. To be sure, their small armies could cope with the terrorist organizations without a great deal of difficulty, the military power of these organizations being very feeble, but these countries are under constant, heavy pressure from the outside, chiefly from Egypt and Syria, which prevents them from employing their full strength against the terrorists. Outside political pressure is brought to bear on them to come to an understanding with the terrorists, as well as the incited pressure of the Moslem population at home in Lebanon and of the refugees and emigrants from Palestine in Jordan. Owing to this, the terrorist organizations have managed to take over several dozen camps of professional refugees (who live, as we have stated, chiefly on American funds, actually provided to them so that they may persist in their refugee status), scattered east of the River Jordan and in Southern Lebanon. By virtue of this take-over, these two countries are in a state of latent civil war, which erupts from time to time in outbreaks of open hostilities.

BEN EZER: What is the realistic political solution for this, in your opinion?

RATOSH: *A Canaan Federation* among Israel, Lebanon Mount Druse and the Beduin east of the Jordan; annexation of southern Lebanon to Israel, which will free Lebanon to a great extent from the Moslem pressure at home and hence also, on the strength of its treaty with Israel, from Pan-Arabist pressure from the outside, the establishment of Druse autonomy at Mount Druse (south of Damascus) and an alliance with the Beduin east of the Jordan. Such a Canaan Federation would be the beginning of the end of

Pan-Arabism and would solve the refugee problem on an individual basis of productive integration and termination of their refugee status, in the same way that refugee problems have been solved all over the world. It would serve as a basis for the Levant Federation that will redeem the entire country and its entire people from medieval Pan-Arabism at home and thus extricate it from the sphere of imperialist designs from the outside.

Our problem is actually a chapter in the national resurgence of the region which is commonly called "the Middle East," including Greece, Turkey, Iran and Egypt. Actually, it is the "world of Levant" [the Hebrew word for which (*Qedem*) incorporates two meanings: "ancient" and "eastern"]. The countries of the world of Levant are all backward countries, to a greater or lesser extent. Their development and the exploitation of their natural resources lag far behind the standards of the developed countries. Their people are backward in their educational level and in their conceptual world. Their view of the world, as well as their attitude, sensibility, or in fact sense-of-belonging, are derived from the principle of clan and religious-community, rather then territorial-and-national organization. In plain language, the entire world of Levant is still to a large extent submerged in the Middle Ages.

The bone of contention in all the countries of Levant, as well as the touchstone as to the degree of their emergence from the confines of the Middle Ages, is the problem of "Who are we?" — of self-determination.

In Greece: a national resurgence relying on the classic period of Hellenic Greece — or continued reliance on the Christian Orthodox Church, whose Holy Tongue is Greek.

In Turkey: a true Turkish state — as against the Ottoman (Moslem) Empire.

In Iran: an Iranian state — as against a Moslem state.

In Egypt: an Egyptian national resurgence relying on the classic Pharaonic period — or a central state in the Moslem, Arab-speaking world.

And in Israel: a new resurgent nation which, its language being Hebrew and itself having arisen in the ancient land of the Hebrews, relies upon the classic period of the ancient Hebrew nation, which antedates Judaism — or a new version of the classic Jewish, Diaspora oriented period known in Jewish historiography as "the Second Temple period." (Incidentally, the expression "First Temple period" is an outright anachronism. The people of the periods of the Judges and the Kings would never have dreamed of naming their period after a temple).

BEN EZER: Could you, perhaps, formulate your distinction between Hebrews, Jews and Israelis?

RATOSH: In the U. S., the English word "Hebrew" serves as a sort of dignified appellation for the Jews, as does the word "Israelite" in French. But "Hebrews," "Israelis" and "Jews" all derive their original meanings from extremely clear and definitive sources.

"*Hebrews*" (*ha'ivrim*) are all the people of '*Eber*, ('*ever*) which is clearly an eponym. It takes in all the people not only of Judea and Israel, but of Moab, Ammon and Aram as well — from the Egyptian boundary to somewhere near the River Tigris. The term "Hebrews," the Hebrew nation, corresponds to the classic, natural complex that takes in the language of the country "Hebrew," and the Biblical terms "the land of the Hebrews" and "the Hebrews." The people of "Israel" in the eyes of foreigners — the Egyptians, for example — were "Hebrews."

At source "*Yehudi*" (the Hebrew word from which the English "Jew", "Jewry" and "Judaism" are derived) meant only a member of the tribe of Judah ("*Yehuda*"), and at later a period a member of the Judean Kingdom (the kingdom of "*Yehuda*"). The first time the term "*Yehudi*" appeared in its present-day sense was in the Persian period: "Mordechai the Jew" in the *Scroll of Esther*. The Persian period was the actual time of the emergence of Judaism. Judaism came into being among the descendants of several thoussand members of the top Judean nobility, who had been exiled 11 years before the destruction of Jerusalem by the Babylonians. These were the Jehoiachin exiles, who looked down upon the "people of the country," all the rest of the people of Judea, not to speak of the Hebrews. Their descendants fitted in well in the Persian kingdom, and preserved nothing but their community identity, like, let us say, the Parsees in India today. The super-structure of their community existence was the Judaism they had originated, and they projected their conception retroactively upon the past.

"Israel" was originally a Hebrew sub-unit, a federation of a number of Hebrew tribes, and, later on, the Kingdom of Israel, more accurately the Kingdom of Samaria. "The land of Israel" of Ezekiel, for example, does not take in Jerusalem, which is in Judea. In the course of time, like many ancient Hebrew terms, the precise meaning of the appellation "Israel" was corrupted, and came to encompass far more than it ever had at the outset. As a matter of fact, the recent choice of the name "Israel" for our state was knowingly and intentionally that of a vague name, selected for its vagueness in order to evade the natural choice which was then actual — between *"Hebrew state"* (the first slogan of the anti-British demonstrations at the time) and *"Jewish state."* The issue of principle was the difference between a national-secular state and a religious-community state.

BEN EZER: Can people utterly ignore their historic past?

RATOSH: When individuals speak loosely of "historic past," just the "historic past" of a "people," and identify that past by association with a specific grouping of people — they are merely proposing their own group self-determination. Furthermore, they are considering themselves to have a sort of natural right to impose that self-determination of theirs on other people. In our case, this is simply a patent attempt to impose denominational affiliation on Israel.

Perhaps I should cite an example from America. President Kennedy was of Irish extraction. Was he Irish by nationality? President Roosevelt was of Dutch extraction. Was he Dutch by nationality? In so far as these were religious people, it stands to reason that each observed the faith of his forebears, while their "historic past" was not the historic past of their forebears, but the historic past of the United States of America. As to the great-grandchildren, grandchildren and children of an Italian who once emigrated to the U. S. — is their historic past, with which they identify, with which they are supposed to identify, the past of Garibaldi and Mazzini, or of Washington and Jefferson?

BEN EZER: Do you agree that there should grow up in Israel a new generation that lacks all interest in the history of the Jewish people? Is that what you want? Is it conceivable, in your opinion, that in the future there should be no link between the Jew in Israel and his fellow-Jew in the Diaspora? Will two different peoples emerge?

RATOSH: Expect for the advocates of cosmopolitanism, who have, until now at least, proved to be Utopians and at the very best may be thought to constitute an attempt to represent a post-national era which has not yet arrived — why, all of us are pupils of the twentieth century, and even more so preservers of the traditions of the nineteenth-century conception. We tend to view mankind as composed of nations, and in every society that possesses its own identity we see a nationality along the lines of the Western European model. It was in keeping with this trend that people who originated in the Jewish ghetto of Eastern Europe and Austro-Hungary (countries which lagged considerably behind the West in terms of national consolidation) — who had emerged from the confines of medieval Judaism but did not wish to or were not able to assimilate entirely among the people of those countries — tended to see in Judaism, too, a nationality.

It is, of course, possible to speak of a Jewish people. It is also possible to speak of "the people of Jerusalem" or of "business people," But Judaism is not and never has been a nationality. The Jews have never counterposed Judaism to "being French" or "being English" but rather to "the nations" (*goyim*) in general — to all that are not Jewish. To be more precise from an historical standpoint, they counterposed Judaism to Christianity or Islam. This definition and view of Judaism as a religious community has been accepted by Jews and by others, at least by the great majority, throughout the generations and is till this day accepted without any doubt by the great majority of Jews outside of Israel. (In Israel, in point of fact, Jews are considered chiefly as material for building the state). Mendes France is undoubtedly, in his own eyes, too, a member of the French nationality. But he is still a Jew. The over-whelming majority of American Jews are considered, and see themselves as members of the American nationality. But they are still Jews.

Judaism is not a nationality. The sociological definition most suitable for it is the "*millet*" of the defunct Ottoman Empire. In that empire there existed a society of a clearcut medieval pattern, composed of a mosaic of religious communities, each a closed, endogamous unit, with its own judiciary system, collective responsibility and religious and secular leadership. Judaism as a religious-community unit, as a "millet," was not exceptional in the Ottoman Empire, just as it was not exceptional in the framework of medieval society, a society based on the religious community. Judaism is not exceptional or a "problem" anywhere except in the new national society that is based on national principles.

The generation that is growing up among us, the large majority of whom are secular, do not feel identified with the history of the Jewish people in the Diaspora. The tie between them and the Diaspora Jews is most slack and is getting slacker. They are aware of a different identity for themselves. That is a fact. This fact is bewailed by numerous Jews and Zionists, who have been alarmed about it for decades, even before the Israeli-born placed the concept of "Zionism" in quotation marks and thereby provided a popular expression for their sense of its foreignness. In recent years the Jewish authorities have introduced "Jewish consciousness" studies into the schools, in the spirit of Jewish and Zionist theory — but to no avail. The estrangement of the Israel-born from "Judaism" is in point of fact a clear testimony to how alien the imposers of "Jewish consciousness" are to the Israel-born.

If we free ourselves from all sorts of Jewish and Zionist theories about what supposedly "should" emerge in this country, and observe the facts themselves, we will be able to see that, as the national idea spread eastward, starting at the beginning of the nineteenth century, there began to spring forth in this country, as in many immigration-based countries in recent centuries, *a new nation, the new Hebrew nation*. This nation emerged, owing to various circumstances, *in the classic Hebrew language*, which was the only common language of the various Jewish communities, and *in the classic country of the Hebrews*, which was a region devoid of nationality under an empire to which nationalism was alien. The formation of the new nation coincided with a phenomenon of national resurgence, whose pattern is familiar from several European countries, relying on the classic Hebrew period: the time of the Judges and Kings, in Biblical terminology. Owing to this juxtaposition, the first new Hebrew generation was imbued already with a sense of unique Hebrew identity, which did not take four or five generations to emerge, as is usual in immigration-based countries.

That, in my opinion, is the reality. Incidentally, people from the New World and from Europe are far more open to viewing things in this spirit than others — with the exception, of course, of many Jews. The main fact is that there is no *national* identity between the natives of this country and other people. And, of course, there cannot be a national identity on our part with people whose nationality is foreign, as the nationality of the Jews of the world usually is. As to history, it can not be, of course, that members of a specific nationality should see any identity between their own national history and the history of some religious community like Jewry.

BEN EZER: In recent years, a different distinction has been made. The Jewish intellectual in the western world has become a symbol of "the stranger," the "outsider" in the world of literature and thought. He has a "message" for the nations and for his people. But the Jewish intellectual in Israel is subjected to the pressures of awareness of siege, wars, and sustained peril to the existence of the state. He has therefore become, whether consciously or not, part of the Establishment sharing the majority's sense of responsibility, and in most cases incapable of a critical, radical stand.

RATOSH: I do not consider myself qualified to discuss the question of whether Western Europe or the western world have in fact gotten past the national era and are now at the dawning of some post-national era. Therefore I will not presume to judge whether that Jewish intellectual you speak of is indeed the bearer of "*a message* for the nations and for his people*," or whether he is just a socially marginal product of degeneration, as were to a great extent those like him between the two world wars, who objectively assisted in the outbreak of the war. This entire discussion is irrelevant from my point of view. What is clear to me is that the world of Levant, and it may be all of what is termed "the third world," in fact the entire world excepting perhaps the classic West, is at the dawning of the age of nationalism. Any judgement by medieval-community or cosmopolitan-post-industrial criteria is alien to it, is incapable of grasping its actual problems, not to speak of the possibility of solving them. I would consider myself absurd were I to presume to preach to Americans, for example, whether Jewish or not, how they should view themselves and how they should deal with their problems according to my view of them.

The danger that I see in the Zionist mentality, here with us, lies in the attempt to impose a Jewish sectarian and international identity upon us. And if there is a problem of "Levantinism" here — *that* is its origin. Levantines are people who are brought up on cultural values that are alien to their experience and to their mental make-up, on the disparity between talk and studies which have become meaningless empty phrases in their application, and the reality of their life and mind. The classic Levantine was not the *fellah*. He was the city-dweller who lived in the feudal Ottoman reality with a superfical, artificial, spurious veneer of "French consciousness."

Incidentally, with all the awarness of siege, wars and sustained peril to the existence of the state, and despite the hardened Establishment in Israel and the direct and indirect establishment control over most of the jobs and sources of livelihood — it seems to me that both of us, you and I, despite all the elementary differences between our approaches but with the fact that characterizes both of us that we are extremely aware of the problems of the society to which we belong — it seems to me that we might serve as a living proof that the intellectual in Israel is definitely capable of an extremely radical, critical stand. And I think that both of us know quite well — your collection of interviews is itself a rather partial evidence of this — that we are not at all the only ones voicing dissident views.

BEN EZER: Isn't it conceivable, in your opinion, that there might evolve within Judaism a new secular people, whose affinity to national self-determination would not be religiously oriented?

RATOSH: It appears to me that the definition of Jewry as a *community*, and the realization that it exists in terms of *sectarianism* are far more basic and essential than any definition or realization of the terms of *religion*, which is its superstructure. Nothing that *can* or is likely to develop *within* Judaism can develop except in these terms — some *community* though it be other, some *religion* though it be different. But what has actually arisen here in this country, though this sociological fact has not yet won general public recognition, is a new *nationality*. The fact that the vast major-

ity of the members of this new *Hebrew* nationality are biologically
the offspring of Jews has nothing to do with their group affiliation,
just as the fact that vast majority of early Americans were the
descendants of Englishmen and Protestants was not capable of
hampering the emergence and existence of the new American
nation.

Viewing Judaism from the outside, there is no positive difference
between the *streimel*-clad Neturei Karta (members of a fanatic
Orthodox religious sect) with their long ear-locks, the "Frenchmen
(or Americans or others) of the Mosaic faith," and the leftist or
other Zionists. Anyone who considers the main thing about Judaism to be not its religious formulas and its religious milieu, but its
sociological community quintessence, cannot see any definitive
importance in all these differences, which are so grave in terms of
the community's subjective existence. These are but intra-commun-
ity problems, which are of no consequence.

BEN EZER: How do you define Zionism, and what is your new
Hebrew outlook's criticism of it?

RATOSH: If we wish to sum up faithfully the common denominator of Zionism from its inception, with all its currents, parties and
conceptions, which quite often discredited each other's Zionism,
it seems to me that we will arrive at a somewhat paradoxical
formulation: Zionism is essentially an attempt to provide an
undefined answer (from a "spiritual center" to an empire) to an
undefined problem (the Jewish question, all depending in the
various attitudes towards the question of what Judaism is) of an
undefined human grouping (all the Jews, according to the various
conceptions of "Who is a Jew?" — or portions thereof) in an
undefined territory (from Western Palestine, or a portion thereof —
to the borders of Egypt and the Euphrates).

If you wish, I shall enumerate the three fundamental premises
of Zionism:

Contrary to the considered opinion of the large majority of
Jews and non-Jews in all periods including our own, all Zionists
hold that Judaism is a nationality. The fact is that from the standpoint of normal nationalism one may find in many nations examples
paralleling the characteristics of Judaism. For example, many
nations have been deprived of national independence. Most of the

Irish live outside their homeland, and their language is a foreign one: English and not Gaelic. In the Zionists' view, such examples confirm the opinion that Judaism is a nationality, too.

All Zionists are convinced that that "Jewish nationality'" has a "national tie" with the "land of Israel" as a "homeland." The question of what a "homeland" is, what the nature of that "national tie" is, and what that country and its boundaries are (some part of the country west of the Jordan without Sinai, both banks of the Jordan, from the Nile to the Euphrates, the borders of 1967 or those of 1947 west of the Jordan) — in these questions, too, just as in the matter of "Who is a Jew?" there is not a trace of agreement among the Zionists.

All Zionists believe that that (undefined) "homeland" is destined to solve that "Jewish problem" (which, as we have noted, is also undefined) either from a physical standpoint for all the Jews or for the "superfluous Jews" in every single country, or in terms of some religious or spiritual problem of Judaism.

Perhaps this is the place to mention that the "Jewish problem" itself has always been the problem of the non-Jews, of the nations of the world. For the Jews, it has only been a problem from the time and to the extent that they emerged from the confines of the traditional life and prior to their assimilating entirely into society at large.

BEN EZER: Do you deny that Zionism brought to pass the establishment of the State of Israel?

RATOSH: It is worth stressing that anyone who represents the establishment of the State of Israel and the evolution of the Hebrew population in this country prior to the establishment of the state, as being the outcome of Zionism is just mistaken. He is, in fact, being deceived by Zionist propaganda. At least till the establishment of the state, Jewish migration to Palestine was in an overwhelming proportion solely the outcome of the Jews' need to migrate, in so far as the ground was slipping away for chances of continued survival in East Europe. The very dates of the waves of migration testify clearly to this link, from the pogroms in Russia in the '80s of the last century till the refugees from Hitler. In all these refugee crises Jews migrated, with no distinction between Zionists and non-Zionists, both to Palestine and to other countries.

And in all other, normal times, the migration to this country, without distinction between Zionists and non-Zionists, was virtually nil. It is worth stressing that till World War I, when the gates of migration were generally open, the Jews who migrated to this country comprised an almost insignificant percentage of the total Jewish migration — in fact no more than the number of Jews who migrated, for example, to Egypt during the same time span, and incomparably less than Jewish migration, not only to the United States or to Latin America, but also to the various Western European countries. The number of those who might be termed immigrant "pilgrims," whether secular or quasi-religious, was perhaps one in a thousand.

Zionism is the product of the Jewish Diaspora. Its protagonists were the lower-middle-class Jew who, following the dissolution of the medieval frameworks of the Jewish ghettos of Western Europe and the *stetls* of Eastern Europe, were unable or unwilling to assimilate entirely into the framework of life of the nations among whom they lived. The objective sociological function of Zionism was to answer the individual need-to-belong of these middle-class Jews, to afford the members of the Jewish community a feeling of a sort of national status in a world that was conceived as a world of nationalities. The Zionist movement (with all its organizations and ideologies), being the product of a religious-community, non-national milieu, could not be and was not a national movement. Its role among the Jews undergoing secularization has been akin to that of the belief in the next world, in the millenium, amongst believers, for the purpose of coming to terms with the Jew's life in this world, a life of Diaspora. As in the Christian world, so too in the Jewish religious world, there have arisen singular individuals, as well as marginal groups, whose belief in the millenium has removed them, usually for a brief span, from a sense of reality and a realization of the realistic function of belief in the millennium for the common weal. But these have been the exceptions. So, too, functional principles, the greater part of Zionist energy and thought has been devoted to current affairs, to enhancing the natural Diaspora life of Jewry. The tie with Palestine has only obliged Zionism to dominate Jewish life in this country as far as possible, and keep it under its sway. The "homeland" of Zionist terminology has been but a secular Jewish surrogate for the "Holy Land" of religious Judaism, and the Zionist monetary support of Israel is of a piece with the traditional Jewish support of the religious contingent in the Holy Land.

BEN EZER: What, in your opinion, are the real chances for the Hebrew outlook to triumph in Israel?

RATOSH: As I have already mentioned, owing to the juxtaposition of the birth of the new Hebrew nation with the process of national resurgence, the sense of Hebrew identity and Hebrew consciousness already formed the first generation of those born in this country at the beginning of this century.

This first generation of Hebrews — whose moving spirit and symbol was Absalom Feinberg, the founder of the Nili organization which (headed by Aaron Aaronson) fought for the liberation of this country at the time of World War I — was repressed by the Zionist Establishment at the time of the mass (by the criteria of those times) migration of the beginning of the '20s.

The emergence of the State of Israel was a direct function of the crystallization of the second Hebrew generation (those who grew up here in the '30s and the '40s) who in large measure were the offspring of the migrants from the beginning of the '20s. It was this generation whose pressure forced the underground movements to be set up to wage the war that ultimately brought about the emergence of the state — this generation that originated the Canaanite theory that crystallized Hebrew awareness to the point of total self-recognition and self-determination, and which was to have a deep influence among the young intelligentisa.

It was this second generation that compelled the Zionist Establishment to declare the state. But — the state was dominated by that same Zionist Establishment, and the large wave of migrants brought to this country immediately upon the establishment of the state swamped this generation and set back for a full generation the formative process of the native-born and of Hebrew self-awareness. (It is as though 200 million people had been introduced in the U.S. all at once, all of them speaking only foreign languages, and the overwhelming majority of them coming from backward countries — and they had immediately been granted the franchise.)

Today, the migrants from the first years of the state are mostly fathers of Israel-born sons; a third Hebrew generation is arising. There will never again come to this country migratory waves sufficiently large to swamp it and its Hebrew national consciousness. In the nature of things, it is going to take its own fate and the fate of its country into its own hands. Zionist consciousness and Jewish consciousness are an obstacle to this natural crystallization, to the taking root of national consciousness in this country, and are the foes of Hebrew self-determination and all it dictates in the sphere of political practice, in culture and in the economy. The war of 1967 effectively demonstrated to the Hebrew youth the horizons open to us since the inception of the new Hebrew nation, and the gravity of the Jewish obstacle — the price that we are required to pay for Zionism, to borrow your term.

God Speaks To Us With Just Two Words — Love and Death

Interview with Pinhas Sadeh

(This interview was held in June, 1970)

BEN EZER: What do you see in the war between Israel and the Arabs?

SADEH: War is neither good nor bad. Nor is peace good or bad. Both must be examined on their own merits. As for war, it is inherent in the makeup of humanity and nature: we didn't create it and we won't do away with it. History and nature are no cocktail party but a continuous, shadowy struggle that expresses the essential condition of man, a condition which includes death, which comes upon all of us sooner or later and is part of the mystery of existence. I think that God speaks to us with just two words — one of them is love and the other death. All the other words are irrelevant. And the more I think about it the harder it is to assume that God needs two different words, so maybe what appear to us as two different words are really only one.

As for the "War of the Jews," it has been the Jewish people's histori> destiny to return to the Land of Israel and to have to fight — for its life, for the soil (and the soil is a very important thing — it is our mother). Then fight we must. And as for death, we will die in the end anyway, with or without wars.

But the question is really this: if you fight then what are you fighting for? And if you live in peace, how is such a life to be lived? I heard that not long ago someone asked the Chief of Staff, Lt. Gen. Haim Barlev, "Is it right for life to be going on the way it is in Tel Aviv while each day soldiers are being killed at the Suez Canal?"

235

To which he answered, "Why, isn't that why the soldiers are fighting on all the borders — so life in Tel Aviv can go on the way it is?"

With all my esteem for the Chief of Staff as an army man, I ask, "Who is he and what is his authority to decide that life here should go on the way it is?" Because if life here is to continue the way it is now, there is nothing worth fighting for. Better to come to some sort of an arrangement with the Arabs whereby they will have pity on us and permit this sort of life in Tel Aviv to go on, and I think they will agree, because this life of ours here is pitiful indeed, and isn't Allah known as "He who is merciful and compassionate."

And still people want to hold onto all this big beautiful country — Bethlehem, Shechem, Hebron and Jerusalem. And this is essentially no different from the first impulse to settle here on the land in the days of Petah Tikva and Degania. Very fine and good. But you have to remember that the impulse and rationale to come here and settle had its roots and origin in the Bible and the Prophets. Nor is any other rationale possible, because living here was another nation, no less human in any respect than the Jews. But now when I look around me I see that the reality of life here is utterly remote from the spirit of the Prophets. So what good is a victory over the Egypt outside of us if we are thralls to the Egypt within, to that "Land of onions and cucumbers," the flesh pot with its golden calf, idols of silver, commercialization and emptiness. Thus people are making a jest of their very rationale for war, and in the long run are cutting the ground out from under their own feet. For this ground is the Land of the Prophets, and if the people will not be loyal to it it will be cut out from under their feet.

BEN EZER: Thus would it be right to say that you consider the State of Israel in its present form an absurdity?

SADEH: There is nothing on earth that does not have something of the absurd about it, nor is there anything devoid of divine significance. Even the feather of a bird does not fall by accident, and since we don't know its significance we also don't know the difference between the fall of a feather and the fall of a kingdom. Of the mighty kingdom of Babylon for instance, there remains today no more than there does of the birds that nested in the trees on the banks of the river Euphrates. So it was and so it always will be, and the same grass will cover both the whorehouses and the houses of parliament. Which goes to prove, incidentally, that in the final analysis spiritual prostitution pays no better than its physical counterpart. At any rate, as far as the State of Israel is concerned, it is necessary, of course, that the Jews at long last have a place in which they can live and survive, but now that this has been taken care of there is no longer anything exalted in the State itself, and it is not an ideal. All States are both stupid and stultifying, and the modern ones even more so than those of antiquity or the middle ages, seeing as they are in essence commercial and mercantile. On the one hand the ideal is to create more, to produce more, to export more, and on the other hand to *consume* more (even "culture" has become a consumer product, its value measured in terms of market demand). This is known at present as "raising the standard of living" (if you can call it living). The State is producing a type of person who is sated and supercilious, and this makes me sick. The State of Israel's ideal is to be a little America, and while its inhabitants may have the right to so desire, it is a jest to maintain that this is the vision of the Prophets. I touched on this in my poem "Jerusalem." I think that the most genuine action the people here in this nation can take with regard to the Bible and themselves is to consign it to the flames. To search out, seize and burn every single copy down to the last one. To completely obliterate.

BEN EZER: In your book *Life as a Parable* you talk about the day in 1948 you enlisted for the War of Independence. I would like to quote the passage:

"I sat lost in thought, wrapped in heavy loneliness. I thought sadly that I was going to die, to die in the wrong battle. That national war had no meaning for me and I did not see anything that I should fight for. My real enemies were lurking for me in another place, in the hidden darkness of the soul. It did not matter to me who reigned in the city, it did not matter to me which soldiers the masses would flock to see parading, it did not matter to me if they burned the theatres, the universities, the post offices and the newspaper offices, it did not matter to me if the ministers and scribes of the State were circumcised or not. For what is the statehood and what is exile? This existence itself is the true exile."

(*Life as a Parable* by Pinhas Sadeh. Translated by Richard Flantz. Anthony Blond. London, 1966. p. 96)

The question is, do you stand behind these words today?

SADEH: I do not attach much value to any answer I may make now, because what is really important is what I felt and expressed at that moment of actual life, not my opinion today about what I lived and felt then. Life and feeling — it is they that are true, nor does their truth depend on anybody's opinion, not even my own. To the point of the matter, the universities, for example, are temples of sophistry, (as Jeremiah put it, "what wisdom is in them?") and I had no urge to die in their defense. (I wanted to live a little longer because I felt the need to write a poem which to my way of feeling was more important from the standpoint of the heritage of the biblical spirit than anything being taught in the universities, and indeed that day I wrote *Parables of the Virgins* and then went out and enlisted). And as for the ministers, organs and culture of the State, Weizmann once said (I believe it was to Balfour) that "We may be the sons of rag pickers but the grandsons of the Prophets." This is all very flattering to everyone concerned but allow me to ask: If we are the grandsons of the Prophets, where are the grandsons of those who persecuted and killed the Prophets, who after all constituted the majority? Did they vanish with the Ten Lost Tribes? The reason I feel so alienated and inconsequential is because the grandsons of the prophet killers have, to use Elijah's phrase, both "killed and also taken possession."

BEN EZER: On June 16, 1970 the parliamentary correspondent of the daily *Ha'Aretz* reported that a cerain non-clerical member of the Knesset quoted with some bitterness a statement by the Lubavitcher Rebbe that on a certain day Israel suffered relatively a high number of casualties at the Suez Canal because of a "breach in the wall" of the laws regarding conversion to Judaism, that is the violation of one of the laws of the Torah in the modern State of Israel. To which one of the Religious members (a rabbi himself) replied that the Rebbe had merely paraphrased Isaiah: "If you are willing and obedient you shall eat the good of the land, but if you refuse and rebel you shall be devoured by the sword." What do you say about this?

SADEH: To my mind the opinion of those who take issue with the Rebbe is of no value, and the Rebbe's opinion is also far from my own, but I will accept what Isaiah said word for word. Perhaps it will sound fantastic and unrealistic now that psychology, academism and journalism have gnawed through the natural mode of thought like an all-consuming eczema, but I hold the view of the Biblical Prophets (for who am I to differ) that if man will be unworthy of the land the land will vomit him up, and if he will violate the laws of the Lord the Lord will raise against him the scepter of his wrath. This will not come about from today to tomorrow — it will not be a one-time miracle. But the situation today will not endure for very long.

On the other hand — and it may be cruel to say this — but if we take a non-humanistic view (and I can cry at the sight of a small child in pain — what I am referring to is not my emotions but my attempts to understand existence, the globe of this earth, during this wink of an eye that we call life) then the greatest value going today in this country is war. As far as I'm concerned the established Jewish religion is emptied of its vitality as are all the artistic, literary, and the other "spiritual" manifestations here. Neither the literature, the art nor the religion here are placing man in juxtaposition with his essential situation — the riddle of death and the question of life. The only thing still expressing itself humanly, expressing the values, is war. War is the real book of life and death, the literature and art of today, now that literature and art are no longer carrying out their function of a constant juxtaposition of man with his essential situation. This is cruel, perhaps, and sad.

BEN EZER: In your opinion, what has been the sin of literature in this respect?

SADEH: From the time I learned to read, Hebrew literature (with the exception of three or four isolated names) has stultified two generations of youngsters and given them a distorted outlook on life. It has been preoccupied with social issues in the most circumscribed and provincial sense, and shows all the corrupt manifestations of self-satisfaction, smugness, and the sort of relationships that arise between members of the Establishment in a small and institutionalized society.

When it paid, socially, to write about the Palmach they wrote about the Palmach, and then about the State or the War of Independence or the kibbutz or the Six Day War and so on and so forth. All of which is despicable, not only from the standpoint of esthetics but morally and fundamentally, and I'll tell you why: because he who does so is thereby brazenly proclaiming his denial of the power, independence, supreme authority and certainly the divine origin of the spirit, that he considers literature a kind of prostitute whose favors are sold in the marketplace, a commercial product whose value depends on consumer demand only. To my innermost feeling this is an atrocity. And the same is true of all the other fashionable kinds of writing intended to supply the public's need. For instance when that public's taste became a bit more refined it felt a need to trade the Palmach scrivening in for something more in keeping with its new mode of life, i. e. writing that is more intellectual, that lets you pick away a bit at its "symbols," "motifs" and other witticisms, while sitting comfortably in your slippers, and of course this has its purveyors as well. This kind of writing is suited for slippers just as that of twenty years ago was suited for sandals. And to do this in the tongue of the Prophets! Why, all this is so remote from life, from love, suffering, compassion, genuine spiritual aspirations, from the essential condition of man; all this demands nothing and arouses nothing except a mild mental titillation among some critics and readers. And the same is true of most — though not all— of the poetry, which today is nothing more than witty feuilletons in verse, and in fact its writers no longer even take the trouble to make it rhyme, as this is no longer in fashion.

And thus people have been living, and dying, in their beds or in the wars — with no understanding, and not only have they not known the answers, they have not even known that the questions existed! Such a literature is a betrayal. And to betray a man is a whole lot more terrible than to betray a State, because the man is God's representative on earth while the State is merely an abstract concept. A literature that flings mud in people's eyes in order to conceal God from them is anti-religious by its very essence. Yet God cannot be concealed, because he manifests himself not in words but in his Being and his deeds, in that a man lives or dies. Nor will these villifiers of the name of Heaven, these false prophets, gain anything by it because there is no profit in sin. In its very essence sin is identified with loss and not with profit. Sin is nothingness.

And since the spirit has not spoken to man, nor those who drape themselves in spiritual pretexts, life itself is what speaks to him, with no go-between. And right now it speaks to him through war. War is the book now being read by young and old. And it tells things the way they are — struggle, death, love, death, death.

BEN EZER: On June 14, 1970 *Ha'Aretz* carried an item about an Israeli raid on Egyptian positions in the northern sector of the Suez Canal, an operation in which four of our men were killed:

> When the Israeli soldiers returned from the invasion of the Egyptian bunkers early Friday morning the first thing they said on reaching shore was "What's the score?"
> The invading troops who had missed the broadcast of the soccer game between Israel and Mexico (in the world cup playoffs) wanted to hear as much as possible about the Israeli showing.
> Next morning during the debriefing the men wanted to hear a rundown of the results on the radio. A transistor radio was brought into the room but its volume was insufficient. A bullhorn was placed in front of it, so that all those present could hear. The debriefing stopped for a number of minutes while the men who took part in the invasion listened to the results from Mexico. Then it continued as before.

In my opinion this merely confirms what the Chief of Staff said. These youngsters are clutching at the straws of everyday life as an escape from the terrors of war. They are fighting in order that life may go on as usual, and to them the soccer scores are a toehold, a way back to a quiet, sane world.

SADEH: To my mind this is not what the Chief of Staff had in mind. Yet I am not prepared to construe what it does mean, though I see in it signs of things to come.

I said that war is the book being read by the young Israeli, one that describes things as they are — struggle, death and love (the absence or remoteness of love are sometimes its manifestations). But since reality is a condition of constant flow and change, a continuous springing up of life from within death, the question is what will the future bring? And this is a riddle. It is known that the Messiah must sit among the poor of Rome, dressed in rags and stinking of pus. That which is holy can only spring from amidst the places of bottom-most darkness. About this Nathan of Gaza wrote in *Derush HaTaninim* ("Treatise on the Dragons") which I quote in *Life as a Parable* at the end of the chapter on Judaism:

> "Know then, that the soul of King Messiah is in the lowest larva, for as the primeval snake came into being in the form of a larva, so too the soul of King Messiah is shaped and comes into being in the infinite Will, and it preceded the creation of the world and exists within the great abyss..." (*Life as a Parable*, 1958. p. 139. Anthony Blond, London, 1966).

It may be that precisely amid a very dark and oppressive reality — perhaps the abyss of the present-day negation (the liquidation of traditional religion, the bankruptcy of culture and literature) perhaps precisely here there lies hidden, like a very tiny seed, the tree and fruit of the future. Such a thing does not come smoothly or easily, and under no circumstances does it ride the wooden horse of statements by intellectuals and journalists; rather it must sprout forth amid terrible pangs of labor and travail, perhaps grave disaster. Because though the divine seed is one of loving kindness, its springing forth from within the earth must be bound up with a terrible struggle, one which appears to be hopeless. Hope may be possible, though at the moment I have no light one way or another. There have been a few isolated moments, though, when the thing seemed to me possible. A certain incident in reality (and I think every man should refer and relate only to what he knows, rather than to sophistries) — and in those moments it really did seem to me that there existed the possibility of affirmation. But there is also the other, and terrible possibility, and the question is which one of them will win out. The forces that are inherent in the Jewish race are certainly not being expressed by anything that is literary or artistic, on the face of it, but perhaps only by the facts of life itself, of which war is one.

BEN EZER: What do you read in this book entitled War?

SADEH: Allow me to quote you a passage from the Bible:

"And Jacob was left alone. And there wrestled a man with him until the breaking of the day. And when the man saw that he prevailed not against Jacob, he touched the hollow of his thigh, and Jacob's thigh was put out of joint as he wrestled with him. And he said, 'Let me go, for the day is breaking.' But Jacob said, 'I will not let you go, unless you bless me.' And he said to him, 'What is your name?' And he said, 'Jacob.' Then he said, 'Your name shall no more be called Jacob, but Israel, for you have striven with God and with men, and have prevailed.' Then Jacob asked him, 'Tell me, I pray, your name.' But he said, 'Why is it that you ask my name?' And there he blessed him. So Jacob called the name of the place Peniel, saying 'For I have seen God face to face and my life is preserved.' And the sun rose upon him. . .'' (Genesis 32; 24–31).

And now I'll tell you what I read in these words:

"And Jacob was left alone." His remaining *alone* is something essential — in fact it is indispensable. "Wrestled until the breaking of the day"—the struggle is shadowy, savage and prolonged. "And Jacob's thigh was put out of joint" — the struggle involved great suffering and agony. "And he said 'I will not let you go unless you bless me' " — Jacob will not forego his struggle merely in order to achieve peace for its own sake; he wants the blessing that will arise from the struggle itself — a blessing that is the fruit of suffering and war. And the angel says to him "For you have striven with God and with men" — the struggle with men is not something in its own right but has another aspect, namely that the struggle is always with God as well. The outward struggle is with men, while within it there is the struggle with the angel of God. Then Jacob says to him, "Tell me, I pray, your name."

Here he errs because of the limitations of his human understanding. He wants the name — the outward, rational appellation. But the angel declines to give it to him because the inward meaning can by no means be within the realm of rational concepts, culture and sophistry. "And there he blessed him." Though he does not tell him the name he gives him the blessing as a result of the night of struggle and terror. And then it says, "So Jacob called the name of the place Peniel" — only after he has gone through the struggle can he give the land a name. He relates to the land not as something to be taken for granted but as a place embodying the divine presence, just as he too now is called by a new name. And then he states "For I have seen God face to face and my life is preserved." Here I think the explanation must be quite the opposite of the conventional, rational one. It is not that his life was preserved *despite* the fact that he saw God face to face, but rather only after he had seen God did his life have any real salvation. And then it says "The sun rose upon him." This is the only real salvation.

BEN EZER: You are trying to give an apocalyptic significance to sad and secular matters like war, death and day-to-day life which somehow always drags on.

SADEH: A short time ago I was in Genoa, in the dining room of a small, cheap hotel. About half a dozen young fellows and girls were sitting around talking. As it happened, at the moment the television had a film about the Warsaw Ghetto. No one there took any interest, because they didn't find it amusing. And you saw an old Jew walking with a yellow Star of David and up comes a German soldier and shoots him in the head. All of a sudden I said to myself, "No! This must never happen again, ever. Even if it means the entire Middle East will be destroyed, or even a nuclear war. By all means!"

Now you know, I have never written a single word, poem or book of patriotism either national or Jewish. I have always lived and written in complete opposition to the society in which I live.

A young woman friend of mine, whose feminine intuition I value highly, once told me that the excitement that seized hold of the entire Christian world on the eve of the Six Day War was really a cover-up for something a whole lot deeper and less conscious, namely a fervent anticipation that here at long last the Jews were going to be liquidated, for good.

Two weeks ago I was in Barcelona for the Corpus Christi ceremony, and I saw just what a living experience it was for the people there, crossing themselves and singing in the streets. And then I understood just how badly hurt they were by the fact that there were Jews in the world, and organized as a nation no less, of whom it could be said, and they could say of themselves, that they were the neighbors of Jesus. For these Christians Jesus is the last hope, their salvation in the next world amid the hardships of this, while for the Jews he is merely their old neighbor from Nazareth. And this is a lot more serious than the crucifixion was, because the crucifixion after all was part and parcel of Jesus' career and way of life, the "cup he had to drink," while the existence of the Jews as such is a fact of profound, abysmal gravity for Christendom and for the individual Christian. And every Christian is a Christian, even if he is a Marxist, etc., just as every Jew is a Jew. Because it really boils down to a matter of race and spirit, of instincts, of the last moment before death (and essentially, every moment is the last one before death).

BEN EZER: So what do you conclude?

SADEH: In view of all this perhaps we can consider the circumstances of the war between the Jews and Arabs in an entirely different light. Contrary to the Arabs' charge about the Jews being agents of the Western world perhaps the strange, fantastic truth is that it is the Arabs who are agents of the Western world, servants of Christianity and imperialism. Actually, the dispute between the Jews and Arabs is a very superficial one. The real conflict is that between the Christians and Jews. The Arabs are the emissaries of the Christian world's need to liquidate the phenomenon of the Jews, especially in its present, incredibly provocative form of the Return to Zion, to Jerusalem and to Nazareth. The Arabs are pandering to the Catholic world's hope of killing the Jews off one by one. While they do not have the strength to eliminate Israel at one blow they express their intentions by the daily killing of three or four of its citizens and by an attempt to liquidate them all every few years in a general war.

And so that all this unconscious activity of theirs, this mission of historic destiny which operates *in profundis* will be understood neither by them nor others, the middle-man in this matter is the strangest one imaginable — Marxist Communism (which in actual fact is impelled by the spirit of Russian Orthodox Christianity). This is the mediator between the Arabs and Christendom in implementing this fantastic historic process. The Arabs are serving the absolute need of the Christian world to destroy the Jews.

I have always had a sense of the central and extreme importance of Jesus, who is an absolute focal point — a keystone — in Jewish history. The historical attempt of the Jews, both at the time and ever since, to place him outside the annals of the nation, did not succeed and was ineffectual. My attitude toward Jesus has always been in the nature of a living, intense, personal experience — in my writing and of course in my life — in the difficult and wonderful hours. Yet now when I consider the question you have raised from the historical standpoint I see that here too there springs forth, and from angles which surprise even me, the figure of Jesus, who in a certain sense, from a viewpoint which is perhaps a Jewish one, is the largest question mark of all, but perhaps, who knows, also the greatest exclamation point of all.

BEN EZER: I recall that in the book *Conversations at Midnight with Pinhas Sadeh* by Yosef Mundy, you said: "In my eyes Jesus is a human being, an Israeli boy who lived in Nazareth or Bethlehem, suffered, loved, said what he said and sometimes even cracked jokes." Could you elaborate?

SADEH: I am surprised that no one has noticed his sense of humor, which was occasionally quite savage. For example one time a beautiful woman (it may have been Mary Magdalene) came to him, poured costly perfume oil on his feet and wiped them dry with her hair. Judas Iscariot, who was the group's treasurer, got angry and said it would have been better to sell the oil and give the money to the poor. To which Jesus replied: "Buddy, the poor won't run away, they'll always be here, but me — here today and tomorrow who knows where I'll be." He didn't use exactly these words, but that was the gist of it. There are other places with humor that is deep and complex, but I won't go into it here. And in the end he was crucified and died. On the other hand, Jesus is also the greatest symbol of man's condition on earth. That is, whether we like it or not he lives inside of every man, myself included. At certain moments in my life I identify with him, insofar as I identify with myself. And inasmuch as I forget myself, I forget him. And I forget myself when the hustle and bustle of the outside world, false and evanescent, confuses and scares me and conspires against me. I try to make a reply to Jesus, a reply to what he says to me. And not only to him but to all who lived in previous generations and have spoken to me. It is they who are my true listeners, my judges and even my critics. The myth of Jesus repeats itself in every man. After all, every man goes through the world bearing his suffering and hoping for redemption and in the end is crucified alone. Jesus was a man just like any other. He was *the* man.

BEN EZER: You said before "or set off a nuclear war." You seem to have a predilection for catastrophe.

SADEH: A few months ago I received a visit from an English chap I had never met before. He was just back from a trip to India. At one time, it seems, he had been a poet, but gave it up. In his opinion Jesus, Beethoven, Christianity — all the previous cultures and religions — were completely dead. He felt we were now living in a new era. He did not believe in individual creation, the written word, but only in living encounters with people, even via the mass communication media. This Englishman had joined a new religious sect whose high priest — for them the embodiment of God on earth — lives in New York. And he had come to Israel, he said, to understand the true significance of what is happening here. The two focal points in the world of the future, he felt, would be China and Israel, and for some reason he came to the instinctive conclusion that if he wanted to understand what was happening here he should come to me. This may be a bit strange, because after all I do not represent anything in this State and hold no position, but this was how he felt, and he came and we talked all night.

One of the things he said was that he did not believe there would ever be a world war or that the H-bomb would be used. He felt that humanity ought simply to push the bomb out of its mind and not believe in its possibility, and it would simply go away. I said that as far as I knew anything that people have ever made has

eventually been used, and if hydrogen bombs existed there was
every possibility they would some day go off. This made him very
sad. So I told him that after all we were both religious people and
so what really mattered was the point of view of God. And what
was he afraid of — if humanity perished God would find Himself
"out of business?" — "Why, you're a religious man, and for somebody like you God alone is what counts. And God will carry on
even without people." This, and perhaps the jesting tone in which
I said it (it was already four a. m., an hour at which my mood
is savage and somewhat metaphysical) he turned white and looked
at me in genuine fear. I felt he saw in what I said an instinctive
expression of what the Jews in Israel would do if the "waters
came in unto their very soul" that is, if they faced annihilation,
for then they would feel justified in dragging the entire world
down with them. If Auschwitz, then all of us together. One's
sense of justice demands it, and justice is a very important thing.

BEN EZER: You said that the conflict between the Arabs and
us is very superficial. What is your attitude toward the Arabs?

SADEH: I love the *Thousand and One Nights*, the quiet, patient
way the Arab sits with his water pipe or cup of coffee, the style
of the Koran, the cries of the muezzin, the autobiography of
Al Ghazzali, the Arab markets and villages. A short while after
the Six Day War I got on an Arab bus going from Jerusalem to
Bethlehem. The driver was quite elderly. At the outskirts of Jerusalem an attractive young Arab woman went up and asked him to
make a detour and pick up a passenger who it seems could not
make it to the bus stop. To my surprise the driver left his route
and drove to the house the girl had indicated. There was no one
there. We went back to the main road. Again she began talking
to him and managed to persuade him that if he made one more
try he was bound to succeed. I could hardly believe my eyes but we
went back there a second time and again found no one. Not one
of the Arabs on board said a thing. When we reached the outskirts of Bethlehem it developed that the girl was looking for an
address but did not know her way about. Again I was surprised
to see the driver stop, get down, and help the girl find what she
was looking for. He got back in and drove us to the station. Now
it occurred to me that this Arab was a rather inefficient bus driver

and certainly inefficient as a tank driver, but he fitted into this country's landscape better than any efficient Israeli driver. He drove between Jerusalem and Bethlehem not as one drives between two points on a map, but as one drives between Jerusalem and Bethlehem. And it also occurred to me that the more the State of Israel expanded, the Land of Israel would contract. Still, there is a war on, and when in war as in war.

BEN EZER: What you are saying bears little resemblance to the usual political, social and national evaluations we hear in Israel. What is your point of departure?

SADEH: I do not look on man as a political animal, like Aristotle, nor an economic animal, like Marx, nor a psychological animal, like Freud. To me man is a religious animal, brooding here on the planet Earth as it floats in space. Usually he is quiet. Sometimes he jabbers something, howls at the stars. On occasion he bites himself. (A few weeks ago in London I saw a performance of mesmerizing beauty by a Negro girl dancer, nude, and then I realized that on occasion man is also a dancing animal. It is very important that this point be added as well.)

The condition of man is a religious one, therefore attitudes too have value only insofar as they are religious. And thus in the final account religion cannot be a conventional establishment, because what it really is — is an ever-renewed attempt to come into contact with the essence and meaning of life. The road can be neither easy or comfortable. Sometimes one must go through the eye of a needle in order to attain the Kingdom of Heaven, or as Jacob Frank said, one has to pass through the sewage canals to reach the Holy City of Jerusalem.

Hence I attach little value to literature, culture, theories or the academic approach, because they do not stand in any true relationship to life. I think that the only — and indeed hardest — way is to try to learn and draw conclusions from those moments in which we are able to open up to life, to the world, to nature and reality. Life is but a parable, it is the reflection of the divine, and the moral of this parable is God. That is why I titled my chief work *Life as a Parable*.

Every word I have ever written is the product of a religious experience, thought or direction, and if this were not so it would be devoid of any value. I am convinced that any world devoid of religion is devoid of existence. One time students in Jerusalem asked me a provocative question — whether the Nazi movement was also a religious movement. I replied: Can you show me any movement whatsoever that is not religious? Why, in that case it would be, as it were, outside of God, in some extraterritorial realm. When a lizard shakes its tail it is a religious movement. When a thief climbs up a drainpipe it is a religious movement. When people go on a pilgrimage to Jerusalem it is a religious movement.

BEN EZER: What is your attitude toward Judaism?

SADEH: Sometimes it occurs to me — and this may be a strange thing to say — that I am the Jew of the Jews. This phrase came to me in a dream, years ago, which I described in the final chapter of *Life as Parable*. Sometimes it seems to me that I have in my character, and thus in my writing as well, an extreme concentration of the qualities of the Jewish race, something which goes back to the really ancient sources, the time of the Bible. And so perhaps my situation among the Jews of today is similar to that of the Jews in the Gentile world. I feel that in my work there is an affinity to that which characterized the Biblical prophets, and it is not that I consider this a privilege of mine but rather I am convinced that it is the only way an author or poet can try to interpret the divine law as it is expressed in our life on earth. Everything else in my eyes is idolatry. Rationalism is the real idolatry and barrenness of life against which the Prophets fought, and not as is mistakenly supposed, the worship of nature. The earth is not the enemy of God. The earth is our mother, and God is our father.

BEN EZER: Have your sources of influence been Jewish ones?

SADEH: My personal sources of influence have not been the conventional Jewish ones. I have said that I attach importance only to situations of inspiration, so now let me tell you what it is I really derived living sustenance from, that which influenced my life. My religious sources are mainly the New Testament, and religious works (not necessarily in the conventional sense) such as Thus Spake Zarathustra, Faust, the poems of Hölderlin, the Koran, Dostoevski, and Knut Hamsun. (I like the nature in Knut Hamsun's stories. I like nature in general. Earth. Grass. Trees. Rivers and streams. Green things especially. Mountains and deserts less.)

As for the Bible, in recent years, but only in recent years, I have been reading and been influenced by it more and more, each day. In my youth it hardly had any influence on me at all, because the conventional mode of study imposed on me at school (and it was a religious school of all things) made me heartily sick of it. As far as I was concerned that book was completely dead. Today the Psalms to me are a manifestation of the divine, and I can hardly understand how a mere fifteen years ago they bored and disgusted me. When I took them at school they were completely divorced from any personal meaning. They did not relate to my own life. The weeping of David was not my own weeping. The Bible was interpreted to me as a national epic only. It took me many years to go back and discover it for myself.

Judaism in itself, on the basis of what I have felt all these years ever since I began thinking, writing and living (and these are questions of life and death for me, because it is now just before midnight and I have no way of knowing if I will not die tonight, or what tomorrow will bring). Judaism as it is today has told me nothing that is vital. That is, as far as I am concerned the conventional Jewish religion is not something alive. To be sure, there are elements, throughout its history, which may belong to the past but are for me completely alive: the Prophets are more alive than the rabbis. And unlike Ecclesiastes I feel that a dead lion is better than a live dog.

Then I go on to Jesus, who is something in his own right. And then I would mention manifestations, experiences of the genuine ancient racial spirit that I feel within me as well, and which fill my writing — the attempts to break out and make contact with life, as with Sabbatai Zevi. Even Jacob Frank, whose attempts to break out and come into contact with life were highly suffused with sexuality. I am not frightened by the contradictions, because it is obvious to me that contradictions create perfection, seeing as God unites all the contradictions.

BEN EZER: I would like to ask you about a very controversial passage in "Life as a Parable," one that aroused a storm of controversy, at least among the critics, when it was first published and in the years since as well. Allow me to quote it:

"The Jew is basically not religious. What is the meaning of being not religious? It is not to treat of the important things of life except in a joking, cunning, bestial manner; not to know even of the possibility that an individual may exist who questions the meaning of all, who suffers the sufferings of all, who bears the responsibility for all his existence, who demands of himself the fulfilment of the divine Idea. For how can what is not personal be religious? Does not life, which is the word of God, turn on the individual? But Judaism has never understood the concept of redemption except in a social context, and this is because it has not understood the concept of guilt except as social guilt, as crime; Judaism has never fathered (for if it had it would have contradicted its nature) a single true genius in the fields of literature, or of art, except for those who, by accident or because of persecution, broke out of its sphere, or at least stood in bitter opposition to its creed; Judaism has broken all of its prophets and poets, whether by slaughtering them between temple and altar or sending them down into the pit, whether by crucifying them or mocking them or sinking them slowly into the smart, cowardly, desperate mire of social life; it peeps through the cracks with cold eyes at anything enthusiastic, innocent, great, serious, poetic, and to preserve itself from these it nurtures in its bowels a culture of intellectual bacteria; Judaism knows how to laugh, to laugh monstrously, and so it is a cruel fate to be born a prophet or a poet within Judaism, but, on the other hand, no fate is more exalted or heroic; Judaism tosses and turns, pouring with sweat, in its long sleep, and its fears are not those of pogroms and slaughter (though what terrible afflictions it has suffered during two thousand years! Enough to turn even Nebuchadnezzar into a servant of God) but the nightmare of a continual fall into the abyss; and yet, who knows? Perhaps it is out of this deepest abyss, out of which redemption is humanly impossible, perhaps out of this very filth and clowning, out of despair and the hardest of afflictions, perhaps out of all this — that is to say, through all this — grace and salvation may come."

(*Life as a Parable*. Anthony Blond, London, 1966. p. 138-9.)

Are you prepared today to sign your name to these words which were written in 1957?

SADEH: I do not retract my signature from anything I have ever written, because what I have written has flowed from my life. And as for the question itself, sometimes I think that Judaism is an anti-religion. The idolatry that existed previously in Canaan was a true religion, that is, the people recognized the divine essence of reality, of every tree, stream, flower and mountain. Then along came Judaism and reduced the concept of God to the figure of a supreme guardian of law and order and social mores. And this is just not so. I think that Jesus sought to restore religion to the Jews and to people in general by reintroducing the image of God into the world, man and nature. I think that even the Prophets who preceded him also aspired to something like this, and in speaking against the idols what they were really getting at was the petrification, corruption and death of a non-religious, godless society. They were the expressers of eternal youth, eternal revolution, eternal religious fervor. Actually, I am prepared to say that any conventional religion, and not only Judaism, is an anti-religion, since religion is the very antithesis of the conventional — it is the eternal human drive to come into an ever-renewed contact with the essence of existence and to investigate it, live it, and break it.

From the historical standpoint Judaism had been in a process of erosion for generations, and its essential crisis was the advent of Jesus. Nor essentially, has Judaism solved this problem to this day. Incidentally, here we have a strange and highly significant combination of events; at the very same time that the Torah was being sealed by Ezra the Scribe prophecy ceased as well. In other words what ceased was personal contact with God. For contact with the Divine, even for the wink of an eye, is very frightening, and the Jews had lost the strength and the vitality to endure it, which is why they were assailed with hysterical fear and hatred at the advent of Jesus.

For man as he is, in his weakness and helplessness, it is very difficult to be in contact, even momentarily, with life, with existence, with God. This is perhaps the true meaning of madness. Even in a dream it is difficult and terrifying. For example, when Jacob was journeying to Haran God appeared to him in a dream and blessed him and was nice to him. And still, when Jacob awoke he said "How dreadful is this place, it is none other than the house of God!"

BEN EZER: Does Zionism have anything to do with this violent opposition of yours to Judaism?

SADEH: Zionism destroyed what was left of Judaism, that is, the anticipation insofar as it still existed, of the Messiah of God, just as the State of Israel destroyed and inherited Zionism. From the Jewish standpoint there perhaps remains only the pathetic phenomenon of the Neturei Karta*—a kind of residue from the past who still await the Messiah and refuse to accept the latter-day substitute. All the rest is, at best meaningless, and at worst negative. Today Judaism lacks vitality or any connection with living creation. It is disintegrating into petty, decadent, atrophied elements of politics and verbiage like our use of the Bible in nationalistic slogans, popular songs and radio readings. Why our life here is an utter contradiction of the vision of the Prophets, in comparison to which everything that is happening here is a veritable caricature of religion.

However, since I am not a professor or publicist lamenting the public condition or the low morale of society, the situation of Judaism does not frighten me one bit.

I do not think that God is alarmed by a shortage of customers. As long as I am alive (and I think this should and must be every man's feeling regarding himself) I am myself the personification of the religious attitude, and when I wonder and struggle over the meaning of my life and life in general, and try to express it, why this in itself is a never-ending religious activity and a manifestation of the Jewish religion. To my way of seeing, man stands alone before God. Therefore I do not suffer from nor am I worried by the condition of the organized Jewish religion. Culture is of no interest to me.

* Translator's note: a fanatic fundamentalist sect in Jerusalem.

BEN EZER: Do you think that separation of religion and the State in the manner proposed by Prof. Leibowitz will restore the Jewish religion's vitality?

SADEH: Man, don't make me laugh. Religion belongs to God, not to us. To argue that separation of religion from the State, or State from religion, or religion from the plastics industry has any essential relation to man's condition in the world and the question of his death is utterly ridiculous. God is not in a bad way because religion hasn't been separated from the State. All these are concepts that belong to the realm of culture, and religion is anti-cultural, and culture is anti-religious. Religion is anti-psychological, too.

BEN EZER: What do you mean by religion being anti-psychological?

SADEH: Psychology is something diabolical in the worst sense of the word. The devil has a knack of passing himself off as a servant and then taking over and becoming a master. This is what is happening today in culture and literature, and so as a reaction we get outbreaks of savage violence, which will yet increase, perhaps even to the point of an atomic-hydrogen apocalypse. And now I will explain myself: The goal of psychology is human and humanitarian — to make man suitable for society, to adapt him, to emasculate the spiritual, the mysterious, the ideal, the religious, the savage within him. In my opinion this makes him subhuman. Whereas the goal of literature is a divine one — to give expression to the religious nature of reality, dreams, love, nature, death, the riddle of existence. Psychology is wrong and literature is right, because our existence is not a human, social, rational and orderly one. When error tries to strangle truth an earthquake must eventually result. Religion says life is a parable and God is its moral, while psychology says God is a parable and life the moral. And this contradiction is sufficient reason to kill and be killed. Hence I feel we must burn all the psychologists and destroy the social and cultural substructure which, like a heap of dung, serves as compost for these poisonous toadstools.

BEN EZER: If I understand you correctly, what you are saying is that the reality that presents itself to the artist, or prophet, has no concreteness of its own but is merely a kind of parable, or raiment, for God, who is the moral of it and the only genuine reality. Your point of departure for understanding man is not man but God. In your opinion man is merely a manifestation — one interpretation out of many — of God. Whereas the psychologists (who in your conception represent the essence of all the other approaches — social, economic, political, national and scientific) consider man's life from the cradle to the grave as the only reality, the only *genuine* reality, the *moral*, and God merely a parable man has invented to explain the world and what transpires in his own soul. In their view God is a psychological projection man has developed for his own needs. Now allow me to ask, how do you know you are right and they are wrong?

SADEH: What are you saying man! Do you realize what you are saying? Everything that I have ever lived, everything I have ever written is guided by and based on the reality of God being self-evident. If, let us assume, you could now, just for a moment, prove to me I am wrong, why I would have to — I would immediately go and leap from the roof. It is easier for me to imagine God without the world than the world without God, and this is because the world is merely a parable and God is its moral — that is God (without my slightest understanding of what He is) is the concrete truth of the reality in back of the world which in itself is merely a passing dream. It is not so terrible if man forgets God (though of course it is no great virtue, but when you come down to it it can't change anything for God) but it is more terrible than anything if God forgets man — forgets his existence, his name, does not want to know about him any longer. For this is the ultimate of terror, loss and nothingness; apparently it is the true meaning of hell. In the story about Abimelech King of Shechem I wrote that "Of course it happens that men in their folly forget God, yet even this is not very important since man's deeds and thoughts are nothing in the eyes of God. It is different if God forgets man. That is the ultimate of terror." (*The Death of Abimelech and his Ascent to Heaven in the Arms of his Mother*, 1969. p. 19).

The same is true of art. Life is raw material, i. e. a parable exhibited to the eyes of the true artist so he will understand the moral, the absolute moral, i. e. God, something of Whose activity is revealed to us in human history. The road to God also passes by way of woman, beauty, dreams, nature and sin. There just must be some connection between the feminine, the eternal, nature and death. I think that the four of them combine to make up the ideal of the woman. This blend of sweetness and severity, savagery and order is very important. Of course if you want to you can argue that in what I am saying there is something — how shall I put it — of the Nazi. But don't forget that this is also what characterizes art and true great creativity — a blend of savagery, intoxicating sweetness, and stern order, and above all it characterizes nature: in the thickest and most savage jungle there is a precise structure of every leaf and flower. In nature, in reality, dream and atom are united.

BEN EZER: What influence does the artist, and literature, have on reality?

SADEH: History proves that there has never been a more powerful weapon than the book and an unknown sermon an unknown fellow made on an unknown hill before an unknown group of people has made its way to every place on the face of the globe, has even felled kingdoms and now, 2000 years later, is to be heard in churches from Alaska to Tierra del Fuego. The same goes for a book named *Capital*, for example, which was written in the British Museum by a certain unknown and starving scholar. Today hundreds of millions of people are threatening to destroy each other on the grounds that they are not Marxist enough.

History has also had not a few horrible holocausts of which no artistic memory remains. For example in two weeks in Bukhara the troops of Ghengis Khan butchered a million and a half men, women and children and piled all the corpses in a heap. I will give one other example of many: Plutarch tells us that a quarter of a million Germans were killed in a defeat at the hands of the Romans. Some of them were killed in battle, others fled and were killed by their wives and mothers and these in turn committed suicide, all in the space of a few short hours. And as for your question itself, just as it is not the purpose of art to serve the public in small matters, that is to supply reading matter to meet the current demands of the market, so it is not its purpose to serve the public in large matters, or to serve the public at all. Rather,

the public, history, the events of time and the phenomena of
life are material, in other words a parable, exhibited before the
true artist so that he may perhaps derive something from the moral
that is within it. To put it another way, everything that occurs is
merely an allusion to the essence of existence, to the divine meaning
that manifests itself in the world.

BEN EZER: Allow me to point out that it seems to me you are
trying to establish an unequivocal position in an ancient and
thorny theological issue — the contradiction between God's
omnipotence and His benevolence. If God is omnipotent, then
evil too must stem from Him, otherwise his omnipotence is not
complete. Now you are choosing unequivocally a faith in God's
omnipotence and thus you are compelled to renounce completely
any moral and human meaning to life — all that distinguishes
good from evil. Your God is a cruel God, one "whose concepts
are not our concepts, in whose eyes good and evil are of no
significance," as you say in your book *Notes on Man's Condition*
(1967). Your philosophy has no room for personal providence,
reward and punishment; it provides no contact between God
and man. Hence there would appear to be no difference between
God's existence as you understand Him and the atheistic outlook
that denies His existence altogether. Your God is so general and
eternal, so remote and indifferent to man's fate that it makes little
difference to man whether or not such a God exists. His existence
or absence alters nothing in the life of man or the universe. In fact
one might say the existence of such a God merely enhances
human despair. Avshalom, the hero of *Notes on Mans' Condition*
remarks that he "esteems as human only that which is super-
human" — that is, he aspires to relate to and operate within the
world and society from a standpoint that is not human but super-
human, or divine, according to what he understands of God
and His conduct in the world. Needless to say, such a standpoint
is an utterly anti-humanistic one. It is somber, despairing God
who has "divorced" the world and has no consideration for man,
the God of the secular man for whom the gates of innocent faith,
prayer and compassion have been shut and before whom there
yawns the full terror of the abyss of the hollow substitutes: State
and nationalism, society, psychology, science, eros, journalism

and false literature. Man's grasp of God is a mystical need, but the God you know has no salvation or mercy, no possibility of explaining the human world, merely a cold supra-temporal gaze condemning to death guilty and innocent alike. A God who is practically indistinguishable from total heresy.

Is it any wonder then that Avshalom, in his desire to be like God, chooses evil, or as you put it, "It is as if he does not want to be restricted by the good, just as he does not want to be restricted by the evil." It appears that Avshalom (like Sabbatai Zevi and the other mystics who sought to "descend into the flesh of defilement" so as to redeem the "sparks of holiness" imprisoned within it) seeks to come into contact with the power of Satan, which in his expression is a "vital and creative force."

SADEH: You are surprised that I attribute to Satan a vital and creative force? But then who if not Mephistopheles gives creative meaning to the life of Faust? It is he who extricates Faust from the point at which he is stalled, from the moment of emptiness; it is he who brings him together with Gretchen and grants them love, redeeming love, and disaster, which also redeems. I think that this was the sort of feeling Faust had when he suddenly yearned to set forth on a journey — like a God descended on earth, and wanders—wanders back to himself—through the world, through the suffering, and the beauty, also the filth—yes, the filth...

To this generations ago in Poland Jacob Frank replied that sometimes the holy city must necessarily be taken via the sewage canals. And who can say which is the sewage canal and which the river of dreams? For example it is sometimes possible in the midst of infamy to feel a profound sweetness, and in the midst of honor, revulsion. Somehow it seems to me that Sabbatai Zevi was right when he said that one must descend into defilement in order to redeem the sparks of holiness. It would seem that in order to arrive at any desired destination one must first pass through the world, through the circles of hell, *hell*, and sometimes, like Faust, in the company of the devil, perhaps even with his help. Everyone knows the dictum of Jesus, "Do not resist evil," but it seems to me our interpretation of it is very mistaken. In my opinion he meant us to take it literally: Do not resist evil, let it come within you and do its work, for your life derives sustenance from evil just as from good. (Incidentally Faust did just this when he opened his door to Mephistopheles). For after all, evil is a religious concept just as good is, hell is precisely like heaven. Only the middle is equally remote from both. In fact the middle is farther removed from heaven than hell is.

BEN EZER: If we are speaking of Satan, naturally there arises the name of Hitler, who was the embodiment of Satan in our age. What does the name Hitler say to you?

SADEH: The name Hitler says a lot to me, more than can be expressed in answer to your question. It says things that are contradictory, that are of the depths, things which are on the border between human nature, and the mystery of existence. Hitler was perhaps the most important phenomenon of our age. One of the questions he poses, for example, is how God allowed him to realize himself and his dreams and nightmares to such a great extent while depriving all the others, all the babies, the girls and the men, of their own little bit of life. Well, this gives rise to the question of God's intentions and concepts as regards human life, good and evil and the essence of reality in general. Under nocircumstances is it possible to avoid this question.

BEN EZER: Could you formulate this question precisely?

SADEH: The question in this case is both simple and cruel: how could God let such a thing happen? After all the final responsibility is His, for I cannot for one moment accept that anything transpires outside of Him. It is inconceivable that Hitler, or Ghengis Khan or any other mortal has taken fate into his own hands and left the realm of God's being. Hence the simple and cruel question is, why did God let such a thing happen? Why did God give the murderer, more than any other man, the opportunity to express himself, to implement his dreams and nightmares, to run amok. Why?

BEN EZER: And have you any possible answer to this question?

SADEH: I would say that God's concepts are not ours, that what is good and evil in our eyes is of no consequence in his.

BEN EZER: Doesn't this imply that man's condition is hopeless?

SADEH: No, it implies something completely different.

BEN EZER: What?

SADEH: I will tell you what it is, what it is that I hear. And I will say it not in the rational words that I can find now at this moment, in this conversation, but in the words of a poem I wrote:

Six Lines: *The Arab Flute*

Suddenly I heard the clear sound of the flute
Coming from the fringe of the desert,
Coming from Syria.
And told me that God sees in the dark.
And swore me to take from my heart the poverty of value
And said,
Your lot, like a sage blossom, cast at the feet of the Lord.
And said, that the universe is unfolding like a flower of light.

Zionism — Dialectic of Continuity and Rebellion

Interview with Gershom G. Scholem

(This interview took place in April and July 1970)

BEN EZER: In recent years, the opinion has been voiced in Israel and among world Jewry, that there is a difference between Jewish intellectuals in the West and those in Israel. The Jewish intellectual in the West has become the epitome of the outsider in literature and thought, with a message for the Gentiles and for his own people. In contrast, the Israeli intellectual, subjected to the pressures of a consciousness of siege, wars and sustained peril to the State, has become willy-nilly part of the Establishment, sharing the majority's sense of responsibility, incapable of a radically critical stance. Is this not part of the price we are paying for the consummation of Zionism—the loss of that fecund alienation and critical outsider slant? Are we really unable to deliver some message outside our narrow sphere?

That, for example, is the opinion of Prof. George Steiner as regards the difference between his own Jewish intellectual cosmopolitanism and our narrow nationalism here in Israel. Steiner considers his outsiderness and his alienation to be a mission and a purpose. What do you think?

SCHOLEM: You are asking about the price of Zionism, while the real question is not *the price of Zionism* but *the price of exile*.

These reproaches by people like George Steiner were being made sixty, seventy years ago. There have always been reproaches against Zionism, and the Zionists have been a minority within the Jewish people. It was only after the Holocaust that the recriminations were silenced for a time. I have no argument with George Steiner. He is trying to live outside of history, while we in Israel are living responsibly, inside of history.

You ask about "outsiderness." We have paid a high price for having been outsiders and aliens during our two thousand years of exile, a price of hatred, persecution, massacre and martyrdom. Today, the outsider is in fashion in the Western world, and the Jewish intellectual seems to be benefiting thereby. But what will happen tomorrow? Won't his Jewish outsiderness be flung in his face pejoratively? In Germany and France it was at one time fashionable for the Jew to belong, and not to be an outsider. The formula was: "a German of the Faith of Moses." At that time the Jews prided themselves on belonging, and not on their foreignness.

If today you are fascinated by the unique charm of the Jewish intellectuals in the Diaspora, I say — you're welcome. Go there. Live among them for five years, and see what price they are paying for exile. Anyone who feels cramped in Israel should go to New York or Cambridge and see if he feels as marvelous there as George Steiner does.

As to the reproaches of intellectuals who to not wish do be identified with any national body—I heard all about that sixty years ago. Then I was looked down upon for belonging to the Zionist movement. These questions are not new, and George Steiner did not invent them. We heard them even before World War I, and afterwards.

Had you asked me fifty years ago how I define myself, I would have told you that I am an Echad-Ha'amist, my outlook being one of practical Zionism, in contrast to the political Zionism initiated by Herzl. Herzl assigned primary importance to the framework. He wished to achieve the establishment of the State by means of wide-scale political activity. Practical Zionism, according to Echad Ha'am's outlook, was conceived of primarily as a Jewish resurgence from within, based on a Jewish society being built up in Palestine. That is why I immigrated to this country. Resurgence is essential for the Jewish people, containing its hope for innovation. Without it, Judaism will degenerate.

I was an Echad-Ha'amist. I believed that Judaism possessed spiritual features that were going to change. Echad Ha'am did not contemplate living according to the dictates of the Rabbis. He educated his children without religious observance. And he certainly thought that there is something in Judaism that would derive its life from the up-building of Zionism. It may be that he did not foresee the Holocaust, but he did foresee the development of Judaism.

Were you to ask me why I came to this country, I would tell you that I came because I thought that Judaism and the Jewish people are of value. I wanted this people to survive. I did not believe in assimilation or in the reproaches of the Jewish intellectuals, who were exactly as they are today. They spoke of their greater perspectives, ridiculing and denouncing our allegedly narrow, provincial perspectives. They told us: "What are you going to create, all told? One more small nation—while we are going to integrate with world development."

I have no argument with George Steiner. For arguing with him admits no possibility of a logical, rational resolution. The resolution is a moral one. For neither position is logical. That is the way history is.What logic is there in the fact that my brother in Germany set out to represent Communist workers who laughed at him? I have never believed in arguing with the Jews from abroad whom the Jewish Agency brings here for symposia. For I know nothing will come of it. It is meaningless.

Steiner's logic is one of intellectual recrimination that does not wish to relinquish its ostensibly "broader" attitude. Why, even then, over sixty years ago, weren't they speaking against that petty cause, Zionism? And we countered their reproaches, replying: "What is that great, worldwide cause that you believe in and speak of? Why, no Gentile speaks that way. Only you. There is no over-all humanity. It exists only in your imaginations." And today, exactly the same thing is recurring.

How dare you say that the Jewish intellectual in Israel has become part of the Establishment, and is therefore incapable of a radically critical stance? I hate that word: Establishment. But if you insist on using it, then I'll have you know that I am part of the Establishment and so are you. And all of us here are the Establishment, including those who sneer at it. And anyone who does not want to be part of the Establishment here should go away. Because the Establishment today is stationed at the Suez Canal. Anyone who doesn't like it should go away.

I have no argument with a Jewish intellectual who gives priority to his personal emotional complexes, over the problem of *historic responsibility*. Let everyone do what he likes. It is not realistic to argue with him. A person who gives priority to his own private, personal troubles, and indulges himself in the creative opportunities of alienation—should go wherever he likes, and live to the best of his understanding.

If Steiner does not wish to bear the burden of responsibility for the State with us — he is right. Let him be a Jew in exile. It may be that some day he will be hit over the head, and will then discover that he does not *really* belong there. For his alienation is not merely an impressive and fashionable pose, but also an extremely bitter historic reality, for which the full price must be paid.

BEN EZER: You said that in the debate with the Jewish intellectual from outside Israel there is no possibility of a logical resolution, but only a moral one. What is the moral resolution?

SCHOLEM: The meaning of the intellectual's moral resolution is that he is concerned first of all with his emotional complexes, and is only thinking of pursuing his own private course. But the overall moral question is whether a living body of several million people who are not only intellectuals, but an entire people, can live that way. The intellectual, by nature, does not desire a common future. He is fascinated by his isolation. And the more isolated he is the better he likes it. Perhaps the person who can not overcome his urge for intellectual isolation is right. But the question is in the sphere of common responsibility for Judaism. I agree that the Jewish people is eminently alive. I do not consider myself alienated from that people. My feeling is that my place is here, and that is why I am here. For me, immigrating to this country was a question of both personal and general resolution. That is why I immigrated to Palestine back in the twenties, before Hitler and prior to the economic problem. I immigrated not because I was unable to cope in Germany but because I had decided that my place is here, both as an individual and as part of the Jewish people.

That is why I say to you that it is impossible to resolve the two moral alternatives. The resolution is in the hands of every individual, personally, insofar as he is capable of being master of his own fate. Does he think he has something in common with his people, or does he consider alienation to be a supreme value? I do not believe in the latter possibility. Alienation is only a faddish concept.

And it will change. That fashion was at its peak ten years ago. And the day may yet come when we Jews will be censured for being "aliens," and will pay a heavy price for being so. Do you think that we will not pay, for example, the full price for the malicious way the Jew's attitude towards Gentile women is presented in Roth's *Portnoy's Complaint*?

BEN EZER: One of the claims of Zionism has been that it will secure Jewish survival. The Holocaust seems to have produced a tragic vindication of that claim. But the threat to survival, and our awareness of that threat, have been powerful, actually inevitable facts of Israel's existence since its inception. To put it brutally, we must ask: What is the advantage of an armed ghetto in the Middle East, whatever its borders may be, still hated by all our neighbors—over Jewish life in the Diaspora at the price of sporadic manifestations of anti-Semitism, but perhaps with no foreseeable danger of annihilation, and without the inexorable trend that threatens physical survival in our country? Wherein lies our superiority, as a Zionist State, in solving the fundamental problems of Jewish survival? Is not the price we are paying, by submerging ourselves in the defense of our survival as a supreme, unifying value, a rather high price, paid at the expense of not realizing other goals of the Zionist vision?

SCHOLEM: You will not find me mentioning a word about Zionism being a solution to the Jewish question. I am not one of those who believe that there is a "solution" to the so-called "Jewish question." When, with your eyes open and your mind resolved, you enter the lists of history you must contend. We have also caused the consolidation of the Arabs as an enemy possessing a common national consciousness, because we have functioned within history. When you are static you achieve nothing. But when you begin to move, you select one course and not the others, and pay the price of your decision and your action. That is the meaning of functioning within history, and not just amusing yourself.

It is hard for me to understand what is bothering you. Why do your questions contain an element of self-disparagement before the Jewish intellectual in the Diaspora? What is hindering you from living your life fully?

BEN EZER: The sustained war; the Arabs; having to consider most of the years of my life—just like the rest of the members of my generation in this country—in terms of military service and extended reserve duty every year, or perhaps it would be more correct to say: intermittent military service all year round. And then, a sense of suffocation and siege accumulates. It is difficult for an Israeli to shut himself up in his own corner and be at liberty to engage in creative intellectual activity.

SCHOLEM: Like that? Fantastic! Why don't I feel it?

BEN EZER: I don't know. Maybe it is because you chose to immigrate to this country, while we were born into a certain historic reality, and are condemned to live within it whether we like it or not, whether out of Zionist consciousness or in lieu of an alternative. Perhaps because my generation, here in this country, were taught that Zionism *would* solve the Jewish question. We were taught that Jewish existence in the Diaspora is fundamentally negative and wrong, and that is why the entire Jewish people has undergone all its tribulations. But here in Israel, thanks to Zionism, the existence of the Jewish people had become normal; a new, healthy generation was growing up; and that normalization was to have secured us against the past troubles of the Diaspora Jews. Time after time, the Arabs' hatred of us destroys anew the dream of the Zionist promise to which we were educated, and sometimes makes us ask whether the price of Zionism is cheaper than that of exile.

SCHOLEM: If you are saying that Zionist education purported to promise the younger generation, your generation, "normalization" and a solution to the Jewish question, a sort of Paradise on earth, then in my opinion that education was wrong. I am, of course, a Zionist, but I am not naive and I do not think like that. My Zionism is hinged on the basic fact that without Zionism the Jewish people can not survive. But I have never thought that survival would not be problematic. There is no solution to the Jewish question in our time. Zionism is a noble attempt to contend with the Jewish problem. And it is impossible in this world to do more than contend with a problem on the historic level. The Zionists have not been afraid to undertake historic responsibility, and that is their greatness. And there is nothing in history for which you do not have to pay a price.

I came here because I thought, and I still think that *Zionism is not a Messianic movement*. Absolutely not. There are, of course, certain Messianic strains accompanying it in the background. As a sort of overtone, there is a sublime melody that accompanies Zionism, for the Jews have been addicted to Messianism for two thousand years. But *the price of Messianism*, of which I have written, was a fundamental weakness of Jewish history, and it was a terrible price that we paid for that weakness. Our faith in the Messianic concept has cost us in terms of the very substance of the Jewish people, debilitating its powers of survival, as in the Sabbatai Zevi affair.

In this sense, the Orthodox Jews were "right" in their criticism of Zionism. The Zionists did, in fact, rebel against their grandfathers, who had said they must wait for the Messiah, and not act within history. The Zionists were right in that they were no longer prepared to pay the price of the terrible fundamental weakness of the Jewish people's position in exile. This, of course, does not matter to the Jewish intellectual, for he is on his own. He is the great individual contending with himself. But Zionism really did rebel.

The difference between Zionism and Messianism resides in the fact that *Zionism is acting within history, while Messianism remained on a Utopian plane*. The Jewish Orthodox theory linked exile with Messianism. For the Orthdox Jew, exile and the coming of the Messiah were mutually exclusive—the people could be either in an exilic state or in a Messianic state. But for a Jew who is not traditionally religious—it is a different matter. For a situation can arise in which, without Messianism, the price of exile must be paid. That is, the price of exile and the price of Messianism are not always necessarily identical.

I think that Zionism really did revolt against something. I do not view Zionism as Ben-Gurion does—as a Messianic movement. I consider Zionism to be a movement that asserts that we must accept the decree of history without a Utopian cover. And, obviously, one must pay for that. One encounters others who have counter interests and rights. The Arabs' hatred of us is not like Hitler's was. They have the basis of a concrete interest which we have injured. Weizmann, for example, knew very well that the

Arabs had a valid case. The question is whether we will be able to hold out until we succeed in coming to terms with them.

BEN EZER: In retrospect, from a historical standpoint, how does Zionism's approach to the Arab question look to you? Aren't we today paying the price of that blindness by virtue of which the State was indeed established, but established without any possibility of peaceful co-existence with the Arab national movement? The romantic, pacifistic approach to the Arabs has always been bankrupt, while only activism, which has perhaps resulted from despair and pessimism, has been proven right in its attitude towards the Arabs, in view of the sustained war. Might we say that the State of Israel and its children were born under the sign of a tragic situation from which there is no exit? Or is there a possibility of an ideological and political renewal in Zionism, which will lead to a solution of these problems? Or might the answer be forthcoming from other quarters?

SCHOLEM: If we study Zionism on the historic plane, it appears that there were indeed Arabs in this country during the time of the Turkish rule, but they did not constitute a decisive factor. If at that time, 150 years ago when the population of Palestine was only a quarter of a million, fantastic historic circumstances had brought half a million Jews to this country, it is reasonable to believe that the entire question would have assumed different proportions. The Arab question could arise on a serious historic plane after the removal of Turkish rule. Had the Turkish authorities deported hundreds of thousand of Arabs as was done with the Armenians, the situation would have been different. I am not saying this nostalgically, but in order to explain to you how fine the thread was on which the Arab question has depended.

Till the Balfour Declaration, all Zionist political activity was conducted only with governments. To blame today the Zionist movement of that time for not having conspired with the Arabs against the Turks—is fantastic! Why, there was no one to talk to, for all their spokesmen were *effendis*. The historical dialectic is a serious matter and not a jest. Your reproach is akin to those being advanced against Zionism these days:"You should have educated the Arab masses." But there was no address then. There was no one to turn to. It would have been like talking to the negroes of the Cameroons at that time, against the Germans or the French. These things are not realistic. Today, now that the emerging dialectic processes of history have disclosed their features, the reality that has been crystallizing in the course of our action has come to light. It is just the same as in modern physics, which must take into account that the experimenter is part of the experiment. It is impossible to complain today about what we did not do sixty years ago. There was simply no address.

Did the Zionist movement miss opportunities? An indication of whether it did may be seen in the fact that several of the Arab leaders who did agree to talk to us were assassinated by their compatriots. Of course, I am not the person to absolve the Zionist leadership of its misdeeds, but in retrospect, as a member of Brith Shalom ("Peace Alliance": a pacifist organization founded in 1925 for the purpose of Arab-Jewish rapprochement — Ed.) at that time, I am today doubtful as to whether it would have made much difference had one thing been done then rather than another.

BEN EZER: There exists among young people in this country a painful, sometimes desperate feeling that we are doomed to face hatred and war on the part of the Arabs for many long years to come. Are we not in danger of becoming fatalists as a result of this situation? We have lost our faith in there being a connection between our good and bad deeds and the Arabs' hatred of us.

SCHOLEM: When we came here without asking the Arabs — Buber or myself, your father or your grandfather—we were being "Fatalists," and you could have asked us the same question. In what way were we fatalists? In that we said that despite the opposition of the Arabs we would seek a way. I am not certain that everything here is a matter of fatality. Perhaps things do function according to human behavior. It is hard to know. It is subject to change under so many circumstances. It is clear that were it not a question of the Russians today, everything would change. I think that were there in Egypt, instead of the Russians, some other traditional power that would not be prepared to invest capital there in order to intrench itself, the situation would be different. The Russians supported us, too, in 1948 against the British. The entire Marxist lexicon that was employed at that time was a sham. Their aid to us had no Marxist significance. It was a Russian imperialist measure. Had it not been for the Russians, you would have no reason to say that we were unable to talk to Jordan and Egypt after '67. It is their doing that made the Arabs strong again.Therefore I am unable to foresee the adventurism of history. And I do not advise the younger generation to despair of things I have not despaired of.

We have no argument with the Arab position that rejects us. If someone tells us, "I don't want you; go back to where you came from,"—then neither I nor Zionism have an answer ready. I can tell him that he is right. He has rights. But I think that the rights of the Jewish people are more important. I want immigration, and I am not asking Mussa 'Alami's permission for Jewish immigration. I think that Mussa 'Alami's nationalist consciousness was evoked by us, because of our activity. And we, as Zionists, were from the outset prepared to meet the consequences of this contest. We did not know that it would be chiefly a military contest. There are other ways to contend, too. It is clear that were we to agree to concede the principle of Jewish immigration to this country, we would be able to make peace with the Arabs this very day. But we would thereby be putting an end to our existence here.

Today, too, you can not tell what upheavals there are going to be in our world. The Egyptians have not always considered themse ves Pan-Arab. We ourselves can remember hearing how Egyptians, insulted at being called Arabs, would reply, "I am not an Arab, I'm an Egyptian!" Our conflict has nothing to do with Egypt. There is no clash. With the inhabitants of Shechem—certainly. But not with the inhabitants of Cairo.

Today there is talk of our misdeeds towards the Arabs. It is said that we—Weizmann, the Zionist movement—should have talked to the people of Shechem and not to the Arab states. In my opinion, it was the right approach to apply to the Arab states. The premise at that time was that, if there is a legitimate conflict, the solution can only be provided by people who do not have a direct interest in it and who are capable of exercising a moderating influence. That is what they were saying forty years ago— that we should seek an agreement with Egypt for what real conflict of interests could there be between us?

They were saying that here in this country a genuine conflict was taking place with which we had to contend. But with others we could reach a compromise. They were seeking a hold on something very real—politically crystallized bodies with whom they had no genuine point of conflict, whose influence could also moderate our friction with the Arabs of this country, and lead to a compromise. Egypt's true problems today have nothing at all to do with us. With the people of Shechem, we never had any hope. We will never be able to incorporate Shechem. But one must not forget that the political question is subject to the vicissitudes of history.

BEN EZER: In several places in your writings you have defined yourself as a *Utopian* in your approach to Jewish history, an *anarchist* from the standpoint of the Jewish religion, and a Zionist in your outlook. What is your Zionist outlook, and how does it fit in with your other two attitudes?

SCHOLEM: Zionism has never really known itself completely—whether it is a movement of continuation and continuity, or a movement of rebellion. From the very beginning of its realization, Zionism has contained two utterly contradictory trends. So long as Zionism was not consummated in practice, these two trends could dwell peaceably together, like two books containing contradictory views, standing together on the same bookshelf. Fundamental intellectual trends do not yet clash on the practical plane so long as things do not come to psychophysical consummation.

In my opinion it is manifestly obvious that these two trends have determined the essence of Zionism as a living thing with a dialectic of its own, and have also determined all the troubles we are confronted with today. Is Zionism a movement that seeks a continuation of what has been the Jewish tradition throughout the generations, or has it come to introduce a change into the historic phenomenon called Judaism? We all know that when we speak of Judaism we are speaking of something that exists, but which it is difficult to define. Nor is there in my opinion any need to define it. The question is whether we have wanted to alter fundamentally the phenomenon called Judaism, or to continue it.

Within the Zionist movement, these two elements have from the outset been confused and opposed from many standpoints. The conflicts were articulated theoretically in extreme form, even before they became actual. The most active part of the Zionist movement which carried out the main part of the implementation, was in favor of rebellion and of an intellectual refurbishment of Judaism. They said: "We are through with Diaspora mentality." But they were not Canaanites. They were speaking of change and not of a fresh start. There were others who said that Zionism is a realization of traditional Judaism. Zionism would afford us the opportunity here to realize such a life as has previously been marred by the exilic milieu. From the start, these two possibilities were incorporated in the living organism called Zionism. The Zionist worker's movement in Palestine, with all its factions, was absolutely antitraditional. Today we tend to forget with what anti-religious pungency they used to write and speak, for they themselves have consigned to oblivion or have forgotten how they spoke and what their opinions were during that period.

It is impossible to ignore this fudamental reality. We today are obliged to pay the price and to contend with the fact that the conflict between these two elements has been operative within Zionism, and in world Jewry, as well. Centrifugal and centripetal trends, away from the center and towards it, exist today both in Israel and in the Diaspora. It is the same dialectic. The alternative is between partial or complete assimilation, and an inner strengthening of Judaism. In the Diaspora this expresses itself, on the one hand, in the form of a pro-Israel Jewish national movement and, on the other hand, in the phenomenon of Jewish intellectuals fleeing from the center, in a centrifugal trend. Here in Israel we may enumerate all the Cananite manifestations as part of the centrifugal trend. They wish to be aloof from the center. As against them, there is the movement for conscious Jewish concentration, which desires a Jewish resurgence here in Israel. The problem is whether or not to break consciously with tradition. And these are the processes which might have been foreseen.

I have no reproach against the non-Zionist Orthodox Jews. Today an attempt is being made to make it look as though all the religious Jews have been Zionists. One should not disparage the Mizrachi people, who envisaged a synthesis between Zionism and religion. But against them were posed the Orthodox, who comprised 90% of religious Jewry, and who were radically opposed to Zionism. Today a conventional lie is current, falsifying history. We are being told how Zionist the Hassidic movement was. It's a lie. They were faithful to the star they were born under: provisional reconciliation to the Diaspora—till the coming of the Redeemer. Perhaps less than one percent of them had a leaning towards us at the beginning. I have no argument with the Neturei Karta and their like, such as the Rabbi from Satmer. They are consistent. But most of the religious camp has adapted itself to the new reality that has come into being as a result of Zionism. Here you can see the extent of Zionism's victory. For all those factors that once hated Zionism are today adapting themselves to it. And all of this has come to pass because Zionism was a dynamic movement. Take the Rabbi from Lubavicz. His predecessors were confirmed enemies of Zionism. Now these circles keep quiet. They have not come to agree with us ideologically, but in practice they are holding their peace.

Zionism has been the vital part of the Jewish people, the part that has been dynamic, and not merely a power of endurance. I am not belittling the Orthodox or the power of endurance. But the young people here today forget how dynamic Zionism has been, the will—or the need—to stand naked before history, to embark on a course. It is clear that the conflict between continuity and rebellion is a determining factor in the destiny of Zionism. Determining in so far as we are able to determine our destiny from within. One must know that there are contradictory trends within Zionism, and that for the time being there is no synthesis between them. To be sure, after the Holocaust the rebels of the Zionist workers movement discovered that they themselves are the torch bearers. They understood the value of continuity.

I am one of those who say that there is no conflict. It is obvious that we are all torch bearers. Except the Canaanites. *But I believe that Judaism is a living thing that is not amenable to a dogmatic definition.* Innovation can not be defined in advance. Because innovation arises, not from denying one's tradition, but from a dialectic, a metamorphosis of tradition. And these two trends have not yet run their course.

I have said that every generation interperts Judaism for itself which implies that one can not conclusively define what Judaism is. I said what I did as a thoroughly anti-theological definition, contrary to the dogmatic trends I do not share in. Because for some time, let us say from 500 till 1800 C.E., there has been or has crystallized a certain Judaism, can we not assume another Judaism, as well?

The criterion must be: What are the living manifestations of the nation's strength that have existed throughout the generations and that are yet going to emerge and crystallize? What Judaism is—is not a definition by religion, though that is the aspiration of the religious people whose conception I do not share. In general, I believe that it is possible to define a historical phenomenon solely from within history. There is here no real uniform content. What has the Judaism that existed at the time of Abraham or of Moses got to do with the Baal-Shem-Tov? The phenomenon called Judaism does not terminate in some given year on some given date, and I do not think it is likely to terminate so long as there exists a living Judaism. If you are asking for a precisely formulated definition, I must say I am incapable of producing one. That is the Almighty's business. Were we to know how to formulate a definition of what Judaism is, we would not be dealing with a comprehensive spiritual phenomenon, but would be faced with a body whose vitality is determined by definition. I reject that conception. I say that in the entirety of life, in the course of the generations, extremely differing trends have developed within Judaism. I do not believe that there will not be more such new expressions in the future. But there is something vital that is beyond dogmatic definition. In other words: In my opinion, *Judaism contains Utopian aspects that have not yet been revealed.* It contains a vital force, which I term, "Utopian aspects."

There are aspects that are oriented backward, i.e. to Knesseth Israel (the Jewish Congregation) of the past. I do not believe that everything it embodies has been discovered. It seems to me that it is still given to discover exalted and obscure things in it which no one has beheld. My belief in a living Judaism is based on this conception. There are manifestations that have been discovered and have assumed an historic form, and there are those who sift out only those manifestations that seem to promise future glory. Beyond such matters they forbid us to go, or even to select such phenomena which do indeed embody a manifestation of our historic essence, but have in the war of the generations been vanquished for some reason, not to speak of those that have been utterly suppressed. In my opinion this approach is wrong. We are not a party to the contradictory trends, nor do we affirm or deny. And we should certainly not say, following the criteria of the rabbinical tradition, that the one side is right and the other wrong. Anyone today who reads the Dead Sea Scrolls knows that one can not comprehend a Jewish reality by the definitions of the authors of the rabbinic code. Here, too, there was a living Judaism, though it was suppressed. The historical fact that other forces overcame it does not invalidate its Jewishness. Can we say that the Sadducees were not Jewish and the Pharisees were? That would be utterly invalid; I myself have no part in such judgements.

As to the future, I am certain that there are possibilities for manifestations of Judaism as a national-spiritual phenomenon. These are the Utopian aspects that are oriented to the future. Were I teaching the young, I would be teaching history as a believer in Judaism as a living thing. I would tell them that we have not yet appreciated all the values and that the manifestations have not stopped coming because in some year or other the *Shulchan Aruch* was composed or the Basel Program was drawn up. This is what I term "Utopian content." Many such things have been set right in the past, and are going to appear in the future, perhaps with added vitality.

BEN EZER: Why are the Canaanite outlook and the Canaanite trends outside the bounds of your view of Judaism and Zionism? Is there no possibility of viewing Canaanitism, too, as a dynamic rebellious development within the dialectic continuity of Jewish history, and as such — as one more of the Utopian aspects of Jewish historical development in our generation?

SCHOLEM: In my opinion, cutting the living tie with the heritage of the generations is educational murder. I admit it. I am down right anti-Canaanite. I will cite an example. I do not share the view of those who wish to "skip" the Diaspora. We all know that there are among us some people who preach that we possess an inner bridge to the period of the Bible, that "exile" is something that we reject. I have no stock in those opinions. The leap to the Bible is purely fictitious, the Bible being a reality that does not exist today. But there is an ideal which we term "the Biblical world" which it is wished to raise up today. That is definitely legitimate, though I believe that this leap is likely to lead to an educational breakdown and from the standpoint of the continuity of the generations which have endowed us with strength and with a tremendous tradition which should be brought up, selected from and made a problem of. From this standpoint, I am a *religious anarchist*, for I am unable to discuss any phenomenon of the past and rule whether they were right or wrong, though it is in place to struggle with the manifestations or ideologies that demand a hearing.

There are people who try to tell us to interrupt the continuity. This Canaanitism has deep roots with Berdichevsky. A process of centrifugality is taking place among us; young fellows dream of cutting their ties with the entire past and of national existence without a tradition—cutting ties with the recent past. Ben-Gurion encouraged the Canaanites because he skipped directly to the Bible and rejected all exile. But he leapt into the moral Bible, while they turned to the pagan Bible. Ben-Gurion has today forgotten the fact that he alienated himself. He thought then that we were returning to a Biblical historical continuity. But such a continuity exists only in books, and not in history. The continuity of the Biblical period existed within a religious reality and not within an historical reality. Ben-Gurion encouraged movements towards cutting off their ties with Judaism here in Israel. But it is impossible to strike roots right into the Bible.

It is impossible to foretell the religious dimensions of the new Jewish life. I am expounding for you the contrasts between the two trends, of continuity and of rebellion in Zionism, not because I think that they are going to fight it out to the death, but because I am certain that there is here a fruitful debate between two different trends with one and the same vital interest. And Judaism, out of a positive inner lawfulness, is likely to assume an aspect we do not know.

BEN EZER: In this connection, I would like to quote a passage from your essay "Reflections on the Possibility of Jewish Mysticism in Our Time":

"Anyone who tries to bring to the community the fruits of his inspiration and mystical awareness, but does not consider himself to be in conscience bound to the one great fundamental principle of the 'Law from on High,' without any reservations whatever, word for word as written—such a person may be considered to be an anarchist. In other words, without strict notation of the Divine origin of Scripture, no new forms of Jewish mysticism of broad significance can evolve. In fact, whoever is unprepared or unable to accept this principle, who lacks the absolute faith of the early believers, having found other beliefs or having been diverted into historical criticism (for many and varied are the forms of doubt in the infallibility of the Torah) is also an anarchist.

"Thus, as far as religion is concerned, we are all of us, to some extent, anarchists today, and this should be plainly stated. Some know it and admit it fully; others of us twist deviously to avoid facing the essential fact that in our time a continuity of Jewish religious awareness is beyond this principle of the 'Law from on High.' Such a conclusion inevitably leads to anarchic forms of religion. Hence the great question at the heart of these reflections: will a clear, objective basis be found for a fresh, contemporary Jewish translation of an experience no less significant than those of other ages? For this generation has been deprived of the fundamental faith upon which earlier generations stood firm.

"That is why, when we ask what form mystical impulses can take in Judaism today, we find ourselves confronted with the fact of Jewish religious anarchism. Consequently, we have no answer to this question." (from *Ariel*. No. 26, Spring 1970).

And now I would like to ask you: what is the place of Jewish religious anarchism here? How does it tie in with the Utopian aspects of Judaism?

SCHOLEM: The anarchistic point enters only in that we do not know who the religious authority is today. Someone who has lost his faith in the Divine origin of the Bible must today resolve the question to the best of his understanding and his conscience. Here, too, is concealed the stumbling block which hinders the crystallization of a publicly meaningful Jewish mysticism today. All of us are anarchists because we do not have an agreed upon authority. A person may be extremely religious and not receive Divine inspiration in the earlier form. And that is the problem of mysticism, which received the Bible and drew extreme conclusions, and was extremely free within the limits of the Kabbalah and of faith in the principle of the Divine origin of the Bible. But today non-acceptance of the Divine origin of the Bible hampers the free development of mysticism.

The problem of authority, the question of which authority dictates to you, has not been solved till this day. It is impossible to know in what form things will appear. I had a debate about this with Buber. Years ago he wrote negatively about the State of Israel, from the standpoint of the attitude of the State towards the continuity of the Jewish religion. And I replied to him: How do you know that the State of Israel has no religious significance? It may be that it has not. I too think that political frameworks have no religious significance. But how do we know what is taking place within the framework, in the living society, in the body that bears the State? Perhaps our concepts are being utterly changed, and not everything which we today consider to be "established" religion is the genuine religious act? We do not know in what form things may appear in the new reincarnation. And that is the price of Zionism, which is being paid for the dialectic it contains from birth, in the clash between two contradictory trends. On the one hand, it debilitates, on the other, it strengthens. That is the dialectic of the development, and we have not yet arrived at any synthesis.

BEN EZER: In the same essay, "Reflections on the Possibility of Jewish Mysticism in Our Time," you also wrote in this connection:

"There is one last point which I must raise, which I cannot avoid touching on briefly—the matter of the secular, or the sanctity of the secular, in our lives, or rather the problem of secularization, and its possible relevance to mysticism in our time. After all, in recent times most of the creative force of Jewry has been invested in building up something different from what was laid down by spiritual tradition. This construction, or reconstruction, of the life of a nation has been extremely arduous, it demands powers of thought and implementation that hardly leave room for any productive expression along traditional patterns. This energy, which in other circumstances might have been largely invested in the world of Jewish mysticism, is today absorbed in affairs which would seem to be devoid of religious sanctity; they appear utterly and completely profane. This is the problem.

"Still, who knows the limits of sanctity? Such was the question Rabbi Kook raised in the most controversial of his teachings. He was not prepared to accept the view, from the orthodox standpoint, that this work of building was profane. Perhaps it only masked the sacred which had not yet been recognized as such? After all that has gone into a life of upbuilding can there be any strength and initiative left over for the creation of forms recognizably belonging to the sphere of holiness, with universal significance for the Jewish people? It is doubtful whether the answer can be in the affirmative. Perhaps a double way is possible, secular and holy, towards which we are evolving? Perhaps this holiness will be revealed at the very heart of the secular, and the mystical is not recognized because it appears in forms which are new to the concepts of tradition? And possibly this mysticism, in its new guise, will not conform to the conservative concepts of the traditional mystics, but will be of secular significance. This is not at all far-fetched. The secular element in our lives and the rebuilding of the nation have been explained by many as reflecting the mystical meaning of the secret of the universe." (from *Ariel*, No. 26, Spring 1970).

My question is this. In the debate over the form of the Knesset decision in the "Who is a Jew?" issue at the beginning of 1970 the camps split chiefly into Orthodox Jews and secular Jews. The claims advanced by the two sides implied that one can only belong to one camp or the other, with no other alternative possible. How do you view the question, in the light of your outlook concerning dialectic continuity and dynamic development in Jewish history, and the possibility of the revelation of sanctity within the secular?

You have said that Judaism contains a Utopian aspect with regard to both the future and the past. Is it possible to apply the Utopian aspect of "living Judaism" to the topical question of "who is a Jew?" What determines the Judaism of a person in Israel? Only his religious faith? His racial affiliation? His free will, to the best of his judgment?

SCHOLEM: You are asking, in fact, can there be Judaism without "I am the Lord?" Why, we have been pondering that problem for over fifty years, since the inception of Zionism. Whether there is an atheistic Judaism, or more precisely, Judaism as a living body with a constellation of historic phenomena and experiments possessing tremendous historical significance. The question is whether a comprehensive atheistic explanation could be feasible. And so, who is a Jew? Just someone who gives Judaism's historical phenomenon a religious interpretation? Why, that would be absurd. Couldn't the spiritual phenomena which were given a tremendous theological, monotheistic interpretation also have other interpretations which might arise to contend with it? It may be that they have no survival value and will pass away from the world. It may be that the Almighty will overcome that, as well. I myself believe in God. But I am a religious anarchist. I do not believe in the Law handed down to Moses on Sinai in the traditional sense. If there is something real to the Almighty, then the very struggle to believe in him has something exalted in it. That is the way it was when Zionism arose, and we knew very well that the constellation of problems of the people and of history also has secular interpretations! I believe that an atheist can be a Jew and that he may offer a correct or incorrect explanation of our historic manifestations, quite legitimately. And, as I have said, only cutting the living tie with the heritage of the generations is in my opinion educational murder, and in that sense I am a thorough anti-Canaanite.

BEN EZER: But I asked whether you have one, formulated definition in the question of "who is a Jew?"

SCHOLEM: I think that there are here two entirely different questions. The first question is whether secular Judaism and religious Judaism can reside together in close proximity, and whether there is something uniting them, My answer is — yes. The national movement in Israel is built on that principle, which asserts that the common denominator that united the Jews is beyond religious clashes.

Religious clashes may be final, or open to development. There are those, particularly in the religious camp, who think that the religious interpretation is final. Nevertheless, they are not excluding the others from Judaism at large, for they consider the secular Jews to be candidates for religious repentance. There is no reason at all why they should not be right in their expectations, but even assuming that they are in error, these expectations afford them in the present a principal possibility for not excluding the non-religious from Judaism at large.

The tie between religious and secular Judaism is one of security and agreement not only as regards their common past, but also in working and struggling for a common future, the future of the people, in the role of a living nation. Even if we today do not know whether this Jewish life will indeed be expressed in a movement away from or towards traditional religion, or in new patterns of religion.

BEN EZER: And what is the second question?

SCHOLEM: The second question relates to the matter of "Who is a Jew?" I have said that in my opinion Judaism is a living phenomenon, and though there are major and specific directions evident in it, it is impossible to foretell how the content of its affairs will evince itself. I am convinced that the religious question in Judaism has not yet arrived at its final, conclusive epiphany, and that secularism is not the last word. I regard Judaism as a religious phenomenon, and I view approvingly even the changing forms within it. Judaism has religious significance for the future, as well, and the crisis of our generations is not the last word. But I am not prepared on my own say so to draw conclusions that are binding on people who do not think as I do, be they Orthodox religious or secular, in the laws of the State. There are also among the secular, those who claim that a change in the framework, such as a separation of religion and the State, would provide some essential solution, though I do not believe that separating religion from the State, one of these days, would lead to a greater division within the people than that which exists in practice today between the observant and the secular.

As to your question of whether we can today determine by law who is a Jew, and whether the legislation already passed is wise, I believe it has been handled most unfortunately. An extremely undesirable and inappropriate step has been taken in an effort to influence the process of creation of historic consciousness, which is undergoing alteration and crystallization, by a legal definition that is ostensibly binding on the inhabitants of the State. And this has been done on the grounds (which appear to me as imaginary or a pretext) of safeguarding the unity of the people.

Till now the intentions of the Israel Government have been based on the fact that its members did not wish to adopt a position on a question that is in dispute between Jews who accept the *Halacha* and those who do not. Quite rightly, the Government has attempted to evade a decision on the administrative and legislative levels, for its members were aware that the process they were confronted with would not result in clearcut crystallization.

BEN EZER: What is your conclusion?

SCHOLEM: In my opinion it was wrong for the Israeli Government to have entered upon "Who is a Jew?" legislation, not to speak of deciding according to the *Halacha*. It is a scandal. It was wrong for the Government to rule on a natural process of change in our historical consciousness, which is part of the soul of Zionism itself, of the dialectic of two contradictory trends within it. These are the two sources of *continuity* and *rebellion* which draw on invisible springs, both of them having made their contributions to our existence. To decide on this today by legislation, and not to allow the historical process of change in our consciousness to arrive at a crystallization, is a fatal error. The plane on which these two trends clash, and on which the historic process is taking place, was made possible after the Holocaust only by the State of Israel. Since then, only twenty five years have passed. There exists an extremely powerful trend which asserts that *changing* the tradition comprises renewing it. I agree with that.

BEN EZER: How does our period differ from preceding periods with regard to the definition of "who is a Jew?"

SCHOLEM: The fact that all of us, up till two or three generations ago, actually accepted the *Halacha definition* emerges from historic reality. That is, anyone who did not wish to be a Jew in the traditional sense of the *Halacha* chose one of the ways to drop out: either by modestly departing from the entire community, or by mixed marriage, which at that time led to the unequivocal outcome of leaving the nation, or by open conversion. The circumstances that caused this dropping out are clear to anyone who looks at the history of the Jews in the nineteenth century.

BEN EZER: When did the question of the definition of a Jew arise?

SCHOLEM: The question could not have arisen before large portions of the Jewish populace were prepared to define themselves as Jews, though they emphatically did not accept the religious premises that determined the world of *Halacha*. That began at about the end of the nineteenth century, and progressed during the following three generations, as the facts of Jewish life were changing fundamentally. A considerable part of the Jewish populace went on identifying with Judaism, while its consciousness was undergoing a process of renovation, which expressed itself not only in its view of our past history, but in its view of our future. From the time that numerous people belonging to the protagonists of this new process entered the ranks of the Zionist movement, it was clear that the question of our Jewish identity was no longer what it has been — as, for example, in the question of inter-marriage.

BEN EZER: How do mixed marriages illustrate the alteration, the innovation, that has taken place in Jewish identity?

SCHOLEM: In this case, there is a most obvious contradiction between the feelings and the consciousness of the followers of the *Halacha*, and the outlook of a large part of the populace to which the most dynamic elements belong, who consider the offspring of a Jewish father and a non-Jewish mother, who wish to belong to the Jewish community, to be undoubtedly Jewish. This is obvious to anyone who cares to look.

BEN EZER: Isn't the approach of the followers of *Halacha* a racist one?

SCHOLEM: It is clear that there is no question of race here, for the religious Jews are not racists. Racism has not even existed in the *Halacha*, since a person who converts to Judaism is entirely a Jew, in all respects, while one can not convert to a race.

BEN EZER: What then is the source of the stern insistence of *Halacha* on defining the offspring of mixed mariage?

SCHOLEM: As to the definition and the pedantic observance of the *Halacha*, these are extremely difficult matters. A mark of this is the intentional and manifest way in which Israel's rabbis refrain from insisting on the laws of bastardy, and their extremely liberal interpretation of the ways in which to avoid all areas defined by *Halacha* as applying to bastards. They have feared ruining themselves and their status, if they are pedantic in questions pertaining to children born of love affairs, who would be defined as bastards according to *Halacha*.

BEN EZER: And what happened?

SCHOLEM: The rabbis muzzled the *Halacha*. They interpreted rules in a manner that enabled them to ignore the matter. They chose to suppress rules which they knew were destructive of the public weal. And it may be said that their behavior was extremely tolerant in refraining from acting on these rules, in matters that were not patently obvious.

On the other hand, in a matter that was patently obvious, like mixed marriage, the rabbis were obdurate. Though everyone knows that a deep change has taken place in Jewish consciousness in this matter, for secular persons and even for a considerable portion of the observant, who consider the son of a Gentile mother and a Jewish father to be not a convert but a Jew. In my opinion there is here a process of change in the public's consciousness, a process that has not yet reached any crystallization, and it should be allowed to develop to the full. The Knesset legislation was not the outcome of a legitimate development in public opinion, but a concession to the Orthodox which was accomplished by opportunistic bargaining and political pressure which, under other circumstances would not have prevailed. In my opinion, this can only have a negative effect, without a trace of positivity.

BEN EZER: The religious do not consider the imposition of Jewish *Halacha* in Israel by parliamentary means to be a political conspiracy, but a reinforcement of religious unity within the nation. It must be admitted that not a few secular politicians and leaders, whose votes and influence served to win a majority for this Knesset decision, also adduced the same national reasons for their decision. Of course, it must be admitted that there has recently been a tendency to use this "national emergency" reasoning to vindicate any decision whatsoever.

SCHOLEM: The Orthodox claim that they have safeguarded the unity of the nation for so many years really means conformity with the requirements of *Halacha*. It should be stressed that this unity has to a great extent been the result of the *existence of the institution of excommunication* (a fact which they generally forget to mention). Excommunication, with all its various degrees, was the severest weapon held by the rabbinical authorities, so long as Gentiles allowed us to exercise internal jurisdiction. Excommunication entailed the application of sanctions, and was a judiciary institution of the rabbis. Whether or not excommunication has done good in Jewish history is a very open question and a grave one, which raises a great deal of doubt and hesitation. There is no truth to the view that excommunication has always been beneficial, as the ideologists of the Jewish idyl claim. *Our historical experience with excommunication and the use that has been made of it has been utterly frightful*, and is demonstrated by the chronicles of the great debates that took place in the world of Jewish ideas and in the wars for public domination. For a thousand years we have known that this dangerous weapon has been used fanatically and without consideration (which shock and revolt anyone reading about them today) even in the battles against the Rambam and the Chassidim, and not only in the famous case of Spinoza's excommunication. The Orthodox today do their best to obscure the unpleasant fact that these excommunications were employed in the most radical manner against Jews who in the forum of religious history itself were later found to be righteous Jews, or even more than that.

At the end of the eighteenth century, the power of excommunication was taken from the rabbis in most countries. Not long thereafter, there developed in the Jewish public streams which had previously been put down, such as Liberal, Conservative and Reform Judaism, and *immediately* sought free expression. This development began at about 1780, from the time the Austrian Kaiser Josef the Second forbade the rabbis to employ excommunication. It must be asked how many movements that were important to the Jewish people were suppressed before their time, and suppressed only because fanatical rabbis did not allow them to raise their heads. The rabbis' opinion was that it was better for non-conformists to convert to another religion, to be expelled, just so they should not remain within the community and exert an influence. It is obvious that had the power of excommunication still been held by the rabbis, why, most of the Orthodox rabbis would have employed it against the up-building of a secular Palestine and the Zionist movement!

BEN EZER: And today?

SCHOLEM: Today the rabbis claim that they are liberal and tolerant, but I fear that they are so only because they do not hold the power of excommunication.

BEN EZER: Perhaps they are trying to regain something of the power of excommunication by imposing the religious *Halacha* in Israel by means of the legal and juridical sanctions that the state is according them.

SCHOLEM: The matter of religious legislation in the State is a sort of substitute for imposing sanctions. The State is giving the institution of the Rabbinate an authority that most of the public would not give it at all. Were it not for the power given to the rabbis (which they do not always employ wisely), I have no doubt and I know that others think as I do that the attraction of the Jewish religion as spiritual force would be far greater in the shaping of our life than it is today.

BEN EZER: You said that cutting the living tie with the heritage of the generations is, in your opinion, educational murder, and that in this sense you are thoroughly anti-Canaanite. What exactly is your criticism of the Canaanite outlook, according to which a new Hebrew nationality has come into being in this country, and that we have nothing to do with the Jews and with Jewish history?

SCHOLEM: What the Canaanites have to say has no documentation and no genuine grounds. Their victory would lead not to the creation of a new Hebrew nation but to the evolution of a small sect which in the tempests of historical dialectics would come to ruin. A Canaanite success would not lead to a fecund dialectical relationship between Israel and the Diaspora but to utter polarization and severance. And this "new people," this sect of Jews, would not have any true strength to cope with the contest of history. The State of Israel is of value only because of the consciousness of Jewish continuity, as regards both past and future. The Canaanites have sought to initiate today a new national identity, relying on the roots of what existed in Israel two thousand years ago. This is a Utopia based on the past of a nation about which we do not know everything. You can see the utter fictitiousness of all this talk. What would have happened if in the Six Day War this new sect (whose spokesmen have expressed themselves about the Jews in a genuinely anti-Semitic manner) had stood alone in the trial? What would have happened? They would have been annihilated, or they would have assimilated among the Arabs, out of their ideology of the Semitic Region.

BEN EZER: They speak of a new Hebrew nationality that will arise in the entire "Euphrates country."

SCHOLEM: You can see the utter fictitiousness, the fictitious character of all their fundamental concepts — "Euphrates country!" As though there were something real about that, and as though a people can cut itself off from its roots. They are denying themselves the substance, the marrow of their lives. And their solution actually means that we would come to assimilation (for Arabs would not move towards a secular nationality of this sort — except in the field of Arab propaganda, which lacks any truthful intentions). They, the Canaanites, would bring the entire Jewish settlement to total assimilation, to oblivion or to emigration. The Canaanites have fictitious concepts as regards the past, the period of the Bible, and the future, too. The fact that we have not been carried away in the tempests of history happens to be a result of anti-Canaan-itism. *I am not interested in a State of Canaan.* It is an empty game of fictions, a sectarian game of a small irresponsible and unserious group. And all of this arises from their unwillingness to admit that Judaism can be a living, growing, developing body. If it is impossible to the People of Israel to exist in the Land of Israel as a body possessing historical vitality, responsible for itself — then what did we come here for? Why do I have to live in a country with a Canaanite government, when the only thing we have in common is that we have both learned Hebrew? The fact of speaking Hebrew is not in itself a redeeming fact. The Arabs will not accept the Canaanite outlook either. The Arabs do indeed live in a reality of fantasy, but not in a fictitious reality as our Canaanites do.

BEN EZER: The Canaanite outlook contains a desire for a secular, democratic revolution in the entire "Euphrates country," which is, in their opinion, the ancient land of the Hebrews.

SCHOLEM: So! So! Nice! Very Nice! They want, like Trotsky, to be the leaders of secular revolution within a foreign people, in the midst of the Arabs. And I ask you, for a person like myself, who has lived the past fifty years — isn't that funny? Why we have argued about this same thing with our Jewish Communist brothers. We have had our fill of the theory that we must be oil on the wheels of the revolution — that is not what we came to this country for! Not in order to be *that kind* of revolutionaries. And I am telling you — the Canaanite outlook will fail here just as the Jewish Communists failed in Russia.

BEN EZER: The Canaanites cite the example of the way a new nation of sons of immigrants came into being in the United States.

SCHOLEM: The Canaanites survive in the Jewish society in Israel for the simple reason that every society permits itself paradoxes. But essentially they are a thoroughly negative thing. They derive their sustenance from having someone to abandon. What can one do if the history of our settlement here does not in the least resemble the United States two hundred years ago? Entirely different circumstances made possible the building of a new nation there, while such circumstances are today inconceivable. What are the Canaanites to do if the Arabs are not Indians?! Perhaps only a few thousand of the Arabs will be able to join the Canaanites in creating a new Levantine nation. It is all nonsense.

BEN EZER: The Canaanite outlook may be viewed as an expression of the way reality is perceived by the younger generation in Israel, who feel that a new Israeli nation has come into being here, essentially secular, striving to liberate itself from the bounds of Jewish *Halacha*.

SCHOLEM: I can understand a secular Jew who does not deny the living link with the Jews of the world. Secular Judaism has been the reality of our lives for the past decades, even though there have been pseudo-religious fulminations among us. But for me secularism is part of the dialectic of the development *within* Judaism.

BEN EZER: Prof. Leibowitz would say that your view of secular Judaism and of secular Jewish nationalism is an essentially Canaanite view.

SCHOLEM: Prof. Leibowitz has a talent for taking everything to the point of absurdity. He asserts that Judaism is a definitive thing, and I say that it is undefined phenomenon, a living phenomenon.

BEN EZER: But the Canaanites see you as holding a thoroughly Jewish view, no less than Prof. Leibowitz and the rabbis, because you view the entire historical development exclusively in terms of Judaism.

SCHOLEM: The entire legitimacy of my outlook resides in the fact that I have related to the Judaism of the past, and relate to the Judaism of the future, as a living undefined phenomenon, whose development possesses a Utopian dimension, and I am not prepared to be a slave to formulations and definitions. I am in the middle of a process, or of a path. I believe that if something is alive, it is in the middle. What has brought me here is no different from what brought other Zionist Jews here. Anyone who denies that like the Canaanites — then there is no reason why his sect should withstand the tempest of history and the Arab world.

BEN EZER: Do you think there is today in Jewish mysticism — in religious, artistic or speculative works — an expression of the decisive historic phenomena of the Holocaust, the national up-building of Israel, the war and the Arab enemy?

SCHOLEM: If you are asking about Kabbalists who are writing today — why, they are seeking to vitalize Kabbalistic creativity and explain Kabbalistic matters, in symbols that have no transparent understandable connection with the problems you are asking about. How does their writing relate to the questions of our life? I have no answer. Because it does not relate. Their writing relates to questions of the deep symbolic world that historical Judaism embodies. In the past, that expressed something, but today I greatly doubt whether the Kabbalah, as it was formulated in previous generations can respond in a vital manner, without a change of form. How can it answer the questions you are asking!

BEN EZER: You have cited the example of Rabbi Kook, who attempted to understand the secular national activity in Palestine by means of the world of symbols of the Kabbalah.

SCHOLEM: But Rabbi Kook was an Orthodox person who believed in the Divine origin of the Bible. He was a living person and sought to find in the Kabbalah a symbolic bridge to the pragmatic world of Zionism.

BEN EZER: You said that the next metamorphosis of Jewish mysticism may possess secular symbolism.

SCHOLEM: You are asking to what extent Jewish mysticism can construct conceptions outside the world of Kabbalah. I can not answer that, for it is not known *how* such a thing can take place, although it is not impossible that it may. Everything that has been done till now has been traditional, or partially traditional, or has been the private world of symbols of isolated individuals who lack the power to express themselves in the symbols that are comprehensible to others, since they are not baked by the authority of tradition that was behind Kabbalistic writing. Can new symbols take shape on the basis of an old tradition? It may be. But I do not know what the new symbols will look like. Attempts by individuals endowed with vision have not helped. For what made the Kabbalah accepted, an historical phenomenon, was a very special thing — that the symbolic language of Jewish mysticism could be conveyed to most of the populace, as well. A movement could be brought into being through its means. Those were symbols, which despite all their depth could be translated into the language of the public. Otherwise it would have remained amorphous and without influence. This transition depends upon the power of the dialectic obtaining between the individual and the public, on the power of the religious experience. And I am certain that even if the world will be atheistic, religious matters will not disappear. As we know, the atheistic world has brought forth a new *religion* — atheism. And so there will also be an atheistic mysticism, which does not require God in order to digest those experiences of inner reality that the religious mystics had. God will appear as non-God. All the divine and symbolic things can also appear in the garb of atheistic mysticism. Something entirely different is even going to come out of Russia's atheism. Even if they keep holding on to what they consider atheism, God will enter it in other ways.

And if you ask whether or not the Kabbalah can fulfil a role here — I can not answer that. There is for example the instance of Walt Whitman's poetry — a poetry that is steeped in elements of naturalistic, atheistic and pantheistic mysticism. But how many of Whitman's readers are aware of the mystical element in his poetry?

BEN EZER: Aren't you afraid of the resurgence of Jewish mysticism possessing religious and extreme nationalistic content, providing a symbolic expression and divine sanction for Jewish domination of "Greater Israel" and the other peoples in the region, and for eternal hatred between them and us? These trends are reverberating in several chauvinistic religious circles in Israel, and sound quite good to many non-religious people among us.

SCHOLEM: I imagine such things may be, and they were not entirely lacking in the Stern movement (Lehi) of the past. But I do not believe that these circles have a real "message." The actual question is another one. *There are* religious and non-religious chauvinists. Of this there can be no doubt for anyone who lives in the reality of this country. How they should be fought, and the question of how to fight them, is a much more serious question. The holders of these views are much closer to the use of Bible passages than to the Kabbalistic world of symbols. But it is not by quoting books that the unavoidable debate with chauvinistic tendencies will be resolved.

BEN EZER: What is the intellectual and national challenge that Judaism in Israel can pose for Jewish youth in the West?

SCHOLEM: The challenge is to act, to be themselves. If they think that they do not need Judaism in order to preserve their self-identity, I fear that they will move towards the same kind of despair and disillusionment that was experienced by European Jewry under entirely different circumstances. If the Jews do not want their own resurgence, then the matter of the State of Israel will not endure. If a new generation will arise today that is not concerned with the matter of Jewish resurgence — I am not certain, I do not know what will happen.

The challenge is to face the facts. And that is precisely what the New Left does not like doing. They, too, like the Canaanites, live in a fictitious world. There are among us those who think that there is a chance to communicate with Jewish members of the New

Left. I do not think there is any point to it. The mutual estrangement has been produced not by their lack of knowledge but chiefly by their unwillingness to know. The Jewish people is losing them just as Socialism and Communism carried away some of the best of our children two generations ago. There is a recurrence of the temptation of a universal cause as against the so-called provincial one. We Zionists have resolved on the provincial side, and they on the universal. But the universal side can be right and just only when the individual knows his place. Jewish members of the New Left do not know their place. They are operating in a vacuum, and that is going to have dire consequences for them.

BEN EZER: Are you hinting at a similarity between what is going to happen to them and what did in fact happen to Jews under the shadow of Nazism and Communism?

SCHOLEM: There are, of course, enormous differences. But it is impossible not to see the powerful aspect of parallelism between the development among the Jews of France and Germany prior to the Holocaust, and what is happening today in the new assimilation within the New Left: the temptation to make a leap to an ostensibly great cause, and not to contend with concrete historic up-building; the view of revolution as redemption, as messianism, as religious redemption, as an alteration of the modulation of the Creation. Why, they are prophesying in just the same way Jews of their type were doing a hundred years ago and fifty years ago. And what have we offered, and are we offering to them? To contend out of concrete responsibility. But who knows? It may be that Zionism too will fail. But the failure of Zionism depends not only on us but on them, too. If a generation arises which does not wish to preserve its Jewish identity—then we will not succeed, nor will they. For the vanguard is of no value without the main camp.

BEN EZER: On behalf of what should we approach them, if we too regard Zionism as capable of failing, as you have said?

SCHOLEM: I do not know whether Zionism proffers a good, an ideal remedy. *I only say that there is no other way.* I do not know whether Zionism is a remedy at all, but that it is the correct analysis — that, to our sorrow, is just as true today as it was fifty-sixty years ago. As regards America, it is truer now than it was then, for it has become clear in the meantime that the melting pot is not in the least a melting pot. Why are most of the members of the New Left Jews!? I can only hope that the Zionist therapy will take effect, and I am certain that there is no better. It is clear that it contains a dialectic, but a fertile and not a destructive dialectic.

BEN EZER: Did the war of June 1967 make an essential change in the attitude of the Diaspora Jews toward Israel?

SCHOLEM: Till the Six Day War they were saying that the real State of Israel is in New York, since the largest and most creative concentration of Jews was located there. Today they have stopped speaking in that style. Something happened to them. They have had the feeling, prior to the Six Day War, that here in Israel there was going to be a second Auschwitz, while their hands were tied and they were unable to do anything. They would not even be able to say afterwards that they didn't know, as they said after the Holocaust, for it was all published in the press, in the Arab propaganda, on television. And that was a severe trauma: the sense of recurring Holocaust that arose among the Jewish intellectuals abroad.

BEN EZER: How did the Israeli victory affect them?

SCHOLEM: After the victory they understood just why the real State of Israel is not in New York. They understood that such a struggle, such a victory, could not take place in New York. That is to say, if the Jews of New York were in a similar situation, they would not have the opportunity to contend with the peril and come out of it as the Israelis did. But I do not think that their deep crisis took the form of imagining what might have happened to them in a similar situation — but in facing the possiblity that there might be a second Auschwitz, this time for the Jews of Israel, within the span of a single generation.

BEN EZER: Would you say that they are living in a sense of catastrophe?

SCHOLEM: Are they living in a sense of catastrophe? Perhaps the term catastrophe is too strong! I would say: distress. Why, they themselves say so explicit. When there appear expressions against "those intellectuals from New York," it is clear to everyone just who is meant, and there is no need to say explicity — the Jews. That is the way it was in Russia, too. They did not explicity say Jews. They just said "the cosmopolitan elements," and everyone knew very well who was meant.

BEN EZER: These are fears that many Israelis and Zionists have tended and still tend to entertain for the Jews of the Diaspora (sometimes, it seems even out of envy). Is not such talk on our part actually harmful to the Diaspora Jews in the eyes of the Gentiles?

SCHOLEM: Is this talk harmful? I do not know. Throughout the years we have said over and over to the Jews who followed Communism and Marxism: "You are making a mistake! Come back, or you will come to a bitter end!" And the results are common knowledge. But can it be said that the catastrophe, the persecution, took place out of any connection with what we said to them and warned them? That is the way it is with the fate of the Jews of America, too. Everything depends to a great extent on the fortuity that exists in history. How will the problem of the Vietnam war be solved? What will engage the consciousness of the public afterwards? Where will it turn? How will the U.S. cope with its internal problems? Will there be an economic crisis or not? And who knows what our fate here in Israel will be. For there is no certainty in history.

The Arab Question as a Jewish Question

Interview with Prof. Akiva Ernst Simon

(This part of the interview was held in September 1966)

BEN EZER: Has the intellectual in Israel lost his fecund state of being an outsider, owing to a sense of responsibility which, consciously or not, is paralyzing him because criticism could be detrimental to the State?

SIMON: When I landed in Israel one of the first things that made me angry was an article by the late Berl Katznelson which said that our group, the "Brit Shalom" was "alienated." In my opinion every intellectual must be alienated at least to a certain extent because if he is bound to reality by every thread of his soul he will not gain the perspective that only distance can give.

BEN EZER: This was the position generally attributed to the Jewish intellectual in the Diaspora.

SIMON: The alienation of Jewish intellectuals in the Diaspora was often too facile, because perhaps unconsciously they felt that the issues they were dealing with were not entirely their own people's. The distance between them and society was exaggerated. That is the way I felt in the days of my youth in Germany. A classic example is the fate of Trotsky, whose career was not only an ideological but also a national tragedy.

One might say that the malady of nonconformist intellectuals in Israel, such as the members of "Brit Shalom" in their time, was that they were far-sighted — that they correctly saw the day after tomorrow while omitting the tomorrow; hence their influence was not real. They knew how to speak but not how to translate this speech into language acceptable to the public at large. On the other hand, with the average intellectual in Israel today just the opposite is true: He is too close to reality and the class, religious, communal or military sector of it with which he identifies. We do not yet have enough people who take a position of *critical identification*. *In the Diaspora criticism won out over identification, while in Israel it is identification which prevails over criticism.* Hence people must be educated to critical identification, which is the aim of a good civic education. As to the concrete viewpoints of such a critical identification one can give no fixed formula because they change with the changing situation. Take our military education for example: We have no choice but to prepare for tomorrow and the eventuality of war; to act otherwise would be suicidal. Yet there is no choice but to prepare for the day after tomorrow as well — for peace; acting otherwise will also be suicidal. The same is true of our present-day political struggle.

Such a highly dialectical standpoint of critical identification is not easy, because identification comes from the language (or logic) of the heart (*l'ordre du coeur* — Pascal) while criticism is of the language (or logic) of the mind (*l'ordre de la raison*). In the intellectual who is also a patriot both things are combined, and his sense of responsibility brings him to oppose the things he considers detrimental. It is a false sense of responsibility that supposes it must always answer "yes," and cannot make the distinction between State and government.

BEN EZER: How does this phenomenon find expression in the Israeli intellectual?

SIMON: I would say in a drastic alternation between one extreme and the other. Only if we have the time and breathing space, and perhaps this is already beginning, will it be possible to achieve an equilibrium around the central value of critical identification. Examples can be found in the first war stories of S. Yizhar and even in his book *Ziklag Days* — these are positions of critical identification.

Unfortunately, it seems writers like S. Yizhar tire quickly. They lacked the perseverance or stamina required to retain this position in the years that followed, and this perseverance is the real test. I have the feeling eventually they settle on only one of the ingredients in the compound — an excessive identification.

BEN EZER: Isn't this excessive identification a consequence of the state of "normality" and "health" in which the young generation is being raised?

SIMON: Health can not be a substitute for matters of the spirit. Health is to a certain extent a condition, but it is not an end. We have made it into an end, and the reason, from the historical standpoint, is obvious: we regarded the Diaspora as an historical and social disease. The transformation of a condition into an aim is a clear sign of a period of transition. Only now we must realize that for those who are growing up in Israel the period of transition is over. However there is a certain conservatism in us and many still tend to consider health the aim. The result is we renounce positions that might be called Jewish ones, and a pathological situation is created in that there is often a nationalistic and chauvinistic awareness without any distinctive historical folk content to go with it. This is one of the definitions of neurosis: an awareness that does not suit the experience.

Buber says that nationhood is an experience; nationalism is an awareness of this experience and sometimes a sign, like temperature in a patient's body, indicating that something is missing in the experience. Chauvinism is an excessive awareness — a symptom of the disease is transformed into the disease itself.

To this I myself would add the distinction that nationhood and chauvinism are not two different rungs on the same ladder but rather mutually contradictory things. The concept of nationhood presupposes organic differences between nations, and it is precisely because of these differences that there is no rivalry between them. Chauvinism on the other hand is something uniform, it is an equalizer. No two groups of people are more similar than the soldiers of two different armies engaged in killing one another. Therefore if nationhood is a variegation that does not necessarily conflict, chauvinism is a uniformity that must result in conflict precisely for that reason, because what separates it into its various units is only territory and borders, i. e. the dimension of place.

BEN EZER: Chauvinism was, and I suspect still is, an element of consequence, whether covert or overt, in Zionism and the Israeli way of life.

SIMON: This is the tremendous difference in Buber's concept of Zionism. He did not think the aim would be accomplished by preaching, but rather by the silent speech of existence itself. And this is what led him to severe criticism of political Zionism, at the time of Herzl, and even later. He believed with a faith that was truly religious that our life in Israel, and its internal affairs and foreign relations, would give the world a new example of how people should and can live. And in this he saw and believed in a very deep historical connection with the fact, that whereas in Greek philosophy the absolute lay in the universal, in the idea — in Judaism it took root in the particular, including the national — that is, precisely in what was different. We are the only nation whose mission from the outset has been collective and whose collectivity from the outset has been missionary. It was in this mission that he wanted to continue.

That is why I feel we must offer so much resistance to any talk, by Ben Gurion or others, of our being a "light unto the Gentiles," because treating a present situation which is far removed from such an aim as if it were the beginning thereof destroys any chances there might be of ever approaching or achieving it. If you abolish the distance, the gap, and unrealistically anticipate a congruence between the desirable and the existing, the result will be that the desired will conceal itself to the point of preventing any possibility of positing it as an aim. Educationally speaking, this is the curse of "patriotic" propaganda. Just as in the extremist Sabbatian movement, where a surrogate miracle (the revocation of certain religious duties) and the sanctification of the present became an expression of the messianic situation, here too the attachment of a messianic quality to a present which is far from such an aim makes a mockery of it.

BEN EZER: On several occasions you said that the Arab question in Israel has become essentially an internal Jewish one. What did you mean?

SIMON: Anti-Semitism is in the nature of a touchstone for the truth of the faith of a true Christian, and the truth of the humanism of the secular humanist, and for both it has in the modern era become a kind of badge of honor in the implementation of their own personal faith or the achievement of the religion in general,

like the importance which is attached to the position of Pope
John XXIII, or Cardinal Bea. The attitude to anti-Semitism has
thus become the test of the Christian and the humanist. Moreover,
both Christianity and humanism live to a very large extent from
the source of Jewish prophecy, whether in its Christian interpretation or in a humanistic secularization.

What is the test confronting us? First and foremost the in-
heritance of the great ideals of the equality of all those who are
created in the Divine image or the messianic vision, of "Love ye
therefore the stranger," of the legend about "My creatures are
drowning in the sea and you would sing" (Talmud, tractate
Megilla 10,2; *Sanhedrin* 38,2). These things are one stream in
Jewish tradition as opposed to a different stream which is chauvinistic, one which is not at all lacking even in a prophet like
Nahum, but was mitigated to a certain extent by our Sages —
and the test is to which of these two totally contradictory streams
our generation will give its hand.

Judaism is not a closed system, nor is its trend unequivocal.
One can explain it in the manner of Uri Zvi Greenberg, and find
support for his outlook in the tradition, and one can explain it
in the manner of Buber, and he too has references in great number.
The dominant explanation, the third text in between these two
contradictory ones, must be the standpoint of the given generation,
every generation, in actual practice. It is in this polarized tension
that Judaism lives, and the Jews must live.

In the Diaspora it was very easy to swim with the prophetic
stream, and in Marxist terms you might say that the excessive
resort to universalist demands was the ideological superstructure
of a social and political situation in the minority. Because inasmuch as those progressive and liberal ideas were adopted by the
alien environment, their price was paid by the Gentile majority
rather than by the Jewish minority that professed them to sub-
stantiate its aspiration for improved conditions, less deprivation
and progress towards equality.

In Israel, for the first time in our history, we have now become
responsible for our own deeds and misdeeds. We have achieved
a very high degree of responsibility for ourselves, and now if we
do not start showing our Arab citizens a universalistic and humane

attitude, not only will the prophetic vision have been lost for this generation but the words of the prophets will — God forbid — have become a dead letter.

The moral authentication of the words of the Prophets now devolves on us, we who have returned to Zion. *And from this standpoint the Arab question has become an internal Jewish question, and the Arab problem can be considered essentially a part of the Jewish problem, just as the Jewish problem was basically a problem of Christianity.* That which ails the Arabs inside and outside of Israel and that wh ch is ailing us is not the self-same malady but two different forms of it. With the Arabs it may be more a matter of hatred and sense of inferiority in the wake of their defeats — a kind of poisoning from within. With us, on the other hand, it is rather a case of disdain and conceit, a groundless assumption of our own superiority, which is no less dangerous. I do not think that we really hate the Arabs; rather we look down on them and will not accept them as equals.

I must admit that when the State was created I thought we would develop a militaristic mentality as a result of our external situation. In this it seems that I was mistaken. I have the impression that the atmosphere here is closer to the English ethos than the German one. We have a readiness to fight but have not developed a militaristic mentality.

BEN EZER: A prevailing Israeli attitude, especially among the young generation but not limited to it is, "If I were an Arab I would do exactly the same thing — I would be fighting us." From this it is only a short step to conclude that the Arabs are right from their standpoint.

SIMON: If I were an Arab I would be striving for an Arab-Jewish peace, rather than for destruction. When different nations — even hostile ones — are located in the same area their mutual influence is analogous to what takes place in inter-connected pipes — this is my credo, even if it is not a rational one. And perhaps that current catchphrase — were I an Arab I would take a stand against us — and the consequent shaping of all our policies and actions, is precisely how we will strengthen the kind of Arabs that do want to destroy us.

Here we have one of the methodological elements which distinguishes between the interpretation of time past and time present. The work of the historian cannot alter what happened in the past. In fact Aristotle says that the past is something even the Gods can not alter — the most it can do is try to understand it anew in the light of present-day concepts — whereas the present is something one can alter by one's opinions. Opinions about the present, to a greater extent than opinions about the past, are an act in themselves. Of course I am aware that what I say about the present is slightly in the realm of wishful thinking, but this too has its justification because it can bring the present closer to what I want it to be. The present is still to a certain extent unshaped matter and is not entirely determined by the burden of heredity, and that is why we are both capable of and obliged to take action from the political standpoint as well.

BEN EZER: But what if peace does not arrive in the foreseeable future? There are those who argue that if we do not succeed in achieving peace and remain in a state of military and political siege and spiritual isolation, there will arise a young generation half of whom are fascists and the other half despairing neurotics.

SIMON: It is sad to see that the older generation of Zionists which started off with a new outlook and made ideas real in a belief that an ideal upheld could change reality, has lost its faith in the transforming force of the ideal and has surrendered to the power of reality as a transformer of ideals, and as a result is infecting part of the youth in two ways:

1. With the feeling of despair that you mention: the feeling that essentially all is lost and life is but fleeting, so let us eat, drink and make do with a substitute for "love," for tomorrow we die. This conclusion is practically inescapable when one's anticipated life span has been drastically foreshortened. This is what I see here in Israel.

2. With cynicism: because ideals have become ideologies, a system of meaningless, high-blown phrases bandied about by political parties. To a certain extent the *cynicism of youth is a legitimate response to the hypocrisy of the adults*, to a calculated and opportunistic exploitation of a myth of State or father figure that has become transparent and naked. Yet this reaction has

justification only as a transitional stage; from cynicism the youth must progress to a new affirmation. And to this end I think the new generation now growing up must set itself three goals:

First: a common decency in interpersonal relations. For instance to be untruthful only to the extent of the most concrete necessity; to see in one's fellow his relative merit and thus to see yourself only in your own relative merit; to listen to what one's fellow has to say, to hear patiently other opinions as well as your own; to observe debating etiquette; to take issue with the argument in front of you rather than the psychological motives you would see behind it, even if there are such. Small virtues such as these have to a considerable extent been lost as a result of collectivization and ideologization.

The second: Active participation in improving the lot of the "Second Israel" whose real crisis will follow its initial economic consolidation, when worries about making a living will lose their acuteness and a surplus of time and energy will seek an outlet and heighten the awareness that the equality that has been achieved is to a large extent in name only. We must prepare for this hour of crisis and do everything possible to forestall it — and not chiefly with words.

And the third: to take a concrete step towards an appeasement of Israel's Arabs. I say "appeasement" because we must admit that no population that has within half a generation been transformed from a majority to a minority can relish its situation, even if economically the level of some and perhaps most of its members has been immeasurably improved.

BEN EZER: How do you view today, from an historical and personal perspective, your position favoring the creation of a bi-national State in Palestine?

SIMON: I have serious self-criticism about the possibility of creating a bi-national State, and I sometimes wonder whether we were right — not only in view of what has happend here but also in view of the situation in Cyprus or even in Canada with its French-speaking minority. But I definitely do adhere to the idea of the Semitic Region. To Buber, for example, the idea of the Region was a lot more important than the bi-national State. He considered the latter merely a local substitute until the idea of the Region could prevail. No real solution to the problem is possible except in terms of the Region. That is why people like Bourguiba should be taken very seriously rather than belittled. It is very disheartening to note that precisely the people who always maintained no Arab would be willing to recognize and admit the existence of the State are now prepared to write off those who are beginning to approach an admission of its existence. And just as I am prepared to reconsider the bi-national concept, my former opponents should take into account the new realities among the Arabs.

One thing is clear to me: History has given us a breathing space. No one can know how long it will last, but we can formulate the conditions that will permit it to continue, the main one being that the factor of our quality so far outweighs the quantitative preponderance of the Arab States that are opposed and inimical to us that in effect they carry less wieght than we do. This condition can not continue indefinitely, because here there comes into play a dialectic that is political, technological and moral as well: when two hostile nations are in competition the one that is industrially and socially less advanced will learn from the other. For example England created the liquidators of its own empire, especially in India. Whether they like it or not, those who have the upper hand are the most effective teachers of those who have the lower.

This is one of the few historical laws from which there is no escape, not even through nuclear power, whether as a deterrent or, God forbid, actual use. Because its use is dependent on geopolitical facts, a country that lacks elbow room is more vulnerable than countries with wide open spaces. Hence Zionist foreign policy must be governed by one basic consideration — that at the end of that breathing space there will be peace. For if not we can expect the worst.

BEN EZER: In your opinion, did Zionism have an alternative course open to it in which such a discrepancy between the fact of the State's existence and its inability to achieve peace with its neighbors would not have arisen?

SIMON: To prophesy about the past is something I am not prepared to do, but I will try to shed light on the question from a different vantage point. The late Dr. Magnes (one of the leaders of the pacifistic Brit Shalom) in our last conversation in New York, a few days before Hoshana Raba* in 1948, and just prior to his death — told me about a farewell conversation he had with Ben Gurion. What Ben Gurion said to him was approximately this: "This difference between us is not so much a matter of basics as a matter of order, of timing. You too never wanted to settle for the Mandatory regime; you too aspired to Statehood. However you believed in a binational State that would come to us by peaceful means, that is you gave peace precedence, chronologically speaking, to the State that you wanted. I could not believe in the possibility of such a State. That is why I gave the State precedence over peace. But I believe that the State will bring us peace."

Our situation today is such that both of them in effect were right in the negative part of their conception. Ben Gurion was right in that peace did not bring us the Jewish State (and here it should be noted that according to Magnes a uninational State was not something we could attain by peaceful means either), while Magnes was right, at least for the present, in that the State has not brought us peace. A supreme effort must now be made to prove that it was Ben Gurion who was right.

BEN EZER: In 1951 you published an essay entitled "Are we still Jews?" an essay which aroused considerable repercussions both then and now. Today I would present the question in a different form — are we already Canaanites?

SIMON: The organizational downfall of the Canaanite movement is an indication of its ideological victory. It is often difficult to preserve a distinctive framework for an idea that rapidly overflows its original format and becomes such a truism that it is no longer formulated or fought over. This appears to me to be the case with several of the fundamental ideas of the Canaanites: a sense of alienation and superiority to the Diaspora, the sanctification of the Sabra inasmuch as he was born here, the severing of historical continuity and a hatred of Jewish tradition, something to which many of that tradition's official representatives

* Part of *Shavuot* festival in spring.

have and are continuing to add considerable fuel, to their own detriment.

Unfortunately, all these negative elements in Canaanism have cut a swath through broad circles despite a slight retreat in recent years, while the main positive idea — the search for the natural affinity with the Arab who was born in this country or in the region — has made considerably less headway.

BEN EZER: If we accept the Canaanite movement not as a desirable end but merely as a form of criticism of the present situation and an exposure of the real gap between Israel and Diaspora Jewry — how will it be possible to progress further and create a new link with the Jews of the world, and without the dead wood of the official Zionist approach?

SIMON: A healthy link cannot develop if one side feels it is giving everything in spirit and taking everything in cash. And this, unfortunately, is the situation on the Israeli side — a spiritual haughtiness and conceit devoid of any foundation, and an economic self-abasement that is also exaggerated. We must enhance our economic strength so as to lessen our financial dependence. The level of our emissaries abroad must be raised as well. But above all the new link must be built on different foundations. The Jews of the Diaspora must be allowed to share Israel's real problems instead of having them covered over with a verbiage of rhetoric and propaganda. Now that the Zionist myth (though not the Zionist ideal) is bankrupt, is shattered, and no longer holds the same naive or heroic magic, the only way we can regain the confidence of the Jews in the Diaspora is to bring them our problems, even the hardest ones of all, unadorned. Only thus will we again offer a challenge to the young Jew ouside of Israel, no less than do the problems of the Negroes or Viet Nam for example. The attempt to present ourselves in a totally rosy and positive light has failed and has no future. Now only a candid revelation of our essential problems, even at the price of some damage, as it were, to our positive image (which is apparently a bit of wishful thinking on our part) can help us regain the confidence of Jewish intellectuals abroad, not a few of whom have developed a rather critical attitude toward Israel in recent years as a result of the discrepancy often revealed between its pronouncements and actions, between its collectivist propaganda "image" and the actual situation and living conditions of thousands of Israelis, and not only those who subsequently emigrated.

There must also be readiness on our part not only to teach the Jews of the Diaspora but also to learn from them, hence the question arises, what can we learn?

Perhaps the situation can be defined in the terms of scholastic philosophy — essence and entity. Here in Israel we have a greater degree of entity, and it appears more secure and self-evident, hence it would seem to require no justification. It is justified by its very existence. In the Diaspora, on the other hand, the entity is growing weaker and is in need of further and deeper justification, i. e. essence. This essence receives what it lacks in the way of entity through contact with Israel. Our Israeli entity, which is not sufficiently problematic in our consciousness, may receive the justification it requires if it is to remain a Jewish entity and not become a public assimilation superseding the individual assimilation of the Diaspora, by seeking out the essence that is in the best of the Jews of the Diaspora, which like any elite are in a small but not inconsequential minority.

BEN EZER: Outside of Israel the influence of the Jewish essence may also be felt in religious influence. Perhaps on this point there is room to learn both spiritually and organizationally from the experience of American Jewry, whose various different trends seem to answer the needs of present-day reality.

SIMON: The Jewish essence in the Diaspora has the great advantage of pluralism in its modes of expression and organization. There are, as you know, three religious trends, each one of which is seeking, often with great seriousness, the justification for its Judaism, whereas here in Israel we have external uniformity and internal fragmentation. It is a truism that in Israel there are no religious Jews but merely Orthodox fundamentalists, but we can safely assume that the majority of those Jews who have no particular attachment or Jewish tradition stand somewhere in between Orthodoxy and a formulated conceptual atheism. And this majority has no organizational expression and very little ideological expression. If to be a "kingdom of priests" and a holy nation is the ultimate goal of Jewish history, and I believe it is, then a kingdom of priests with no holy nation is our present situation, another name for which is clericalism. In the United States there is no clericalism because of the multiplicity of different trends, and this is an example we should aspire to here in Israel.

BEN EZER: Do you belive that among the young generation in Israel, growing up in proximity and association with the Biblical landscapes, archeology (Masada for instance) and language, there is a Judaism that goes without saying?

SIMON: I will make bold to say that even a knowledge of Hebrew and understanding of the Scriptures is not something completely positive. The Israeli child who comes to the first chapter of Ezekiel (1,4) and sees there the word *hashmal* ("amber") is hindered in his understanding by his knowledge of its modern Hevrew usage ("electricity"). In this case the teacher has to make what is familiar remote in order to explain it. The Talmud (*Hagiga* 13,1) relates that a boy was burned while expounding the mysterious word "hashmal." It was a word with a magic aura that inspired fear of heaven and a fear of death. Yet today it is one of the words a child learns at the end of his second year of life, and is something utterly secular.

Hence the Jewish child is liable to a misunderstanding that cannot occur to someone whose mother tongue is not Hebrew. In its prophetic sense this word, which appears in this form in only one place in the Bible, refers to an object with a brilliant luster. Later it became identified with amber, and the Suptuagint translated it as "electron" ("amber" in Greek). The use of amber in creating static electricity gave rise to the word's modern use in Hebrew. To arrive at a precise understanding of its Biblical origins, the modern Israeli child must make a long journey back through the history of the word's evolution. That is why in ancient and sacred texts the teacher often has to take what is familiar and make it remote so as to make the meaning near, whereas outside of Israel his task is to make familiar what is remote; for there the gap between the Bible and the concrete experience of country and language is a given fact, and the task is one of bringing them together. Hence in the case of the Diaspora we must overcome an excessive distance, while the danger that lies on our own doorstep is an excessive familiarity, which is also likely to cause trouble.

(This part of the interview was held in May 1970)

BEN EZER: Has your appraisal of the Israeli-Arab conflict changed since the war of June 1967?

SIMON: I have started to doubt whether the distinction between a readiness for self-defense on the one hand and militarism, on the other, a distinction I made in the first part of this interview, is still completely valid. The prolonged military and combat experience will not pass over many youngsters without leaving psychic wounds and scars. Perhaps a part of them is getting hardened and habituated to the danger of death and the situation in which the alternative is to kill or be killed. Bloodshed is being transformed from an exception and necessary evil to practically a daily affair.

The excessive use, and often deliberate misuse of the phrase "national security" on every issue, relevant or not, is also liable to impair Israeli democracy and the possibilities of free debate within it.

The Six Day War, which to the best of my knowledge and feeling was forced upon us, has brought with it another dangerous development as well: The Jewish-Arab conflict has now entered in full force the world arena of global conflict, and sometimes I am afraid that Israel and its region may become the Spain that precedes World War Three.

Yet it may be that precisely the intensification of the danger, with all its inherent technological possibilities, including the use of nuclear weapons, will enable the discerning minority in Israel which today is in a state of reticence, whether voluntary or not, to raise its head, and the same goes for the discerning minority which no doubt exists in the Arab countries as well, and is condemned to practically total silence. Together they may be able to parlay the little bit of influence they have to the point of an agreement, not necessarily in the form of a signed peace treaty, but one which will be a first step toward saving the lives of all peoples concerned.

BEN EZER: From your view point as a religious person does it appear to you that in recent years the Jewish faith has been playing a positive and vital role in the State of Israel or rather is it venturing onto dangerous paths like the sanctification of military force and nationalist extremism? These are trends which stand in complete contradiction to the hopes of the "discerning minority" that you mention.

SIMON: The political influence of the established Jewish religion is chauvinistic and reactionary, with the possible exception of minorities in the National Religious Party and especially the religious kibbutzim. In the last political discussion I had with Buber, in the final year of his life (1965), I expressed the fear that Dayan's political following, which is secular in its outlook, together with the right-of-center Herut-Liberal bloc (Gahal), one of whose most prominent leaders is the observant Jew Menachem Begin and which has many religious members, whether from the petit-bourgeoisie or the Oriental communities, together with the overwhelming majority of members of the religious parties themselves, would join to create an extremist alternative of a chauvinist-religious hue. Buber replied, "Not to such an extent!"

Of course, the danger has not materialized the way I foresaw, but it has been embodied, and still exists, in the National Unity Government which was formed on the eve of the Six Day War and continues to this day, and it influences every single action of that government, good and bad.

BEN EZER: What do you think are the factors giving rise to this situation?

SIMON: I will mention two: First the unity of outlook between the nationalistic and religious elements in the Jewish people's historic structure; second, the fact that outstanding or disastrous events like the Holocaust, the creation of the State and its wars tend to stress the nationalist element in this amalgam of religion and nationalism and to extract from the religious element the prophetic component of collective self-criticism.

BEN EZER: Would you say that religious rulings are being imposed by secular means on the non-religious majority of the Israeli people, as for example in the Knesset decision on the "Who is a Jew"? question?

SIMON: The Knesset's majority decision on the "Who is a Jew"? question I regard as one of the consequences of this unholy alliance between chauvinism and religion. Precisely because, as a Conservative Jew, I belong to the religious camp, I am revolted by religious legislation, such as the State imposing on men and women who throughout their lives and under conditions of the greatest danger have expressed identification with the Jewish people, religious rituals of conversion which to those like myself, who believe in them, may have true sanctity but which become blasphemous when performed with no inner feeling of their significance.

It is obvious to me that the historical continuity of the *halacha* cannot suddenly be suspended, nor are the Orthodox rabbis at liberty to absolve themselves of the responsibility for that continuity. Yet the gates of exegesis are not yet shut, and they have played an important role in the history of the *halacha*, one that has made for flexibility on the part of its carriers, the Poskim (rabbinical authorities) especially in times of political and economic crisis. Examples are Hillel's "prozbol" regulations (exempting loans from being cancelled automatically during the Sabbatical Year) and the *heter iska* (allowing interest to be taken on loans by making the lender a "partner" of the borrower).

In the 1920's I was present at a meeting between the late Mrs. Bertha Pappenheim, President of the Jewish Women's League of Germany, and a number of Frankfurt rabbis regarding the problem of *agunot* (deserted wives who cannot remarry until their husbands can be found and made to give them a divorce). Mrs. Pappenheim demanded redress for these unfortunate women. The rabbis did not harden their hearts but shrugged their shoulders in despair, saying "What can we do? That is the law." Whereupon she answered, "When the capitalist system required of your predecessors, gentlemen, that they enable the Jewish merchant to lend money with interest, you found a way to circumvent an explicit prohibition in the Torah, because there was sufficient pressure. However the pressure of these poor women is apparently not sufficient."

In the Second World War there was hardly any such cases of *agunot*, and for this much credit is due to a man with almost all of whose opinions I differ. I am referring to Rabbi Shlomo Goren, who found ways in the *halacha* of resolving this question, which was till then insoluble. In my opinion, pressure of this type should also be applied on behalf of those non-Jewish women who have come here with their Jewish husbands and in many cases saved the lives of both them and their children to find a suitable solution in the *halacha* for them as well.

BEN EZER: What do you think of the tendency in Israeli nationalist religious circles (and not in them alone) to identify the Arabs with the Amalek of the Bible and to view our relations with them in the light of an eternal enmity?

SIMON: I believe in our being a Chosen People and in our Covenant with God, and my attitude to the Bible is in keeping with this. Yet today everyone quotes the Bible as an authority for his political views, including those *who do not believe*. The latter, like all the others, are capitalizing on the political concepts of a "chosen people," "promised land" and the like. Yet there is a catch to it. The Covenant is being interpreted by many as a Bill of Rights, unconnected, as it were, with the observance of religious duties. I do not imagine it to be the desire of the Holy One Blessed Be He that we deviate from the course of general history and digress into a path that is negative and egoistic, buttressed in its sequestered singularity. The truth is quite the contrary; the destiny set aside for the Jewish people is one of increased responsibility and obligations, towards ourselves and towards the outside world.

I took issue with David Ben Gurion when he spoke of Israel in terms of a "light unto the Gentiles" (*Isaiah* 42,6; 49,6). I do not feel that we are on the way to becoming a light unto the nations. Rather I am certain that the religious and national goal of the State of Israel is to provide an example and to emphasize our difference from other nations, not only because the conditions of our existence are far from normal but because it is our duty to be *a nation that is more than normal under normal conditions*. In effect, this is my faith in redemption. Practically all through the Exile, the attitude of "Thou has chosen us out from among all the nations" was too facile, because it was mainly interpreted as a demand from the Gentiles. The only place where we have to pay the full price of being "chosen" is here in Israel. From this my feelings toward the Arab minority and all my other attitudes in this connection can also be understood.

The historical truth of those words of the Prophets we quote so often is bound up with the implementation of religious humanism, which it is incumbent on us to practice here. Judaism can be interpreted as a humanistic religion in the sense of an appreciation of Man in that he is Man.

True, in Judaism there are anti-humanistic elements as well, more conspicuously in the Scriptures than in the Oral Law. I refer to the conquests and acts of destruction. Joshua's conquests are described in the Bible as the fulfillment of an express commandment by God, while our Sages ventured to mitigate its severity. Yet of late we are quoting these verses in their scriptural sense only, for the purposes of topical political argument. Often suggestions are heard that are even worse, for example, in the letters columns of newspapers mention is made, *en passant*, of the Seven Nations the Torah commanded be destroyed as an example of how we should act regarding the Arab inhabitants of the territories under our control. Yet the fact is that the *halachic* ruling on this question is clear and unequivocal. It served as the subject of a famous debate between Rabban Gamliel and Rabbi Yehoshua. Rabban Gamliel had forbidden an Ammonite proselyte named Yehuda to "enter the assembly of the Lord" i. e. to marry an Israelite woman. Rabbi Yehoshua said to him "You may." The conflict was resolved by a Rabbi Yehuda, who ruled that "Sennacherib the King of Assyria came and confounded all the nations" (*Yadayim* 4,4; *Brakhot* 28,1). What this means is that the seven nations mentioned in the Bible no longer exist, or as Maimonides said, the nations that live there in their place today are "different people."

Anyone who today toys with the thought that the non-Jewish population of the Land of Israel is in any way similar to the seven nations is like someone who says that what is forbidden is permitted. Yet there are in Israel Orthodox Jews who are using the Bible to buttress their political positions in the manner of the Karaites*, in express contradiction to the ruling of Chief Rabbi Nissim, who found that the term "Amalek" does not apply today to any nation.

---

* A sect that believes in interpreting the Bible literally word for word.

We should also be mindful of the way the Bible is studied in Israeli elementary and high schools. The verses on the Torah which are given to interpretation in a Karaite spirit I would supplement by means of concepts and principles from the Oral Law which mitigate their severity. Injunctions like "thou shalt leave alive nothing that breathes" are no longer relevant today, and caution should be exercised when teaching them.

BEN EZER: How do you regard the education of humanistic values in Israel in a period marked by protracted warfare?

SIMON: Education is something that never ends. We are enjoined to educate even in time of war. The task of the educator of morality in time of emergency is to inculcate values from the Jewish heritage which are not topical nor accepted by the mass media or Israeli public opinion. This is the prophetic standpoint at its peak, things which it is hard to listen to but are the foundation stones of eternity.

War alters values. Murder and killing become a positive commandment. As Jews the question is extremely acute for us. Throughout our history we were takers of offense rather than its givers. But have the good qualities we possessed in the Diaspora been reinforced here in Israel?

I believe in the heroism of faith in the Lord our God even to the point of martyrdom. I believe in the perfect heroism of the Jewish ghettos, in both the active and passive varieties of heroism. (The latter is something we no longer want to hear about, because the young generation in Israel accepts as heroism only war on the battlefield.) War is a sin. By its very existence it attests to an unredeemed world and an unreformed society. And in a democracy every citizen is a partner to this sin.

As far as I am concerned, all war is sin, but I am not a dogmatic pacifist. It is axiomatic that there is no one in the world who is totally just. We all sin. Man's very existence is bound up with the concept of sin, nor is there any way this link can be done away with. Yet we do have the possibility not to do that which is not essential, i. e. to commit a *transgressiom* which differs from a sin in that we do not overstep the bounds of unavoidable evil.

BEN EZER: The young generation in Israel sees its entire life in terms of war and is in danger of being reduced to fatalism and loss of faith in education.

SIMON: I am not a fatalist, perhaps thanks to my childhood, in that I was able to live my first fifteen years in a period of relative peace, which implanted in me the idea that continuous war is not necessarily an inescapable fact of modern history. The situation in which we have been living lately is not so much a state of war as a warlike state. For the youth it is something of a routine. The prolonged continuation of the conditions with which we are all familiar has led the youth to feel as if it is living a normal life. I still remember days of peace before the outbreak of the First World War, and I understand the pain of young people who have never known times of peace, whose memories and a large part of their parents' are steeped in the terrors of two world wars, memories of pogroms and persecution, flight and expulsion.

BEN EZER: "People think it is simpler to win by force. The same is true of air raids. They thought Egypt would break. Yet history teaches that bombing makes a nation rally around its leader. This seems to be what is happening in Egypt. The triumphant Israeli is a phenomenon I encounter at school. Our State is militaristic. At school there is an atmosphere of 'We're going out to get killed.' There are jokes like 'See you in the obituaries' and 'Cemetery plots cheap, get them while they last.' A friend of mine, sitting here tells me his parents bought him an apartment. So I say, 'Is it going to have a memorial room?' This sort of spirit is contagious."

This was part of an interview with an eighteen-year-old in his last year of high school and on the eve of his induction into the army, published in the daily *HaAretz*, April 30, 1970.

What is your opinion? At one time you said that the Arabs and Jews are fashioning each other in a negative way. Isn't this process taking place in its fullest severity before our very eyes?

SIMON: For the educational process to be successful, the educator must posit the pupil a horizon or space of time in which to realize the human values he has been taught. Education in Israel today is completely under the shadow of the lengthy term of military service and the never-ending war, and what develops in the educational process is a kind of short circuit. The pupil sees no horizon or space of time in which to fulfill himself in the light of the values he is receiving, and accordingly loses faith in these values. There develops a crisis of confidence between him and the educator. The educator feels that he is working in a vacuum, that what he says has no connection with reality, while with the young people the effect of this gap may be an inability to accept the harshness of such a reality and an escape to delusions and unreality on the one hand, or despair and cynicism on the other.

The words of this lad are a symptom of the crisis in education, which cannot provide the space of time necessary in order to implement the humanistic values it professes.

It is not within the capacity of education to change society to the point of bringing peace, yet if and when social and political forces do succeed in altering the situation for the better, the well educated young person must be prepared to accept this development and do everything to bring it about, rather than offer resistance.

The theoretical side of education to peace in a warlike situation is education in two dimensions of time simultaneously. We have no choice but to educate in the present for survival under warlike conditions which are not likely to change soon and for which we must be equipped (and it may be that in this respect we are doing too much); however if we desire to live we must at the same time, even in the army, educate toward that longed-for day after tomorrow when, we must believe, there will be peace. Moreover we must reject any element or action which might be detrimental to this education for the day-after-tomorrow.

BEN EZER: How is the young individualist to find his way through this complex maze of concepts?

SIMON: This is a question which each person is asked individually, therefore there is no single all-embracing answer to it. Yet it is permissible, perhaps, to indicate a few signposts which may help a few individuals find their way through the maze. I myself, for instance, have found it profitable to ask myself each evening, before I fall asleep, questions such as these:

What did I do today that involved an unnecessary release of aggression? What did I do today which promoted a rapprochement between antagonists? What opportunities did I miss to bring about mutual understanding, or help someone who needed my assistance, whether or not he asked for it explicitly?

Such "exercises of the soul" which are known to various systems of morality — Jewish, Christian and Asiatic, generally tend to reinforce the positive qualities inherent in a person and help restrain the negative ones. Yet such a method of self-education has its limits. Since its application is generally limited to a person's day-to-day experience, its conclusions usually apply only to those people who belong to his social group or at most to those who share his outlook, religion or nationality. In other words, they lose their practical effectiveness precisely where interpersonal relations have their severest test, in disputes of a public and supra-personal nature.

In order to overcome this barrier safely and "smuggle" beyond it at least part of the moral content that has been acquired and strengthened by these nightly examinations of the heart, one must continuously and systematically educate the imaginative faculty. Only a rich and well developed imagination can carry us out to realms remote from our origins and upbringing. Accordingly, there is no better teacher than to read great works of literature. Not only does it fill the individual's vital need to participate, in his short lifetime, in human experiences he has not known himself and has little likelihood of knowing, it also makes him an emotional partner to the joys and sorrows of people unknown or even alien to himself.

A practical example: Someone who has read one of the good books about the Holocaust will perhaps no longer feel disdain for the "Diaspora Jew" and when he meets one of them his attitude, we may hope, will be more tolerant and sympathetic. And anyone who has read *Hirbet Hiz'a* and *The Prisoner* by S. Yizhar will perhaps harbor a different and finer attitude toward our Arab neighbors.

"The world is all one,"said our Sages, and the soul of man insofar as he is human is also the same the world over. The man of enlightenment who learns this fact will continue to defend his home in time of need, will continue to mourn his brothers, kinsmen and countrymen who fall victim in war, yet no longer will he rejoice at the death of his enemies. On the contrary, he will pray for the day and will strive by his present conduct and his actions projected on future dimension to bring it near, when peace will reign in Israel and its surroundings.

Let Us Not Betray Zionism

Interview with Avraham B. Yehoshua
(This interview was held in June 1970)

BEN EZER: As a young Israeli author and the scion of an old
family that has been living in Jerusalem for five generations
how would you define your position toward Zionism today?

YEHOSHUA: I believe that the basic aim of Zionism has been
fulfilled. I do not consider Zionism an all-embracing ideology,
neither a way of life nor some kind of social philosophy, but first
and foremost a historical act, the aim of which was to bring about a
certain normalization of the Jewish problem by concentrating part
of the Jewish people, territorially, in a State of their own. Had we
not become involved as we did with the Arabs, Zionism would
indeed have brought this normalization to the Jewish people, and
its main task would be almost completely fulfilled.

BEN EZER: Have you a feeling that today you are a Zionist
from lack of choice? Perhaps involvement with the Arabs does
not leave us the possibility of any position other than Zionism?
How can you say then that Zionism's main task has been fulfilled?

YEHOSHUA: You are asking in what sense I am a Zionist today?
In that I accept the necessity and legitimacy of the entire Zionist
enterprise as it began more than ninety years ago, and its aim —
the creation of a safe refuge for the Jewish people. I regard my position not in terms of a lack of choice, but in a historical perspective.
Zionism developed as a necessary process within the Jewish dilemma of a century ago. Today I consider the process practically complete, and accept it as historical fact. On the other hand, I do not
think that the *entire* Jewish people has to come to the Land of
Israel, nor am I certain that this was the real aim of Zionism.
The existence of part of the Jewish people outside the Land of
Israel is apparently a basic possibility inherent in Judaism's

very nature and substance. And just as in the period of the Second Temple large parts of the nation were dispersed outside the Land of Israel, there is no reason why today as well parts of the nation should not live in the Diaspora. It seems that it is precisely the religious element in Judaism which makes this dispersal possible, *and after the truimph of Zionism the Diaspora does not frighten me the way it did the first Zionists who rebelled against it.*

I want to reduce the scope of Zionism in our lives, even from the point of view of ideology, because I do not want to see in Zionism what isn't there. Zionism does not stand before me as a question which I must decide this very day: to be or not to be a Zionist, but as historical fact. I refer to Zionism the way a Frenchman speaks of the period of Napoleon. I see its necessity, its legitimacy, but also where it ends. Nor does it make any difference to me if even today we are engaged in a debate with trends outside of Zionism; this debate has been going on for the past seventy years, and the answer Zionism made back then seems good to me even today. That is to say, I reject any attempt to bring about a de-Zionization of the State of Israel, to sever the link between the State and world Jewry. I consider the State as something that belongs to the Jewish people, and its only raison d'etre that it is a Zionist State i.e. a potential refuge for any Jew who may be rejected by his environment, period.

If anyone thinks that the entire Jewish people must be in the Land of Israel — for him Zionism is still unfinished. If anyone says there is no solution for the Jewish people other than Zionism — for him Zionism is still unfinished. For me it is finished. Because I do not feel that the entire Jewish people must immigrate to Israel.

Were it not for the conflict with the Arabs, the fact of the existence of a tranquil prosperous and secure Jewish State, alongside Jewish life in the Diaspora, would certainly provide the necessary security at the moment of danger of a Holocaust or other calamity. For that there is no need to bring the entire Jewish people to Israel in advance. Nor do I consider that the separate existence of the entire Jewish people is a supreme value; because a separate existence is not a value itself. If Jews wish to live as Jews they should be permitted to do so. But if they want to cease being Jews, and assimilate — I do not see in it any negative value or evil. The fact that part of the Jewish people will willingly and happily, totally integrate in the world of the Gentiles gives me cause for regret both personally and nationally, but I cannot say that it is an *absolute evil*. In Jewish history immense parts of the nation have assimilated beyond recognition. Were it not for assimilation, I was told by the historian Dr. Schatzmueller, we should now number a hundred million. Yet can I say this is an absolute evil? It is a loss for us and a gain for other nations but as far as I am concerned it has no value, because for me nationalism is not the supreme criterion by which to judge all things.

BEN EZER: Let us examine what Zionism means for that part of the Jewish people that resides in Israel. Do you feel the evolving phenomena of a loss of Jewish sensitivity, an inability to see our society with a critical eye from the standpoint of an outsider, and a disturbing contraction which finds expression in an almost total solidarity with the opinion of the majority, with ourselves as a State, on almost every issue?

YEHOSHUA: You are arguing that the price of Zionism for the nation dwelling in Israel has been the loss of Jewish sensitivity, the ascendancy of the consciousness of the majority, the fact that the existential position of an outsider hardly exists any more, the loss of cosmopolitan character and a certain reduction in our inspiration from Europe. In my opinion the loss of these things is a very small price to have paid for Zionism, a price that is tiny in comparison to the rescue of 400,000 Jews from the crematoria of Auschwitz or the early rescue of the Jews of the Arab States from the dilemma of a conflict with their environment. To my mind any physical rescue of Jews as human beings balances the loss of any spiritual attribute, and I admit that we have indeed lost some spiritual attributes.

Where the price of Zionism is most onerous and hardest to bear is in connection with the Israeli-Arab conflicts, but this price is not only the fault of Zionism. Several factors have been at work here, of which Zionism is only one. In effect there has developed here a kind of interaction between ourselves and the environment. Certainly part of this interaction is the result of our mentality and character, but the phenomenon as a whole is bound up with a very much broader historical constellation and it is part of the price that nations pay for living in a given historical reality. In life you cannot avoid friction, destruction and ruin.

From the outset the Arabs did not grasp the essence of Zionism, its might, vitality and necessity, which is why their extreme opposition to it has given rise to such a terrible conflict, the price of which rises from day to day. Yet it is hard to argue that Zionism has been directly responsible for that price. Arab history and other factors, such as world powers and various interests must enter the picture. The developments in our region have not been a direct consequence of any one factor alone. The responsibility of Zionism is merely part of a complex of factors, actions, and reactions.

BEN EZER: How would you explain this complex?

YEHOSHUA: The conflict in our region has a character which is uniquely harsh and bitter, and there is no doubt that the Arabs' interaction with us is growing harsher and more terrible from day to day. I once said in an interview that there is something in us that arouses an "insanity" among other nations, and certain people were deeply shocked by this assertion of mine. I do not know if the word "insanity" is appropriate. I do not have a better one. Yet it is obvious to me that the Germans had a kind of insane attitude regarding the Jews, that the Arabs are living this insanity day by day, and among the Russians a new insanity towards us is now developing. I will try to explain.

Perhaps there is something exceptional in all our Jewishness, in all the risk we take upon ourselves, in the fact that we live on the brink of an abyss and know how to do so.

To us our Jewish nature is clear and we can feel it — but it is hard to say that the world can understand it, and by a certain kind of logic one can even justify this lack of understanding, because when you come right down to it the phenomenon of the "Jew" is not an easy one to understand. For nations which encounter us in a certain historical situation, like the Germans and the Arabs, our very existence and the uncertainty of our nature in their eyes could provide the spark for whatever kind of insanity was afflicting them at the time. Take Hitler: At a time when his forces were retreating from Russia and everything was disintegrating in his campaigns, he still employed crack S.S. units to destroy Jews, assigning for this purpose trains he needed for military efforts. Obviously this was insanity on his part, something that does not enter at all into the framework of utilitarian considerations and *realpolitik*.

While Nasser is enslaving his country to the Soviets, an enslavement for generations to come, he is likewise doing so because of an insanity of which he is a captive. The Arabs' attitude to the State of Israel brings them to do things they would never do among their own states. One can understand the motives of the Egyptian intervention in Yemen (though not agree with them) as well as the war between the Iraqis and the Kurds in Iraq. But the war between the Arabs and us is motivated largely by drives which are not at all rational. This applies also to Nasser's decision in May of 1967 to blockade the Straits of Tiran. In my opinion we should make an effort to understand the nature and motives of this insanity which has caused us so much harm, just as we have tried to understand the motives of modern anti-Semitism.

Anti-Semitism may be understood and find justification for itself within the structure of the modern state, which cannot tolerate or digest the Jew as a foreign element. After all, an understanding of the motives of anti-Semitism (though we don't justify them) are part of our Zionist ideology here. We have known that a Jew who maintains contact with the outside is in effect a thoroughly anarchistic phenomenon that no modern national state can digest. We ourselves would not be able to digest a similar phenomenon in Israel. For example, we would not be able to understand the mass identification of part of our citizenry with another state, say Chile. I remember the way masses of Jews ran down the Champs Elysee in Paris on the eve of the Six Day War, holding the Israeli flag and shouting identification. It must have been shock to the French. As Jews we know that the connection with the outside is designed merely to protect Jews, and it is not dangerous. But it is hard to prove this to the world. It is hard to expect the Gentile to understand it, and one can understand the lack of confidence that he feels toward the Jew. I am certain that the Jew has never endangered the true interests of any state in which he lived. Yet I understand the Gentile who cannot persuade himself that this is really so. Only in a state which has arrived at

true and full democracy, a pluralistic outlook and a great deal
of tolerance, can the Jew find peace and status. But how many
such states are there?

BEN EZER: How can Zionism reduce the irrational forces that
arise against it?

YEHOSHUA: First and foremost by precisely defining its standpoints and aims. In my opinion, what Zionism stands for is the
creation of a safe refuge for the Jewish people, and not necessarily
a return to the Ancient Homeland. The ancient homeland concept
is a spiritual superstructure that without doubt had some connection with the roots of the Zionist enterprise. Yet inestimably
more important than that was the establishment of a safe refuge,
the creation of a New Homeland. In Zionist history it is
always difficult to explain the Uganda episode to young people.
How could Herzl and other leaders at a certain moment have
considered creating a Jewish State in Uganda? But to me the
Uganda chapter of the Zionist movement is completely obvious.
The most important thing of all was not a return to the ancient
homeland but the creation of a *Jewish State*, a *state of refuge*.
And when they thought they would not be able to settle in the Land
of Israel they began look elsewhere. Of course the Ugandan concept
could not appeal to the hearts of the people but did the Zionist
concept of the Land of Israel appeal to the heart of the masses?

The great disappointment that followed the Balfour Declaration
was when Jews who had the chance to immigrate here did not
come. After all, Zionism, which was a movement supported by
only a minority, materialized at the last opportune moment provided
by history. Had Herzl awoken to the Zionist cause twenty years
later, perhaps we would not have come here. We arrived at
that last moment before the Palestinians were strong enough to
resist us, though unfortunately they were already not weak enough
to accept us. Even the Soviet Jews today are attracted not by an
Ancient Homeland, but by the desire to live Jewish lives in a
Jewish State.

Therefore I do not consider Zionism a messianic movement of
national revival, revolution and total change. The Jewish people
has been alive in all the centuries and all the eras. Was the Jewish
people in the Golden Era of Spain dead or culturally atrophied?

On the contrary, Jewish history teaches us to respect our profound spiritual manifestations and to consider the nation living and expressing itself in every generation.

Zionism's strength lies in the fact that it is a *prosaic rescue movement*. The entire national myth with its slogans of ancient Homeland, Greater Israel and the Land of the Fathers has not brought us many Jews, just as today it is not creating *aliya*. Were it not for an urgent need to find refuge from a conflagration no one would have come here. I do not believe in the historic right to the Land of Israel as the sole justification of Zionism. And for this reason I think that Jewish settlement now in Hebron is an act that is anti-Zionist, a betrayal of Zionism. No one went running to Hebron or Jerusalem back in the first days of Zionism; what the first pioneers were looking for was a *territory*, preferably as empty as possible: Ben Gurion was speaking for many years mainly about the Negev, about that empty place available for settlement. This was the most important thing and it was from this that Zionism derived its strength. Had the Zionist enterprise started off with Hebron and Jerusalem and places densely populated by Arabs — nothing would have come of it. Therefore it is not true that what we are looking for is a homeland. Even in Jaffa we were not looking for a homeland; that we looked for in the swamps of Umm Jouni where Degania, the first kibbutz, was founded.

BEN EZER: Is it correct to say that from its very beginning there was in Zionism blindness to the question of our relations with the Arabs?

YEHOSHUA: It is not correct that there was a blindness. On the contrary, the first Zionists saw the problems and tried to remain aware of them as much as possible, and to restrict the damage as much as possible without renouncing their settlement activity. It is one thing if you repress the consequences of your action towards the Arabs, ignore them, and then what is repressed bursts out all of a sudden and can frighten you like a nightmare. But if you have been watching the evil with an open eye, knowing its limitations and its aims, you could arrive at that level where, despite a tactical and temporary blindness, there remained some kind of moral purity in all your conquest. And I do not flinch from the word "conquest." Sometimes it seems to me as if a latter day page from the Middle Ages has found its way into our modern history, or that we are repeating the conquest of the United States from the Indians.

BEN EZER: In your story *Facing the Forests* you describe an Israeli forest that has been planted on the site of the ruins of an Arab village abandoned in the war. The forest goes up in flames as a result of vengeance by an Arab laborer who was an inhabitant of that village. The young Israeli who has been sent to guard the forest against fires cannot cope with the psychological tension, terror and nightmare that surround him, and there is a feeling that he too looks forward to the fire as a psychological release and escape from responsibility.

YEHOSHUA: We have in our lives some extremely serious repressions regarding the Israeli-Arab problem, the entire problem of our existence here. Literature has a socio-psychological function to perform, a cathartic one which lies first and foremost in the release of our repressions. This is what happens in my story; I considered this story one of the ways of resolving an existential problem that was oppressing me, of releasing the repression, seeing reality with an open eye and freeing myself from the nightmare.

Let us return to the matter of the conquest. Our dancing in the streets on November 29, 1947, when we learned of the Partition Resolution adopted by the U. N., was sincere and genuine because the resolution had promised us a Jewish State, and in a division of the country we saw no contradiction of Zionism. Compromise was what gave us the ability to get where we are today. Maximalistic notions would not have got us far. Today we are in effect denying the basic aims and essence of Zionism with talk of Israel's "integrity," Greater Israel and a Return to the Ancient Homeland. It is as if we are reverting to our old Jewish bad habits. This is also seen in the "Who is a Jew" definition the Knesset adopted this year as law. What we are doing is formulating Zionist ideology in messianic terms and giving it aspects which place us in total conflict with the world.

BEN EZER: I am afraid that the Knesset's decision on the "Who is a Jew" question and the way it was made can be considered a victory not for the Jews but for the Arabs. Had the Arabs not exhausted our mental capacity and caused us to become xenophobic, semi-racist, introverts indentifying with ourselves alone and nationalistic to a fanatical and uncritical degree, they would not have succeeded in getting us to push through a decision that disavows all the humanistic values and secular aims of the Zionist vision that brought us here. It was a decision adopted under pressure of the hysteria of a state of war and seige that continues without end. And it is not true that the majority of the nation opposed it. The "quiet majority" agrees with it, because in the face of the nightmare from without it has nothing to hold onto except a desperate internal cohesion.

YEHOSHUA: I am not as fatalistic as you are. Zionism, says Prof. Gershom Scholem, was a return into history, after Judaism had spent long periods outside of it. In Zionism there was an act of renunciation — a renunciation of messianism, religious salvation, and the vision of the End of Days. Accordingly, the contrast and the debate between Judaism and Zionism was proper and substantial. Zionism was accused of seeking a small earthly happiness — and that was true. The renunciation of everything else was worth it in the saving of life.

Today, in trying to reformulate the aims of Zionism in such Jewish terms as *Ancient Homeland* or *restoration of Israel's integrity*, and in using the concepts of messianic salvation — we are introducing into it elements that again place us outside of history and in grave conflict with the world. Zionism enjoyed tremendous support; it was one of the national movements with the most world support, whereas what we are doing today is reverting to the dangerous "Jewish" situation of a conflict with the world — with one difference: Our distinguishing marks now are our airplanes not our caftans. What Zionism wanted was to put a stop to this dangerous Jewish conflict with the entire world.

Nor can we say that only the Arabs are to blame. It is not likely that our part in this situation — where Soviets and Chinese and Arabs are all here to destroy us — has been merely passive and that we have done nothing to exacerbate the differences. It is hardly likely that it has all been imposed on us as fate. Why, even in the time of the Second Temple we were loathed by all our enemies and clashed with all the nations in our environment.

BEN EZER: Perhaps your objection to the idea that the conflict with other nations has been imposed on us by fate is the native born

Israeli's psychological inability to admit that this Jewish fate is something he cannot avoid. And this despite his national-secular education which all these years has taught him that the implementation of Zionism would eliminate the reasons for the Diaspora Jew's constant conflict, reasons which according to the Zionist view resulted as it were from the abnormality and distortions of Jewish life.

YEHOSHUA: Here we are, a state of two and a half million Jews practically at war with the Russians; even Chairman Mao with his 700 million Chinese does not forget to mention us in his rare speeches; practically all of Eastern Europe is against us, to say nothing of all the Arab States. To come and say that this situation is part of the price of *realpolitik* is difficult, very difficult. True, as a nation we have not lived in a vacuum — and one can always explain why other nations have arrived at such an insane degree of conflict with us — beginning with the ancient Egyptians, Assyrians, Babylonians, Greeks and Romans. But by the same token we on our part have been creating here the same Jewish interaction; we have been acting in accordance with our Jewish history rather than with the Zionist vision that wanted to dispel the tension. Moreover, all the Jews are now being dragged into the global conflict in which we have involved ourselves.

BEN EZER: Yet the conventional Zionist view that led to the foundation of the State, takes a position that is quite the opposite. Jewish history has meant passivity, weakness, an unhealthy existence in exile, whereas Zionist Israeli history means activism, taking our fate into our own hands, and the war as an expression of historic activism.

YEHOSHUA: It is not true that all our activity is in the name of political expediency, or that through it we have re-entered history. I think that already in our activity we can find processes that are anomalous and irregular, that amount to reintroduction into our lives of Jewish messianic elements.

In Zionism there was a delicate balance — on the one hand it wanted the Jews to remain Jews, in a State that would preserve its Jewish character, the link with other Jews and the readiness to rescue them. On the other hand it sought to combat something in our Jewish nature, to create a new synthesis. It acted on the assumption that we could indeed be changed; that our Jewish nature was not a decree imposed on us that could not be touched or altered. And the result? The Israeli is nothing more than a super Jew, and the Jew has always been the prodigy — first in the talmudic academy, then Einstein and now in the Israeli Air Force — always the best.

Anyone who thinks the Israeli is different and does not have typical Jewish traits is mistaken. I can see, in the Israeli, fundamental characteristics of the Jewish outlook: *The same exaggerated self-confidence — while living on the edge of an abyss.* Here I fill with despair, because just as one speaks of an Arab mentality one can speak of a Jewish mentality. And one of the hallmarks of the Jewish mentality is a kind of spiritual exaltation and ascendancy in the thick of conflict, on the brink of catastrophe, on the edge of an abyss.

BEN EZER: Most of your stories, like *Facing the Forests* that I mentioned before are marked by a typical Israeli feeling that is similar. The heroes are imprisoned within themselves in a world of inner malaise and distress, with desperate longing for catastrophe and an attempt to avoid it. Yet it is precisely the disaster, the drastic change, that seems to solve their problems, release the accumlated psychological tension, redeem and free them from the monotony of their former lives and give meaning to their existence. Your play *A Night In May* is set on the eve of the war of June 1967, and its impending outbreak seems to provide a way out from the characters' psychological impasse.

YEHOSHUA: I do not want to be a racist and argue that our love of disaster is something predetermined and imposed on us. But it seems to me that the way we are linked with catastrophic situations is no coincidence — we are positively attracted to them, and then have to use our powers to the full or else we fall. I do not know if the period of the Crusades, with its brutal pogroms against Jews could not have been gotten through in peace without the terrible slaughter, if we had temporarily lowered our heads. Perhaps we could have yielded on some point and weathered the wave of slaughter and destruction. And perhaps we chose deliberately to be obstinate and that is why the catastrophe came about. I am not certain that the confrontations were necessary and unavoidable. In the same way I am not certain that the Zealots'

rebellion against the Romans was a historical necessity that stem-
med from the Romans alone, without any exacerbation on our
part. The same applies to our relations with the Russians today.
We seem to be one of the factors that are creating this situation.
What would happen if we withdrew five kilometers from the
Suez Canal and permitted it to reopen, thus avoiding the conflict
and the sacrifices? We, who know how much contingency there
is in history, cannot ignore the contingencies arising from our
own actions.

The Holocaust brought upon us by Hitler was the only case in
our history where we were one hundred per cent passive. One
cannot say that the Holocaust came about as a result of our
obstinacy or that it could have been weathered by temporarily
lowering our heads. For the same reason the Holocaust did not
enable us to prove ourselves, to draw inspiration and arrive at a
spiritual ascendancy and the utilization of all our strength, but
we were merely condemned to greyness and slaughter, whereas
in the Crusades, or today in the war with the Arabs, we found a
source for the ascendancy of our spiritual forces, though not particularly our cultural forces.

At times the increase in the danger also answers to the Jewish
feeling of megalomania. You see with what pleasure the young
people in Israel are now singing the popular song "The Whole
World Is Against Us." It is as if they enjoy the feeling that the whole
world is anti-Semitic and opposed to us, but we will show them all
the same, we will show the entire world. When we learned that
the Russian pilots had entered Egypt there were a few days of anxiety here. But look how fast we have gotten used to that as well.
Perhaps there is even a hidden pride in it — look who we are and
how important we must be to have as our rivals the Russians, a
world power. I think that all these feelings are fundamentally
anti-Zionist and contradict the Zionist aim.

BEN EZER: I am afraid that the war of June 1967 undermined
my ability to believe in a connection between our good and bad
actions and the Arabs' attitude toward us. I am afraid that consequently I have become a fatalist without realizing it. The more
realistic I become the more I am a fatalist. And the fatalism within
me becomes a silent consent to the murky burgeoning of a national-

istic pseudo-religiousness and a religious pseudo-nationalism. The other alternative — the utopian position, faith in the possibility of peace, an optimistic outlook, belief in our moral and political capacity to alter our situation — is going bankrupt before my very eyes, with each new war.

I am afraid that even now a new young generation is arising for whom the war of June 1967 does not appear to have been something necessary and unavoidable, and that in this new generation our self-accusations about our lack of desire to arrive at a peace settlement with the Arabs are gaining weight. And I am afraid that only another war will prove to these young people that they are mistaken. And so on and so forth, just as the wars of 1948 and 1956 proved to their predecessors that peace objectively is beyond our grasp.

I am afraid that "proofs" of this nature will mean the emasculation of all the aware, rebelling and thinking forces in every new generation growing up in Israel. And I am afraid that the answer of the young people will be an escape to drugs and fantasies, or to madness or mindless conformity, because of their inability to recognize the element of fatalistic truth in our reality, or accept it over the long run as the sole perspective of their entire lives.

YEHOSHUA: I do not agree that there is no connection between our good and bad actions and the Arabs' hatred, their entire attitude toward us. It is true we have a kind of intimacy about us that makes it difficult to understand or establish contact with us, but I think that these isolationist elements in our national character are catastrophic, and we have not done enough to destroy them.

And this is the betrayal of Zionism. Zionism had a nice idea — here the Jews would live together among themselves, and no longer be in conflict with the entire world. Well, we had several years like that before the war of June 1967 — and what did they contain? The Lavon Affair, the recession, large-scale emigration, "sick jokes" about the impending end of the State, and so on and so forth. This was the greatest disappointment of all, because here we had been saying that everything would be okay if we were only left alone; that our spiritual strength was not necessarily founded on confrontations with the world.

And I am afraid that this thesis is being revived now once again, that we are in danger of arriving at the degree of isolation in which the Jew lived in the Middle Ages. And now, after the Holocaust, we must not arrive at such a state, for the risk now is too terrible and diabolical. It will no longer give us strength and spiritual power such as came in the wake of the Crusades. From the Holocaust there came no spiritual strength, but only terror. That is why I am afraid of the confrontation with the world which we are heading for willy-nilly.

BEN EZER: Let me tell you something else: I am afraid we have stopped being afraid; that we have accepted the nightmare as the only reality, that we have resigned ourselves to words of regret, a "religion of rote," about the daily carnage on the borders, so as to hide the depth of the cynical and fatalistic despair that is strangling each and every one of us individually. I am afraid we have stopped telling the truth — to each other and to the public at large, because our heart is not prepared to reveal to our lips to what extent our situation — that of each and every one of us — is not more than that of a "sheep in a flock, without cause or value, only terror and doom" (as Pinhas Sadeh puts it in his book, *Death of Abimelech*).

I am afraid we have become hardened, and not only on the outside but each towards himself and to the fate of those around him. And thus our lives have lost their dimension of reality and become a quiet nightmare. I am afraid that Israeli nationalism has become something that is sacrosanct, and that is why we tell each other only what we feel is worthy of being heard in public. Through self-restraint — a sense of responsibility and fear — we speak only at the level of the lowest common denominator. And I am afraid that there are people taking good advantage of the situation of untruth in which we all find ourselves to impose and brainwash us with false and dangerous "truths" of their own.

YEHOSHUA: At a certain stage there was pleasure to be taken in the Israeli schizophrenia that characterized our generation, in the fact of a life of peace existing alongside a life of war. The fact that each one of us is also a soldier most of his life, a reservist who doffs his uniform and reverts to being a civilian. The fact that we are a country at war and at the same time linked to the West, trying to take the best it has to offer and refusing to forgo the link. In this balanced schizophrenia there was even an element of pride when we compared it to the lack of challenge facing the youth in the West, to the high rate of suicides there, the alcoholics and the drug addicts.

It seems to me that lately this delicate balance has begun to be tipped. And tipped on the bad side — that of the war which is coming to dominate our lives. And suddenly we begin to grasp how dangerous our situation really is.

The most terrible thing that is happening to us is our inability to give meaning to death, to cover it with words, explanations, faith. This will be the source of great evil to our life and culture, if we repress death and begin putting it into a statistical framework, such as we do with traffic accidents. After all, traffic accidents exist in any case, and death in war does not replace, but comes in addition to them. Yet all the same there are those who are using this excuse to give some dimension of normalcy, of routine, to the reality of our lives.

But we must not forget that our most profound value is not death but the preservation of life. How can we prevent the process that is now taking place? How can we stop it? We, who have such a long history of bloodshed, for whom every drop is precious and something we cannot afford to lose after the Holocaust in which six million Jews perished. Even for the blood shed in the Holocaust we have been able to provide no explanation, especially not in the framework of religious belief. Perhaps the non-religious person, who believes in randomness finds it easier to explain the Holocaust to himself, but the Holocaust's randomness is precisely what confutes the truly religious person.

Today we are hobbling along behind death, managing less and less to cover it up or to explain it. And this is one of the things that is seeping into the foundations of our being and will shatter entirely the delicate and happy balance of the Israeli schizophrenia which has existed since the War of Independence, a period of twenty years. And the problem is even more severe, because not only have we found no meaning for the death that is raging in our midst, but we are unwilling to admit that in many cases there simply *is no meaning* to *our* deaths nor to those we are causing the Arabs, that both they and we are dying for no reason.

BEN EZER: I am afraid we are all living in a state of semi-delirium, a state of nightmare. A state which is developing in us and in our national and public environment, reactions of submission and anxiety, a sense of helplessness and resignation and an inability to speak the truth. I am afraid that these dangerous symptoms resemble the reality in Russia and the nations of other semitotalitarian States. There is one difference though — our situation is better than that of the Russians, and at the same time worse, because the most terrible thing of all is that our nightmare is real, that no one is deluding us. Those who want to destroy us mean it in all seriousness. They are not a diabolical invention of the Israeli leadership.

On the other hand, a situation is developing whereby someone who isn't a man on horseback, a senior Israeli army officer, will have little chance of attaining a position of leadership and decision, to say nothing of entering the Cabinet. It is easy to imagine a situation in which the factor of one's former rank will be what gives the authority in future Israeli governments. And the appeal to the instincts of the masses, at the level of the lowest common denominator, will tighten the noose of negative reciprocity. No longer will we have the phenomenon of an Israeli leader who is not a former senior army officer — a leader who will set government policy and whose political and personal authority will be above that of army and ex-army personnel, as it is in the world's more advanced countries.

The dilemma in which we are all being ground down, in our collective way, is the choice between a blindness that is blissful as-it-were, and a sobriety that leads to despair. Both are equally dangerous. Yet there is no other way. Because whether it is by a sudden plunge into the abyss of reality or a lengthy adjustment that undermines one's inner faith, we are all to be driven to a position of fatalistic activism, of delirious activity, whereupon our honesty becomes a sober recognition of the hopelessness, the impasse and the impossibility of changing the situation. The realism and pragmatism in which we glory becomes a profound pessimism; and our strength — something which drains our blood and our souls, and the Arabs — our sole raison d'etre, a negative one.

- What will be the end?

I am afraid we have grown accustomed even to that question. I am afraid we are all so much in the same boat that each of us has lost his unique visage, his personal destiny, and his horizons as an individual. As if it is possible to live only as part of the nation, and only to die alone. It is not so hard to be sober and realistic. It is a lot harder to go back to being stupid and innocent. I wish I still had my naive faith that there *is* a connection between our actions good and bad and the Arabs' attitude toward us.

YEHOSHUA: I do not agree with your assertion. I think that there is a connection between our actions and the Arabs attitude toward us and their desire for a peace treaty with us. Especially today, when more than a million Arabs are under our direct control, there is a connection between our actions good and bad, and hence a new literature should also evolve. It is hard, and not pleasant, to preach the need for writing a literature that will deal with moral problems. But I think that a literature that is genuine and serious can also cope with moral problems and deal with the Arab-Israeli problem also through the use of moral instruments without being forced into a position that is passive and fatalistic. It will have to return to the same point of departure as S. Yizhar, but with a complex of problems that are completely different. When Yizhar wrote his story *The Prisoner* there was perhaps one prisoner he had encountered in an Arab village at the start of the Israeli conquest in the war of '48. Today the problems are much broader. The question is how to come to grips with them in literature. And this, in my opinion, will be the acid test of the literature — if it will be able now to pass to a new stage, as something that releases repressions, that releases many things that we don't want to talk about, and as something with the strength to present the truth to our face. And this truth in the final account will bear very real fruit.

On the other hand, it is true that because our spiritual life today can not revolve around anything but these questions, when you engage in them without end you cannot spare yourself spiritually, for other things. Nor can you attain the true solitude that is a condition and prerequisite of creation, the source and its strength. Rather, you are continuously summoned to solidarity, summoned from within yourself rather than by any external compulsion, because you live from one newscast to the next, and it becomes a solidarity that is technical, automatic from the standpoint of its emotional reaction, because by now you are completely built to react that way and to live in tension. Your emotional reactions to any piece of news about an Israeli casualty, a plane shot down, are predetermined. You are no longer able to think whether the bombing itself was justified, because operating inside of you are mechanisms which create the automatic solidarity. Hence the lack of solitude, the inability to be alone in the spiritual sense, and to arrive at a life of intellectual creativity.

A further reason responsible for the fact that you have no perspective with regard to the events taking place around you is that in the Six Day War you suddenly had a good feeling that here you were linked to a great event, to a historic wave, that you were at one with its flow. That feeling was a pleasant and elevating one. Today, with the lack of a feeling of purpose and the fact that you cannot see the end of the war, you lose this sensation of being borne on the wave-motion of history, but neither do you achieve the quiet of the Dane or the Norwegian; you do not achieve peace from history. The feeling of being swept along and of uncertainty as regards the future prevents you from seeing things in any perspective whatsoever. And there is a state of perpetual frustration as a result of the inability to see what is happening. You live the moment, without any perspective, but you cannot break free of the moment, forget the moment. You cannot cut yourself off and not read newspapers or stop hearing the news over the radio for weeks on end, as you could six or seven years ago.

From this there also spring the phenomena which are most prominent on the surface: the internal censorship, the public pressure, the mounting chauvinism. And that betrayal of Zionism which sees settlement in all the territories of Greater Israel as a value that is messianic and sacrosanct, which sees not the Jewish people's survival and normalization as the main thing, but a situation of expansion and territorial settlement, and a life in continuous conflict with the Arabs, and hence with the entire world.

BEN EZER: It seems to me we are in a serious dilemma: Those

among us who are fighting to defend the borders, and all of whose
strength is mobilized for the military and security effort which
includes the occupation of the conquered territories, are unable
to stop and think critically about what they are doing and the
explanation for all that is happening here. Whereas the Israeli
intellectual lives with a constant feeling that it is only thanks
to those warriors that his life and well being are assured, and,
so even he, who might perhaps be capable of analytic thought
feels he lacks the internal moral justification to regard reality
in a radically critical way and to express his opinion without
misgivings. Moreover when he serves in the reserves (a service
the duration of which is increasing from year to year) he himself
becomes a soldier and partner in the security effort, and in all
his actions is required to identify completely with the aims of the
State. Hence even during those months of the year when he is
free of military service, he is paralyzed by the atmosphere of a
state of war which drags on and on, and he lives without any
perspective for the future, neither as to his fate as an individual
nor in everything connected with the spiritual conditions which
make creative activity at all possible.

YEHOSHUA: We are living today in an atmosphere which is
more and more dangerous, and less and less is it possible to speak.
At certain stages there is some kind of hand that has you by the
neck — an *internal* hand, not a hand of the authorities, and this
is all the more terrible. There is a public atmosphere in which
one cannot say everything or deliver oneself of everything. I think
there is much blessing in the release that literature provides for
the feelings of nightmare and distress, anxiety and wrong-doing
and this entire fabric of the Israeli-Arab problem, which, as I
said, we are repressing, and have no choice but to repress. In
this, the literature plays an important psychological role from
the standpoint of our mental health. A story like S. Yizhar's
The Prisoner played a decisive role with regard to our attitude
to the Arabs; the moral and ideological resolution it provided for
that problem was of tremendous blessing with regard to many
of our actions. There must be no taboo as regards literature,
nor must we preclude ourselves from discussing the Israeli-Arab
problem from any aspect whatsoever.

Biographical Notes

SHULAMIT ALONI: Born in Tel Aviv in 1928, she served in the Palmach during the War of Independence and was in the siege of the Old City of Jerusalem. A teacher and lawyer by profession, and a member of the Sixth Knesset for the Mapai Labor Party, she was not accorded a position with a realistic chance to be elected in the party's list for the Seventh Knesset because of her non-conformist attitudes and opinions. She writes a regular column in the evening paper, *Yediot Aharonot*, entitled "Outside Office Hours," and previously edited a program of the same name on Israel Radio. At the time the broadcast filled the role of an Israeli Ombudsman. She also publishes articles on social and legal topics in the Israeli press, and was elected to the Eighth Knesset, heading her own new party.

Books: *The Citizen and His State* (1958, 1962), serves as an auxiliary citizenship text in Israeli high schools.
The Rights of the Child in the Laws of the State of Israel (1964).
The Arrangement — from a State of Law to a State of Halacha (1970), a book dedicated by the author to the members of her people who have suffered discrimination and frustration because of religious coercion in Israel.

PROF. SHLOMO AVINERI: Born in 1933, he is chairman of the Department of Political Science at the Hebrew University of Jerusalem. He is a graduate of the Hebrew University and the London School of Economics, and during 1966–68 was visiting professor at Yale University.

His publications include: *The Social and Political Thought of Karl Marx* (Cambridge, 1968); *Karl Marx on Colonialism and Modernization* (New York, 1968), as well as a number of books on political theory in Hebrew. He also translated Marx's *Early Writings* into Hebrew. His articles have appeared in *Commentary, Encounter, Journal of the History of Ideas, Review of Politics, Review of Metaphysics, Parliamentary Affairs* and *Jewish Social Studies*. He is now a member of the editorial board of the *American Political Science Review*.

DAVID BEN GURION: Born in Plonsk, Poland, in 1886, educated in *cheder*, while simultaneously studying secular subjects and languages; he was active in *Poalei Zion* in his town. He immigrated to Palestine in 1906. At the start worked in Petah Tikva; and at the beginning of 1908 he moved to Sejera, where he worked in agriculture and as a watchman. In 1910 was called upon to work on the editorial staff of *Ha'achdut*, a weekly in Jerusalem. In 1912 traveled to Salonika and to Istanbul to study law, returned to Palestine in 1914. Expelled from the country at the beginning of World War I, he went to the U. S. There he was one of the organizers of the Hechalutz movement and of other activities connected with Palestine and Zionism. Together with Izhak Ben-Zvi, he organized the volunteers for the Jewish battalions and came to Palestine with them, via England. In 1919 the *Achdut Ha'avoda* party was established, of which he was one of the ideological leaders. From 1931 to 1935 he presided as secretary-general of the Histadrut. In 1933 he was elected as a member of the Jewish Agency Executive, and was its head from 1935 till the establishment of the State. He was the moving-spirit in the passing of the Biltmore Declaration (1942) concerning the establishment of a Jewish state. From the time the Israel Workers' Party (Mapai) was established in 1930, he was one of its chief leaders and shapers of its path. Upon the establishment of the State of Israel in 1948, he became Prime Minister and Minister of Defense, holding these offices in all the governments till 1963, excepting the period of his retirement in 1953-54 when he resided in Sde Boker. Upon his final retirement from the Government, he returned to live in Sde Boker and Tel Aviv intermittently. He headed the

Rafi list in the elections to the Sixth Knesset, and in 1970 he also retired from his membership in the Knesset, in order to devote all his time to writing history books and memoirs dealing with the period of his public activity. His books include: *We and Our Neighbors* (1931); *From a Class to a People* (1933); *When Israel Fights* (1950); *Israel's Eternity* (1964); *Meetings with Arab Leaders* (1967). This last book as well as his moderate position on the question of annexation of the territories and his vigorous stand in questions of the separation of religion and state restored to him in recent years a portion of the sympathy of the public and the youth, which was damaged following the well-known Lavon Affair of 1960–61, an affair which not inconsiderably hastened his retirement from the administration a few years later. He died on December 1973 and was buried in Sde Boker.

Prof. SHMUEL HUGO BERGMAN: Born in Prague in 1883, he was a childhood friend of Franz Kafka. He studied at the Universities of Prague and Berlin and received his doctorate in Prague in 1905. From 1907 to 1919 he was a librarian at the University of Prague, and was active in a student Zionist organization named *Bar Kochba*. It was at this time that he met Buber and A. D. Gordon, who had considerable influence on his Jewish thinking. In 1919 he moved to London, where he served as Director of the Cultural Department of the Zionist Federation. In 1920 he came to Israel and from then until 1935 was Director of the National and University Library in Jerusalem. A member of *HaPoel HaTsa'ir*, he attended the founding convention of the Histadrut federation of labor. In 1925 he was one of the founders of *Brit Shalom*, a society for Jewish-Arab rapprochement. In 1928 he was appointed lecturer in the Department of Philosophy at the Hebrew University, and became a full professor in 1935 and Rector of the University, 1935–38. His humanistic-religious approach was of considerable influence in Jewish life, and he is widely known for his moderate approach to Jewish-Arab problems.

In 1903 he began publishing papers in philosophy, Jewish affairs, Zionism and Hebrew literature. For many years he has contributed to newspapers and literary symposiums. The following of his books have been translated into English: *Faith and Reason*, B'nai B'rith Hillel Foundation, Washington, D. C. 1961. *The Philosophy of Solomon Maimon*, Magnes Press, The Hebrew University, Jerusalem, 1967.

The Quality of Faith, the Youth and Hechalutz Department of the World Zionist Organization, Jerusalem 1970.

Together with Prof. Nathan Rottenstreich he translated into Hebrew Kant's *Critique of Pure Reason* and *Critique of Judgment*. He has trained generations of teachers and pupils of philosophy, and his books and translations are mainstays of modern Hebrew philosophic literature.

MORDECHAI MARTIN BUBER: Born in Vienna, 1878, from age three to fourteen he was educated by his grandfather, the talmudic scholar Shlomo Buber of Lwow. He attended a Polish high school and in 1896 enrolled at the University of Vienna to study philosophy and the history of art. He also studied at Leipzig, Zurich and Berlin, and received his doctorate in 1900. He joined the Zionist Movement in 1898. A year later he was a delegate at the Third Zionist Congress and in 1901 was appointed by Herzl as the editor of *Die Welt*, the weekly organ of the Zionist Federation. Under his influence Zionist awareness was deepened by an emphasis on cultural activity. He was one of the founders of the *Jüdischer Verlag* publishing house which brought out a series of highly influential books on Zionism in the West.

In 1904 there came a turning point in his life when he discovered the world of Hasidism. In 1906 he published in German the first of a number of books on that subject. In 1909–1911 he delivered before the *Bar Kochba* Jewish students' society in Prague a series of "Addresses on Judaism" in which he attempted to infuse content and substance into a Western Jewish life that became devitalized and superficial.

From then on his position was secure as spiritual leader and guide of Western Jewry, especially in the nationalist movement and youth movements. In 1916 he founded *Der Jude*, a periodical on Western Jewish thought. In 1920 he resumed public Zionist activity as a delegate to the Twelfth Zionist Congress, the first after the war, where he raised the question of Jewish-Arab relations, and the ways of realizing the profound content of Zionism.

In 1925 there began to appear a new translation of the Bible into German, on which he collaborated with his friend Franz Rosenzweig until the latter's death in 1929, in the middle of the Book of Isaiah. The project was suspended with the rise of the Nazis, and was only completed in 1961, in Jerusalem. Meanwhile there began appearing in German, and later in Hebrew, Buber's studies and works on the Bible. The rise of the Nazis forced him to resign as Professor of Religious Studies at Frankfurt University. Until his settlement in Palestine in 1938 he directed the Jewish adult education project in Germany along the lines of spiritual resistance. From 1938 to 1951 he taught Cultural Sociology and Social Philosophy at the Hebrew University of Jerusalem. He was also active in groups such as *Ihud* which sought Jewish-Arab rapprochement. In his last years he directed a number of literary and scientific projects such as the translation of the world's literary classics into Hebrew, the Encyclopedia of Education, etc. He died in 1965 and was buried in Jerusalem.

His major works (in the order of their appearance in Hebrew) include: *The Demand of the Spirit and Historical Reality* (1938); *Spirit and Reality* (1942); *The Problem of Man* (1943); *Gog and Magog, the Scroll of the Days* (1944); *In the Orchard of Hasidism* (1945); *Between Nation and Land* (1945); *Moses* (1946); *The Hidden Light: Hasidic Stories* (1947); *Paths into Utopia* (1957); *The Way of Man According to Hasidism* (1957), *The Crisis of the Spirit: Three Addresses on Judaism* (1953).

His selected essays and articles have been published in Hebrew in four volumes. Two of them contain his philosophic writings: 1. *Secrets of the Dialogue: man and his position vis à vis experience* (1959) — contains the following books which were published originally in German: *I and Thou* (1923), *Dialogue* (1932), *The Question the Individual is Asked* (1936) and *The Educational Act* (1925). The second volume *The Face of Man: Studies in Anthropological Philosophy* (1962) is likewise a collection of philosophical essays, and contains among other things his important work *Guilt and Guilt Feeling*. Of the two volumes entitled *Te'udah V' Ye'ud* (Deposition and Destiny) (1960–61) the first is devoted to *Questions of Judaism* and the second, *Am V'Olam* (Nation and World) to Buber's Zionist and political thought. His collected articles on biblical topics appeared in *The Way of the Bible* (1964) and in *Kingdom of Heaven* — studies in the Books of Judges and Samuel (1965). A bibliography of Buber's writings in all languages, 1897–1957, edited by Moshe Katan, was published by the Bialik Institute in 1961.

A. ELI: The nom de plume of Eli Allon, a young poet of Kibbutz Ein Shemer in Samaria. He was born in 1935, the second generation of his family on that kibbutz. After completing his military service he took a five-year leave of absence to hitchhike around the world. At present he is married and has two children. His professions are shepherd and poultryman. He has also served as editor of the weekly bulletin of the *HaShomer HaTsa'ir* kibbutz movement, *HaKibbutz HaArtzi*. An animal lover, he keeps beside his door either a dog, a lamb or else a chicken with a name and personality all its own — in protest against the kibbutz poultry-raising methods, which he feels are little better than a meat factory. He served in the 1956 Sinai Campaign, and, in the tank corps, in the Six Day War.

Collections of poems:
The Story of Jacob (1966)
Mount of Quietudes (1969)

BOAZ EVRON: Born in Jerusalem in 1927. His father, David Hamburger was a member of a veteran family that has been in Palestine since the first half of the nineteenth century. He completed his secondary studies at the Herzliya High School in Tel Aviv and studied at the Hebrew University in Jerusalem. He was a member of Lechi (the "Stern Gang"), and on a mission of that organization spent the years 1947–1951 in the U. S. When he returned to Israel, he began to work at *Ha'aretz*, a newspaper where he wrote literary criticism and a weekly radio review column that was the first of its kind in the Israeli press and set a style of criticism which combines a theoretical essay with a topical polemic approach. In 1964 he went over to the newspaper *Yediot Aharonot* where he has a regular weekly publicistic column and writes drama criticism. For some time he also edited that paper's literary section. His weekly articles have considerable political and cultural influence on Israeli public opinion. In recent years he studied philosophy and history at Tel Aviv University, and is now also Acting Director of the School of Theater Art in Ramat Gan, where he resides. At one time known for his Canaanite views, he was editor of the non-comformist bi-weekly magazine *Etgar* ("Challenge") which appeared in the years before the Six Day War and took a stand for Israeli integration in the "Semitic region."

His publications include criticism of Israeli literature in the Parisian *Le Monde*, and an essay on the situation of Israel and Zionism today in the French liberal-Catholic journal *Esprit* (September 1966). Translations of his articles have appeared from time to time in the foreign press. He recently completed a book on *The Concept of Liberty as an Integrative Factor*.

PROF. YESHAYAHU LEIBOWITZ: Born in 1903 in Riga, Latvia. His family moved to Germany after the First World War and in 1924 he completed his studies in chemistry at the University of Berlin. He subsequently studied medicine at Basle, Switzerland, and worked in the Department of Chemistry at Berlin, the Institute of Biochemistry at Berlin Dahlem and the Department of Physiology at Cologne. He came to Israel in 1934 and has been teaching at the Hebrew University of Jerusalem ever since. In 1955 he became Associate Professor of Biochemistry and in 1961 Professor and Head of the Department of Organic-Chemistry and Biochemistry.

Prof. Leibowitz is one of the senior editors of the *Hebrew Encyclopedia*, and was a leader of the Religious Worker Movement and the *Shurat HaMitnadvim* (a civic volunteers league). He is a keen polemicist and a far-ranging scientist and thinker. He has published works in organic chemistry, biochemistry, physiology and cybernetics, as well as on current affairs, Judaism and problems of religion.

His books include *Education for Torah and Mitzvoth* (with A. Eliner) 1943; *What is Heredity?* — 1945; *Torah and Mitzvoth at these Times* (a collection of lectures and articles) — 1954.

YONATAN RATOSH: The nom de plume of Uriel Shelah, a publicist, a thinker and one of the best, most original Hebrew poets of our generation. He has translated from English and French, and edited a very large number of books, and his own literary work has profoundly influenced the development of the renascent Hebrew language. A controversial figure in the political and cultural life of Israel, his relatively late recognition as a poet was more the result of his views than of his poetic innovations.

At the time of the Mandate, Ratosh was the first to publicly brand the British as the principal enemy of the Hebrew community, and to pronounce the fight against them as the condition for the establishment of the State. He was to a considerable extent responsible for the decision of Avraham Stern ("Yair") to set up a terrorist underground movement. He is also considered the father of the "Canaanites," who had a great influence on the young Hebrew intelligentsia during the '40s and the beginning of the '50s, and who in recent years have resumed their activity.

Born in Russia in 1908, he was brought up in a home where Hebrew was spoken exclusively. His parents emigrated to Palestine in 1919. A graduate of the Herzliya High School, he took law for one year, then went to Paris to study linguistics. He worked for several years on the editorial staff of *Hayarden* (a newspaper published by the Revisionist party), becoming its editor in 1937. He was ultimately dismissed because of his views. He was also the first editor of the underground newspaper, *Baherev* (1937). In 1939 he set up the "Committee for the Consolidation of the Hebrew Youth" which he headed, and founded *Alef*, the Canaanite organ which appeared from 1948 till 1953 and is now again appearing as an occasional publication.

Following the Six Day War, he wrote a book entitled *1967— And What Next* (*Pax Ebraica*). His volumes of poetry are: *Black Wedding Canopy* (1941); *Yochemed* — (1952); *Rib* — (1959); *Poems of Account* — (1963); *Poems of Reality* — (1965); *Walker in Darkness* — (1965); *Poems of the Sword*, 1930–1964 — (1968).

PINHAS SADEH: Born in 1929 in Lemberg, Poland (now Russia). He came to Israel with his parents at the age of four, attended school in Tel Aviv and at Kibbutz Sarid in the Valley of Yisre'el. At one time or another he worked as shepherd, office clerk, librarian and night watchman in the Negev desert. He served in the War of Independence, spent a year in London and several years in Jerusalem. At present he lives in Ramat Gan.

Sadeh's poems have been translated into English, Arabic, French, Hungarian, German and other languages. A survey of his work in English may be found in Herbert Howarth's essay in *Commentary*, August, 1956. Sadeh is a leading Israeli author.

His books include *The Burden of Duma* (poems) 1951; *Life as a Parable* (autobiography) 1958, 1968; *Notes on Man's Condition* (novel) 1967; *The Death of Abimelech and his Ascent to Heaven in the Arms of his Mother* (Biblical novel) 1969; *Collected Poems* 1947–1970, and *Journey* 1971. The book by Yosef Mundy, *Conversations at Midnight with Pinhas Sadeh* appeared in 1971. An English version of *Life as a Parable* was published by Anthony Blond, London, 1966. The book has also been made into a play, produced in Israel in 1968.

PROF. GERSHOM SCHOLEM: Born in Berlin in 1897, studied mathematics, philosophy and Semitic philology at various German and Swiss universities. In 1923, he published his first major research work on the Kabbalah. Since then, Scholem has published hundreds of articles, by no means limiting himself to the Kabbalah. His books are considered the most authoritative in the field.

Gershom Scholem was the first to subject Jewish mysticism to exact scientific treatment; and his approach was scrupulously unprejudiced, systematic and thorough. It was he who restored the Kabbalah to its rightful place in history and religion, both within the realms of Jewish studies and in the study of religion and mysticism in general.

Scholem came to Israel from Germany in 1923, to take up duties as head of the Jewish Department of the National Library of the Hebrew University. In 1946, he was charged with rescuing what remained of Europe's Jewish libraries. From 1925 until his retirement in 1965, Scholem was Professor of Jewish Mysticism. In his teaching he not only gave of his vast knowledge to his students, he also trained them in method of accurate scientific study, with particular emphasis on intellectual honesty which he possesses to an unparalleled degree. Numerous honours and awards have been conferred on Scholem, among them the Israel Prize and the Rothschild Prize for Jewish Scholarship. Recently he was awarded the Reuchlin Prize for Humanities by the Municipality of Pforzheim. At present, he holds the office of President of the Israel Academy of Sciences and Humanities.

Prof. Scholem has published books and papers in numerous languages especially in Hebrew, English and German. He is the author of *Major Trends in Jewish Mysticism*; *Bibliographia Kabbalistica*; *Zohar: The Book of Splendor*; *The Beginnings of Kabbalah*; *Sabbatai Zevi and the Sabbatian Movement During His Lifetime*; *Jewish Gnosticism, Merkabah Mysticism and the Talmudic Tradition*; *on the Kabbalah and its Symbolism*; and numerous monographs in the Eranos yearbooks and in other publications.

PROF. AKIVA ERNST SIMON: Born in Berlin in 1899 he served in World War One and was seriously injured at Verdun in the summer of 1916. He studied history, philosophy, sociology and Hebrew at the Universities of Berlin and Frankfurt, and received his doctorate at Heidelberg in 1932. He was influenced by Buber and by Franz Rosenzweig. Together with Buber he edited the periodical *Der Jude*. Coming to Israel in 1928 he taught in Jerusalem and Haifa. In 1934 he returned to Germany to train teachers and organize Jewish adult education under the nose of the Nazi regime. Since 1935 he has been Professor of Education at the Hebrew University of Jerusalem; in 1966 he became Director of the School of Education and in 1967 Professor Emeritus. One of the leaders in the movement for Jewish-Arab rapprochement, he had been a member of *Brit Shalom, Ihud* and the *League for Jewish Arab Rapprochement and Peace*. At present he is active in the *Peace and Security Movement*.

Professor Simon has published in German, Hebrew and English. His main books in German are *Ranke and Hegal* — 1928; *Value Judgements in the Teaching of History* — 1931; *Reconstruction during Destruction* — *Jewish Adult Education in Nazi Germany as Spiritual Resistance* — 1953; and *Bridges and Selected Essays* — 1965. In Hebrew he published a book on the great Swiss educator J. H. Pestalozzi and his doctrines. Of his English essays the following appeared in a book edited by Dr. E. Jospe for the Hillel Foundation of B'nai B'rith: *Tradition and Contemporary Experience* divided into *Law and Observance in Jewish Experience* and *On the Meaning of Prayer*. Also his essays in Yearbook I-III of the Leo Baeck Institute, London: *Jewish Spiritual Resistance* and *Martin Buber and German Jewry*.

AVRAHAM B. YEHOSHUA: Born in Jerusalem in 1936, he is the fifth generation of his family in that city. He served as a paratrooper in the Israel army and graduated the Hebrew University of Jerusalem in philosophy and Hebrew Literature. He taught in Jerusalem, was the headmaster of an Israeli school in

Paris and the Secretary of the World Union of Jewish Students. Since 1967 he has served as Dean of Students at Haifa University.

His first book of stories, *The Death of an Old Man*, appeared in 1962; the second, *Facing the Forests* is 1968. His play *A Night in May* was produced in 1969. The Israeli film *Three Days and a Child* was based on his story of the same name. Yehoshua is considered one of the outstanding young writers in Israel. His stories have been translated into English, Danish, Norwegian, French and Spanish and are included in numerous anthologies. A collection of his stories was brought out by Doubleday, New York, in 1970.

PROF. ROBERT ALTER: is Associate Professor of Comparative Literature at the University of California, Berkeley. He was educated at Colombia and Harvard Universities. He is the author of *Rogue's Progress: Studies in the Picaresque Novel; Fielding and the Nature of the Novel* (both Harvard University Press Books), and *After the Tradition: Essays on Modern Jewish Writing* (E.P. Dutton & Co., Inc.). He writes on a variety of literary and cultural subjects for *Commentary* and other national magazines.

EHUD BEN EZER: was born in 1936 in Petah Tikva where his family has been rooted since 1878 when that first Jewish colony in the country was founded. He is a former member of Kibbutz Ein Gedi on the Dead Sea shore, and was a teacher in new settlements of oriental immigrants. He read Philosophy and Kabbalah at the Hebrew University of Jerusalem. Since 1966 he has been living in Tel Aviv.

His writings include a variety of short-stories, poems, critical pieces, radio plays, lectures and essays on Hebrew literature, children's stories, and a weekly column in the *Ha'aretz* newspaper on rare Hebrew books. His novels *The Quarry* (1963), *The People of Sodom* (1968), *Nor the Battle to the Strong* (1971), and a children's book *A Night in the Sleeping Vegetable Garden* (1971) have been widely circulated in Israel.

Acknowdlegements

YIGAL SHENKMAN: translated the interviews with Shulamit Aloni, Shlomo Avineri, Boaz Evron, Yonatan Ratosh, David Ben Gurion, and Gershom G. Scholem.

UZI NYSTAR: translated the interviews with Shmuel Hugo Bergman, Mordechai Martin Buber, A. Eli, Yeshayahu Leibowitz, Pinhas Sadeh, Akiva Ernst Simon, Avraham B. Yehoshua, as well as the introduction by Ehud Ben Ezer.

The poems of A. Eli are taken from his books *This is the Story of Jacob* and *Mount of Quietudes*, and are published here with the kind permission of Sifirat Poalim Publishing House, Tel Aviv.

The first parts of the interviews with Shlomo Avineri, David Ben Gurion, Shmuel Hugo Bergman, and Yeshayahu Leibowitz are published here with the kind permission of the Hebrew Writers Association and the Editorial Board of *Moznayim*, Tel Aviv.